—THE—
SPANISH ARMADA

Also by Robert Hutchinson

The Last Days of Henry VIII
Elizabeth's Spymaster
Thomas Cromwell
House of Treason
Young Henry

–THE–
SPANISH ARMADA

ROBERT HUTCHINSON

Thomas Dunne Books
St. Martin's Press
New York

THOMAS DUNNE BOOKS.
An imprint of St. Martin's Press.

THE SPANISH ARMADA. Copyright © 2013 by Robert Hutchinson. All rights reserved. Printed in the United States of America. For information, address St. Martin's Press, 175 Fifth Avenue, New York, N.Y. 10010.

www.thomasdunnebooks.com
www.stmartins.com

Library of Congress Cataloging-in-Publication Data

Hutchinson, Robert, 1948–
  The Spanish Armada / Robert Hutchinson. — First U.S. edition.
    p. cm.
  Includes bibliographical references and index.
  ISBN 978-1-250-04712-0 (hardcover)
  ISBN 978-1-4668-4748-4 (e-book)
  1. Armada, 1588. 2. Spain. Armada—History—16th century. 3. Spain—History—Philip II, 1556–1598. 4. Great Britain—History, Naval—Tudors, 1485–1603. 5. Spain—History, Naval. 6. Spain. Armada—History. 7. Spain—History—Ferdinand and Isabella, 1479–1516. I. Title.
  DA360.H88 2013
  942.05'5—dc23

                                                        2014003178

St. Martin's Press books may be purchased for educational, business, or promotional use. For information on bulk purchases, please contact Macmillan Corporate and Premium Sales Department at 1-800-221-7945, extension 5442, or write specialmarkets@macmillan.com.

First published in Great Britain by Weidenfeld & Nicolson

First U.S. Edition: June 2014

10 9 8 7 6 5 4 3 2 1

To Alicia and the young ones:

Marcel, Julian and Giselle,
Alison and Sylvia

CONTENTS

LIST OF ILLUSTRATIONS

Princess Elizabeth as a young teenager (attributed to William Scrots, *c.*1546) (*Royal Collection Trust/© Her Majesty, Queen Elizabeth II 2013*).

Mary I painted by Hans Eworth in 1554 (*Society of Antiquaries of London/Bridgeman*).

Mary Queen of Scots by François Clouet, *c.*1558-60 (*Royal Collection Trust/© Her Majesty Queen Elizabeth II 2013*).

Philip II of Spain, painted by an unknown artist, after 1580 (© *National Portrait Gallery, London*).

Don Alonso Pérez de Guzmán, Seventh Duke of Medina Sidonia, the reluctant commander of the Armada, sixteenth-century engraving (*The Granger Collection, New York*).

Alessandro Farnese, Duke of Parma, Hispano-Dutch school, *c.*1585 (*Philip Mould Ltd/Bridgeman*).

Pope Sixtus V. Italian school, sixteenth century (*Chateau de Versailles/Giraudon/Bridgeman*).

Elizabeth's new 'race built' warships (from *Fragments of Ancient Shipwrightery* by Matthew Baker. © *The Pepys Library, Magdalene College, Cambridge*).

Howard's flagship *Ark Royal* (*Bridgeman*).

Sir Francis Walsingham, Elizabeth's secretary of state and spymaster. John Critz the Elder, *c.*1585 (© *National Portrait Gallery, London*).

Dorset warning beacons, showing their construction (© *The British Library Board, Cotton Augustus I/i*).

Sir William Cecil, Lord Burghley, Elizabeth's lord treasurer (© *National Portrait Gallery, London*).

Charles Howard, Second Baron Effingham (*His Grace the Duke of Norfolk/Bridgeman*).

Sir Francis Drake, unknown artist, *c.*1580 (© *National Portrait Gallery, London*).

AUTHOR'S NOTE

The Spanish Armada campaign of 1588 changed the course of European history. If the Spanish captain-general Medina Sidonia had managed to successfully escort the Duke of Parma's invasion force across the narrow seas from Flanders, the future of Elizabeth I's government and Protestant England would have looked very black indeed.

It is one of history's greatest 'what ifs'.

If those experienced and battle-hardened Spanish troops had landed near Margate on the Kent coast, it is likely that they would have been in the poorly defended streets of London within a week and the queen and her ministers apprehended. England would have reverted to the Catholic faith and there may have not been a British Empire to come.

Of course, despite his very best efforts, Medina Sidonia failed utterly in his mission – and experienced one of the most signal catastrophes in naval annals.

Much has been written about this myth-ridden campaign. This book indeed provides a blow-by-blow account of the naval skirmishes up the English Channel, culminating in the fireship attack off Calais, the Battle of Gravelines and the Armada's subsequent terrible destruction on the west coast of Ireland.

But what is not so well-known is the fact that Elizabeth faced opposition within her own realm to her efforts to defend her crown against the Spanish. There were many who were less than enthusiastic about the coming fight. Some were reluctant to pay for it, or voted with their feet like the gentry shifting their families and moveable wealth away from the coast, rather than standing and fighting. Her ill-trained and ill-armed militia mutinied in the frontline on the Channel coast. The Dorset troops were thought more likely to fight each other than the Spaniards. Patriotism, despite the Tudor propaganda, was not as pervasive as popular perception suggests.

The Armada was the climax to a war of religion, the Catholic Church *versus* the fledgling Protestant state of England, and Elizabeth's Ministers feared that the Catholic majority amongst her subjects would immediately rise up in support of the invaders. There were also English Catholics on board the Spanish ships who hated the English queen as a cruel oppressor of their faith and were sailing joyfully to depose her.

Philip II of Spain, having early on been rudely shunned as a prospective husband by Elizabeth, was spurred to spend enormous sums of money in what he saw as a holy crusade against heretic England. But he also had a more prosaic motivation: despite his protestations, Philip was very conscious of his claim on the crown of England. Thus, the Anglo-Spanish war of the 1580s was a very personal conflict between two monarchs who reviled each other but were frustratingly strapped for cash. The surprising maverick in all this was Pope Sixtus V, who cared 'more for ducats than devotion', and often expressed an embarrassingly public admiration for the English queen.

The Armada campaign was the first modern conflict as we would understand it. A largely unexplored aspect has been the intense intelligence war fought by both sides, employing many of the espionage techniques familiar today. Black propaganda was also used to vilify each other and sap the morale of their adversaries, in publications that Joseph Goebbels, Hitler's 'Information Minister' almost four centuries later, would have been proud to write and distribute.

Because of the state of Elizabeth's exchequer and her natural parsimony, the English ships were starved of gunpowder and ammunition and failed to land the killer blow on the 'Great and Most Fortunate Navy'.

England's own Protestant God was thought responsible for His divine hand in stopping the Armada. We now suspect it was probably climate change that blew apart Philip's flawed plans for the conquest of England.

Much of the source material for this book has been drawn from contemporary documents, where possible employing the written or reported spoken words used by those living at the time.

Throughout, the dates are expressed in the 'New Style' or Gregorian calendar, introduced by Pope Gregory XIII in 1582 and used by most of Western Europe from 1587. England naturally refused to conform and did so for more than another century; their old Julian calendar running ten days behind.

ACKNOWLEDGEMENTS

This book could not have been written without the tireless and enthusiastic support of my dear wife Sally who, appropriately as the daughter of a sea captain, has helped me with the complexities of naval warfare in the sixteenth-century as well as the mysteries and dilemmas of both the English and Spanish orders of battle in the campaign.

A great number of friends and colleagues have very kindly given invaluable support and help in tracking down manuscripts and rare books in Britain and in Europe. As always my particular thanks go to Robin Harcourt Williams for his generous help with the Cecil Papers held in the archives of the Marquis of Salisbury at Hatfield House. I am also very grateful to Heather Rowland, head of library and collections, and Adrian James, assistant librarian, at the Society of Antiquaries at Burlington House, London; Kay Walters and her team at the incomparable library at The Athenæum in Pall Mall; the ever-willing staff at the University of Sussex library at Falmer, Sussex and the always helpful teams at The National Archives at Kew and in the Rare Books, Manuscripts and Humanities reading rooms of the British Library at St Pancras.

At Weidenfeld & Nicolson, Alan Samson has, as ever, been very encouraging and helpful, as has Lucinda McNeile, and I would like to record my grateful thanks to my editor Anne O'Brien and Douglas Matthews for compiling a complex index. I am also grateful to my agent Andrew Lownie.

As always, any errors or omissions are entirely my own responsibility.

Robert Hutchinson
West Sussex 2013

PROLOGUE

The law of nature moves me to sorrow for my sister. The burden that is fallen upon me makes me amazed and yet ... ordained to obey His appointment, I will thereto yield, desiring from the bottom of my heart that I may have the assistance of His Grace to be the minister of His heavenly will in this office now committed to me.

Elizabeth I, on hearing of her accession to the throne of England. Hatfield, 17 November 1558.[1]

Elizabeth Tudor's long years of torment, anxiety and fear finally ended just before noon on 17 November 1558, reputedly beneath the spreading branches of a gnarled old oak tree in the verdant grounds of Hatfield Palace, in Hertfordshire, 20 miles (32.2 km) north of London.

Six senior members of Queen Mary I's Privy Council, accompanied by Sir William Cordell, speaker of the House of Commons,[2] had cantered breathlessly across the greensward to bring her the news she had long dreamt of receiving – but in her dark days of despair, feared would never come.

After hastily dismounting, they knelt on the grass before the princess, who had been walking outside in the chill November air, and solemnly informed her of her half-sister's death.

Elizabeth, the twenty-five-year-old red-headed daughter of Anne Boleyn and King Henry VIII, had succeeded at last as Queen of England.

Although the fateful message from London had been expected almost hourly, its import still stunned her. She too fell to her knees and must have breathed a prayer of profound thanks both for her survival and her safe accession. At length, after 'a good time of respiration', exaltation flooded through her body and she spoke her first words as monarch, choosing, in Latin, verse twenty-three from the Old Testament's Psalm 118: *'Domino factum est istud, et est miribile in oculis nostris'* – 'This is the Lord's doing; it is marvellous in our eyes'.[3]

Around seven o'clock that morning, Mary had died in St James' Palace, London, only moments after the sacred Host had been solemnly elevated during a Mass celebrated in her bedchamber. Drifting in and out of consciousness, she died in great pain from the ovarian cysts or uterine cancer that finally killed her. Death was energetically stalking abroad that day. An epidemic of influenza (or more probably the 'English Sweating Sickness' a form of viral pneumonia),[4] which had carried off up to a fifth of her subjects over the previous two years, still claimed its victims, including Cardinal Reginald Pole, her Archbishop of Canterbury, who succumbed to its fevers within twelve hours of his sovereign's passing.

Elizabeth had become the last of Henry's disparate brood to occupy the throne of England. Many believed it was something of a miracle that she had lived long enough to wear the crown: no wonder those words of praise to God for His infinite mercy were chosen as her first public reaction to her accession. Doubtless the phrases were carefully rehearsed beforehand, with a typical Tudor eye to history's judgement.

Her path to the throne had been perilous and strewn with lethal pitfalls.

Her despotic father's obsessive infatuation with her feisty mother, driven by his restless longing for a lusty male heir, had been the root cause of a cataclysmic rupture with Rome that created a renegade church in England in the 1530s which was briefly returned to papal authority during Mary's reign. Henry's fixation and its aftermath spawned decades of religious discord that brutally cost the lives of hundreds of men and women who remained faithful to their creeds on both sides of the Catholic–Protestant divide.

Three months after Elizabeth's birth (on 7 September 1533 at Greenwich Palace) she had been moved to Hatfield with her own household. She was joined there shortly afterwards by seventeen-year-old Mary (the only child of Henry VIII and his Spanish wife Katherine of Aragon), who was now legally bastardised and formally stripped of her royal rank of princess because of the divisive annulment of the king's marriage with her mother.

Thomas Howard, Third Duke of Norfolk and uncle to Anne Boleyn, mischievously asked her on her arrival if she would like to 'see and pay court to the princess'. Mary snapped back defiantly that 'she knew of no other princess in England but herself ... The daughter of Madame de Pembroke [Anne Boleyn was created Marchioness of Pembroke before she became queen] is no princess at all. This is a title that belongs to me by right and no one else.' Mary lumped Elizabeth in with Henry's bastard son, Henry Fitzroy, Duke of Richmond (by Bessie Blount, one of Katherine's maids of honour); they were simply her illegitimate brother and sister. Did she have any message for the king? 'None,' said Mary, 'except that the Princess of Wales, his daughter, asks for his blessing.' Norfolk dared not return to court with such a dangerous message; 'Then go away and leave me alone,' Mary ordered imperiously.[5]

One of the last times Elizabeth saw her mother was in January 1536, but as a toddler, she probably would not have retained any memory of her visit. News of Katherine of Aragon's lonely death, exiled in spartan Kimbolton Castle, Huntingdonshire, had been received joyously at Henry's court. Queen Anne rewarded the messenger with 'a handsome present' and her father, Thomas Boleyn, Earl of Wiltshire, commented sardonically that it was a pity that Mary 'did not keep company with her [mother]'. The then Spanish ambassador, Eustace Chapuys (never a friend to Elizabeth), reported that the king 'sent for his Little Bastard and carrying her in his arms, he showed her first to one and then another'.[6]

Those happy red-letter days withered on the tortured vine of Henry's determination to safeguard the Tudor dynasty and his fury at being continually thwarted by his lack of sons. Despite three pregnancies, the queen failed wretchedly in her primary duty: to deliver a healthy prince.

That year, Anne Boleyn was competently beheaded by a specially hired French executioner on Tower Green on Friday 19 May for treason, adultery and alleged incest with her brother George. Four days before, Thomas Cranmer, newly appointed Archbishop of Canterbury, had annulled Anne's marriage with Henry, thus rendering Elizabeth, in her turn, a bastard. A new Act of Succession decreed that as she was illegitimate, she was 'utterly foreclosed, excluded and banned to claim, challenge or demand any inheritance as lawful heir ... to [the king] by lineal descent'.[7] But nothing was ever certain during the Tudor period: a further Act of 1543 reinstated Elizabeth and Mary to the succession and stipulated that if Edward died childless, the crown would pass to Mary. If she too died without issue, it would then pass on to Elizabeth.[8]

Her education was directed by religiously reformist scholars from St John's College, Cambridge and she later admitted to Mary 'that she had never been taught the doctrine of the ancient [Catholic] faith'.[9] Elizabeth became fluent in French, Italian, Greek and Latin, but she did not begin to study Spanish until her twenties. When Henry died in January 1547, her priggish half-brother Edward, son of Henry's third queen, Jane Seymour, wrote to her: 'There is very little need of my consoling you, most dear sister, because from your learning you know what you ought to do ... I perceive you think of our father's death with a calm mind.'[10]

The radical Protestant policies of Edward VI's short reign swept English and Welsh parish churches and cathedrals clean of popish imagery, opportunely recycling many of these fixtures and fittings into hard cash for the young king's embarrassingly empty exchequer. Daringly, Mary continued to hear Catholic Masses in her household and when told to cease and desist by Edward's outraged Privy Council, her reaction was predictably forthright:

> You accuse me of breaking the laws and disobeying them by keeping to my own religion – but I reply that my faith and my religion are those held by the whole of Christendom, formerly confessed by this kingdom under the late king, my father, until you altered them with your laws ... This is my final answer to any letters that you may write me on matters of religion.[11]

After Edward's death from a bizarre combination of tuberculosis, measles and the unhelpful ministrations of a 'wise woman', Mary determinedly saw off the challenge of her half-brother's preferred Protestant heir, Lady Jane Grey, and entered London in triumph as queen on 3 August 1553. She swiftly returned England to Catholicism, although incongruously, she initially retained her father's title of Supreme Head of the Church in England (until early 1554, when use of the title was phased out in official documents) and early on continued to benefit from the sacrilegious sale of church goods.[12] Giovanni Michiel, the departing Venetian ambassador in London, reported in 1557 that seven new monasteries had been opened;[13] 'the churches are frequented, the images replaced and all the ancient Catholic rites and ceremonies performed as they used to be, the heretical being suppressed'.[14] 'Suppressed' was too feeble or facile a word to describe what was happening. Mary burned two hundred and eighty-three Protestants at the stake for refusing to recant their beliefs during just four years – hence history's pejorative soubriquet 'Bloody Mary'.

On 8 September 1553, the feast of the Nativity of the Virgin Mary, Elizabeth heard her first Mass but attended such services only erratically thereafter. The Spanish ambassador, Simon Renard, believed her Catholic fervour was mere show and that her heart was not in her conversion. He reported acidly: 'she complained loudly all the way to church and that her stomach ached' and during the liturgy, she 'wore a suffering air'.[15]

Elizabeth was always her father's daughter: characterised by the red hair; her imperious manner; the Tudor rages; the love of magnificence and of gaudy ceremony. Despite her mother's execution, she continued to cherish Henry's memory and to model herself upon him. The princess, the Venetian envoy observed, 'prides herself on her father and glories in him; everybody says that she also resembles him more than the queen does'.[16]

But Mary hated Elizabeth with a black sibling passion. She feared her as a younger rival waiting threateningly in the wings to wear the crown of England once she died or was deposed. Michiel was well aware of the queen's 'evil disposition towards ... my lady Elizabeth, which although dissembled, it cannot be denied that she displays in many ways the scorn and ill she bears her'.[17] Mary's suspicions intensified when she was faced by an uprising in 1554 over her projected marriage with Philip, son of the Emperor Charles V of Spain. Mary's Lord Chancellor, the sinister Stephen Gardiner, Bishop of Winchester, had led the religiously conservative party during Henry VIII's reign, and now feared Elizabeth would become the focal point of a Protestant resurgence. The prelate confided to Renard that 'he had no hope of seeing the kingdom at peace' while the princess lived and he urged Mary to consign her to the Tower – even before rumour had implicated her in the abortive Wyatt rebellion.

Gardiner's unease was justified. On 14 March, thousands flocked to London's Aldersgate Street to hear a miraculous 'voice in the wall' which when people cried 'God save Queen Mary' stayed silent, but as the shouts changed to 'God save the Lady Elizabeth' it responded: 'So be it!' When one mischief-maker asked: 'What is the Mass?' the 'spirit' replied: 'Idolatry!' The perpetrator of this hoax was Elizabeth Croft, 'a wench about the age of eighteen', who was imprisoned in the Tower and subsequently executed:

> There was a new scaffold made [at St Paul's Cathedral] for the maid that spoke in the wall and *whistled* in Aldersgate Street ... She wept piteously, knelt and asked [for] God's mercy and the queen and bade all people be aware of false teaching for she said that ... many good things [had been promised] to her.[18]

Following the defeat of the rebels at the western gates of the City of London, the queen ordered Elizabeth to be taken to the Tower. To prevent the inevitable outbursts of popular support that her progress through the city's streets would incite, the Marquis of Winchester and the Earl of Sussex were instructed to convey Elizabeth to the fortress by boat.

Knowing her life now hung in the balance, she immediately wrote a heartfelt, pleading letter to her sister in her neat, easily read italic handwriting:

> If any did try this old saying – that a king's word was more than another man's oath – I most humbly beseech your majesty to verify it in me and to remember your last promise and my last demand; that I be not condemned without answer and due proof.
>
> It seems that now I am, for without cause proved, I am by your Council from you commanded to go unto the Tower, a place more [accustomed] to a false traitor than a true subject ...
>
> I know I deserve it not, yet in the face of all this realm, it appears it is proved. Which I pray God I may die the [most] shameful death that ever any died before I may mean any such thing ...
>
> I protest before God ... I never practised, counselled or consented to anything that might be prejudicial to you or dangerous to the state ...

Pardon my boldness which innocency procures me to do, together with hope of your natural kindness. I have heard in my time of many cast away for want of coming to their prince ... I pray God ... evil persuasions persuade not one sister against the other ... I humbly crave to speak with your highness.

As for the traitor Wyatt, he might [by chance] write me a letter but on my faith, I never received any from him.[19]

Fearing that she might be incriminated by the surreptitious addition of a forged postscript, Elizabeth wisely scored a diagonal line across the blank two-thirds of a page at the end of her letter.

While she was writing to Mary, 'the tide rose so high that it was no longer possible to pass under London Bridge' from Westminster to the Tower – so her grim journey by river was postponed to the next day, Palm Sunday, 18 March.[20] En route, Elizabeth was almost tipped into the water as her boat shot the race through one of the nineteen arches of the medieval London Bridge. She flatly refused to disembark at the Tower's privy stairs and sat down in protest at her arrest, announcing, 'It is better sitting here than in a worse place.'[21] It was raining hard and perhaps it was the inclement weather rather than the entreaties of her discomfited escorts that finally persuaded her to struggle out of the boat declaring: 'Here lands as true a subject, being a prisoner, as ever landed [here].' Entering across the drawbridge, the sight of the forbidding grey outer walls, dwarfed by the White Tower within, terrified her. She believed that she would now suffer the same fate as her mother had there eighteen years earlier. Her fears were magnified when she passed the scaffold on Tower Green on which Lady Jane Grey had been beheaded five weeks before.

During her incarceration, Elizabeth wrote this prayer; its bleak words eloquently describing her feelings of isolation and hopelessness:

Help me now O God for I have none other friends but Thee alone.

And suffer me not (I beseech Thee) to build my foundation on the sands but on the rock whereby all blasts of blustering weather may have no power against me.[22]

Her despairing cry in the dark was seemingly heard as her trials and travails were now about to be eased. Sir Thomas Wyatt was taken in chains to a scaffold at Hay Hill beside Hyde Park on 11 April, and there he was hung, drawn and quartered, along with three other rebel leaders. Portions of his torso were hung up at the approaches to the City of London as an awful demonstration of the fate of traitors.[23] He went to his death adamantly refusing to implicate the princess in his conspiracy.

Despite strenuous efforts, no solid evidence proving Elizabeth's involvement in the rebellion was ever uncovered to warrant her following him to the executioner's block. Much to Gardiner's chagrin, she was released on Saturday 19 May[24] and taken to the royal hunting lodge at Woodstock in Oxfordshire, where she remained under house arrest. During those tedious, listless days, she used one of her diamond rings to scratch this verse on a pane of window glass there:

> Much suspected by me
> Nothing proved by me
> Quod [said] Elizabeth the prisoner.[25]

Mary had meanwhile married Philip of Spain, enveloping him with a love of unexpected passion. After he ascended the Spanish throne on his father's abdication in 1556, the couple assumed the extravagant style and title of 'Philip and Mary, by the Grace of God, King and Queen of England, Spain, France, Jerusalem, both the Scillies and Ireland,[26] Defenders of the Faith, Archdukes of Austria, Dukes of Burgundy, Milan and Brabant, Counts of Habsburg, Flanders and Tyrol'. Mary not only became Queen Consort of Spain but also 'Queen of the Spanish East and West Indies and of the Islands and Mainland of the Ocean Sea'.

Mary's bridegroom regarded his marriage as a loveless match of mere diplomatic convenience. The queen was eleven years older than him; had been betrothed briefly to his father in the 1520s and her love was unfortunately unrequited. His eyes may have roved lasciviously over his wife's ladies at court: tall and blonde Magdalene Dacre whispered that the king had reached through a window and tried to fondle her breasts as she was washing herself one morning. She grabbed a conveniently placed stick (was this something always kept handy indoors by Tudor ladies in *déshabille*?) and struck his outstretched arm to cool his ardour, prompting his polite praise for her modesty.[27]

Both Philip's heart and head had no roots in England and he stayed just long enough in his new dominions for appearances' sake. There were hopes that he had begat a child and in April 1555 Elizabeth was recalled to Hampton Court to witness the happy birth of Mary's heir.

She was not yet wholly rehabilitated in the queen's affections and was patently a despondent and reluctant prospective aunt. It did not help that her household had a reputation as a hotbed of Protestant subversion: in July 1554, one of her servants had been imprisoned for sedition; a second followed him into gaol in April 1555 and the following month, Elizabeth's Italian tutor, Battista Castiglione, was sent to the Tower on suspicion of distributing treasonous literature in London. However, he maintained stoutly that he was in the city only to buy new strings for his mistress's lute[28] and was grudgingly released. The princess was therefore still held under arrest – 'the doors being shut upon her, the soldiers in the ancient posture of watch and guard'.[29]

Mary did not produce her heir, having suffered a phantom pregnancy, and her grief and humiliation were deepened by her husband's departure from England soon afterwards. Beforehand, he had urged the queen to offer Elizabeth better treatment as her heiress presumptive and had dissuaded her from yet again declaring Elizabeth a bastard – or exiling her abroad. Behind Philip's outward kindness lay a hard-nosed pragmatism: if Mary's half-sister did not succeed her, the French would certainly press the claims to the English throne of Mary Queen of Scots, who had been betrothed to François, Dauphin of France, the son of King Henri II. Under no circumstances could Spain ever countenance an England in the thrall of France.

Elizabeth was sent back to Hatfield, where she rejected several offers of marriage suggested by her half-sister over the coming years as a means of ridding this troublesome cuckoo from Mary's uncomfortable nest.

In August 1558, the queen, now aged forty-two, was afflicted by bouts of fever and those around her began, hesitantly and tentatively, to consider the thorny problem of her successor. Others were voting with their feet. The Venetian diplomat Michiel Surian told the Doge in November that 'many personages of the kingdom flock to the house of my lady Elizabeth, the crowd constantly increasing with great frequency'.[30] Although these consultations were carried out covertly, it was plain as a pikestaff that plans for her accession were being quietly drawn up. The Spanish envoy Renard observed that she was 'honoured and recognised' [as heiress to the crown] and it would be almost impossible to debar her. He urged Philip to find her a husband overseas – perhaps the Duke of Savoy, 'a man true to God and your majesty'.[31]

Even Mary knew deep down of the unspoken reality that she would never conceive a child and that she should grasp the nettle of the succession to the throne. But she still shied away from naming her half-sister as heir apparent. On 28 October she signed a codicil to her will that acknowledged that 'God has hitherto sent me no fruit nor heir of my body' and requested her 'next heir and successor' to honour the terms of her will, particularly those relating to religious houses and the founding of a military hospital.[32] The successor's name was conspicuous by its absence.

Time was running out for Mary and she began to suffer frequent bouts of delirium. On 6 November, the Privy Council finally convinced her to name Elizabeth to succeed her. Jane Dormer, one of the queen's ladies, took some of her jewels to Hatfield with her fervent request that the Catholic religion should continue in England. Years afterwards Jane remembered that Elizabeth had promised 'that the earth might open and swallow her up alive' if she was not a true Catholic – but others recalled a very different, less explicit pledge: 'I promise this much, that I will not change it, provided only that it can be proved by the word of God, which shall be the only foundation and rule of my religion.'[33]

Another visitor was a special Spanish envoy, Gómez Suárez de Figueroa, Fifth Count de Feria, who, on behalf of his king, wanted to sound out Elizabeth's views on continuing England's alliance with Spain. When he suggested that her brother-in-law Philip was responsible for her belated recognition by Mary, she immediately retorted that she 'owed her crown not to Philip ... but to the attachment of the people of England'. The envoy told his master:

> Madam Elizabeth [has] come to the conclusion that she would have succeeded even if your majesty and the queen opposed it [so] she does not feel indebted to your majesty in the matter.

It is impossible to persuade [her] otherwise that the kingdom will
not consent to anything else and would take up arms on her behalf.

The new queen, Feria concluded, was 'determined to be governed by
no one'. She was 'a very vain and clever woman. She must have been
thoroughly schooled in the manner in which her father conducted
his affairs and I am much afraid that she will not be well-disposed in
matters of religion for I see her inclined to govern through men who
are believed to be heretics and I am told that all the women around
her definitely are,' he ruefully reported.[34]

In Flanders, Philip, who had lost his title as King of England under
the terms of his marriage treaty, jotted down his reactions to his
wife's passing, almost as a footnote to the business of his day: 'I
felt a reasonable regret for her death. I shall miss her even on this
account.'[35] He seemed more exercised about the potential loss of gold,
jewels and resplendent robes belonging to the Order of the Garter
that he had left in England 'packed in a trunk that was ... deposited,
locked, in the late Queen's chamber' in the Palace of Whitehall and
in his own hand, amended two lists of those items to be reclaimed.[36]

Elizabeth joyfully grasped the levers of power. She charged her
new council always to offer 'good advice and counsel' and required
'nothing more than faithful hearts in such service as ... shall be
in your powers towards the preservation of me and this common-
wealth'. She appointed Sir William Cecil, formerly the administrator
of her estates, as her secretary of state, telling him:

This judgement I have of you: that you will not be corrupted with
any manner of gift and that you will be faithful to the state and that
without respect of my private will, you will give me that counsel
that you think best and if you shall know anything necessary to be
declared to me of secrecy you shall show it to myself only.[37]

He was to serve his queen faithfully for forty years until his death
in 1598.

There were some scores that had to be settled. Count de Feria
was aghast at the immediate and radical changes: 'The kingdom
is entirely in the hands of young folks, heretics and traitors, and
the Queen does not favour a single man whom her majesty, who is
now in heaven, would have received. [She] will take no one into her

service who served her sister when she was Lady Mary.' The elderly and the Catholics were dissatisfied 'but dare not open their lips'.

She seems to me incomparably more feared than her sister and gives her orders and has her way as absolutely as her father did.

He added: 'What can be expected from a country governed by a queen, and she a young lass, who although sharp, is without prudence and is everyday standing up against religion more sharply.'[38]

Elizabeth was crowned queen at Westminster Abbey on Sunday 15 January 1559, tartly ordering its monks to remove the popish altar candles as 'she had enough light to see by'.[39]

Sir John Hayward wrote admiringly of the new queen:

Nature had bestowed … [on her] many of her fairest favours. [She is] of stature mean, slender, straight and amiably composed. Every motion of her seems to bear majesty … in her forehead large and fair, her eyes lively and sweet but short-sighted,[40] her nose somewhat rising in [the middle]. Her virtues are such as might suffice to make an Ethiopian beautiful which the more a man knows and understands, the more he shall admire and love.[41]

With the Tudor dynasty's recurrent nightmare about succession in many people's minds, Elizabeth was soon beset with questions about her marrying. Philip instructed de Feria to formally throw his own feathered and bejewelled cap into the ring as a suitor for the hand of his sister-in-law. He admitted to some troublesome doubts about Elizabeth; he believed her unsound in religion 'and it would not look well for me to marry her unless she were a Catholic. Besides … such a marriage would appear like entering upon a perpetual war with France, seeing the claims that the Queen of Scots has to the English crown.' Philip also fretted about having to pay for 'the costly entertainment necessary' in England when his own exchequer was so depleted. But on the whole, it was more important that England remained Catholic and he was prepared to 'sacrifice my private inclination' and marry Elizabeth, if only in the service of God. Confronted by the prospects of such a marriage, Philip 'felt like a condemned man awaiting his fate'. These were scarcely the words of an eager, blushing bridegroom.[42]

Elizabeth kept the Spanish envoy waiting on tenterhooks for her answer to this less than munificent offer of marriage. In February, she discovered an important impediment to her acceptance – the fact that she would be marrying her half-sister's husband. There was more than a little piquancy in suggesting this as a stumbling block; the queen was deploying the Biblical arguments contained in Leviticus 20:21, 'If a man shall take his brother's wife, it is an unclean thing. He hath uncovered his brother's nakedness; they shall be childless.' This was the self-same argument used by Henry VIII to justify the annulment of his marriage to Katherine of Aragon. How could she therefore marry Philip? It would dishonour the memory of her father. Moreover, no dispensation from the Pope could be sought, as 'she denied point-blank' the authority of Rome.

How she must have savoured the irony of this response! In addition, she had been warned that after marrying Philip, he would return to Spain 'directly'. The Count told his master: 'This she said with great laughter as if she could read [my] secret thoughts. She is so well informed about this it looks as if she has seen your majesty's letters.'[43]

At last that March, Elizabeth gave her final and definitive answer. It teetered on the coquettish; whilst she had no wish to offend 'her good brother' she could not marry him because she was a heretic. The queen, reported de Feria, was 'disturbed and excited and resolved to restore religion as her father left it ... [She said that] so much money was taken out of the country for the Pope every year that she must put an end to it and the bishops were lazy poltroons.'[44] The envoy was horrified: 'This country ... has fallen into the hands of a woman, who is the daughter of the Devil, and the greatest scoundrels and heretics in the land.'[45] Instead, a doubtless relieved Philip the following year married the French princess, Elizabeth of Valois, eldest daughter of Henri II of France and his wife Catherine de Medici, in yet another union of diplomatic advantage.[46]

Although there were other more enthusiastic suitors, Elizabeth had no plans for marriage. She assured Parliament that 'the realm shall not remain destitute of an heir' and promised to deal with selecting a suitable husband 'in convenient time' – but at present she was determined to remain single.[47]

One matter that could not wait was a decision on what would be the state religion for England. The queen sometimes appeared bored by the endless wrangling over liturgical minutia and testily told one French envoy: 'There is only one Jesus Christ and one faith and all the rest that they dispute [are] but trifles.[48] That faith would be Protestantism in her realm, but Elizabeth tried not to alienate or disaffect her Catholic subjects. The compromise that was achieved was based on Edward VI's Protestant settlement but permitted ecclesiastical vestments to be used during the liturgy. She had to accept the title of Supreme Governor of the Church of England, rather than her father's more ostentatious 'Supreme Head', which many (in those unenlightened days) believed was unacceptable for a woman to bear. The religious changes were enshrined in the Act of Supremacy[49] and the Act of Uniformity,[50] which made attendance at church compulsory for all. The 1552 Prayer Book in English became the only liturgy allowed in England and Wales.

Unwittingly, the foundations had been laid for decades of religious turbulence. In Elizabeth's name, more than two hundred Catholics and their priests were executed during the forty-four years of her reign – not burnt at the stake, but butchered on the scaffold as traitors to her crown.

The yawning schism with Rome also became the catalyst for a cripplingly expensive nineteen-year war with Spain that threatened invasion of her realm and day and night made her an assassin's target.

– 1 –

THE ENEMY WITHIN

*We (poor wretches) ... are reported ... to be evilly
affected towards your royal person ... and that upon the
vile action ... of every lewd person, we all must be condemned to bear traitorous minds ... We are most odi-
ously termed 'bloodsuckers' ... and it is published that
your majesty is to fear so many deaths as there be papists
in the land.*

An appeal to the queen from her loyal Catholic subjects,
March 1585.[1]

At seven o'clock on the evening of Sunday 16 May 1568, Elizabeth I's personal nemesis entered her uncertain realm, stepping wearily ashore on a remote windswept beach in north-west England.

Her Catholic cousin Mary Queen of Scots landed from a small fishing boat near Workington in Cumbria after fleeing Scotland across the treacherously shoaled waters of the Solway Firth. She was dirty, penniless, and like other benighted refugees from civil war, possessed only the grubby clothes she stood up in. But despite her many hardships, the thrice-married,[2] twenty-five-year-old auburn-haired woman – at 5 feet 11 inches (1.80 metres) tall, towering over her handful of exhausted, dispirited attendants – still exuded the dignity and deportment of a queen. Only the vivacity of her hazel-brown eyes was diminished, sapped by months of fear, heartbreak and privation.

Three days before, it had taken just forty-five minutes for her army of six thousand men to be roundly defeated at Langside (now in south Glasgow),[3] by a smaller force fighting for the Scottish Protestant nobility led by her illegitimate half-brother, James Stewart, Earl of Moray.[4] She had earlier been forced to abdicate so that her baby son could ascend the Scottish throne as King James VI, with Moray as all-powerful regent. Now, as dawn broke the following morning, Mary wrote plaintively to Elizabeth, craving an immediate private audience to seek English military assistance both to recover her crown and wreak bloody vengeance on those who had rebelled against her.

She was hardly a welcome visitor. Her personal heraldry proudly quartered the arms of England with those of France and Scotland, symbolising her claims to be the strongest heir presumptive to the English throne through her direct descent from Henry VIII's eldest sister, Margaret, one-time Queen of Scotland.[5]

Even though Elizabeth enjoyed less than harmonious relations with Mary and had resolutely rejected her as her successor, she sympathised with her sister queen's unhappy fate, believing that her Scottish neighbours had wickedly deposed a monarch anointed by God Himself. But she knew full well that her own Catholic subjects believed her a heretic, the bastard daughter of Anne Boleyn who had bigamously married Henry before the death of his saintly wife, Katherine of Aragon. She was also conscious that many prayed earnestly that ere long, Mary would wear the crown of England rather than her.

Her chief minister, William Cecil, did not share Elizabeth's regal sympathy or her constitutional concerns about the inviolable divine right of monarchs. To him, Mary Queen of Scots' presence on English soil posed a grave threat to his mistress's throne and his own political and personal survival. In his view, her Catholic loyalties also imperilled England's fledgling Protestant faith that had been forged in the cruel fires of martyrdom of Mary I's reign. No surprise then, that within hours the Scottish queen found herself in comfortable quarters in the south-east tower of Carlisle Castle – but under strict twenty-four-hour guard. Even in her worst nightmares, she could not have dreamt that she was to be sequestered from the outside world for the next eighteen years as Elizabeth's unwanted guest. Mary might be allowed to enjoy the title and a few trappings of a queen, but the cruel reality was that she was to remain a closely guarded prisoner in five-star captivity in a succession of fortified houses in northern England and the Midlands.

Cecil's uneasiness stemmed from his uncomfortable knowledge

that large swathes of England remained staunchly Catholic, with perhaps more than half of Elizabeth's three million subjects still clinging stubbornly to that faith. Lancashire, for example, was to retain a Catholic majority until very late into the sixteenth century.[6] In the strategically important maritime counties of Sussex and Hampshire, bordering the English Channel, the heart of the old religion was yet beating strongly, nurtured by conservative gentry and fugitive priests. Many rood screens[7] stood in Sussex chancels in defiance of government order; and where they had been dismantled, 'the wood lies still ... ready to be set up again', according to a disquieting official report of 1568. Holy images were hidden, not destroyed, and 'other popish ornaments [were concealed] to set up the Mass again within twenty-four hours'. Chalices were secreted to await the happy return of the ancient ritual. Parishioners still brought their Latin missals with them to Protestant services and women and the elderly openly said their rosary beads, ignoring the benefits of both God's Word and those of the dark-clad ministers wearing sober Geneva bands at their throats.[8] In Hampshire, Bishop Robert Horne had great difficulty in finding ministers who would preach 'sound doctrine' and complained indignantly that some priests even in Winchester Cathedral were still stubbornly 'inculcating popery and superstition'.[9]

Events were to justify Cecil's hard-nosed assessment of the ramifications of Mary Queen of Scots' ill-omened arrival in England. By the middle of the following year, 1569, Thomas Howard, Fourth Duke of Norfolk, the egotistical premier peer of England, was up to his innocent eyes in plans to marry the imprisoned Scottish queen, motivated by fevered dreams of becoming king consort of Scotland one day, if not of England the next. Mary herself also proved a compulsive conspirator. Not content with pledging her love for the naïve duke as a possible means of escaping Elizabeth's unwelcome and unwilling hospitality, she had written secretly to the Catholic earls of Northumberland and Westmorland seeking their assistance in freeing her, by force of arms if necessary.

Generations of sixteenth-century Howards had been flawed by a fatal arrogance and Norfolk's pride inescapably became his downfall. Describing his fabulous wealth and his opulent palace at Norwich, he bragged shamelessly that his annual revenues were 'not much less than those of Scotland ... and when he was in his tennis court at Norwich, he thought himself equal with some kings'. If he had hopes of reassuring the mistrustful and always penny-pinching Elizabeth, these were hardly appropriate blandishments. Peremptory royal summonses to Norfolk to attend court were seemingly wilfully disobeyed and the queen suspected that the duke's suspicious absence was a curtain-raiser to rebellion by her Catholic subjects, with him as their noble figurehead. Inevitably, that October Norfolk was arrested en route to Windsor and carted off to the Tower of London, where so many of his family had been incarcerated before him and where his father had been executed in January 1547 for conceitedly (and treasonably) including the royal arms of Edward the Confessor in his heraldry.[10]

As in many rural counties, the Elizabethan religious settlement of 1559 had made little difference to the beliefs of the traditionalist populations of those immediately south of the Scottish border. Northumberland, Durham and Yorkshire were a world way from London and the carefully contrived splendour of the royal court. The much-loved pre-Reformation rituals continued habitually as if Mary I was still occupying the throne, with holy water, rosaries, images and devotional candles being used in defiance of official Protestant doctrine.[11] It was only a matter of time before the cauldron that was the Catholic north, containing a heady, seething mix of religion, resentment and reaction, finally boiled over.

On 9 November 1569, Thomas Percy, Seventh Earl of Northumberland and Charles Neville, Sixth Earl of Westmorland, rose in revolt – church bells being rung backwards to warn their tenantry to muster. They intended to head south to free Mary Queen of Scots from her new prison at Tutbury Castle, Staffordshire, 'as next heir, failing issue of Her Majesty' and return England to Catholicism.[12] On 14 November they arrived in Durham, marching, with heavy symbolism, behind the banner of the Five Wounds of Christ, last carried by rebels in the Pilgrimage of Grace against Elizabeth's father thirty-two years before. They swept through the eleventh-century cathedral, tearing down any emblem of Protestantism they could find and triumphantly burnt the English prayer books and Bible in an iconoclastic pyre. They then joyfully celebrated Mass.

The Lord President of the North, Thomas Radcliffe, Third Earl of Sussex, had only four hundred badly armed cavalry with him at

York and was fearful of facing the rebels on the battlefield with such a small force of perhaps doubtful loyalty. For Elizabeth, 265 miles (425 km) away in firmly Protestant London, the insurrection was a startling recurrence of the perilous threats that had persistently haunted her Tudor forebears and siblings.[13] Her grandfather, Henry VII, whose claim to the crown was in reality of only paper-thin legality, had faced a series of uprisings after his victory over Richard III at Bosworth Field in 1485. Her father Henry VIII put down rebellions against the dissolution of the monasteries in the north in 1536–7, but only with the greatest difficulty. Her teenage half-brother, Edward VI, was forced to hide in Windsor Castle during the dangerous revolts in the West Country, the south, midlands and in Yorkshire in 1549 over the introduction of the English prayer book, and also had to counter Kett's Rebellion in Norfolk that same year. Further insurrections followed in Nottinghamshire, Leicestershire and Rutland in 1551, involving 'light knaves, horse-coursers and craftsmen'. Finally, Mary I had defeated rebel forces in London in 1554 over her planned marriage with Philip of Spain. Now it was Elizabeth's turn to face the anger and rude weapons of the commons and, with characteristic Tudor truculence, she raged at delays in confronting and crushing them on the field of battle.

In York, Sir Ralph Sadler, chancellor of the Duchy of Lancaster, explained patiently to Cecil why Sussex could not risk fighting the rebel forces immediately. 'The ancient faith', he counselled, 'still lies like lees at the bottom of men's hearts and if the vessel is ever so little stirred, comes to the top.'

There are not ten gentlemen in all this country that favour her [Elizabeth's] proceedings in the cause of religion.

The common people are ignorant, superstitious and altogether blinded with the old popish doctrine, and therefore so favour the cause which the rebels make the colour of their rebellion that, although their persons be here with us, their hearts are with them ...

If we should go to the field with this northern force only, they would fight faintly.

For if the father be on this side, the son is on the other and one brother with us and the other with the rebels.[14]

The earls paused on their way south on 16 November at Darlington, County Durham, to issue a proclamation seeking popular support to safeguard England's ancient customs and Catholic religion. It contained a compelling message, resonant both of patriotism and religious faith, designed to appeal to the region's sullen conservative masses. Declaring themselves 'the Queen's most true and lawful subjects', they railed against the *arriviste* upstarts surrounding Elizabeth who, they claimed, daily sought the overthrow 'of the ancient nobility' and had for ten years 'maintained a new-found religion and heresy, contrary to God's word'. Foreign powers, they warned darkly, would force England to return to Catholicism at the point of the sword and intended 'shortly to invade this realm, which will be to our utter destruction, if we do not ourselves speedily [achieve] the same'.

> We are now constrained at this time ... to ... redress it ourselves, which if we should not do so and foreigners enter upon us, we should be all made slaves and bondsmen to them.
>
> [We] therefore will and require ... every one of you ... above the age of sixteen years and not [yet] sixty, as your duty towards God binds you, for the setting forth of his true and catholic religion and as you tender [value] the common wealth of your country, to come ... to us with all speed with all such armour and furniture [weapons] as you ... have.
>
> This fail you not ... as you will answer to the contrary at your peril.[15]

The proclamation ended, somewhat ambiguously, with the traditional words: 'God save the Queen'.

However, beyond the two earls' tenantry, there was little enthusiasm for rebellion – perhaps painful memories of Henry VIII's vicious retribution against the Pilgrimage of Grace three decades before lingered on amongst the yeomen's grandsires. So when the insurgents concentrated at Bramham Moor, west of Tadcaster, north Yorkshire, on 16 November, only 3,800 ill-armed infantry and 1,600 better equipped cavalry could be mustered.[16] The raggle-taggle foot soldiers hardly resembled an all-conquering army and Northumberland and Westmorland began to be assailed by doubts. Discretion being the better part of valour, they decided to head home with barely a shot fired.

Meanwhile, the new Spanish ambassador in London, the wily Don Guerau de Spes, was aghast that the rebels had not marched on the capital, as he sensed something approaching panic in Elizabeth's government's reaction to the uprising. The City of London had raised two thousand men 'of mean sort' for the royalist army now gathering in Leicestershire; there was a shortage of horses and the queen was trying desperately to borrow money from foreign merchants to pay for her hastily recruited army.[17] There were whispers that Elizabeth planned to establish a last-ditch redoubt at Windsor Castle and had ordered infantry there as her bodyguard. Frustrated at the slow progress in restoring her rule in the north, the queen could only order the removal of Northumberland's banner as a traitor from his stall as a Garter Knight in St George's Chapel, Windsor.[18]

Would the uprising spread? 'The Catholics in Wales and the west have not yet followed the example of those in the north, although it is said they are about to do so,' de Spes reported to Philip in Spain.[19] The Spanish king pondered over the ambassador's dispatch as he sat in his austerely furnished study within the palace of San Lorenzo de El Escorial in the Sierra de Guadarrama, 28 miles (45 km) north-west of Madrid. He had regarded English Catholics as special kindred since his marriage to Mary I, so he was cautiously pleased by news of the uprising. Philip wrote immediately to his captain-general, Fernando Álvarez de Toledo, Duke of Alba, busy suppressing Protestantism in the Spanish Netherlands, musing that force might now be needed to drag Elizabeth back to the Catholic faith:

> We are beginning to lose [our] reputation by deferring so long to provide a remedy for the great grievance done by this woman to my subjects, friends and allies.
>
> [God's] holy religion may be restored ... and the Catholics and good Christians thus rescued from the oppression in which they live.
>
> In case her obstinacy and hardness of heart may continue, you will take into your consideration the best direction to be given to this.
>
> We think here that the best course will be to encourage, with money and secret favour, the Catholics of the north and to help those in Ireland to take up arms against the heretics and deliver the crown to the Queen of Scotland, to whom it belongs by succession.

Philip was hardly delighted that Mary Queen of Scots, with her close ties to the French monarchy, could now become Queen of England – but his unqualified fidelity to Holy Mother Church overrode such diplomatic misgivings. Her accession, he declared, 'would be very agreeable to the Pope and all Christendom and would encounter no opposition from anyone'.[20]

Back in England, despite their retreat, the northern rebellion was still alive and kicking. In the first week of December, more than 4,500 rebels besieged Sir George Bowes, a grizzled veteran of the Scottish border wars, in Barnard Castle where he suffered a mass desertion by troops of his garrison who jumped over the low walls of his defensive outworks, some killing themselves in the process. Others treacherously opened his gates to the insurgents and he was forced to surrender on generous terms that permitted him to take four hundred of his men unmolested into Yorkshire.[21] Another rebel victory came with the easy capture of the port of Hartlepool, where the ruinous defensive walls had collapsed in places. The rebels hoped that Spanish troops would soon land there as reinforcements. These were forlorn hopes indeed.

Elizabeth's revenge was drawing ever nearer.

Advance elements of her ten-thousand-strong army reached the freezing banks of the River Tees on 16 December and the demoralised earls stood down their infantry and fled first to Hexham, then across the Scottish border, seeking sanctuary from their queen's retribution. Cecil wrote to Sadler on Christmas Day, employing a contrived hunting analogy to describe the royalist forces' pursuit of the fugitives:

> The vermin flee into a foreign covert where I fear thieves and murderers will be their hosts and maintainers of our rebels until the hunters be gone and then they will pass [overseas].[22]

Even now, there was optimism amongst England's enemies that this flight was merely a timely strategic withdrawal. The Venetian ambassador in France, Alvise Contarini, reported as late as mid-January 1570 that the insurgents were marching on the border town of Berwick to establish a winter base there 'and seeing that every day their forces continue to augment, they expect to be stronger ... by the spring'.[23] De Spes in London soon realised the bleak truth: 'The

Catholics are ... ashamed that their enterprises should have turned out so vain ... [They] are lost by bad guidance and although they are undertaken with impetus, they are not carried through with constancy,' he admitted ruefully.[24]

The brutal aftermath was that Northumberland was betrayed to the Earl of Moray and ignominiously handed over to the English authorities in return for £2,000 in coin. He was beheaded at York in 1572.[25] Westmorland fled to the Spanish Netherlands and, his estates forfeited, survived only on hand-outs from Spain.[26] Elizabeth jubilantly informed the French ambassador that she had completely defeated the rebels and pardoned the population in Yorkshire and Durham,[27] claiming to 'have always been of our own nature inclined to mercy'. But behind the polite language of diplomacy, she had demanded bloodshed and urged her generals to put to death, under martial law, any captured rebels. More than eight hundred were executed, mainly those 'of the meanest sort'.[28]

Sussex feared it was taking too long to hang the miscreants and dreaded that 'the queen's majesty will find cause [for] offence'. He told Bowes on 19 January that 'the queen does much marvel ... that she does not hear from me that the executions [are] not ended. Therefore I heartily pray you to expedition for I feel this lingering will breed [her] displeasure to us both.' The scale of vengeance was such that Sir Thomas Gargrave suspected that these judicial killings 'will leave many places naked and without inhabitants'.[29] The fearful destruction visited upon the homes and property of the insurgents ensured that the economy of this part of England would not recover for almost two centuries.

The danger to the crown posed by Mary Queen of Scots may have been averted but Cecil knew it remained dormant and ever-present. Elizabeth's cousin, Lord Hunsdon, lived up to his reputation for plain-speaking by warning her bluntly on 30 January 1570:

> Assure yourself that if you do not take heed of that Scottish queen, she will put you in peril ... for there are many practices [conspiracies] abroad.[30]

As in much of the Vatican's dealings with the Tudor monarchy, Pope Pius V acted too slowly to assist the abortive Catholic uprising. On 25 February 1570 he signed the papal bull *Regnans in Excelsis*, which excommunicated Elizabeth – 'that servant of all iniquity' – and deprived her of any 'pretended right' to the English throne that she had so 'monstrously usurped'. This was not only a religious sanction but also a very personal attack. Pius carefully catalogued Elizabeth's every sin in a veritable litany of heresy and cruelty. By 'main force' she had destroyed the true religion; oppressed 'the professors of the Catholic faith'; compelled her subjects 'to submit to her accursed laws to abhor the authority of the Roman pontiff and to acknowledge herself alone as mistress in both temporal and spiritual matters'. She had 'cast many bishops and prelates into prison, where after many sufferings they had miserably perished'. Furthermore, Pius declared:

> We command and interdict all and every one of her barons, subjects, people and others that they shall not dare to obey either her, or her laws and commandments, and he who shall do otherwise shall incur the same sentence of malediction.[31]

So, in wielding his sword of anathema, the Pope had instructed Elizabeth's Catholic subjects that to obey her or her laws would automatically invoke their own excommunication – 'utter separation from the unity of the body of Christ'. With this admonition, the Holy Father had sown sedition in the green fields of England and made every English Catholic a potential traitor in the eyes of the queen's ministers. Some, they reasoned, could become her assassins.

Publication of the bull was naturally prohibited in England but a few months later, a copy was cheekily nailed on to the garden gate of the Bishop of London's home in St Paul's churchyard in the small hours of the morning. The perpetrator was John Felton of Southwark, a prosperous Catholic gentleman whose wife had been a maid of honour to Mary I. Felton, a 'man of little stature and of a black complexion', was arrested within twenty-four hours, tortured, and executed near where he pinned up the felonious document. He reportedly cried out Jesus' name when the public hangman held aloft his still beating heart, as the grim sentence meted out to traitors – hanging, drawing and quartering – was bloodily carried out.[32]

New penal laws were passed in April 1570 to isolate and prosecute the religious zealots. The Second Treasons Act of Elizabeth's reign broadened the crime of treason to encompass the 'imagining, inventing, devising, or intending the death or destruction, or any bodily harm' to the queen 'or to deprive or depose her' from the 'style, honour or kingly name of the imperial crown of this realm'. It also became treasonous to claim that Elizabeth was 'a heretic, schismatic, tyrant, infidel or a usurper of the crown'.[33] A second Act of the same Parliamentary session criminalised the importation of papal bulls or 'writings, instruments and other superstitious things from the See of Rome'.[34] Non-attendance at church services was now viewed in more sinister light and regular worship according to Protestant rites became a test of loyalty.[35]

The papal attack on Elizabeth coincided with another plot to overthrow her. Within days of the Duke of Norfolk's release in August 1570 from the Tower into house arrest at his London townhouse at the former Carthusian monastery in Charterhouse Square, he was reluctantly embroiled in a plot involving the Florentine double agent Roberto Ridolphi, who begged him to write to the Duke of Alba, to seek assistance for Mary Queen of Scots. She was still outwardly keen to wed Norfolk, encouraging him to escape on 31 January 1571 – 'as she would do [herself], notwithstanding any danger' – so that they could be swiftly married.[36]

On 12 April, Charles Bailly, a young Fleming in her service, was arrested in the Channel port of Dover and found to be carrying seditious books from Catholic exiles. Two letters, 'hid behind his back secretly', were addressed to one of Mary's agents, John Leslie, Bishop of Ross, and sent from Ridolphi, now safely living in Brussels. Under torture, Bailly admitted that the Italian had departed England on 25 March carrying Mary's appeals to Alba, Philip and the Pope urging a Spanish invasion of England. A copy of the invasion plan had been lodged with Norfolk, together with a damning list of forty nobles, identified as Mary's secret supporters. Alongside each name was a number, to be used in coded correspondence by the duke.[37]

Ridolphi's loquacious efforts to convince Alba to invade England fell on stony ground. During a somewhat one-sided conversation, he talked enthusiastically of how Spain should supply six thousand men equipped with twenty-five cannon to reinforce an English Catholic army (led by Norfolk) which would free Mary and seize Elizabeth. Alba was singularly unimpressed, reporting to Philip that Ridolphi was a 'great babbler' and had learned his lessons 'parrot fashion'. A better strategy, he suggested, would be that Spanish military assistance should be provided only after the English Catholics had risen and when Elizabeth was already 'dead ... or else a prisoner'. He added: 'We may tell [Norfolk] that these conditions being fulfilled, he shall have what he wants.'[38]

Agents working for Cecil, now raised to the peerage as Lord Burghley, scoured Norfolk's London home, Howard House, for evidence of his guilt, watched haughtily by a silent but fretful duke. Their search was soon successful: his codebook was discovered hidden under some roof tiles, and deciphered documents were found beneath a rug outside the duke's bedchamber. Sir Ralph Sadler warned a 'submissive' Norfolk that for 'his obstinate dealing and denial of his great faults, her majesty was sore offended ... and had determined to use him more severely'.[39]

The duke was duly returned to the Tower. As Norfolk sat desolately considering his fate, his retainers were questioned in less salubrious accommodation within the grim fortress. Old William Barker, one of the duke's secretaries, was 'three or four times examined but hitherto showed [himself] obstinate and a fool', Sadler reported. Threatened with the terrors of the rack, Barker's resistance and loyalty disappeared like snow melting in the sunshine. This hellish contraption was the first choice of torture in the sixteenth century to persuade obdurate prisoners to cooperate. It had two windlasses or capstans positioned at each end of a long wooden table, attached to chains and shackles for the victim's arms and legs. Turning them agonisingly stretched and dislocated the limbs of those undergoing interrogation. The first Elizabethan rackmaster was Thomas Norton, a lawyer turned playwright and poet, nicknamed with Tudor black humour, 'the pincher with pains'. He enjoyed his work and was later accused of leaving the Jesuit priest Alexander Briant 'one good foot longer than ever God made him' after a session on the rack.[40] The Spanish ambassador in London reported that it was also common practice to drive iron spikes between the fingernails and the quick – a torture that his countrymen imagined 'would be employed by the Anti-Christ, as the most dreadfully cruel of all'.[41]

No wonder that Barker talked, his words tumbling out in his anxiety to please his questioners. The old man revealed Ridolphi's pie-in-the-sky plans for invasion: Spanish troops would land at

Dumbarton in Scotland, at Leith, near Edinburgh, and at the Essex port of Harwich.[42] Perhaps Scottish Protestants were going to taste Spanish Toledo steel as well as their English cousins.

Norfolk was doomed. Only the grim formalities of legal process stood between him and the scaffold. He was found guilty of treason by his peers at Westminster Hall on 16 January 1572, despite his claims of perjured evidence by his servants, and he was executed on Tower Hill on 2 June that year – mercifully with just one blow of the headsman's axe. He had told the crowd around the scaffold:

> I take God to witness, I am not, nor never was a Papist, since I knew what religion meant. I have never been addicted to Popery ... but have always been averse from Popish doctrines ... Yet, I cannot deny but that I have had amongst my servants and familiars some that have been addicted to Popish religion.[43]

De Spes, the Spanish ambassador, was expelled from England after Elizabeth admonished him angrily that he was 'secretly seek[ing] to inflame our realm with firebrands'.

Notwithstanding the vehemence of Pius V's rhetoric, Elizabeth and her council were opposed to persecuting her Catholic subjects on the basis of their religion alone. Their policies drew a sharp distinction between the fanatical papist who worked assiduously to return England to Rome's jurisdiction and those who secretly professed the Catholic faith and did not acknowledge the queen's spiritual supremacy but remained passive, or at best neutral, about papal authority.[44]

Despite this relatively moderate stance, by 1572, the substantial number of Catholics imprisoned in London was beginning to trouble Elizabeth's Privy Council, which feared that hotbeds of Catholic disaffection were being created within the capital's many gaols.[45] Banishing obstinate recusants overseas would only provide unfettered opportunity for them to plot against queen and state. The solution was to establish what today we would recognise as internment camps to hold potential troublemakers at times of especial danger to the state. This plan, first tabled in March 1572, suggested the dilapidated Wisbech Castle, in the Isle of Ely, as a suitable prison.[46] There Catholics could be confined under guard, and as Elizabeth was always reluctant to dip into her exchequer, they would have to pay for their own accommodation and food.

Internationally, England had now become a beleaguered Protestant bulwark off the coast of Europe. The Spanish reign of terror against Protestants in the Low Countries increased forebodings within Elizabeth's government, which felt isolated and under constant threat from the Catholic powers. Her spies in the Netherlands reported that Alba was determined to assist English Catholics,[47] and de la Mothe Fénelon, the French ambassador in London, believed Alba's agent in the city was in constant touch with prominent Catholic families.[48] More than fifty people within the royal court were said to be in his pay.

Catholic exiles were also actively working against Elizabeth, supported and encouraged by the governments that sheltered them. *A Treatise of Treasons*, published at Louvain (in modern-day Belgium) in 1572, declared that heresy alone was creating disorder in England and would eventually lead to the destruction of all civilisation there. As a riposte, Burghley's proclamation of 1573 was the first to employ a palpable national threat as a means of appealing to the patriotism of Elizabeth's subjects:

> Certain obstinate and irrepentent traitors, after their notorious rebellion made against their native country, have fled out of the same and remained in foreign parts with the continual and wilful determination ... to contrive all the mischief that they can imagine, to impeach and subvert the universal quietness and peace of this realm ...[49]

Some exiles were baffled why Spain had not yet attacked England to restore their faith. The Welshman Maurice Clenock, one of the colony in Louvain, explained their willingness to accept foreign invasion:

> They are not to be listened to who would persuade us that the English cannot be forced under the yoke of foreign domination.
>
> The oppression is so severe and grows still more severe daily that the confessors of the true faith hope for freedom from foreigners alone.
>
> Better to attain eternal blessedness under a foreign lord than to be cast into the nethermost hell by an enemy at home.[50]

His eagerness for an invasion was probably atypical among

English Catholics. Although they sought foreign assistance in their cause, most remained suspicious of the motives in providing such help. Niccolò Ormanteo, Papal Nuncio to Spain, acknowledged that they 'refuse all aid from abroad which might bring them under subjection, but desire only just sufficient for the overthrow of their self-styled queen and for replacing her by the other one from Scotland'.[51]

An embittered memorandum in the Vatican archives, written in September 1570, probably by an exile living in Brussels, illustrates graphically both their consuming hatred for Elizabeth and the resentful frustration of a lost existence amongst strangers in a lonely foreign land:

> Verily, she is the whore depicted in the Apocalypse with the wine of whose prostitution the kings of the earth are drunk.
>
> Seeing that meanwhile she is drunk with the blood of the martyrs of Jesus, significant indeed is the figure of that whore and yet more confirmed in that belief would they be who knew that in the time of Queen Mary[52] of happy memory, she would have lost her life for complicity of treason, but that one of the chief nobles of the land intervened to save it.[53]
>
> Therefore, seeing that Elizabeth is now of evil odour – not only with God but also with men – we demand … that Catholic princes cease to accord her regal honour.
>
> How shameful it is that princes so great should be afraid of a heretical and excommunicated woman …[54]

Sometimes, the long arm of Elizabeth's intelligence network could reach out and strike at these Catholic fugitives. An easy target was Dr John Story, Regius Professor of Canon Law at Oxford, who had used his home in Greyfriars, London, to interrogate Protestant suspects during Mary's short reign. According to the evangelical polemicist John Foxe, Story boasted in 1555 that 'there has been yet never one burnt but I have spoken with and have been a cause of his dispatch'.[55] He escaped from the Marshalsea gaol and fled to Flanders in 1563, renounced his allegiance to Elizabeth and served as a customs officer in the Spanish Netherlands, receiving a pension from Philip. In 1570, he was lured by English agents on to a ship in Antwerp harbour and was landed at the Norfolk port of Great Yarmouth. At his trial in May 1571 he faced charges of high treason for supporting the

1569 rebellion and encouraging a Spanish invasion. Story claimed he was now a Spanish subject, citing the Biblical precedent: 'God commanded Abraham to go forth from the land and country where he was born, from his friends and kinfolks into another country.' He had followed the prophet's example to allay his conscience and 'so forsake his country and the laws of this realm ...' 'Every man is born free,' Story declared, 'and he has the whole face of the earth before him to dwell and abide in where he likes best.'[56] Vengeance was not to be denied. His plea was rejected and he was hanged, drawn and quartered at Tyburn on 1 June 1571.[57]

Burghley also tried to discourage those considering fleeing the country by introducing legislation to confiscate their property. The Fugitives Act of 1571 declared that any subject who departed England without licence and did not return within six months would forfeit the profits from their property, as well as losing their goods and chattels.[58] But no legislation can quench the fire of religious faith. By 1575, there was a two-hundred-strong company of exiles, commanded by an English captain, in the Spanish army in the Netherlands, all of whom had sworn allegiance to Philip. Their ranks were later swelled by Irish and Scottish Catholics.[59]

Another, more single-minded opponent of the Catholic cause in England now began to manipulate events. On 20 December 1573, Sir Francis Walsingham was appointed joint principal secretary of state with Burghley, who was also lord treasurer. As a devout and radical Protestant he, like around a thousand others, had fled England after Mary's accession to the throne, fearing persecution. Elizabeth, whose own Protestant beliefs were insipid by comparison,[60] believed him a 'rank puritan' and sometimes unfairly castigated him for caring more for his fellow evangelicals than he did for England. The queen nicknamed him her 'dark Moor' because of his swarthy, brooding appearance.

She had little grasp of what febrile nightmares haunted him. As English ambassador to the French court, he had been a horrified witness to the terrors of the St Bartholomew's Day massacre of Huguenots in Paris on Sunday 24 August 1572. More than three thousand Protestants were shot or hacked to death by a Catholic mob and disciplined troops of soldiers in a carefully planned pogrom that began at dawn. The carnage continued into October with seventy thousand killed in Toulouse, Bordeaux, Lyons, Rouen and Orléans. So many corpses floated in the Rhône at Lyons that the river water was not drunk for three months.

Walsingham, together with a number of terrified fugitives, was besieged in his residency in the quai des Bernardins in Faubourg St Germain.[61] The Huguenot general François de Beauvais was dragged out of the building and lynched by the Parisians.[62] Eventually the ambassador was granted protection by soldiers sent by the French king Charles IX[63] and he managed to smuggle his wife and four-year-old daughter safely out of the city.

In Rome, a new Pope, Gregory XIII, triumphantly called for public rejoicing and had a *Te Deum* sung to celebrate this famous victory over the heretics. He struck a medal to commemorate the event with an image on its reverse of an avenging angel, armed with a cross and drawn sword, slaying the Huguenots.[64] Giorgio Vasari was commissioned to paint three frescoes portraying the destruction of the Protestants on the south wall of the Vatican's Sala Regia state reception room, an antechamber to the Sistine Chapel.[65]

Given Walsingham's harrowing experience, it was predictable that after his appointment there would be strenuous efforts by Elizabeth's government to punish Catholic recusants. Their arrests and punishments increased by leaps and bounds.[66]

In addition to his role as secretary of state, Walsingham served as the queen's spymaster. He created an astonishing organisation for covert action against enemies of the state, as well as for counter-intelligence and espionage. He also established a network of informers to defeat domestic threats.[67]

But all these efforts failed to suppress recusancy in England, now bolstered and succoured by a succession of singularly brave seminary priests, smuggled into the realm to shore up the harassed faithful.

The first to be captured was Father Cuthbert Mayne, arrested on 8 June 1577 in Probus, Cornwall.[68] Papers found on him declared that if

> any Catholic prince took in hand to invade any realm to reform the same to the authority of the See of Rome that the Catholics in that realm should be ready to assist and help them.[69]

Many more priests followed him to the traitor's scaffold after being betrayed by Walsingham's agents or hunted down by his questing pursuivants in the narrow, stinking streets of London or in cramped, cunningly disguised hiding places in country houses.

That same month, the new Bishop of London, John Aylmer, wrote to the secretary, warning that Catholicism was enjoying a worrying resurgence; he and the Archbishop of Canterbury, Edmund Grindal, had received complaints from their brother bishops that 'the Papists do marvellously increase, both in number and in [the] obstinate withdrawing of themselves from the Church and service of God'.[70]

Perhaps religious indoctrination would stem this Romish tide flooding across England? A group of recusants were taken to York Cathedral in August 1580 where they were exhorted to 'forsake your vain and erroneous opinions of Popery and conform yourself with all dutiful obedience to [the] true religion now established'. This appeal was rudely ignored and the prisoners tried to avoid listening by holding their hands over their ears and coughing loudly. After refusing to recite the Lord's Prayer in English, they were packed off to York Castle.[71]

It was increasingly apparent that measures to counter Catholicism were failing signally. On 18 March 1581, an Act to 'retain the Queen's Majesty's subjects in their due Obedience'[72] was passed that imposed punitive fines of £20 per month on those not attending divine service, limits on their travel and on communicating with other Catholics. Stunned and traumatised Catholics offered Elizabeth the gigantic bribe of 150,000 crowns (£37,500, or more than £95 million in 2013 spending power) to drop the legislation. She refused. The new Spanish ambassador in London, Bernardino de Mendoza, warned that 'it was evident to them that God is about to punish them with greater calamities and persecutions than ever'. He feared the legislation would 'root out the Catholic religion in this country' and passed on their pleas to Philip 'as buttress and defender of the Catholic Church, humbly beseeching you to turn your eyes upon their affliction and to succour them until God should complete their liberation'. Specifically, they wanted the Spanish king to use his good offices to ensure the appointment of an English Cardinal in Rome:

They seek the notification to his Holiness of the great importance (in order to prevent the vile weed of heresy from quite choking the good seed sown here by the seminarists), that an English cardinal should be appointed.[73]

In the spring of 1582, Walsingham considered a novel plan to transport recusants to a new colony in North America, thousands of miles away from the dangers they posed to England or the welcoming arms of a Catholic Europe. In our terms, this seems almost as outlandish as sending Catholics to the moon, given just how little known the American continent was then. But for Walsingham, the plan was the ideal solution to many of Elizabethan England's domestic and international ills. Doubtless, he cynically believed that if they did not drown during the perilous transatlantic voyage, it would be only a matter of time before native Americans, disease or starvation would kill them all off.

Paradoxically, this proposal for a Catholic homeland in Florida seemingly emanated from Sir George Peckham,[74] a Buckinghamshire squire who had been imprisoned in the winter of 1580–1 for distributing alms to jailed Catholics in London, and Sir Thomas Gerard, a notorious papist who had been an unhappy guest of her majesty for a botched attempt to free Mary Queen of Scots. However, Walsingham undoubtedly masterminded the plan. It can surely be no coincidence that Sir Philip Sidney, who sought to marry Walsingham's sixteen-year-old daughter Frances, had valuable rights to lands in America and Sidney sold these to Peckham in July 1583, providing the cash to pay off some of his debts and allow the marriage to go ahead that September.[75] The acceptable face of the expedition was supplied by the forty-four-year-old adventurer Sir Humphrey Gilbert (half-brother to Sir Walter Raleigh), who had earlier requested a royal licence for a voyage of discovery to the other side of the Atlantic.

Petitions were presented to Elizabeth and she generously granted them a patent under the Great Seal of England to colonise nine million acres (36,000 km^2) in Florida on the banks of the 'River Norumbega'. Unknown to its organisers, there were inherent problems with the expedition. Firstly, the river belonged to legend, and today can be identified with the mighty Penobscot in Maine, rather than in Florida. Secondly, Gilbert had some unfortunate personality traits, verging on mental instability. Thirdly, Florida was claimed by Philip and was occupied by Spanish troops. Those issues aside, the promoters also had not reckoned with the machinations of the Spanish ambassador Mendoza, who argued that establishing such a colony would weaken Catholic resolve to fight against the Protestant state. He reported to Philip on 11 July 1582 that as Peckham and Gerard

> were desirous of living as Catholics, without endangering their lives, they thought the proposal was a good one and they gave an account to other Catholics who ... offered to aid the enterprise with money ...
>
> They are to be allowed to live as their consciences dictate and enjoy such revenues as they may possess in England.
>
> This privilege is not confined to those who leave here for the purpose of colonisation but is extended to all Englishmen away from England, even to those who may have been declared rebels and whom the Queen now restores to her grace and favour, embracing them once more as loyal subjects.

The ambassador fumed:

> The only object of this is to weaken and destroy [the Catholics] ... since they have now discovered that persecution, imprisonment and the shedding of martyrs' blood only increase the number of Catholics; and if the proposed measure be adopted, the seminaries abroad cannot be maintained, nor would it be possible for the priests who come hither to continue their propaganda if there were no persons here to shelter and support them.
>
> By this means, what little blood be left in this diseased body would be drained.

Mendoza went to great pains to reveal the stark truth behind Elizabeth's generosity. Florida belonged to Spain and was defended by fortresses – 'so directly they landed they would be slaughtered'. As a result, some withdrew from the expedition but others 'persist in their intentions, believing it is not really against your majesty because on the map the country is called "New France" which, they say, proves it was discovered by Frenchmen and that since Cortés[76] fitted out ships ... to go and conquer countries for the Catholic church, they could do the same'.[77]

Despite Mendoza's best efforts, the plan failed for other reasons.

Eleven months later Gilbert sailed from Plymouth with five ships on a reconnaissance mission that proved disastrous, mainly due to him capriciously ignoring wise advice in seamanship. One vessel returned home early because it ran out of supplies. Then, instead of sunny Florida, Gilbert found himself off Newfoundland and he lost two ships during the voyage home. *Delight* ran aground and sank, drowning all but one of her crew of sixteen. The brand-new *Squirrel* disappeared in mountainous seas with all hands, including Gilbert himself. It is not hard to imagine the scale of Walsingham's wrath that his adroit plan to dump recusants in the New World had failed.

Plots to invade England meanwhile continued to be hatched with varying degrees of credibility. In July 1572, the madcap adventurer and privateer Sir Thomas Stukeley suggested a hopelessly optimistic scheme to Philip of Spain to overthrow Elizabeth:

> [Sir Leonard] Dacres offers for the hire of six thousand soldiers, one thousand being foreign harquebusiers,[78] in six months to wrest the kingdom [of England] from the pretended [queen], or at least to wrest from her [the counties of] Cumberland, Westmorland, Northumberland, Durham, Yorkshire and Lancashire, and make of them a safe refuge and, as it were, a realm free and independent, wither all Catholics may repair.[79]

This plan was conceived in a fantasy world. Stukeley was either unaware of the depredations inflicted upon the northern counties following the 1569 rebellion, or his sanguinity was unconnected with reality. Could he really believe that Elizabeth's ministers would allow part of her realm to be hived off to become a safe haven for her Catholic subjects? Would they permit it to survive as a secure base from which the rest of England could be conquered? His confidence was astonishing: if Philip entertained any doubts about this plan, Stukeley could capture and occupy the Isle of Wight, Portsmouth and Southampton instead 'because these places are in that part of England where there are many Catholics'. These three objectives could be seized 'at a stroke, in a single night and in less than twelve hours. From thence to London is not a two days' journey and one can march straight upon the city.' Not for nothing was Philip nick-named 'the Prudent' by his subjects. He ignored Stukeley.

The adventurer was not discouraged. Moving from Madrid to Louvain, Stukeley drew up proposals for a new papal policy on military action against England, urging Gregory to promote an attack, when, he pledged, 'a vast number [of Catholics] will join the invader and very few will oppose him'. He emphasised: 'His Holiness should not desert the cause of the Queen of Scots, who after suffering much and sorely for so many years for the Catholic faith ought now not [to] be deprived of her realm.'[80]

In 1575–6, another scheme for invasion was proposed by English exiles in Rome, amongst them the peripatetic Stukeley; Sir Richard Shelley, prior of the Order of St John of Jerusalem in England; and Sir Francis Englefield, Mary Queen of Scots' agent in Spain. They craved papal blessing and support for their enterprise and Gregory graciously provided them with special crucifixes and ten separate indulgences to those who treated the conspirators 'with reverence or devotion'. These graces included:

> For each time that prayer is made before any one of them for the prosperity of Holy Mother Church and the exaltation of the Holy Catholic Faith and the preservation and liberation of Mary Queen of Scots and the reduction of the realms of England, Scotland and Ireland and the extirpation of the heretics ... fifty days and on feast [days] one hundred days' indulgence.[81]

Like the others, this plan came to nought.

Two that did get off the ground were successive attempts to raise Ireland against Elizabeth's rule. The exiled priest Nicholas Sanders won papal support for an invasion involving the Irish noble James Fitzmaurice Fitzgerald of Desmond in Munster and Stukeley in 1578. Unfortunately, the tiny force was unexpectedly diverted to Morocco to support the campaign by King Sebastian of Portugal against the infidel Turks, and Stukeley was killed at the Battle of Alcácer Quibir that year, when a cannonball tore off his legs.

Another expedition with just fifty soldiers landed in Ireland the following year, accompanied by Sanders as papal commissary. Gregory had already named his own illegitimate son, Giacomo Boncampagni, as King of Ireland if the invasion and a rebellion by Irish feudal lords succeeded. Reinforcements of six hundred papal troops – Irish, Italian and Spanish mercenaries under Sebastiano di San Guiseppe

– landed in Smerwick harbour (now called Ard na Caithne) on Kerry's Dingle Peninsula on 10 September 1580. However, William Wynter's English naval squadron captured the papal ships and blocked the invaders' escape by sea. Undaunted, they refortified the nearby Iron Age earthwork, Dún an Óir ('Fort of Gold') and Sanders proudly unfurled the papal banner above the earth ramparts.

It took some time for the English authorities in Dublin to react, but when their vengeance came, it was predictably brutal. After a ten-day siege that October, the Lord Deputy of Ireland, Arthur Grey, Fourteenth Baron Grey of Wilton, courteously accepted the invaders' surrender and then beheaded every one of the garrison and their women. The rebellion collapsed after the English burnt crops and laid waste most of Munster. Subsequently, famine and disease killed up to a third of the county's population. Sanders escaped and spent months as a fugitive in the wilds of south-west Ireland before dying of dysentery and starvation in the spring of 1581.

Walsingham uncovered a plot in 1583 involving Mendoza, his French counterpart Michel Castelnau, and twenty-nine-year-old Francis Throckmorton to land French troops at the port of Arundel in West Sussex, liberate Mary Queen of Scots and return England to Catholicism. Throckmorton was arrested on 4 November and papers found at his home identified a number of Catholic noblemen and an illegal pedigree of the descent of the crown of England, demonstrating the justice of Mary's claim to the throne. The invasion had been delayed only by lack of funding, despite the promises of Pope Gregory and Philip to underwrite the costs of the expedition.

Mendoza was given fifteen days to leave England and he angrily retorted: 'Bernardino Mendoza was born not to disturb kingdoms but to conquer them.'[82] For all his bluster, he departed quietly. The following November he took up a new position as the Spanish ambassador in Paris.

Throckmorton was executed at Tyburn on 11 July 1584[83] and there was a general round-up of the usual suspects. Henry Percy, Eighth Earl of Northumberland (brother of the leader of the 1569 rebellion), was arrested but committed suicide in the Tower on 20 June 1585 by shooting himself with a pistol loaded with three bullets for good measure.

There is little doubt that Elizabeth's life was frequently endangered by Catholic fanatics. On 17 July 1579, William Appletree, a serving man at court, fired a gun during Elizabeth's stately progress by barge up the Thames, hitting one of her watermen in both arms. 'She saw him hurt; she saw him fall, yet shrank not at the same. Neither made she any fearful show to seem dismayed,' according to a contemporary ballad. The queen dramatically exercised her prerogative of mercy at the last minute as Appletree stood on the ladder of the gallows.[84]

Despite a rash of assassination conspiracies, Elizabeth developed an obstinate dislike of security precautions to protect her sacred person – much to Walsingham's fury.

In October 1583, some of the prisoners held in the Tower were interrogated about 'certain speeches against the queen's majesty supposed to have been spoken by John Somerfield' when he protested against the treatment of Catholics. He announced that he intended to 'shoot her through with his dagg [pistol] and hoped to see her head set on a pole [because] she was a serpent and viper'.[85] He hanged himself with 'his own garters' in his cell in Newgate prison twenty-four hours before his execution; but one of Walsingham's agents alleged he was killed 'to avoid a greater evil' by Catholic sympathisers.[86]

Assassination fears were heightened by the murder on 10 July 1584 of the Dutch Protestant leader William of Orange in Delft in the Netherlands by Balthazar Gérard, a French Catholic. The result was the so-called *Bond of Association,* aimed at neutralising the threat of Mary Queen of Scots, as it decreed that anyone involved in Elizabeth's death would be ineligible to succeed her as ruler. Those who 'procured' the queen's assassination would also be executed, whether or not they were aware of the conspiracy to take the queen's life.[87] Furthermore, the Bond was to be signed by loyal subjects who pledged themselves to 'act [with] the utmost revenge' on any heirs to the pretender to the throne for 'their utter overthrow and extirpation'. In essence, it was lynch law, but its impact was rather dissipated when Mary happily signed it herself on 5 January 1585, promising to be 'an enemy to all those that attempt anything against Queen Elizabeth's life'.[88]

The Bond was enshrined in law in an Act for the Surety of the Queen's Person, passed in March 1585, which created a commission of privy councillors and judges to hear evidence of the guilt of a claimant to the throne alleged to be complicit in any assassination plot or in plans for rebellion or foreign invasion. If guilty, they faced death.[89] Far-sighted Burghley also tried to introduce a Parliamentary Bill to authorise the creation of an interregnum government led by a 'Great Council' in the event of Elizabeth's murder. But the queen felt this impinged dangerously on her God-given right to rule, so she vetoed his proposals.[90]

The same year, the deranged William Parry was executed for conspiring to kill the queen while she was riding in St James'. A special prayer of thanksgiving was written for Elizabeth's safe deliverance which described Parry as a

> miserable, wretched, natural-born subject, a man of no religion [who] … determined very often most desperately to have with his own cursed hand destroyed her majesty's sacred person.

Fortunately, God had protected her and had 'diverted [Parry's] desperate heart and bloody hand'.[91] Parry expected to be reprieved at the last minute, pledging on the scaffold:

> If I might be made Duke of Lancaster and have all the possessions belonging thereunto, yet I would never consent to shed the least drop of blood out of the tops of any of her [the Queen's] fingers.

The crowd were having none of his protestations of innocence. They chanted: 'Away with him', urging the executioner to get on with his bloody business.[92]

Walsingham was determined to entrap Mary Queen of Scots, 'that devilish woman', as he called her, and finally destroy the threat she posed to England. Elizabeth ostensibly shared his opinions of her; in 1578 she told a French envoy who came to London to plead on Mary's behalf, that her 'head should have been cut off years ago'.[93] Walsingham's opportunity came when he intercepted and decoded letters to and from the Scottish Queen which discussed an invasion, her rescue and Elizabeth's murder. Anthony Babington, the naïve twenty-five-year-old leader of the plot and his fourteen fellow conspirators were executed 20–21 September 1586.[94]

For all her grave misgivings about taking the life of an anointed queen, Elizabeth was finally persuaded to sign a death warrant authorising the execution of Mary Queen of Scots on 1 February

1587. She dropped broad hints that it would be far more convenient if Mary was assassinated, but her gaoler, Sir Amyas Paulet, was having no truck with such illegalities, despite his sovereign's fury at his non-cooperation.[95] Elizabeth's Privy Council, fearful that she would change her mind and spare her cousin, hastened to execute her, sending down Bull, the Tower's executioner, in disguise to Fotheringay Castle, Northamptonshire, where Mary was imprisoned. He agreed a price of £10 (or £1,880 at today's prices) for the job and duly completed the grisly task on 8 February, holding aloft her severed head and crying out: 'God save the queen!'

Mary was wearing an auburn wig, and the head fell from his grasp and rolled across the scaffold, grey-haired and nearly bald, leaving a shocked Bull with only her dainty white cap and wig in his hand.[96] Horribly, with the nerves in her dead face still twitching, her lips continued to move soundlessly as her blood soaked the straw and black cloth of the platform.

She had enjoyed the very last word.

RUMOURS OF WAR

I cannot but ... advise Your Majesty to prepare every
way for the worst ... Set out a very strong navy to keep
the seas forthwith ... [and] provide, by your subjects, ...
to have a store of money which is the sinew to hold all by.

Robert Dudley, Earl of Leicester, to Elizabeth I;
Flushing, 21 November 1587.[1]

Francis Drake hated the Spanish with a burning, all-consuming passion, born out of a humiliating naval defeat, snatched dishonourably by his foes in the harbour of San Juan de Ulúa, off Veracruz in Mexico,[2] in September 1568. He and his second cousin and fellow privateer John Hawkins had been illegally trading with Spanish settlers in the New World – exchanging slaves from Sierra Leone for commodities[3] – when their flotilla put into the port for repairs. A thirteen-strong Spanish fleet arrived and after agreeing a gentlemanly truce of convenience, sailed into the harbour. Several days later, they attacked the English and, exploiting their advantage of surprise, destroyed four vessels. Hawkins and Drake ignominiously fled in the *Minion* and *Judith* respectively, arriving in Plymouth with only a handful of survivors. There was more than a hint of animosity in Hawkins' later statement that 'the barque *Judith*, the same night, forsook us in our misery'.[4]

Drake swore to inflict a heavy revenge on the Spanish nation and embarked enthusiastically upon a lucrative career of preying on the treasure looted from their new empire across the Atlantic – producing a highly profitable return for his financial backers of £47 for every £1 they had invested.[5] These fortunate speculators included Elizabeth herself, who showered honours upon him, including a knighthood. Philip of Spain was enraged, reportedly offering a bounty of 20,000 ducats (£15,000,000 at current prices) on Drake's head, dead or alive.

The Spanish king was, however, more preoccupied with building a powerful navy with which to defend his country's burgeoning colonial interests around the globe, rather than with scratching away the irritant that Drake's forays represented. In August 1580, Lisbon was captured and Portugal swiftly annexed. This not only provided an important new maritime base on the Iberian peninsula's Atlantic coast, but the conquest of his neighbour also brought its well-equipped fleet to augment existing Spanish sea power. As if to underline this tectonic shift in Europe's strategic balance, almost two years later, his admiral, Álvaro de Bazán, First Marquis of Santa Cruz, defeated a largely French mercenary squadron supporting Dom Antonio, Prior of Crato and pretender to the Portuguese crown, at the Battle of Sâo Miguel off the Azores.

On the diplomatic front, Philip sought to further isolate Elizabeth's realm, with France the first target of his behind-the-scenes plotting. At the end of December 1584, the Spanish king had secretly signed the Treaty of Joinville between Spain and Henri, Third Duke of Guise (cousin of Mary Queen of Scots) and the French 'Catholic League', promising support for the Catholic cause in France.

It was not only Drake's predatory raids on the gold and silver extracted from the New World that incensed Philip; Elizabeth was now also overtly assisting the Protestant rebels in his possessions in the Low Countries, believing it was better to fight the Spanish on someone else's territory rather than on English soil. Her frontline against Spain would therefore be drawn in the Spanish Netherlands. In August 1585, the queen had signed the Anglo-Dutch Treaty of Nonsuch, which committed her to assist the rebel Dutch provinces. As well as providing a generous annual subsidy of 600,000 florins (£181,000,000 in current spending power), she later sent a seven-thousand-strong English army to the Low Countries under her favourite, Robert Dudley, Earl of Leicester. Its operational costs were to be paid by the Dutch. Unfortunately they turned out to be less-than-prompt payers. Moreover, corruption and rampant fraud ensured that her soldiers remained unpaid and sometimes starving. No wonder she exclaimed petulantly that her Dutch war was 'a sieve, that spends as it receives, to little purpose'.[6]

Drake's brief occupation of ports in Galicia in north-west Spain the following October (when he gleefully sacked local churches) and his later raids on the Canary and Cape Verde Islands and efficient burning and pillaging of Spanish towns in the Caribbean, sealed Philip's determination to invade England.[7]

Never one to be dragooned into unconsidered action, he mulled over the problem carefully for nearly two months. That December, he invited his nephew Alexander Farnese, Duke of Parma, the successful general who had defeated the Dutch in Brabant and Flanders, to draw up plans for an expeditionary force to cross the narrow seas to invade England.

Santa Cruz, his confidence buoyed by naval victories in the Azores, meanwhile boasted that he could easily defeat England at sea, if only Philip chose to give the order. He offered to 'serve your majesty in the enterprise in the firm hope that ... I will emerge just as victorious from it as in the other things I have done for you'.[8] It was probably to the admiral's subsequent dismay that the king readily took him at his word. In January 1586 he was ordered to produce estimates of the extent of forces necessary to successfully invade England and finally eradicate this Protestant bulwark that had become so troublesome to Spain's interests and ambitions.

Philip knew that to defeat England meant he had to destroy its navy to enable him to control the sea. Thirty years before, when he had been such an unenthusiastic husband to Elizabeth's half-sister, he had noted: 'The kingdom of England is and must always remain strong at sea, since upon this the safety of the realm depends.'[9] He was now destined to test the veracity of his maxim.

The Spanish king was no warmonger, however. The exiled English priest Robert Persons acknowledged that Philip 'fears war as a burned child dreads the fire'.[10] But that fear emanated from more prosaic issues rather than simple scruples over the shedding of Christian blood. Philip, always debt-ridden, was more worried about the costs involved and the economic consequences of war.

His very worst misgivings were realised when Santa Cruz submitted his ambitious estimates on 12 March 1586, asking for one hundred and fifty-six ships plus 55,000 troops to land in England, supported by four hundred auxiliary vessels. Like any modern military planner he had built in extra contingencies in case his requirements for the invasion force were cut back, but he had carefully worked out that such a military operation would cost an eye-watering four million ducats (about £3 billion at today's prices). Philip probably gasped in pain when he saw the row of noughts on the paper before him, rather than from the agonising gout that frequently afflicted him.

Parma, in his twenty-eight-page plan delivered that June, envisaged a thirty-thousand-strong force plus five hundred cavalry transported in flat-bottomed barges launching a surprise attack on the Kent coast between Dover and Margate, before assaulting London, 67 miles (107 km) inland. The crossing, the general declared confidently, would probably take around ten or twelve hours – or less, with a following wind. Naval protection was only necessary if Elizabeth's government had learned of the invasion plans beforehand, but either way, Spanish ships could lure the English fleet away from the Straits of Dover. Sceptical that surprise could be achieved, Philip scrawled 'Hardly possible!' alongside this requirement in Parma's plan.

Other strategies were submitted to the Escorial Palace. Bernardino de Escalante, who was a member of the entourage accompanying Philip to England for his marriage to Mary I in 1554, had fought as a soldier in the Netherlands in 1555–8 before becoming a priest two decades later. In June 1586, he drew up a campaign map, urging a diversionary attack on Waterford in southern Ireland by thirty-two thousand men to decoy Elizabeth's fleet from the English Channel, so allowing a landing in Kent by Spanish troops from Flanders. The invaders could then mount a swift and decisive seizure of London, which was only defended by the 'E Greet Tuura', the great Tower of London.[11] The ill-trained English militias would in any case melt away before the onslaught of Parma's battle-hardened veterans.

One of Philip's advisers, Don Juan de Zúñiga, charged with coordinating the now weighty range of invasion plans, was impressed by the priest's strategy, appending only the sensible requirement for reinforcements and supplies to be delivered as soon as the queen's navy had been neutralised. This 'Enterprise of England', he suggested, should be launched in August or September 1587.

However, some disquieting uncertainties remained about the consequences of a successful landing. Once London had been captured,

Zúñiga urged that Parma should set up an interim government, pending the coronation of a new Catholic monarch – why not Mary Queen of Scots? – who should then marry a reliable and steadfast Catholic prince, perhaps even Parma himself. If stout English resistance prevented the subjugation of the entire nation, important concessions could be wrung from the rump Tudor state: freedom of worship for English Catholics; the surrender of English garrisons in the Low Countries (plus repatriation of English forces), and Spanish troops to continue to occupy the conquered regions until payment of hefty war reparations to Madrid.[12]

While the precise strategy was being worked out, early military preparations were put in hand.

Intelligence reaching Walsingham in London had dried up following Philip's seizure of English and Dutch ships in Spanish ports in retaliation for Elizabeth's support for the Dutch rebels. The earliest intimation of the Armada threat came via a north German ship that docked in Plymouth from Lisbon in the first week of January 1585. Her master suggested that 'the King of Spain had taken up all the masts for shipping, both great and small, so there is likely [to be] war[s]'.[13] A message to the Privy Council from the English merchant William Melsam on 4 February 1586 reported gossip that 'immense quantities of grain, wine and military stores' were being collected by Philip, who was also increasing the size of his fleet and mobilising 'land forces from various parts'. Melsam added:

> They [are] saying ... that the Pope does send fifty-thousand men out of his diocese which shall come with twelve galleasses and other shipping.
>
> More, the King of Spain prepares [an]other fifty-thousand men [for] which he has taken up many soldiers in the country, as the poor people say ...
>
> They do mean to land in the Isle of Wight fifty-thousand men, [another] fifty-thousand men into Ireland, fifty-thousand men also in the backside of Scotland ... For one of these three armies, the Pope has ordained that the King of France or Duke of Guise should make ready.
>
> Moreover, they say that the king [Philip] has more friends in England than the Queen's majesty which is a grievous hearing.

God preserve her grace and send her long to reign and to confound her enemies.[14]

In April, a Bristol merchant was told that a 'great fleet' was being prepared at Lisbon and the Amsterdam trader William Peterson reported 'great naval preparations' – but difficulty in manning their navy.[15]

All these straws in the wind were discounted in London, as the government was preoccupied by purely domestic issues such as its campaign against recusants, hunting fugitive seminary priests and the dire consequences of a failed harvest. In Gloucestershire, a mob of 'common people' looted a ship with a cargo of malt intended for Wales and local magistrates reported that 'the people declare they are driven to the last extremity by famine and [are] forced to feed their children with cats, dogs and roots of nettles'. Other violent disturbances were reported elsewhere.[16]

Leicester confidently told Burghley in January 1586 that the rumours of Philip's war preparations were 'made the greater to terrify her majesty' and the Dutch rebels. 'But thanks be to God, her majesty has little cause to fear him.' In the Low Countries 'they esteem no more of his power by sea than I do of six fishermen's boats of Rye'.[17] Walsingham, also unconvinced of the immediacy of the military threat, dismissed stories of naval movements and warlike preparations as mere 'Spanish brag'. He wrote to Leicester on 24 March predicting that the danger of invasion 'will prove nothing this year and I hope less the next'.[18] Walsingham feared that such alarmist reports could distract Elizabeth from fully prosecuting the war against the Spanish in the Low Countries: 'I would to God', he confided to Leicester, that 'her majesty would put on a good countenance for only four months and I doubt not but Spain would seek peace greatly to her majesty's honour and advantage'.[19]

But as the days passed, nagging doubts began to gnaw at his mind and prudently he despatched one of his agents, Antony Poyntz,[20] to Spain to collect more reliable information. In July, he drew up a list of Englishmen who would support 'any foreign power [which] should come to invade this realm'. Ominously, his catalogue of treason contained the names of six peers, seven knights, forty-two esquires and gentlemen, aside from yeomen, farmers and 'priests at liberty'.[21]

Fresh in Walsingham's mind was the arraignment, two months before, of Philip Howard, Earl of Arundel, on charges that he tried to flee England without royal permission; that he had been secretly converted to Rome and was conspiring to be restored as Fifth Duke of Norfolk. He was fined £10,000 and imprisoned in the Tower of London 'during the Queen's pleasure'. The spymaster did not know that according to Mendoza, the Spanish ambassador in Paris, the earl had undertaken 'with the assistance of a few men to make himself master of the Tower' whilst 'Lord Harry Howard', his uncle, would raise troops and would be joined by the earl's half-brother Thomas. The latter was not a Catholic, but sought to avenge the death of his father, the Fourth Duke of Norfolk. All this was claimed to be part of a wider conspiracy in England and Ireland against Elizabeth but, like many of Mendoza's Machiavellian pipedreams, came to nothing.

The King of Spain meanwhile had finalised his strategy for invasion. Copies of the final shape of his naval and military expeditionary force were sent to Brussels and Lisbon on 26 July 1586. A naval armada, with land artillery embarked, would sail from Lisbon in the summer of 1587 to seize and hold a beachhead in southern Ireland with the objective of luring Elizabeth's navy into battle in Irish waters. After two months, the Spanish naval element would sail into the English Channel and patrol the Dover Straits to protect a fleet of small ships collected secretly in Flanders to carry Parma's thirty-thousand men to their landing beaches near Margate in Kent. The troops would then march triumphantly on London to capture the queen and her government of heretics. It was a compromise, and like all such compromises suffered from troubling weaknesses. Timing was everything and the plan depended totally on achieving complete success in all its phases. There was no account taken of the impact of the weather, the problems of re-supply, or the potential loss of surprise.

Although this invasion plan was only the first version of Philip's 'Enterprise of England', orders were drafted immediately to raise the necessary troops and buy the ordnance, ammunition and victuals.[22]

Then Elizabeth's Privy Council unwittingly removed a major drawback to the Spanish plans – by beheading Mary Queen of Scots.

In Madrid, Philip II was stunned by the execution. But with the Francophile candidate for Elizabeth's crown now safely dead, at least a successful invasion would not disastrously unite France and England, which was possible if Mary Stuart had been installed by her Spanish allies. That alarming outcome conveniently averted by her blood being split so copiously at Fotheringay, the shrewd king felt free to pursue his own political ambitions in Spain's interests. In February 1587, he wrote to his ambassador in Rome, Enrique de Guzmán, Count de Olivares, instructing him to secretly brief the new Pope, Sixtus V, on his own tenuous claim to the English throne:

> Failing the Queen of Scotland, the right to the English crown falls to me.
>
> My claim rests upon my descent from the House of Lancaster and upon the will made by the Queen of Scotland and mentioned in a letter from her, of which [a] copy is enclosed ...
>
> You will impress upon his Holiness that I cannot undertake a war in England for the purpose merely of placing upon the throne a young heretic like the King of Scotland, who ... is by his heresy incapacitated to succeed.
>
> His Holiness must be assured that I have no intention of adding England to my dominions but to settle the crown upon my daughter, the Infanta.[23]

Appearances had to be maintained. Another letter to Rome spoke of his grief at the Scottish queen's death 'since she would have been the most suitable instrument for leading those countries [England and Scotland] back to the Catholic faith. But since God in His wisdom has ordained otherwise, He will raise up other instruments for the triumph of His cause.'[24] The Spanish Armada, for example.

Mendoza, oozing sycophancy, was not only hopelessly optimistic but unaware of the new policy on who would succeed Elizabeth after she was deposed. 'It would seem to be God's obvious design to bestow upon your majesty the crowns of these two kingdoms,' he unctuously told the king.

But one nightmare remained ever-present, haunting Philip's every waking hour: the lack of money. The cost of the Armada preparations was a huge drain on his already mortgaged exchequer and he was forced to rein back government expenditure in many areas. The king had already turned down pressing requests to strengthen the defences of Spanish towns and bases in the Caribbean, writing:

As you can imagine, no one resents the damage [done by Drake] more than I do and no one desires more to repair it, if only there was a way to execute it as we wish.

But your plans create a lot of problems and the biggest one is the lack of money with which to pay for it all.

His puppet Portuguese administration had also postponed an assault on the sultanate of Atjeh in Sumatra and its plans to build a fortress at Mombasa in modern-day Kenya, because of the financial drain caused by the Armada.[25]

Walsingham in London was fully aware of Spain's fiscal woes[26] and reasoned that economic warfare might delay or cripple the projected invasion. He suggested, via the London financiers, that the great banking houses of northern Italy, like the Crosinis, and the gold exchanges of Genoa and Florence, should refuse to extend any credit to the King of Spain, thereby starving the Armada of necessary funds. Thomas Sutton, the merchant, banker and founder of the Charterhouse almshouses in London, may have been one of his agents in persuading his Italian counterparts to turn down or at least prevaricate over Philip's increasingly imperative requests for loans.[27]

Thus stymied, the Spanish king reluctantly and regretfully had to turn to the Vatican for financial assistance in 1587. Not only was he suffering the mortification of having to go cap in hand to the Pope, but he was simultaneously seeking another indulgence: the award of a cardinal's hat to the English exiled priest William Allen to provide a Catholic figurehead for the faithful in England.

Count de Olivares, Philip's ambassador in Rome, was far from sanguine at the prospect of Sixtus making a generous contribution to the Spanish war chest: 'When it comes to getting money out of him, it is like squeezing his life blood,' he reported despondently to his royal master.[28]

Sixtus had succeeded his political enemy Gregory XIII in April 1585 and had quickly restored the straitened papal finances by levying harsh new taxes and selling off appointments to the highest bidder. He was notoriously proud of his gigantic hoard of gold and silver, held securely in the papal fortress of Castel di Sant'Angelo on the River Tiber, and was reluctant to part with a single coin unless it was spent on defending the Holy See or in a crusade against the infidel Turks. Olivares sneered that he cared more for ducats than devotion. Despite his miserliness, Sixtus spent huge sums on public works, including draining 9,500 acres (38 km²) of Rome's Pontine Marshes, piping fresh water to parts of the city and completing the dome of St Peter's. The new Pope was impulsive, irascible, obstinate and autocratic. He also held a jaundiced view of Philip and thoroughly mistrusted him, while unfortunately expressing an almost unbridled admiration for Elizabeth I. In this view, he was at odds with Allen, who predicted grimly that March that the Armada would 'chastise our heretics and that woman hated by God and man'.[29]

In March 1587, Olivares reported on his discussions on the loan and Allen's hat with Cardinal Antonio Carrafa, the papal secretary of state, who agreed to put the requests to the pontiff: 'The next day, being Holy Wednesday, he postponed it as he thought it would not be a good time to find the Pope in a favourable temper. He therefore decided to go again on Holy Saturday when the *Hallelujah* was sung.'[30] Its soaring notes did not help the Spanish requests; Sixtus merely prevaricated. In June, Olivares reported some startling shenanigans in the Vatican: 'His Holiness was in a great rage at table, railing at those who served him and throwing the crockery about furiously, which he is rather in the habit of doing but not often so violently as this.'[31]

The Pope nurtured doubts about the validity of Philip's claim to the throne of England and his true motives in sending the Armada. His suspicions probably focused on Mary Queen of Scots' supposed eleventh-hour will in which she named the Spanish king as her heir to the English crown. A Spanish memorandum submitted to Sixtus in June maintained that, although the new will 'had been concealed by the Queen of England', Philip possessed an autographed letter from Mary to Mendoza, dated 20 May 1586, in which she declared her intentions about the succession 'in case her son should not be converted to Catholicism at the time of her death'. The document emphasised that Philip's claim was more valid 'than that of any other claimant who could arise' and anyway, he would enjoy 'the right of conquest in a war whose justice is evident, even if the queen were not a heretic which of itself would justify it'.

Then, just in one brief paragraph, comes a fleeting glimpse of

Philip's hidden agenda: 'The possession of these dominions is of the most vital importance for the maintenance of the States of Flanders in union with the crown of Spain and also for the preservation of the Spanish Indies.' It ends piously:

> His majesty prays His Holiness to consider the question ... as his opinion, dictated by prudence and aided by the Holy Spirit, will have great weight with the king, who desires to hold or dispose of that realm [England] for the service of the Apostolic See and the Catholic faith with the blessing and approval of His Holiness.[32]

An unexpected and unlikely complication to Philip's plans for the crown of England arose that June with the appearance in Madrid of a twenty-seven-year-old Catholic youth named Arthur Dudley, who claimed sensationally to be the illegitimate child of Elizabeth and Robert Dudley, Earl of Leicester. He was interrogated by another exile, Sir Francis Englefield, now the king's English secretary, and the story superficially rang true, or at least was carefully constructed. Dudley recounted how he was brought up by Robert Southern, a servant of the queen's old governess Catherine ('Kat') Ashley, after he was asked by a lady of Elizabeth's court to obtain a nurse for a 'new-born child of a lady who had been so careless of her honour that if it became known, it would bring great shame upon all the company and would highly displease the Queen if she knew of it'.

Dudley was well cared for and expensively educated, and Southern, on his death-bed, 'told him secretly that he was the son of the Earl of Leicester and the queen ... Arthur begged him to give him the confession in writing but he could not write as his hand was paralysed.' The youth later met Leicester, 'whereby his tears, words and other demonstrations, he showed so much affection for Arthur that the latter believed he understood the earl's deep intentions towards him'. According to Dudley, Leicester had warned him: 'You are like a ship under full sail at sea, pretty to look upon but dangerous to deal with.' After many adventures the young man was shipwrecked on the Biscayan coast, apprehended by the Spanish and taken to Madrid.

Englefield was suspicious, advising Philip that the youth's revelations 'may originate in the Queen of England and her Council and possibly with an object that Arthur himself does not yet understand

... They may be making use of him for their iniquitous ends.' He urged that Arthur

> should not be allowed to get away but should be kept very secure to prevent his escape. It is true that at present his claim amounts to nothing but with the example of Dom Antonio [the pretender to the Portuguese throne] before us, it cannot be doubted that France and the English heretics ... might turn to their own advantage or at least make it a pretext for obstructing the reformation of religion in England (for I look upon him as a very feigned Catholic) and the inheritance of the crown by its legitimate master.

The king noted in the margin: 'It would be certainly safest to make sure of his [Dudley's] person until we know more about it.'[33] The youth was therefore confined in a monastery near Madrid and his subsequent fate is unknown.[34]

There was a further source of friction with the Vatican caused by Philip's decision to unilaterally nominate Spaniards as new Catholic archbishops and bishops once England had been subjugated. This was an intolerable infringement of papal powers and Sixtus wrote to the Spanish king – addressing him as 'Dear Son in Christ' – to object:

> On undertaking this enterprise [the Armada] I exhort your majesty first to reconcile yourself with God the Father, for the sins of princes destroy peoples and no sin is so heinous in the eyes of the Lord as the usurpation of the divine jurisdiction, as is proved by history, sacred and profane.
>
> Your majesty has been advised to embrace in your edict, bishops, archbishops and cardinals and this is a grievous sin.
>
> Erase from the edict, these ministers of God and repent – or otherwise a great scourge may fall upon you ...
>
> I have shed many tears over this great sin of yours and I trust you will amend it and that God may pardon you.[35]

The ecclesiastical spoils from a Spanish victory over England caused other problems in Rome that year. Olivares complained to the king that the English priest Robert Parsons was 'worrying me to death to get the Pope to make him Archbishop of Canterbury ... He greatly exalts the dignity of the office and urges the desirability of the [cardinal's] hat going with it. I have not countenanced this as it would divert the Pope from the matter of the cardinalate [for Allen].'[36]

Eventually Sixtus promised Philip 1,000,000 gold ducats (£662,000,000 in 2013 spending power) but cannily stipulated that the first half was only to be paid when Spanish forces actually set foot in England with the remainder in equal instalments every two months thereafter. On 29 July 1587, the sum was transferred to two Roman bankers with strict instructions that it was only to be paid once a public notary had verified that the invasion of England had taken place.[37] Olivares reported: 'Until the men are landed it will be impossible to get anything out of His Holiness ... Everybody believes that the real object is to make peace and nothing will shake the Pope's belief in this respect. The small trust that can be placed in him may be judged by the little trust he places in us.'[38] In return, Philip could bestow the crown of England on whomever he wished, providing that the new monarch pledged that the defeated realm would be immediately returned to the Catholic faith. The Church's properties and rights, alienated since the time of Henry VIII, were also to be restored.[39] Allen was finally made a cardinal on 7 August.

With no advance on the papal subsidy forthcoming, Philip was still confronted by problems in paying for the Armada preparations. These were partially solved that September when the Spanish plate fleet, escorted by Santa Cruz's warships, arrived safely from the West Indies with 16,000,000 gold ducats on board, of which 25 per cent went straight into the king's depleted exchequer.

Olivares, whose patience in dealing with Sixtus approached saint-like proportions, was also worried that the Vatican's institutional passion for gossip could compromise the Spanish invasion plans: 'I tremble at the Pope's lack of secrecy,' he confided to Philip. One probably apocryphal story, first written eighty years after Walsingham's death, tells how the spymaster learned of a letter from Philip to Sixtus, written in his own hand, briefing him on the Armada strategy. English agents in Rome were alerted and they bribed, threatened or somehow induced one of the gentlemen of the pontiff's bedchamber to copy the Spanish king's letter, safely locked up in the Pope's writing desk. This was achieved by stealing Sixtus's keys out of his robes while he slept.[40]

Certainly, confirmation of the extent of the 'Enterprise of England' did come from Rome immediately after the college of cardinals were told of Philip's plans in case the sixty-seven-year-old Pope suddenly died.[41] Moreover, a correspondent from the same city told Burghley that the Spanish plan was to capture Elizabeth alive and send her as a prisoner to the Vatican:

> He heard the cardinal say that the King of Spain gave great charge ... to all the captains that in no way they should harm the person of the queen.
>
> Upon taking her, use the same with reverence, looking well to the custody of her.
>
> And further ... take order for the conveyance of her person to Rome, to the purpose that His Holiness the Pope should dispose thereof in sort, as it should please him.[42]

In February and March 1587, fresh intelligence reached Walsingham about the extent of the Armada preparations. The first report came from Hans Frederick, a merchant from Danzig, who counted three hundred 'sail of shipping stayed in south Spain'. At Lisbon 'they have taken up all the victuals in every ship that comes out of Holland or the [Baltic nations], both bacon and beef, butter and cheese and whatsoever else. They encourage all strangers, affirming that the Catholics will yield up [England] unto the king without bloodshed.'[43] The second was submitted by a Portuguese citizen in Nantes in France, who had a kinsman involved in provisioning the Spanish fleet. The report spoke of four hundred ships and fifty galleys docked in and around Lisbon, with seventy-four thousand soldiers being recruited or mustered in Italy, Spain, Portugal and Flanders. The provisions already accumulated included 184,557 quintals of biscuit, 23,000 quintals of bacon, 23,000 butts of wine, 11,000 quintals of beef and 43,000 quintals of hard cheese.[44]

In England, nerves were becoming frayed. In January, there was a false report of Spanish forces landing in Milford Haven in Wales, and the following month there were rumours of 'foreign preparations' for an attack on the Isle of Wight.[45] During the summer, a gentleman reported a fleet of one hundred and twenty ships off the Scilly Isles and the Privy Council ordered an alert in the West Country 'with as little bruit [rumour] and trouble to the people that shall be occupied in harvest'.[46]

The Tudor administrative machine creakily moved up a gear in preparation for war with much scurrying about by hard-pressed officials. In February and March alone, a census was taken of all available civilian ships that could be pressed into the queen's service. She herself examined a list of almost two hundred captains regarded as 'fit for service'. Calculations were made on how much powder, lead and match should be sent to the counties bordering the English Channel 'at the rate of one pound (0.45 kg) each sort per man for six days' and what artillery was available for these vulnerable areas. The stores of dusty old armour and weapons in the armouries of the Tower of London, Woolwich, Greenwich, Hampton Court and Windsor were carefully inventoried. Possible landing places on the Hampshire coast from Portsmouth to Bournemouth were surveyed and the cost estimated of arming and provisioning twenty-four of the queen's ships, together with their 6,200 crewmen.[47]

It was obvious that England could not afford to remain danger-ously supine, waiting meekly like a sacrificial lamb for an easy slaugh-ter by the invading Armada. John Hawkins, now Treasurer of the Navy, wrote to Walsingham on 1 February calling for a naval recon-naissance expedition of six warships to Spain which could impede progress in Spanish preparations for war by imposing a blockade.

> Having of long time seen the malicious practices of the papists ... to alter the government of this realm and bring it to papistry and consequently to servitude, poverty and slavery, I have good will ... to do ... something as I could have credit to impeach their purpose.
>
> If we stand at this point in a mammering [hesitation] and at a stay, we consume [burn in a fire] and our commonwealth utterly decays ...
>
> Therefore, in my mind, our profit and best assurance is to seek our peace by a determined and resolute war, which in doubt would be both less charge, more assurance of safety and would best dis-cern our friends from our foes ... abroad and at home and satisfy the people generally throughout the whole realm.[48]

Sir Francis Drake also argued vociferously for urgent action, main-taining that a pre-emptive strike on the Spanish fleet was vital to buy time for the defences of the realm to be strengthened both on land and sea. Walsingham, Leicester and the Lord High Admiral, Howard of Effingham, supported his plans for an immediate, decisive blow. Drake should be sent with a squadron of warships, ostensibly to support Dom Antonio, the claimant to the usurped Portuguese crown, but in reality, to destroy as much enemy shipping as he could or, at worst, disrupt the invasion plans to win England the precious commodity of time. Sir Walter Raleigh, if later reports by a Spanish spy are to be believed, was a covert but strident opponent of the plan.[49]

After much characteristic havering, Elizabeth grudgingly agreed to Drake's mission on 25 March, but would only allow four of her own warships – *Elizabeth Bonaventure, Golden Lion, Dreadnought* and *Rainbow*[50] – and two fifty-ton pinnaces, *Spy* and *Makeshift*, to take part. This decision was not driven by her natural frugality alone; the queen was understandably wary of risking too many of her precious ships, her first line of defence, on such a dangerous venture.

The remainder of Drake's fleet of twenty-five vessels would be fitted out and paid for by nineteen London merchants as a speculative venture in the fond hope of rich pickings in plunder.[51] The eager sponsors scenting profit from this venture included grocers, drapers, fishmongers, haberdashers and skinners. Drake's agreement with these 'Merchant Adventurers', signed three days later, laid down that 'whatsoever commodity in goods, money, treasure, merchandise or other benefit ... shall happen to be taken by all or any of the aforesaid ships or their company either by land or sea, shall be equally proportioned, man for man and ton for ton, [and will] be divided at sea ... as soon as wind and weather will permit'.[52] Some may define such an enterprise as an act of war. But there was no hiding behind the lawyer's formal turn of phrase; it was legalised pillage in the queen's name.

The striking force included three ships owned by the Levant Company of London, displacing almost 500 tons each, and seven lesser vessels of up to 200 tons. The rest were smaller ships of lighter draught, to be deployed for reconnaissance, conveying messages or undertaking shallow water operations close to shore.

Elizabeth's government took immense pains to conceal the preparations for the naval expedition. Its purpose was kept secret from all but its most senior officers and the southern English ports were temporarily closed to prevent word of Drake's mission leaking out. Afterwards, the Spanish claimed that:

so much cunning was employed that even Secretary Walsingham refrained from sending hither [Paris] a dispatch from his mistress [Elizabeth] so that the courier might not say anything about it.[53]

Inevitably (and belatedly) the Spanish heard rumours of the fleet's departure. One of their agents talked to a French merchant in Rouen, who had arrived the previous day from England. He provided somewhat inflated estimates of its order of battle to the ambassador in Paris:

> Captain Drake left the Thames with forty well-armed ships, five belonging to the queen, of 800 or 900 tons each and carrying five thousand men.
>
> The merchant saw the fleet pass before Rye [in Sussex] on the way to Falmouth where they are to join forty or fifty more ...
>
> The rumour was that this fleet was going to encounter the [West] Indian flotilla.
>
> We are astonished at the great diligence and secrecy with which this fleet has been equipped, for up to the moment, not a word of it has reached us here.[54]

Drake put into Plymouth for a week to collect the ships assembled there and to provision his fleet. Speed was of the essence, as he had justifiable fears that his assault on Spain could be halted by fresh orders from London before it had even sailed. His flag captain, Thomas Fenner in *Dreadnought,* told Walsingham that Drake 'does all he can to hasten the service and sticks at no charge to further the same and lays out a great store of money to soldiers and mariners to stir up their minds'.[55]

The admiral was signally unperturbed by the embarrassingly large-scale desertion by his sailors on the very eve of his departure, blaming subversion by those at Elizabeth's court who opposed his operation. 'We all think [this was caused] by some practice of some adversaries to the action by letters written. They are mostly mariners. We have soldiers in their place,' he assured Walsingham.[56] Stocked up with food, water and munitions, Drake departed Plymouth on 12 April, his 600-ton flagship, *Elizabeth Bonaventure*, leading out the fleet. He penned a typically flamboyant, swashbuckling letter to Walsingham at the very last minute:

Let me beseech your honour to hold a good opinion not only of myself but of all these servitors in this action ...

The wind commands me away.

Our ships are under sail.

God grant we may so live in His fear as the enemy may have cause to say that God fights for Her Majesty as well abroad as at home. Haste![57]

Out in the south-west approaches to the English Channel, Drake encountered two vessels from Lyme Regis in Dorset, who readily agreed to join the expedition, making his fleet twenty-seven strong. They sighted the Spanish coast of Galicia on 15 April, but forty-eight hours later were struck by five days of violent storms off Finisterre which dispersed the fleet and sank the pinnace *Martigo*.

Elizabeth meanwhile was having second thoughts about the wisdom of Drake's adventure. Reports reached her that preparations for the Spanish invasion were slowing down and Andreas de Loo, an envoy from the Duke of Parma, arrived with tempting promises of peace. Nine days after Drake had left Plymouth, she sent new and urgent instructions,[58] dispatched by a fast pinnace. These ordered him to:

forbear to enter forcibly into any of [King Philip's] ports or havens, or to offer violence to any of his towns or shipping within harbours or to do any act of hostility upon the land.

And yet ... her pleasure is that ... you should do your best endeavour to get into your possession (avoiding as much ... effusion of Christian blood) such shipping of the said king's ... as you shall find at sea, either going from thence to the East or West Indies or returning from the said Indies to Spain and such as shall fall into your hands, to bring them into this realm.[59]

No warlike activity allowed then, but privateering, or more accurately, piracy, was still perfectly acceptable to a queen always worried about the paucity of cash in her coffers.

The pinnace, delayed by the same storms that scattered Drake's ships, never caught up with him. Perhaps the crew did not try too hard: sometime during the voyage they captured a ship which yielded £5,000 in prize money when they arrived back in Plymouth.

Walsingham wrote to Sir Edward Stafford, Elizabeth's ambassador in Paris, informing him of the sudden change in orders issued to Drake. Stafford (whose stepmother was Mary Boleyn, the queen's late aunt) enjoyed a spendthrift lifestyle, including accumulating substantial gambling debts through unwisely playing cards with the French king's brother, François, Duke of Alençon. His consequent financial problems had forced him in January 1587 to traitorously approach Bernardino de Mendoza, his Spanish opposite number, offering his services to Spain for hard cash. He was willing to supply any intelligence, short of that which might jeopardise the life of his queen.[60] Mendoza, delighted with this espionage coup, may have assigned him the codename 'Julio'. Walsingham thoroughly mistrusted Stafford, even sending one of his agents, Thomas Rogers (alias Nicholas Berden), the previous year, to monitor the ambassador's untoward relationship with the exiled English Catholics in France. Elizabeth's spymaster may therefore have used him as an unwitting conduit to feed information, false or otherwise, to the Spanish. After his mistress's mercurial change of heart, it was imperative to emphasise that England was not bent on attacking the Spanish mainland. He informed Stafford: 'There is a new order sent unto Sir Francis Drake to take a milder course, for that he was before particularly directed to distress the ships within the havens themselves.'[61]

From bitter experience, Drake understood very well that no fleet could operate effectively without adequate stores of food, water and ammunition. Therefore, instead of striking at heavily defended Lisbon, where the Armada ships were mobilising, he planned to attack the main supply base at Cadiz in Andalusia. Two Dutch merchantmen, which he had intercepted, had reported a large concentration of Armada provision ships there and this information confirmed his choice of target. Cadiz, reputedly the oldest inhabited city in Europe, stands on a narrow humpbacked peninsula at the mouth of the River Guadalquivir, which provides shipping with safe shelter from the Atlantic weather and tides.[62] Because of reefs and shifting sandbanks, there was only one entrance channel for large ships and this had to pass under the guns on the city walls.

At around four in the afternoon of Wednesday 29 April, a council of war was held in *Elizabeth Bonaventure* as a brisk southwesterly breeze filled the fleet's canvas sails. William Borough,

Drake's veteran vice-admiral and the commander of the queen's ship *Golden Lion*, privately and forcibly argued against an immediate attack on the Spanish. Drake would have none of it – 'Action this day' was ever his motto. 'That is my opinion,' he declared to his captains, 'though there are some would have us stay until morning. We shall not stay at all.'[63]

Drake's fleet arrived outside Cadiz about one hour before sunset. His ships were under strict orders to fly no flags until the very last moment to confuse the lookouts positioned on the walls and atop the masts of the ships inside the harbour. It was a typical warm spring evening and its inhabitants were taking their leisure. The central square was packed with spectators watching an athletic tumbler turn his acrobatic tricks. Nearby, others roared with laughter at a bawdy comedy performed by some itinerant actors in the open air. Then word spread slowly through the crowds that a line of ships was approaching the harbour entrance. What was the nationality of these mystery vessels? Were they friend or foe?

The first English cannon shots booming across the bay provided the definitive answer.

In Drake's words, written soon afterwards, he sighted 'thirty-two great ships of exceeding great burden [displacement] loaded ... with provisions and prepared to furnish the king's navy, intended with all speed against England'. Another account reported sixty ships, of which twenty were French, who immediately hoisted sail and fled, as did six Dutch hulks. The English ships fell upon the helpless anchored vessels like the wolf on the fold.

The first defensive shots were fired from eight oar-propelled galleys, commanded by Don Pedro de Acuña, which had providently arrived from a patrol near Gibraltar a few days before.[64] Inside the panic-stricken city, the mayor ordered women and children to take refuge within Matagorda Castle, but its captain slammed shut the fortress gates in their faces and twenty-seven were suffocated or pressed to death in the crush.[65] The galleys, although highly manoeuvrable in the calm waters in the lee of the peninsula, were no match for Drake's heavily armed warships. Two were badly damaged[66] in a failed attempt to lure the English ships on to sandbanks off the eastern shore and their commander was forced to retreat to St Mary's Port, four miles (6.44 km) to the north, which was protected by a network of treacherous shoals that required the local knowledge of a pilot for safe entry.

At nine that night Francisco de Benito de Maiora, in St Mary Port, wrote to officials in Seville reporting that:

> about four of the clock, we heard a great noise of ordnance in the bay and saw many sails of ships ...
>
> Within two hours, there came hither the *Galliota* which brought ten men very sore hurt.
>
> The people of this town are in arms. There are in the bay two or three ships set on fire but what they are we know not. This is all that we can yet learn.[67]

Over the next two days, Drake's sailors set ablaze the supply vessels, while under constant fire from 'thundering shot' from the shore batteries and from the galleys when they sallied out in attack. Drake sank a Genoese 'argosy' or merchantman loaded with a cargo of logwood, hides, wool and cochineal destined for Italy, and also captured four provision ships.[68] The vessel displaced about 1,000 tons, was armed with thirty-six brass guns, and was 'very richly laden'.

The following morning, Drake took advantage of the flood tide to lead a flotilla of pinnaces and frigates (supported by the London ship, *Merchant Royal*, commanded by Robert Flick), to cut out and sink a 1,500-ton galleon owned by Santa Cruz that was moored in the inner harbour of Cadiz. The ship, valued at 18,000 ducats, was burned to the waterline.

The arrival of Don Alonso Pérez de Guzmán, Seventh Duke of Medina Sidonia, leading six-thousand hurriedly mustered local militia, deterred any English landing on the inner harbour. Artillery batteries were wheeled into position along the shoreline – but their subsequent fire only managed to damage the English vice-flagship *Golden Lion*. Borough warped the ship out of harm's way and then fought off an assault from the marauding galleys. Although that manoeuvre saved the ship, he was later to face charges of desertion and cowardice levelled by Drake.

That night, the Spanish used some of the smaller vessels in the harbour as fireships to float out on the tide, but these were towed away by the English sailors and harmlessly beached in shallow waters.

One of the admiral's volunteer 'gentleman adventurers' estimated that twenty-eight barques had been burned, totalling 13,000 tons:

> We continually fired their ships as the flood [tide] came in ... the sight of the terrible fires were to us very pleasant and mitigated the burden of our continual travail [from enemy fire]. We were busy for two nights and one day in discharging, firing and [un]loading of provisions.

Drake's ships were restocked with Spanish provisions: wine, oil, biscuit and dried fruits, while around 500 tons of bread were set alight, along with 400 tons of wheat. One important coup was the destruction of a year's supply of iron hoops and wooden staves for making barrels. This alone was later to prove a tactical disaster for the Armada; food and water had to be stored in unseasoned, leaky casks that depleted water supplies and quickly rotted the food stored within.

Official Spanish estimates of their losses totalled twenty-four ships, valued at 172,000 ducats or more than £750,000 (£137,000,000 at current prices).[69] Philip, in Madrid, was horrified when he read the news from Cadiz. With typical understatement, he noted: 'The loss was not very great but the daring of the attempt was very great indeed.'[70]

All this was achieved with remarkably few casualties: the master gunner of the *Golden Lion* suffered a broken leg smashed by a cannon shot fired from the town's fortifications. The volunteer soldier commented:

> It may seem strange or rather miraculous that so great an exploit should be performed with so small [a] loss, the place to damage us so convenient and their force so great ... from whom were shot at us at the least two hundred culverin and cannon shot.
>
> But in all this ... our actions, though dangerously attempted [were] yet happily performed. Our good God has and daily does make his power manifest to all papists and His name by us His servants continually honoured.[71]

A brief truce offered by Don Pedro de Acuña, commander of the galley squadron, allowed the exchange of prisoners. Drake's captives were swapped for Englishmen amongst the galley slaves and a five-man prize crew that had been captured in the course of the first night's fighting. The courtly Spaniard sent his barge with chivalrous gifts of wine and 'sucket' – a type of sweetmeat – during this break in hostilities.[72] Drake had interrogated one Spanish sailor who boasted that the Armada now numbered more than two hundred warships. Bravado and swagger were second nature to Drake and he easily brushed aside such Spanish bluster. Shrugging his shoulders, he replied: '*No es mucho*' – 'That's not a lot'.[73]

Then the English ships sailed off westwards, leaving behind them confusion (today we would call it 'shock and awe') and a welter of panic-stricken messages dispatched post haste around Spain and Portugal warning of the danger that Drake still posed. Medina Sidonia also sent a ship to the West Indies ordering the treasure fleet to stay in Havana, Cuba, until he was known to be safely back in England.[74]

Where would *El Draque* – the Dragon – as the Spanish called Drake – now strike? He searched in vain for a squadron of seven Biscayan ships and five pinnaces commanded by the redoubtable Juan Martinez de Recalde, but orders retrieved from a captured dispatch boat indicated that the enemy vessels had run for shelter at Lisbon. Drake therefore cast around for other targets of opportunity. His deputy, William Borough, wrote him an angry letter on 7 May, during a gale off Cape St Vincent, strongly advising against landing on Spanish soil.

> Her Majesty's pleasure is ... that you, with these ships now under your charge, should come hither ... upon this coast and seek by all the best means you can to impeach their purpose and stop their meeting at Lisbon, whereof the manner how is referred to your discretion ...
>
> I do not find by your instructions an advice to land but I remember a special caveat and advice given you to the contrary by the Lord High Admiral.[75]

In front of his personal chaplain and flag captain, Drake charged Borough with insubordination and seeking to dictate his duty. Captain John Marchant was ordered to take command of the *Golden Lion* and Borough, despite offering to destroy his letter, was locked in his cabin in his own ship. He was also clapped in irons to ensure there was no chance of further mischief.[76] There he stayed 'ever in doubt of my life and expecting daily when the admiral would have executed upon me his bloodthirsty desire'.[77]

Ignoring such faint hearts, on 14 May Drake landed eleven hundred men on a sandy beach near Lagos and they marched inland through the cornfields and vineyards for five miles until they came to the town. It was better defended than they had been told and its three-thousand-strong garrison opened fire with cannon, wounding some of the English soldiers. Drake's men retreated to their ships and they sailed on to Cape Sagres in search of easier pickings. The admiral personally led eight hundred men in an attack on the Avelera fort, perched seemingly unassailable on a high rock. Timber, pitch and bundles of firewood were piled against its wooden gates, protected by four towers, under cover of small-arms fire. But before the blaze could permit a forced entry, the fort surrendered under flag of truce. The same day, the English captured Valliera castle at Cape St Vincent and a nearby fortified monastery. All three fortresses were set ablaze and local churches ransacked.

The English fleet moved on to anchor audaciously off Cascaes, north of Lisbon. Santa Cruz commanded the castle of St Julian and Drake sneered at his impotence in not coming out to fight: 'The marqués of Santa Cruz was with his galleys, seeing us chase his ships ashore ... and was content to suffer us there quietly to tarry and never charged us with one cannon shot.'[78] Although Santa Cruz sent a message assuring him, as a gentleman, that the King of Spain was not ready to send the Armada 'this year', letters were found on a Portuguese prisoner repeating a Spanish proclamation that promised that Philip would invade England in 1587 'and would not leave one alive of mankind above the age of seven years'.[79]

Enemy shipping continued to be attacked along the Spanish and Portuguese coasts as Drake imposed a virtual blockade. His dispatch to Walsingham on 27 May was jubilant.

> It has pleased God that we have taken forts, barques, caravels and divers other vessels more than a hundred, most laden, some with oars for galleys, planks and timber for ships and pinnaces, hoops and pipe-staves for casks with many other provisions for this great army ...

All I commanded to be consumed into smoke and ashes by fire which will be to the king no small waste of his provisions, besides the want of his barques.

His triumph was tinged with foreboding about the scale of the Spanish invasion plans:

I dare not almost write unto your honour of the great forces we hear the King of Spain has out in the Straits.

Prepare in England strongly and most by sea.

Stop him now and stop him ever.

Look well to the coast of Sussex.[80]

Drake was undoubtedly receiving some intelligence about shipping movements, probably from disgruntled Portuguese. One piece of information must have made his eyes glint: the carrack *San Felipe* was shortly to arrive from the East Indies after wintering in Mozambique. The ship, laden with expensive exotic spices, was of especial concern to Philip, who suspected that the English admiral had spies ashore.[81] Drake therefore headed out into the Atlantic on a south-westerly course, hoping to intercept the Portuguese ship. After sending home some of his sick crewmen, the depleted fleet hit bad weather with a three-day gale almost sinking the *Elizabeth Bonaventure*. The crew of the *Golden Lion* had suffered enough: short of water and rations, they wanted to return home rather than continue with Drake's adventurers. Marchant, their captain, returned to the flagship in the pinnace *Spy* and informed his admiral of his crew's disobedience. Drake was incandescent with anger and summoned a court martial to try the mutineers. He sentenced Borough and the officers of the ship to death *in absentia* as the *Golden Lion* disappeared below the horizon.[82]

But the prospect of loot and profit soon brought the smile back to Drake's face. On 18 June he sighted the *San Felipe* loaded with gold, precious stones, silks and spices (pepper, cinnamon, cloves, mace) worth £108,049 13s 11d in today's money – a handsome return for his investors.

Elizabeth, her doubts now happily evaporated, told the French ambassador Châteauneuf that she had heard on 13 May that Drake had 'burnt the ships at Cadiz and had sacked the country'. The envoy was astonished and disbelieving, but she told him bluntly: 'Then you do not believe what is possible.'

One of Walsingham's agents reported the fear and trepidation that Drake's incursion engendered among the Spanish. His exploits 'make them all to tremble' and his sack of Cadiz and the damage caused had cost 'more than a million crowns'.[83]

The English squadron arrived back with the *San Felipe* in Plymouth on 26 June 1587 to an outburst of national hero-worship for 'singeing the King of Spain's beard', as government propaganda had it. Drake had destroyed well over 10,000 tons of Spanish shipping, much of the Armada's provisions, and delayed its sailing for at least twelve months. There were also the rich pickings from the Portuguese carrack to savour.

Walsingham, ever the man for action, urged that Drake should return to the Azores to attack the lumbering wide-bellied treasure ships bringing back bullion from the Spanish empire in the Americas. The best way 'to bridle their malice is the interruption of the Indian fleets', he told Burghley on 16 July.[84]

Unsurprisingly, Elizabeth, desperately hoping for an elusive peace, rejected the idea.

But the days of peace were running out. As Leicester, embattled in the Low Countries, warned the queen that November:

> The world was never so dangerous, nor never so full of treasons and treacheries as at this day. God, for his mercy's sake, preserve and keep you from them all.[85]

– 3 –

RAMPARTS OF EARTH
AND MANURE

Many of the justices refuse to furnish petronels [cavalry pistols] *using, for their defence, some nice and curious reason which might have been forborne in this time of special service.*

Lord North to Sir Francis Walsingham,
Kirtling, Cambridgeshire, 20 May 1588.[1]

Elizabeth had no standing army of fully armed and trained soldiers to fight against the Spanish invaders, other than the small permanent garrisons in Berwick on the Scottish border, and in Dover Castle on the English Channel coast. Her fortifications were broken down and decayed, her exchequer impecunious and her nation divided by religious dissent. Outwardly, only her small but powerful navy and the skill and determination of her sea captains stood between her and the threatened all-conquering might of the Spanish Armada.

The more superstitious amongst her increasingly apprehensive subjects considered the two eclipses of the moon predicted for March and August 1588 as alarming portents of catastrophe. Additionally, in the noisy alehouses and around the bustling market stalls, many talked of the fifteenth-century mathematician and astronomer Regiomontanus of Königsburg[2] who had prophesied grimly that the same year the world would 'suffer upheavals, empires will dwindle and from everywhere will be great lamentation'.[3]

Overseas there were equally ominous omens of dark days to come for England. On 4 August 1587, the battle-weary survivors of the English garrison of the port of Sluis in the Low Countries surrendered to Parma's forces after a brutal siege of fifty-three days, having expended all their gunpowder. The Spanish butcher's bill may have been almost seven hundred killed and many more wounded, but Parma now held a deep-water port in Flanders, seemingly a convenient base from which to invade England.

France was an object lesson in the likely fate of a nation riven by widespread and violent religious discord which King Henri III seemed powerless to resolve. Elizabeth's neighbour had been wracked by a series of bloody civil wars between the Protestant Huguenots and Catholics since 1562. As far as the queen was concerned, the stakes in France were high: a victory for the Catholic League and a pro-Spanish regime in Paris could well gift the Armada a vital strategic prize: the use of its harbours up and down the English Channel.

In April 1587, three towns in Picardy (on the then Netherlands border), were seized by French Catholic troops but they failed in their primary objective of capturing the port of Boulogne. The end of that summer's campaigning saw Huguenot forces under Henri of Navarre crush the Catholic army at the Battle of Coutras in Aquitaine on 20 October. Little quarter was offered by the victors and more than three thousand Catholic soldiers were slaughtered, including three hundred of noble blood. Protestant celebrations were short-lived. Six days later the Huguenots' German and Swiss mercenary allies (who were liberally subsidised by Elizabeth) were roundly defeated at the Battle of Vimory, in Loiret, central France. The *reiters* retreated in good order to the walled town of Auneau, ten miles (16.1 km) east of Chartres in Eure-et-Loire, but were routed on 24 November. Catholic Paris was ready to take to the streets in support of their hero, Henri Guise, Third Duke of Guise, and to topple the king. As Mendoza jubilantly told King Philip: 'Events here could hardly have gone more happily for your majesty's affairs. The people of Paris can be relied on at any time. They are more deeply than ever in obedience of the Duke of Guise.'

Elizabeth had written to James VI of Scotland after the execution of his mother, Mary Queen of Scots, protesting her innocence in the matter and describing the 'extreme dolour that overwhelms my mind for that miserable *accident* which, far contrary to my feeling' had befallen the exiled queen. She assured him that no one would 'watch more carefully to preserve you and your estate' than her.[4] Those soft words might have mollified the young king, but reports of widespread pro-Spanish sentiment in Scotland so troubled the queen that in September 1587 she hurriedly sent 6,500 speedily-recruited troops to secure her northern border.[5] Despite this prudent deployment, the situation worsened with John, Seventh Lord Maxwell, launching an abortive Catholic insurrection in Dumfries and Galloway in south-west Scotland in the spring of 1588, with the aim of providing the Spanish with a northern base.[6]

Compounding all Elizabeth's other troubles, attempts on her life remained an ever-present threat. In March 1586, information was received of a plot by 'certain Jesuits against the queen's majesty, one having come to England to do a desperate enterprise upon her ... even as was done upon the Prince of Orange'. Concurrently, there was a conspiracy to kill the Earl of Leicester 'either by poison or other violent means'.[7] Danger could also lurk close to home. Walsingham heard in April that Peter Wilcox, purveyor of the queen's buttery, 'was a great dealer with priests and papists'.[8] The spymaster sent one of his agents, Stephen Paul, to Venice early the following year to pick up news in the city state. In November, he reported that Michael Giraldi, from Bergamo in Lombardy, had left for England, disguised as a merchant:

It is thought ... [he is] to poison her majesty at the instigation of the Pope.

The Pope, under pretence of supporting the war against the heretics and for performing some great enterprise, has enriched himself exceedingly.[9]

And in May 1588, one of the prisoners interrogated in the Tower of London was 'Andrew van Metico, a Dutchman, suspected [of] being sent over to poison the queen'.[10]

There were some among Elizabeth's subjects who placed profit ahead of patriotism. Sometime in 1587, Elizabeth's government learned that twelve English merchants – most from Bristol – had been supplying the Armada, 'to the hurt of her majesty and undoing of the realm, if not redressed'. Their nine sizeable cargoes of contraband, valued between £300 and £2,000, were not just provisions but also supplies of ammunition, gunpowder, muskets and ordnance. What happened to these traders (were they Catholics?) is unknown, but in those anxious and edgy times, they would be unlikely to have enjoyed the queen's mercy.[11]

Walsingham was still hampered by a crippling lack of intelligence assets in Spain, and was forced to rely on merchants providing eye-witness accounts or just plain gossip. These brave men were easily compromised: in April 1587, Mendoza told Philip that he had heard from a 'good quarter' (?the treacherous Stafford) that

> a Scots merchant, who says he is the King of Scotland's banker, is in Spain with twelve well-fitted English boats freighted with merchandise from England – the mariners also being English.
>
> It would be well for your majesty to send orders to the ports to have this merchant arrested.
>
> His name is Hunter.[12]

The spy, based in Lisbon, was detained, put on trial as an English agent and supporter of heretics and imprisoned in the city. A much later letter from him confirmed Mendoza's suspicions. He described his incarceration but then boldly appended details of the munitions and ordnance still stored in the city. Although he used a tiny sketch of a hunting horn to identify himself as the writer, the letter's true provenance is revealed by Walsingham's marginal note, scribbled back in London: 'From Mr Hunter of Lisbon.'[13]

Nicholas Ousley in Malaga smuggled his reports to England hidden in wine casks. Mendoza again uncovered the English spy in a note to Madrid on 12 July 1587:

> Ousley ... sends advertisements [news] to the queen and on Walsingham receiving certain letters from him, said he was one of the cleverest men he knew and the queen was much indebted to him from his regular and trustworthy information.[14]

Ousley was arrested but managed to bribe his way out of gaol and was still sending his reports to England as late as April 1588.[15]

Walsingham's most effective agent overseas was the Catholic Anthony Standen, who operated under the somewhat grandiose alias of Pompeo Pellegrini, or sometimes the more mundane initials 'B.C.'. He had been a member of the household of Henry Stuart, Lord Darnley (Mary Queen of Scots' murdered second husband) and later lived in Tuscany. Standen befriended Giovanni Figliazzi, the Duke of Tuscany's ambassador in Madrid, and used this friendship to garner Spanish military intelligence. Standen's efforts produced an impressive espionage *coup de théâtre* in May 1587. In a coded letter, he told Walsingham:

> Since your last [letter] in which you desire intelligence on Spanish matters, I have borrowed one hundred crowns and dispatched to Lisbon a Fleming who has a brother in service with the Marqués of Santa Cruz and of his chamber.
>
> I have given him [the] address for his letters to me at the [Tuscan] ambassador's house in Madrid who straight [away] will send them to me.
>
> He is a proper fellow and writes well and I sent him away with these four [Genoese] galleys [who have sailed for Spain to join the Armada].[16]

Given the painfully slow transportation resources available in the sixteenth century, there would always be inevitable delays in receiving the information, but Walsingham now had a spy within the household of the Armada commander-in-chief himself. One of the first fruits was a copy of Santa Cruz's most recent order of battle, dated 22 March 1587, complete with the wages bill of the fleet, signed by the captain-general himself and the navy secretary Barnaby de Pedrosa. Three months later, Standen reported that Spanish preparations would not be completed in time that year to take advantage of the best weather to launch the invasion. A relieved Walsingham passed this letter on to Burghley with the comment: 'I humbly pray your lordship that Pompeo's letter may be reserved to yourself. I would be loath [sic] the gentleman should have any harm through my default.'[17]

The spymaster's maxim was that the acquisition of knowledge is 'never too dear' and his espionage network was becoming increasingly expensive. The queen grudgingly granted £3,300 (£600,000 at current prices)[18] in March and June 1587, and a further £2,000 the following year towards the cost of Walsingham's secret service activities. Considering the scale of his network of spies and informers, it seems certain that he had to supplement this spending out of his own purse.

Another weapon in his secret war against Spain was the black art of propaganda and psychological warfare. In July 1587, Mendoza complained about English newsletters 'written by one of Walsingham's officers ... the son of a Spanish friar who fled many years ago from St Isidro in Seville with a nun of Utera to whom he is married. The son is a much worse heretic than the father ... I mention this matter to your majesty that you understand that although these reports have some appearance of probability, they are really hatched by Walsingham's knavery.'[19] The spymaster also printed almanacs in Amsterdam and Paris that forecast damaging storms for the summer of 1588 and great disaster for the Armada. These morale-sapping prophecies damaged recruitment to the Spanish army and in Lisbon an astrologer was arrested for making 'false and discouraging predictions'.[20]

In Madrid, Philip was rewriting the invasion plan. On 4 September 1587, he instructed the Duke of Parma that once the Spanish treasure fleet had been safely escorted to Cape St Vincent, Santa Cruz should collect all his ships and 'sail directly, in the name of God, to the English Channel, proceeding along it until they drop anchor off Margate point [Kent][21] having first sent notice to you ... of his approach'.

> When you see the passage assured by the arrival of the fleet at Margate, or at the mouth of the Thames, you will, if the weather permits, immediately cross with the whole army in the boats which you will have ready.
>
> You and the marqués will then cooperate, the one on land and the other afloat, and with the help of God, will carry the main business through successfully.
>
> Until you have crossed over with the army, the marqués is not to allow himself to be diverted from assuring your safe passage and keeping at bay any force of the enemy which may come out to prevent it ...
>
> When you have landed (the marqués giving you 6,000 selected Spanish infantry as ordered) I am inclined to leave to the discretion of both of you what would be the best for the marqués to do with the fleet.

Should Santa Cruz continue to protect the sea lanes from Flanders or capture 'some port' or 'seize some English ships ... to deprive them of maritime forces which are their principal strength'? After both commanders had considered these options, Santa Cruz should carry out the joint decision 'and you will hasten to the front ... I trust in God, in whose service it is done, that success may attend the enterprise and that yours may be the hand to execute it.'[22]

The king badgered his admiral to complete repairs to his ships and be ready to sail on 25 October. His patience was fast running out and he told Santa Cruz on 10 October: 'There is no more time to waste on requests and replies. Just get on with the job and see if you cannot advance the agreed departure date by a few days.' As the departure date loomed nearer, Philip became increasingly agitated and frustrated: 'So much time has been lost already that every further hour of delay causes me more grief than you could imagine. I charge and command you most strictly to leave before the end of the month.'[23] But his increasingly strident and imperious orders alone could not alter the harsh reality: the Armada was very far from being ready to sail.

Unlike many dilemmas in the history of intelligence, the English were in a position to build up a picture of Philip's military capabilities as well as correctly gauging his hostile intentions. But they could only guess where the Spanish intended to land. An assessment of the potential danger areas was included in a document entitled *Such means as are considered to put the forces of the Realm in order to Withstand an Invasion*. Milford Haven (Pembrokeshire), Falmouth, Helford, Plymouth (Cornwall), Torbay (Devon), Portsmouth and the Isle of Wight were singled out as places of especial danger and 'the places following are apparent for the army of Flanders to land in: Sussex, the Downs and Margate in Kent, the River Thames, Harwich, Yarmouth, Hull [and] Scotland:

> It is unlikely that the King of Spain will engage his fleet too far ... before he has mastered [a] good harbour of which Plymouth is nearest to Spain. [It is] easy to be won, speedily to be by him fortified and situated convenient to find succour unto, either out of Spain or France.
>
> Portland [Dorset] is a great harbour for all his ships to ride in; a good landing for men [and] this isle [having] being won, is a strong place for retreat.
>
> The reason why the Downs, Margate and the Thames are thought fit for landing places is in respect of the commodity of landing and nearness to the Prince of Parma, of whose forces the King of Spain [is] reported [to have] special trust.[24]

Available intelligence was inevitably confusing and contradictory. Thomas Dence 'a pensioner of the King of Spain, a great papist, but not yet wishing the destruction of England' believed that the Armada would seize Milford Haven and fortify it, as well as Lambay Island, off the east coast of Finegal in Ireland.[25] As late as May 1588, there were reports that the Spanish 'would rather land in the Isle of Wight than in any other place in England'.[26]

Elizabeth's government sought professional advice about the size and nature of a successful invading force from Sir William Wynter, the English naval surveyor and commander. He replied:

> Whereas it is said that [Parma's] strength is thirty thousand soldiers, then I assure your honour, it is no mean quality of shipping that must serve for transporting that number [of men] and that which appertains to them, without the which I do not think they will put forth; three hundred sail must be the least.
>
> For I well remember that in the journey made to Scotland in the queen's majesty's father's time, when we burned Leith and Edinburgh[27] there was in that expedition two hundred and sixty sail of ships and yet we were not able to land above eleven-thousand men and we then [were] in fear of none that could impeach us by sea.[28]

Walsingham suspected that most 'mischief' was likely to come from Scotland 'where the employment of two thousand men by the enemy, with some portion of treasure, may more annoy us more than thirty thousand men landed in any part of this realm'.[29]

Unaware that Parma planned to land on the Kent coast, Elizabeth's military advisers eventually selected Essex as the most likely place where the Spanish would storm ashore and the focus of defensive effort was switched there. Fears of an east coast landing were reinforced in March 1588 when three suspicious ships were seen off Yarmouth 'sounding the depths at diverse places'.[30]

The Thames estuary had a wide channel leading straight to the heart of the capital. On either side there were expanses of shallow mudflats that posed a serious obstacle to a vessel of any draught. Therefore, the defensive plans included the installation of an iron chain across the river's fairway at Gravesend in Kent, designed by the Italian engineer Fedrigo Giambelli. This boom, supported by one hundred and twenty ship's masts (costing £6 apiece) driven into the riverbed and anchored to lighters, was intended to stop enemy ships penetrating upriver to London. Unfortunately the first flood tide broke the barrier.[31] A contemporary map of the Thames defences, drawn by Robert Adam, shows the raking fields of fire from cannon on both banks and a second boom (or bridge of boats) further west at Lees Ness, before Blackwall Reach.[32] A similar boom was stretched across the River Medway from the new fort at Upnor, Kent, in 1586 to protect the safe anchorage there.[33]

Mobilising England's defences imposed an immense administrative burden on the Tudor government. After years of neglect there was so much to do and so little time in which to do it. A detailed survey of potential invasion beaches along the English Channel produced an alarming catalogue of vulnerability. In Dorset alone, eleven bays and coves were listed, with annotations such as: 'Chideock and Charmouth are two beaches to land boats but it must be very fair weather and the wind northerly'. Swanage Bay could 'hold one hundred ships and [the anchorage is able] to land men with two hundred boats and to retire again without danger of low water at any time'.[34] Further east in Hampshire, 'from Calshot to Lymington, [there are] good landing in two places, between Stansgore and Lepe and at Pits Deep and Siblers Lane'. The coast from Christchurch harbour to Bournemouth had 'for the most part good landing with small boats and their shipping may safely ride with[in] half a mile (804 m) of the shore in great number'.[35] In Sussex, the breach in the coastal defence works at Bletchington Hill caused during a French raid forty-three years before remained unrepaired.[36]

Lacking money and resources, Elizabeth's government decided that only the most dangerous beaches would be defended by wooden stakes rammed into the sand and shingle as boat obstacles, or by deep trenches excavated above the high-water mark. Earth ramparts were also thrown up to protect the few cannon available[37] or troops armed with harquebuses or bows and arrows. Those earthworks on the Isle of Wight were to be at least four feet (1.22 m) high and eight feet (2.44 m) thick, with sharpened poles driven into their face and with a wide ditch in front. Despite his frequent and vociferous complaints to London, the island's governor, Sir George Carey, had just four mounted guns and enough gunpowder for only one day's use.[38] He wrote testily: 'If this place be of so small importance to be thought worthy of no better provision, having discharged my duty in declaration of my wants, I will perform what I may with my small strength and wish better success than I have reason to expect.'[39] Carey also criticised plans to reinforce the island with raw recruits from the Hampshire militia – 'a brand of men termed trained, who I find rather so in name than in deed'. Carey suspected, not unreasonably, that the irascible Henry Radcliffe, Fourth Earl of Sussex, in charge of the defence of Portsmouth, would retain the best men to fulfil his own responsibilities.[40]

At Portsmouth itself, the strength and design of the newly built ramparts to defend the land approaches to the town had been severely criticised by Sir Walter Raleigh and were therefore demolished, much to Elizabeth's indignation at this waste of her money. New earth walls were constructed in just four months by eight hundred labourers and these were protected by five stone arrow-head-shaped bastions[41] behind a flooded ditch. Yet, more than half the garrison were rated 'by age and impotency by no way serviceable' and the Earl of Sussex happily escaped unhurt when an old iron gun, supposedly one of his best cannon, exploded into smithereens in front of him.[42] In November 1587, Sussex complained that the town's seaward tower was 'so old and rotten' that he dared not fire one gun to loyally celebrate the anniversary of the queen's accession to the throne.[43]

In eastern England, the walls of Great Yarmouth were heightened by ramparts in 1587 'at which time they were ... very fully and formally finished to the top ... with earth and manure more than forty feet (12.9 m) in breadth, resistible by God's help against any [gun] battery whatsoever'. The following year, an earth mount or mound was enclosed with brick and stone walls and 'a great piece of ordnance' placed on top.[44] Harwich, in Essex, was reported in a 'weak state [with] an open situation' in February 1587, so Elizabeth contributed £1,000 towards its fortification with the remainder of the cost expected to be stumped up by local people. Its citizens were pointedly reminded that 'the particular welfare of every private person requires them (as to favour the public weal [good] of their country and their own security), to yield some reasonable contribution'.[45]

Elizabeth's government was well aware of the lack of training amongst the militia who might have to fight Parma's veterans, many of them foreign mercenaries. A proclamation in 1580 had sought to improve military training by banning 'unlawful games' and, instead of wasting their time on gambling, encouraging fathers to bring up their sons 'in the knowledge of shooting'. It decreed that

> every man, having a male child ... of the age of seven years and above, till the age of seventeen, shall provide, ordain and have in his house, a bow and two shafts [arrows] to induce and learn them and bring them up in shooting.
>
> No person ... shall for his gain, lucre or living, keep, have hold, occupy, exercise or maintain any common house, alley or place of bowling ... coils, half-bowl, tennis, dicing, table or carding or any other manner of game prohibited by statute ... or any game new invented.

Playing bowls 'or any other unlawful game in the fields' would incur a fine of 6s 8d for each offence, or being gaoled.[46]

As early as 1577, the total manpower capable of being placed in the field was estimated at just fewer than 324,000 men aged between sixteen and sixty in England and Wales. This may seem an impressive figure, but it belies the quality of the forces that could fight to defend England's honour. A census eleven years later revealed only one hundred experienced 'martial men' available, and as some had fought in Henry VIII's French and Scottish wars more than forty years before, these old sweats were considered *hors de combat*. The infantry and cavalry were drawn from trained bands, volunteers, and a handful of conscripted personnel with special skills, such as the thousand veterans from the English army in the Netherlands who were hurriedly recalled to stiffen the ranks. Many of these, however, soon deserted and hid in the crowded streets and tenements of the Cinque Ports of Kent.[47]

The militia officers were noblemen, esquires and gentlemen whose motivation was not only defence of their country but defence of their personal property too.[48] As such they may have been 'natural guardians' of the land in which they dwelt, but they were largely amateurs.[49] Some who lived near the coast believed it more expedient to shift their households and movable wealth inland to places of greater safety, but this defeatism plainly cut across government policy. A proclamation of November 1587 ordered them to return 'on pain of her majesty's indignation, besides such forfeiture of [their] lands and goods ... No excuse shall be allowed as any just cause for non performance ...'[50]

Like so many of the gentry and some clergy, Walsingham paid personally for a contingent of troops – fifty mounted lancers, twenty cavalry, armed with pistols, and two hundred foot soldiers[51] as well as ordering himself new armour from the Low Countries. Not everyone was prepared to give wholehearted support to the defence of Elizabeth's realm. Even the Protestant clergy were less than willing to fund the militia, and in May 1588, the Privy Council was forced to write to John Whitgift, Archbishop of Canterbury, to ginger them up:

> Their lordships were given to understand that ... [the] clergy in most parts of the realm, although they have good and sufficient livings, refuse to find and show at the musters any lances [cavalry] or light horse, desiring to exempt themselves from that charge ...
>
> The present time requires that those of the clergy should rather by their forwardness encourage others in these public services towards the general defence of the realm than withdraw themselves from any manner of necessary charge.[52]

The bishops eventually contributed money for surprisingly small contingents: Chichester paid for thirteen soldiers, Salisbury, twenty-three, Peterborough, twenty-three. Their clergy also paid for troops. The diocese of Canterbury supplied a total of one hundred and sixty-five; London, two hundred and twenty-three and Winchester two hundred and seven.[53]

Amateurs have little place in repelling an invasion. The defence of Hampshire was plagued by a personal feud between the Fourth Earl of Sussex and the even more petulant William Paulet, Third Marquis of Winchester. At one planning meeting, the two nobles clashed publicly. Sussex found fault with the deployment of the Portsmouth forces, saying he could see neither sense nor reason in the orders. Unfortunately, the troops' disposition was Paulet's own idea and he snatched the vellum on which the orders were written, snapping: 'I will read the same myself and if I cannot find therein both sense and reason, then say I have no more brains than a woodcock.'[54] The marquis then bickered with seventy-year-old Thomas Cooper,

Bishop of Winchester, complaining that his clergy had promised much in arming the militia but had delivered nothing. The bishop, who had contributed £100 of his own money, huffily retorted that he had personally mustered the clergy's men under Paulet's very nose at Winchester. 'Albeit I am well-nosed' came the marquis's riposte, 'yet not so long [as] to reach or smell from Tidworth to Winchester, being twenty-six miles distant'.[55]

A professional soldier, Captain Nicholas Dawtrey, who had been sent to train the Hampshire militia, warned Walsingham in January 1588 that if three thousand infantry went across the Solent to defend the Isle of Wight, the Marquis of Winchester would be left 'utterly without force of footmen other than a few billmen[56] to guard and answer all dangerous places'. Local people complained about being posted away from home: they and their servants being compelled 'to go either to Portsmouth or Wight upon every sudden alarm, whereby their houses, wives and children shall be left without guard and left open by their universal absence to all manner of spoil'. Dawtrey emphasised that 'many of the common sort [were] recusants. My lord bishop [of Winchester] was able to give me a note of two hundred in a little corner. I do perceive that many of these people inhabit the sea coast.'[57]

Hampshire eventually raised a remarkable total of 9,088 men, but Dawtrey pointed out that 'many ... [were] very poorly furnished; some lack a head-piece [helmet], some a sword, some one thing or other that is evil, unfit or [unseemly] about him'.[58] Discipline was also problematic: the commander of the 3,159-strong Dorset militia (1,800 of them completely untrained) firmly believed they would 'sooner kill one another than annoy the enemy'.[59] Compared to these Elizabethan militia, the raw but enthusiastic Local Defence Volunteers (later the Home Guard) of the German invasion scare of the 1940s appears a finely honed military force.

An anonymous correspondent suggested to Walsingham that the most effective means of resisting enemy landings was to resort to 'our natural weapon' – the bow and arrow. It had destroyed the French at Agincourt in 1415; why not the Spanish in 1588? One can imagine an old buffer, bristling at the threat to queen and country and hearth and home, offering up advice that the bow and cross-bow were 'terrible weapons' which Parma's veterans were unused to. After further reflection, he concluded that 'the most powerful weapon of all against this enemy was the fear of God'.[60]

In reality, despite strenuous efforts to buy weapons in Germany and harquebuses from Holland at 23s 4d (£1.17) each, many militiamen did have to be content with only bows and arrows with which to face the enemy. Kent had 12,654 available men, of whom 2,958 were 'trained' infantry and 4,166 untrained, including 1,662 archers and 1,762 'shot',[61] armed with harquebuses and calivers, but these had little 'powder, match, lead, nags and carts'.[62] Equipment shortages were endemic and the old, rusty armour and weapons brought out of store did little to improve morale or create an aggressive *esprit de corps* within the militia. The Earl of Leicester complained that:

A number of burgonets[63] have arrived from the Tower but not a man will buy one, being ashamed to wear it.

The armoury must be better looked to. [There is] a great want of powder and munitions, which is known abroad.[64]

Gradually, out of the administrative chaos grew order and organisation. As in the dark days of 1940, when Britain faced the prospect of a Nazi invasion, it was realised in 1587–8 that, rather than attempting to defend every inch of the coastline, it would be much better to concentrate forces to stand and fight at the most dangerous landing places. The veteran soldier Sir John ('Black Jack') Norris was commissioned to travel to the southern maritime counties and identify sites where invading troops could be 'impeached' and 'some apt and fit places for retreat of forces to withstand' the enemy 'and the erecting of a body of an army to make head against him'. Norris had with him only men of 'skill and trust' for 'there should not be many acquainted with the danger and weakness of the said places'. In vulnerable Kent, probable landing places were identified on the Isles of Sheppey and Thanet, in the Downs, at Sheerness on Romney Marsh and along the broad Thames estuary. [65] Parties of local militia were stationed at these possible invasion beaches, but as they rarely numbered more than two hundred strong, they were very much 'forlorn hopes' – expendable sacrifices to buy time to allow larger forces to be concentrated inland, rather than seriously intended to halt the Spanish on the high-water mark. Kent's defence plan also listed the 'fittest places to be put into defence to hinder the enemy' at Canterbury, Sandwich, Rochester, Aylesford and Maidstone.

Throughout the south and south-west of England, the militia would therefore be concentrated near major ports and would counter-attack if possible, but in retreat, would practise a 'scorched earth policy', destroying bridges, burning crops and driving off farm animals to deny the invader sustenance from the land. Kent was to send four thousand men to any port or part of Sussex threatened and if Sheppey was attacked, four thousand reinforcements from Essex would join the men of Kent.[66] In March 1587, the southern counties were warned to ensure that their militia were ready to repel an invasion: 'The trained bands are to be [re]viewed and put in strength and to repair to such places as were formerly instructed within an hour's warning.'[67]

The main army was divided into two groups. The first, under the Earl of Leicester, with 27,000 infantry and 2,418 cavalry, would engage the enemy once he had landed in force. The second, under Lord Hunsdon, the Lord Chamberlain, numbered 28,900 infantry and 4,400 cavalry, would defend the sacred person of the queen herself, who would probably remain in London, with Windsor Castle as a handy bolt-hole if the capital fell.

On 8 March 1588 Elizabeth wrote to the City of London, ordering them to provide men and weapons as part of this personal bodyguard:

> Upon information given us of great preparations made in foreign parts with intent to attempt somewhat against this our realm, we gave present order that our realm should be put in order of defence
> ...
> Within our said City, our pleasure is there be forthwith put in readiness for defence of our own person ... the number of ten thousand able men furnished with armour and weapons convenient ... of which number ... six thousand be enrolled under captains and ensigns and to be trained at times convenient ...

The trained men were divided into four regiments, each 1,500 strong, armed with harquebuses, pikes and halberds with which they drilled twice a week. Those untrained were also mustered into four regiments.[68]

As well as fears about how an invasion could be driven back into the sea, there remained nagging doubts about the loyalty of Elizabeth's

Catholic subjects if or when the Spanish arrived. Burghley and Walsingham were plainly as afraid of a Catholic rising as Cardinal Allen was confident of it happening.[69] These worries were reinforced in early June 1586 by reports of an intended rebellion 'in the country near Portsmouth'. Within days, the Earl of Sussex reported that he had quelled it and had arrested a number of its leaders, adding on 13 June that 'some recusants, privy to the insurrection, were going to sea' and that he would attempt to detain them.[70] Raleigh reported in December 1587 that several of his commissioners in Devon were 'infected in religion and vehemently malcontent'. The citizens of Exeter had refused to pay their contribution towards the cost of defending the county.[71] The same month, a list of English captains who had served under the Spanish flag in the Low Countries was submitted to the Privy Council. Apparently realigning their loyalties, they wanted passports to return to England but they were described as 'most dangerous papists and thought to be bloody men, not fit to have any liberty in England'.[72]

Roger Walton reported that English priests would enter England and 'raise a Catholic party' at the invasion. The chief agent for the plan was said to be Thomas Hole, the tutor in the Earl of Northumberland's household. Walton talked darkly of a plan to capture a blockhouse between Rye and Winchelsea. The papist Thomas Dence also warned of 'great rejoicings and preparations' by Catholics in advance of the Armada's arrival.[73] Perhaps of more concern were reports of disaffection below decks in Elizabeth's warships. After a scare on board Lord Edmund Sheffield's *Bear*, the 'barber and three or four others have taken the oath [of allegiance] and renounced the Pope's authority'.[74]

Following Walsingham's old internment plan, dangerous recusants and priests were now confined in a number of fortresses. Quarrels over living conditions broke out between the Jesuit and other seminary priests imprisoned in Wisbech Castle. The Jesuit leader William Weston demanded that the internees should follow a stricter discipline as more fitting to their vocation and accused the others of loose living and immorality. Relations were not improved by the Jesuits receiving the lion's share of alms sent in by the faithful outside the walls.[75] Security was so lax that one prisoner was able to secretly celebrate Mass within the castle:

In the dead of night, we were able to obtain vestments by a rope which was let down from [a] window [above] and in the early morning, before the wardens and other prisoners were awake, we returned them in the same manner.[76]

Under the slipshod regime of Thomas Gray, keeper of the recusants, matters had grown so lax that Wisbech became a kind of unofficial ecclesiastical college, a forum for debating theological issues, as well as a place of pilgrimage for the Catholic laity. What was worse, the priests could unlock each other's doors, and they interrupted Gray's own evangelical prayers by whistling and stamping on the floorboards of the room above. His daughter, Ursula, had even become a Catholic convert. Furthermore, two of the recusants, Charles Borne and Nicholas Scroope, had beaten Gray's wife and servants while he was away. Enough was enough. A commission of local justices recommended that 'trustworthy townsmen' should be selected to assist the keeper, who was not permitted to absent himself without written permission. Visits were stopped; letters censored and no communication between prisoners was allowed except at meal times. The only snippet of good news for Walsingham in this sorry tale was that one of the prisoners, Thomas Travers, who had complained of his 'hard treatment' at Gray's hands, now submitted to Elizabeth's government and promised to attend Protestant church services.[77]

Throughout England, recusants were being 'restrained'. In Norfolk, Sir Edward Clere and Sir William Heydon complained that many had ominously 'absented themselves from their houses'. In Bedfordshire, the Earl of Kent asked innocently how he was to proceed with female recusants 'married to husbands that are conformable in religion'.[78] Godfrey Foljambe arrested his own grandmother, Lady Constance, 'and now have her in my custody whom ... I shall safely keep and have forthcoming when she will be called for'.[79]

Sensibly, the armour and weapons held by recusants had been collected and confiscated for use by the queen's militia. With nice English respect for the rights of property, money from those items sold would be handed back to the original owners.

First warning of the enemy's arrival was to come from a number of pinnaces or fishing smacks patrolling far out to sea. On land, a complex network of warning beacons had been located on high points throughout the southern counties of England since at least the early fourteenth century and the system was now overhauled.[80] These beacons consisted of iron fire baskets mounted atop a tall wooden structure, normally positioned on an earth mound, situated some fifteen miles (24.14 km) apart. Kent had forty-three beacon sites, as did Devon; Essex twenty-six; Norfolk sixteen.[81] There were twenty-four in and around the coastal region of Sussex and a similar number in Hampshire, the latter positioned so that Somerset, Oxfordshire and Berkshire could spot the warning signals. News of a landing on the south coast could, with luck, reach London within the hour, with fuller details following on, carried by a string of post horses.

The beacons were normally manned during the more clement weather of March to October by two 'wise, vigilant and discreet' men in twelve-hour shifts (nearby villages taking it in turns to provide the watchers), although at times of crisis this could be extended.[82] Each man received eight pence (just over 3p) per day for his pains. The watchers were subject to surprise inspections to ensure their diligence, and were sternly prohibited from having dogs with them, for fear of distraction.

It was a tedious and uncomfortable patriotic duty. A new shelter was built near one Kent beacon when the old wooden hut fell down. This was only intended to protect the sentinels from bad weather and had no 'seats or place of ease lest they should fall asleep. [They] should stand upright in ... a hole [looking] towards the beacon.' Not everyone spent their time scanning the horizon: two watchers at Stanway beacon in north-east Essex preferred catching partridges in a cornfield and were hauled up in court.[83] There were other cases of opportunism. In July 1586, five men were accused of plotting to maliciously fire the Hampshire beacons 'upon a [false] report of the appearance of the Spanish fleet' and in the ensuing tumult, to steal food 'to redress the current dearth of corn', engage in a little light burglary of gentlemen's houses and liberate imprisoned recusants at Winchester. Most were gaoled, but some were sent to London for further interrogation, in case there was a wider conspiracy.[84]

Instructions on what to do once ships were sighted varied from county to county. No beacon could be lit without the presence of local justices. On the Isle of Wight, if up to twenty vessels were seen heading towards the coast, one of the watchmen had to pant down the steep hill to the nearest church and ring the bells. Surrey justices were instructed in 'a certain and direct' method to spot beacons at night or in misty weather that enabled them to decide 'whether the beacon in which [they] have regard … be on fire or not and how we may discern that fire from any other fire'.[85] Naturally, there were false alarms. In 1579, the Portsdown beacon, high above Portsmouth, was lit and in response the local militia were quickly mobilised. However it transpired that the watchers had reacted to smoke caused by huntsmen trying to flush out a badger from its sett.[86]

The first line of defence was naturally the queen's navy, augmented by ships taken up from trade or hired for the duration of the war. Obtaining these vessels sometimes proved difficult.

Sir John Gilbert, brother to the petulant Sir Humphrey, refused permission for his ships to join Drake's western squadron and allowed them to sail on their planned voyage in March 1588 in defiance of naval orders.[87] At the same time, there was also corporate reluctance to furnish ships to serve alongside the navy, and a litany of excuses began to flow from coastal town councils. William Bray, mayor of Hull, pleaded with the Privy Council 'that they were unable to furnish the two ships and a pinnace', as directed, as 'all their best ships are at present on distant voyages abroad' and their mariners had been pressed into naval service. (Later, after some ships returned from Newcastle and London, they contributed two ships and a pinnace.) John Harris, mayor of the north Devon town of Barnstaple, could not supply the required two ships and 'a handsome pinnace in warlike manner' having 'suffered so much from the prohibitions of the King of Spain' – the Spanish embargoes on English shipping.

John Berryman, mayor of Poole in Dorset, asked to be excused from paying for 'one great ship and a pinnace' because of their 'inability' to raise the money.[88] In mitigation he reported that they had detained the *Primrose* of Poole, bound for Newfoundland (Peter Cox, one of the ship's owners, was imprisoned after she sailed to avoid joining the English fleet) and the pinnace *Elephant*, which when 'fitted up' could be employed in naval service.[89] The good burghers of Southampton were also unable to supply ships 'on account of the decay of their town and commerce and the great charges they had [paid] for providing the powder, repairs and fortifications' of the town. In addition there was a shortage of sailors – more than one hundred had already been pressed into the queen's service.[90] In East Anglia, the inhabitants of East Bergholt asked to be excused their payment towards the cost of Colchester's ship 'by reason of the prohibition of the exportation of Suffolk cloth'.[91] Coggeshall and Dedham also sought exemption. Meanwhile the villages of Blackney, Wiston and Cley in Norfolk complained bitterly that they had been overcharged in their contribution by the corporation of [King's] Lynn.[92]

The thirty-eight ships and pinnaces in Elizabeth's navy, displacing a total of 12,990 tons, were mobilised on 5 October 1587[93] in response to reports that the Armada was ready to sail. Fifty-one-year-old Charles Howard, Second Baron Effingham, was appointed Lord High Admiral on 21 December with Drake as his vice-admiral. On board the queen's ship *Bear* the next day, Howard found his sailors in rags. He told Burghley:

Here is a very sufficient and able company of sailors as ever were seen and because of their long journeys out of all places in this realm and this bad season makes them unprovided of apparel and such necessaries, it were good for their relief to pay them one month's wages before hand.[94]

Although four ships dated from the reign of Henry VIII, eleven had been built since 1584 and a further twelve had been rebuilt to modern standards.[95] The new-builds and refits were to an innovative English design of warship, called 'race-built', which lowered the raised platforms or 'castles' at the bows and stern, lengthened the gun-deck and produced a sleeker hull. This made them faster and more manoeuvrable and enabled them to bring a heavier armament to bear upon the enemy.[96] It was to prove a decisive factor in the battles to come.

Several warships were designed specifically for naval operations in the shoaled waters of the narrow seas between England and Flanders. *Rainbow* and *Vanguard* both had shallow draughts, drawing only twelve to thirteen feet (3.66–3.96 metres) and this made them roll alarmingly in heavy seas. Sir Henry Seymour, who flew his flag in *Rainbow*, acknowledged that 'my summer ship ... will not be able to go to the North, Irish or Spanish seas without harm and spoil of our people by sickness'.[97]

But thanks to the maintenance programme developed by the navy treasurer John Hawkins, the major ships were in good fettle. Howard was delighted at their condition. He told Burghley:

I have been aboard every ship that goes out with me and in every place where any may creep and I do thank God that they be in the estate they be in.

There is never one of them that knows what a leak means.

Therefore I dare presume greatly that those that have been made [built] in her majesty's time be very good and serviceable and shall prove them arrant liars that have reported the contrary.[98]

He was particularly pleased with his newly built flagship, *Ark Royal*.

I think there were never in any place in the world worthier ships than these are for so many.

And as few as we are, if the King of Spain forces be not hundreds, we will make good sport with them.

I pray your lordship, tell her majesty from me that her money was well given for the *Ark Royal* [99] for I think her the [best] ship in the world for all conditions and truly I think there can be no great ship make me change and go out of her.[100]

Drake, in Plymouth, was chafing at the bit, desperate to strike at the Armada before it reached the shores of England. On 30 March 1588, he wrote to the Privy Council, urging another pre-emptive strike on the Spanish fleet. Striking a first blow would

put great heart into her majesty's loving subjects, both abroad and home for they will be persuaded in conscience that the Lord of all strengths will put into her majesty and her people, courage and boldness, not to fear any invasion in her own country but to seek God's enemies and her majesty's where they may be found.

For the Lord is on our side, whereby we may assure ourselves, our numbers are greater than theirs …

With fifty sail of shipping, we shall do more good upon their own coast than a great many more will do here at home.

The sooner we are gone, the better we shall be able to impeach them.

He was also indignant at a report that the Biscayan warships had red crosses on their sails like the English flag, 'which is a great presumption, proceeding from the haughtiness and pride of the Spaniard and not to be tolerated'.[101]

He would soon have his chance to cut the Armada down to size.

THE GREAT AND MOST
FORTUNATE NAVY

Pray to God, that in England, He gives me a house of
some very rich merchant where I may place my ensign,
which the owner thereof do ransom ... me 30,000 ducats.
Antonio de Taso Aquereis, commander of two hundred
Spanish troops, writing home from Lisbon.[1]

Santa Cruz, the commander of the Armada, died in Lisbon on 9
February 1588 from 'ship's fever' (or typhus) after being purged
and bled for eleven days by his physicians. The sixty-two-year-
old admiral had been exhausted both by his struggles to bring the
Spanish fleet up to a full war footing and by the torrent of instructions from a fixated, pedantic and bureaucratic monarch who sought
to micromanage every detail of the invasion plans. Some whispered
that the malicious criticism of the admiral prevalent at Philip's court
had also contributed to his death.[2] Few mourned the passing of this
egotistical grandee of the ocean: only four persons accompanied the
coffin to his grave in the parish church of El Viso in Córdoba.[3]

Two days later, Philip appointed Spain's premier duke, Don Alonso
Pérez de Guzmán, 'el Bueno' [the Good], Seventh Duke of Medina
Sidonia, as Santa Cruz's successor and his captain-general of the
ocean. After the exasperating delays in readying the ships, the king
was sanguine about the impact of Santa Cruz's death, maintaining
coldly that 'God had shown him a favour by removing the marqués
now, rather than when the Armada was at sea'.[4]

For months Philip had been vacillating over when to launch his
'Enterprise of England'. At the end of September 1587, he had urged
Parma to immediately (and single-handedly) invade enemy soil when
the English fleet concentrated at Plymouth leaving the Thames

estuary vulnerable to Spanish attack. The duke had given assurances that he would be ready to put to sea on 25 November, but then Philip, suddenly overtaken by his legendary caution, realised with chilling clarity that his troops, once ashore, could find themselves marooned without naval support and their supply lifelines threatened. He therefore ordered Santa Cruz to sail immediately to protect Parma's invasion barges, despite the lateness of the season, the uncertainty of the weather and the fact that only thirty-five of his warships were ready.

A powerful cyclonic storm on 16 November had badly damaged many of the Armada's vessels and one hundred and four were now rated unseaworthy. A number were beached for repairs, leaving the admiral with only thirteen 'great ships' – and the hull of one of these was so rotten he harboured grave doubts whether it could survive the outward voyage.[5] What's more, the food loaded on board or waiting on the quayside was putrid, and soldiers and sailors were dying like flies from typhus and other diseases. Santa Cruz pleaded that sailing should be delayed until the spring, predicting that if the fleet attacked England 'with all this disease ... there is great danger that after a month at sea, especially in this cold season, it will be either destroyed or seriously damaged'.

The well-informed Venetian ambassador to Madrid, Hieronimo Lippomano, reported in December that the Armada preparations were 'not going on as vigorously as previously, although they are still fitting out some vessels, and putting ammunition on board, squadron by squadron'. He confirmed that, through sickness and desertion, the number of troops and sailors 'will be far less than they thought, to such an extent that his majesty will be forced to raise new levies'.[6] The envoy had also heard of more bad news for Philip: the flagship of the 'new Spanish squadron, in clearing the River Tagus at Sacavém, [had been driven] on to the rocks'.[7]

For all his self-possession, the king could not conceal his chagrin at these continuing delays. He dispatched the Count of Fuentes to Lisbon to accelerate the pace of preparations, beginning with the embarkation of the siege artillery, partly in the mighty 1,100-ton *Trinidad Valencera*.[8] Lippomano reported in February: 'They have embarked twelve heavy siege guns and forty-eight smaller ones with a double supply of gun carriages and wheels for the field batteries and six hundred mules. In addition, there is a large quantity of iron and wood for the construction of a fort.'[9] Fuentes was outspoken in his criticism of the commissariat and artillery 'because they were not prompt in their preparations', but now he began provisioning the ships for eight months' service and every day new recruits marched into Portugal to replace the dead or those who had deserted.[10]

Philip's furious spate of energy and the anxiety of those uncertain weeks at the end of 1587 had sapped his health and he took to his bed suffering from another attack of gout in the hand, together with stomach pains and fever, and was reported 'very languid and weak'. Orders were, however, sent to Santa Cruz early in January, granting him permission to fight the English fleet off Margate – but only to ensure Parma's safe passage to England.

> If this can be done without fighting, either by stratagem or other-
> wise, it would be better so to manage it and keep our forces intact
> ... You must not land or act alone or on your own opinion without
> the concurrence of the duke, the engaging of the enemy on the sea
> ... being the only thing in which you are to act independently.

Following a successful invasion, Santa Cruz could return home with the Armada, 'calling in on Ireland on his way' and transporting Parma's Italian and German mercenaries 'who may appear necessary for the Irish business'.[11]

Parma was appalled that the secret plans for the invasion had become common knowledge: 'from Spain, Italy and all parts come, not only news of the expedition, but full details of it'. His arrival in Bruges 'and the stay of troops in the neighbourhood have given rise to much talk. The affair is so public that I can assure your majesty there is not a soldier [who] has not something to say about it ...' So much for the secrecy which he had insisted was a prerequisite for the success of his landing in Kent.

The duke still nurtured considerable resentment and rage at the strategic folly of his monarch's opportunism of November and December in urging him to invade across the Straits of Dover without the Armada's protection.

> Your majesty is perfectly aware that without the support of the fleet
> I could not cross over to England with these boats and you very

prudently ordered me in your letter of 4 September not to attempt to do so until the marqués arrived. If the marqués had come then, the crossing would have been easily effected with God's help ...

You know also that ... Santa Cruz has not come and the reason for his delay and yet, notwithstanding all this, you suppose that I may be there [?in England].

I must confess that has caused me great sorrow.

Your majesty has the right to give absolute orders ... but for you to write ... with a presumption diametrically opposite to the orders sent naturally causes me great pain.

Parma added sniffily: 'I humbly beg your majesty to do me the great favour of instructing me how I am to act. I shall make no difficulties in anything, even if I have only a pinnace to take me across.'[12]

Philip's choice of successor to Santa Cruz was curious. The new captain-general had never been to sea. He was the first to reinforce Cadiz during Drake's raid on the city the previous April, and had been appointed captain-general of Andalusia as 'conspicuous proof' of the king's favour.[13] The new admiral's skills lay purely in organisation; he was an experienced administrator who had been involved in equipping the Armada warships in Andalusia as well as raising army recruits in the region. His personal qualities were also exemplary: Lippomano described him as not only 'prudent and brave but of a nature of extreme goodness and benignity'. Medina Sidonia, he told the Doge of Venice, was 'generally beloved'.[14]

However, the Armada's new commander was reluctant to take up the post – the king put this down to his natural modesty – and pleaded poor health and poverty as excuses in a letter that may have been long and rambling but at least smacked of honesty and realism:

I humbly thank his majesty for having thought of me for such a great task and I wish I possessed the talents and strength necessary for it.

But sir, I have not health for the sea, for I know by the small experience that I have had afloat that I soon become sea-sick and have many humours [fevers] ...

Since I have no experience either of the sea or of war, I cannot feel that I ought to command so important an enterprise.

I know nothing of what the marqués of Santa Cruz has been

doing or of what intelligence he has of England, so I feel I should give but a bad account of myself, commanding thus blindly and being obliged to rely on the advice of others without knowing good from bad – or which of my advisers might want to deceive me or displace me.

On top of this, he was stony broke – this at a time when commanders were expected to help fund expeditions. 'I am in great need, so much so that when I have had to go to Madrid, I have been obliged to borrow money for the journey. My house [family] owes 900,000 ducats (£225,000) and I am therefore quite unable to accept the command. I have not a single *real*[15] I can spend on the expedition.'[16]

After considering the matter for two days, Medina Sidonia made clear his absolute conviction that the Armada was a grave mistake that had little hope of success. Only a miracle, he added in this frank and outspoken second missive, could save it.[17] The king's councillors, horror-struck at its contents, dared not show the letter to Philip: 'Do not depress us with fears for the fate of the Armada because in such a cause, God will make sure it succeeds,' they begged. As for his suitability for the command, 'nobody knows more about naval affairs than you,' they assured him. Then their tone became menacing: 'Remember that the reputation and esteem you currently enjoy for courage and wisdom would entirely be forfeited if what you wrote to us became generally known (although we shall keep it secret).'[18] Doggedly, the new commander sought an audience with the king, but his request was refused.

Happily ignorant of his new admiral's misgivings, Philip ordered him to Lisbon with instructions to ensure that the Armada sailed on 1 March 'at latest'. Rather more encouragingly, in a second letter he declared: 'I am quite confident that thanks to your great zeal and care, you will succeed very well.' Unconsciously echoing his advisers' pious hopes, the king added: 'It cannot be otherwise in a cause so entirely devoted to God as this. There is no reason for you to trouble about anything but the preparation of the expedition and I am quite sure you will be diligent in this respect.'[19]

Whether or not his doubts were assuaged, the new commander began his task by reviewing his fleet of one hundred and twenty large ships, with 1,730 sailors and 12,810 troops, excluding volunteers.

He recruited the experienced Don Diego de Maldonado and Captain Marolín de Juan. They, together with his squadron commanders, Pedro de Valdés, Juan Martínez de Recalde and Miguel de Oquendo, formed the beginnings of his operational council of war.[20]

At the end of February 1588, Philip imposed an embargo on all shipping in Spanish and Portuguese waters, seizing vessels to augment the strength of the Armada. The English military commander in the Low Countries, Peregrine Bertie, Thirteenth Baron Willoughby de Eresby,[21] heard that a 'great and infinite number of merchant ships [had been] pressed and embarked for this service [from] diverse other nations as well as Spanish, the French only excepted ... There was chase given to fourteen sail of English, Scottish, Flemish and French ships as they came out of the [Gibraltar] Straits ... whereof five were taken.'[22]

A powerful 960-ton galleon belonging to the Duke of Tuscany had earlier been sequestered and renamed the *San Francesco de Florencia*. Now the Spanish commandeered two Venetian ships, the *Ragazona*, 1,294 tons, and the *Lavia*, 728 tons, which were waiting to unload cargoes of sugar in Lisbon harbour.[23] Philip's commissioners reported that they were 'the finest, best armed and manned of all that lay in Lisbon ... and were so powerful that they could give battle to ten or twelve English [ships]'.[24] Around twelve galleons were also 'requisitioned' from Ragusa (present-day Dubrovnik) – probably a diplomatic euphemism to disguise Ragusan support for the Armada, thus avoiding retribution from their Turkish suzerains.[25] The Spanish continued the ruse by choosing new names for the ships that suggested they were of Italian origin.

Despite these reinforcements, the Spanish king was growing frantic about the slow progress in dispatching the Armada. New departure dates such as 18 April (Palm Sunday) came and went, and Philip began to shed his customary caution and circumspection. The spring weather did not help. As well as constant rain, another 'great storm' in early March tore at the ships moored in the harbour, causing 'the loss of many anchors and the destruction of many cables'.

All these problems were swept aside by a king who had gambled his personal prestige and that of his kingdom on the success of this sacred mission. There was never any question of scrapping the invasion plan. Philip was determined that it would sail 'as he was convinced there is no other remedy for the ills [done by England] except to strike at the head of the queen'.[26] The Armada had become a personal obsession, driven by the 'mortal hate' he felt for Elizabeth, 'from whom he receives daily injuries inflicted with base ingratitude, for he freed her from prison when he was in England', according to Lippomano.[27] For all his penny-pinching intransigence over funding the mission, Sixtus V freely acknowledged that 'His majesty has God's justice and pity on his side – God's justice for he is defending God's cause; God's pity, for it is to be held that God will extend His pity to the many poor Christians who are in the kingdom of England and will not leave them a prey to that woman.'[28]

After twenty months of preparations, Philip's financial position was again critical.[29] Despite the Pope's vocal support, it seemed unlikely that the Vatican would tide the king over with an advance on the agreed subsidy, part payable on Spanish troops landing in England. Olivares, Philip's long-suffering ambassador in Rome, was still sparring with an intractable Pope on the issue, even prostrating himself at the papal feet in desperate supplication. The envoy was pessimistic of any prospect of an immediate loan: Sixtus was 'so fond of money that he would rather lose the interest than let it go out of the castle [his treasury in Castel di Sant' Angelo in Rome]', he declared.[30] A few days later, Olivares reported the Pope's angry reaction to news that the invasion plan was really in earnest and that the Armada was moving towards departure. The prospect that Sixtus would have to pay his 1,000,000 gold ducats had caused him 'extreme and extraordinary perturbation':

> The things he says about it are very strange. He does not sleep at night. His manners to all are more than ordinarily abrupt.
>
> He talks to himself and generally conducts himself most shamefully.

In addition, the Pope was also complaining about 'the mint of money' he had been forced to shell out for the new English cardinal, Dr William Allen, 'whereas, all he has given is a thousand ducats for his outfit and a hundred a month for his maintenance'. The days in the Vatican dragged wearily on for Olivares, with a pervasive and ominous papal silence about any advance. 'We might as well cry for the moon as ask for it before. I am trembling for fear that [Sixtus] may give me many a bitter pill even before I can get it, seeing how he seems to love this money,'[31] he admitted despondently.

Philip was now spending 700,000 crowns (£187,500 or £40,000,000 at 2013 prices) each month on preparing for war – 'a thing truly almost incredible' to the Venetians. He tried again to raise money from the Italian banks belonging to the Spinola, Cantanei and Grimaldi families and also sent appeals for cash to his dominions in Italy and Flanders. Closer to home, he sought subsidies from the Spanish clergy to help him pay for 'this cause of God and state'. Gaspar de Quiroga y Vela, Cardinal Archbishop of Toledo, alone faced a demand for £250,000.[32]

For the preoccupied and worried king, there were tensions and unrest everywhere. In the Spanish Netherlands, Parma complained vociferously about the setback in the Armada's sailing date. 'This delay is causing the total ruin of the province of Flanders and is hardly less disastrous to the rest,' he told Philip that January.[33] In annexed Portugal, merchants were losing money through English privateer attacks on their shipping. Its citizens were restive under the burden of supplying grain to the Armada and were now 'at their wits' end'. A number of conspiracies against Spanish rule were also uncovered[34] and Philip, 'greatly disturbed', saw 'no possibility of winning the affection of that people by kindness'. He briefly considered policing his new dominion with six thousand additional Spanish and German soldiers and charging the cost of their maintenance to the Portuguese. Instead he ordered his nobility to mobilise troops to reinforce his garrisons in Portugal once the Armada had sailed.[35]

In London that February, Elizabeth had her own frustrations and fears. She had been enraged by a request for more financial assistance from the rebel Dutch States (or parliament), and fell into a typical Tudor tantrum:

> It is very strange they should ask for further aid without giving her any account of what had been done for them before.
>
> She swore by the living God it was terrible and she does not believe such ungrateful people ... live upon the earth. She has sent them thousands of men, whom they have not paid but let die of hunger and despair or else desert to the enemy. Was that not enough to

exasperate England? Were not the States ashamed that Englishmen say they had found greater civility from Spaniards than from them?

She cannot suffer such conduct and in future shall please herself. She can do without them!

They are not to think she is obliged to help them for her own safety: nothing of the sort.

It is true she does not want Spaniards for her near neighbours as they are her enemies at present, but why should she not live at peace and be friendly with the King of Spain, as she was originally.

He has always desired her friendship and has even sought her in marriage.

Therein lies the clue to the cause of Elizabeth's robust response. She had been caught out secretly seeking peace with Spain. Beneath her bluster and regal indignation was a tacit acknowledgement that she sought negotiations to avert the threat of invasion and to end her costly war in the Low Countries. The Dutch States may have issued an edict forbidding the discussion of peace but, after all, compared to princes, they were just ordinary people: 'Princes can discuss matters together as private persons cannot do.' But she did promise they would not suffer: 'Let princes act as they think fit ...' Whatever else she may do for them in future, she expected to be better treated in return.[36]

Elizabeth's efforts to find a peaceful solution arose from a letter from Parma the previous November. Walsingham believed it a trick to lower England's guard and told Leicester that the letter 'has bred in her such a dangerous security as all advertisements of perils and danger are neglected'. Plainly depressed by developments, he added:

The manner of our cold and careless proceeding, in this time of peril and danger, makes me take no comfort [from] my recovery of health.[37]

Unless it shall please God, in mercy, and miraculously, to save us, we cannot long stand.[38]

A well-placed Spanish spy in London heard that Elizabeth was 'determined to make peace at any cost, it being most important for her to be sure of Spain, now that France is in so disturbed state'. Walsingham and Leicester, whilst vehemently arguing against any peace negotiations, insisted, as a fallback, that any treaty terms should be honourable.

> At eleven o'clock at night, after the queen had heard a comedy, she flew into a passion with the Earl of Leicester and told him that it behoved her at any cost to be friendly with the king of Spain 'because I see that he has great preparations made on all sides. My ships have put to sea and if any evil fortune should befall them, all would be lost for I shall have lost the walls of my realm.'[39]

At the end of January, Parma informed Philip that intelligence he had received 'seems to prove that the Queen of England really desires to conclude peace and that her alarm and the expense that she is incurring are grieving her greatly ... It cannot be believed that she is turning good except under the stress of necessity ... If the negotiations are opened at once, we shall at least be able to see what they are up to.'[40]

Unbeknown to Elizabeth, the peace process had turned into a meaningless charade. Philip, unswervingly committed to invasion, instructed Parma not to agree a treaty on any terms. The five English commissioners to the negotiations crossed from Dover to Ostend that March and began the plenary discussions at Bourbourg, near Dunkirk, on 23 May. In the weary weeks ahead, they faced constant and deliberate delaying tactics by the Spanish.[41] But the queen's fervour for peace remained undiminished, her fears doubly increased by events in France.

On 12 May, the largely Catholic population in Paris rose in rebellion after the French king Henri III deployed his Swiss Guard to preserve order in the capital. Barricades were thrown up on street corners and by nightfall the king had fled, defiantly vowing his revenge on the city: 'When next I enter you, it shall be through a breach in your walls.' The Duke of Guise, with his Spanish-subsidised Catholic League – Philip had recently handed over 100,000 ducats (£25,000) – was left in control and afterwards the damaged monarch was forced unwillingly to appoint him lieutenant-general of the kingdom. The French ambassador in Madrid warned Henri that June: 'The corruption of these times and Spanish money will make a scar on the subjects of your majesty that will not easily be effaced and a wound in your kingdom that will not heal.'[42]

In March, Sixtus boldly voiced his sneaking admiration for the Queen of England. He had heard that Elizabeth had promised the Turks a bribe of 300,000 ducats (£75,000) to send their fleet out into the Mediterranean as a diversionary tactic against the Spanish. 'She is a great woman,' he announced, 'and were she only Catholic she would be without her match and we would esteem her highly. She omits nothing in the government of her kingdom and is now endeavouring, by way of Constantinople, to divert the King of Spain from his enterprise.'[43] Later that month, the Pope learned that the English were fully ready to repel any Spanish invasion. Embarrassingly, he then launched into another bout of panegyric praise of Elizabeth. 'She certainly is a great queen,' he told his increasingly disconcerted audience. 'Were she only a Catholic, she would be our dearly beloved.' His eulogy became ever more enthusiastic:

> Just look how well she governs. She is only a woman – only mistress of half an island – and yet she makes herself feared by Spain, by France, by the [Holy Roman] Empire,[44] by all. She enriches her kingdom by Spanish booty, besides depriving Spain of Holland and Zeeland.

The Pope, reported Giovanni Gritti, the Venetian ambassador to the Holy See, went on 'with pleasure to dwell on the praises and valour of the queen', much to the astonishment and confusion of his listeners.[45]

In July 1588, Sixtus acknowledged to several cardinals that he had done all that he could to persuade Elizabeth to return to the Catholic faith. He had offered a new 'investiture of her kingdom, in spite of the deprivation pronounced by Pope Pius V and to give her the bishops she might approve'. It all came to nothing: the queen characteristically replied that 'the Pope would do well to give her some of his money'.[46] Therefore Sixtus (perhaps regretfully) renewed her excommunication and transferred all her titles to Philip, who now became King of England and Ireland and protector of the Catholic faith in those countries, according to the Vatican, at least.[47]

This new declaration of anathema against the queen was not the sole weapon in the Church's campaign of words against Elizabeth. Cardinal Allen published a pamphlet in Antwerp that was extraordinarily vituperative. His *Admonition to the Nobility and People of*

England and Ireland Concerning the Present Wars repeated Sixtus's confirmation of excommunication 'concerning her illegitimation and usurpation and deprivation in respect of her heresy, sacrilege and abominable life'. No one in England could obey or defend Elizabeth but should be ready 'at the arrival of his Catholic majesty's forces ... to join the said army ... to help towards his restoring of the Catholic faith and deposing the usurper ... as by the General of this holy war shall be appointed'. The queen was 'an incestuous bastard, begotten and born in sin of an infamous courtesan'. Her kingdom was 'a place of refuge and sanctuary of all atheists, Anabaptists,[48] heretics and rebellious of all nations'.

Oozing malice, Allen went on to describe Elizabeth's crimes against God and mankind and denounced both her public and private life. English Catholics, he urged, must now show whether they will endure 'an infamous, depraved, accursed excommunicate heretic; the very shame of her sex and princely name; the chief spectacle of sin and abomination in this our age and the only poison, calamity and destruction of our noble church and country'. They should not fight the Spanish invaders:

> Fight not, for God's love. Fight not in that quarrel, in which, if you die, you are sure to be damned.
> Fight not against all your ancestors' souls and faith, nor against the salvation of all our dearest wives [and] children.
> This is the hour of God's wrath against her and all her partakers.
> Forsake her therefore ... that you be not enwrapped in all her sins, punishment and damnation.[49]

Vitriolic stuff! Olivares sent a copy to Parma, who planned to have it printed 'and spread all over England at the time of the invasion'.[50] As the peace negotiations dragged on, Dr Valentine Dale, one of the English commissioners – 'an old man, very stout and heavy' – formally complained about Allen's pamphlet to Parma. The duke 'excused it as well as I could by saying I did not understand the language, nor was I acquainted with the secret information which might justify [Allen's] statements'.[51] He was of course dissembling.

If Walsingham worked long and hard to build a network of spies to monitor the Armada's progress, the Spanish too had agents in London who produced remarkably accurate reports on Elizabeth's defences. A Portuguese spy, Antonio de Vega, was one of the most energetic and possessed good contacts at court, but in late April he heard of inquiries being made about him by Walsingham and begged permission to leave England before the spymaster's net closed on him.

Other agents fed intelligence through Bernardino Mendoza in Paris, who may have coloured his digests with some wishful thinking, or in the hope of providing the news that his master would be pleased to read. On 23 February he told Philip that every gun had been taken out of the Tower of London to arm the queen's ships 'and they even brought down the pieces which were mounted in the White Tower, as they call it. The queen's arsenals and all the country is very short of [gun]powder.' On 5 April, Mendoza reported a cannon exploding on board Drake's flagship, the *Revenge*, killing thirty-five men and wounding seven; the English, he said, looked upon this as 'an evil omen'.[52] Another spy's report at the end of March claimed that Plymouth was 'badly defended at present as the [crews] have been landed to save the victuals in the ships ... Colonel Norris exercises and drills his troops every day in London. They are not very handy yet but will really become so in time. There is therefore danger in delay.' The agent went on to report some of the government propaganda that was being distributed in England:

> The ministers of the false religion in their preaching frequently repeat that the King of Spain exercises great tyranny in all his dominions and swear that if he enters England by force of arms he will leave no English person alive between the ages of seven and seventy.[53]

The contents of these intelligence reports did not always cover the bustle and clamour of military activity. On 1 April (a significant date perhaps?), one Spanish agent could not resist reporting that 'a vast number of fleas collected' on the window of the queen's presence chamber and 'thirty great fish, commonly called porpoises, came up the river [Thames] to the Watergate of the queen's court'. This dispatch was read and annotated by Philip himself.[54]

Questioned about what he had seen in England, Francisco de Valverde, a released Spanish prisoner, reported new bulwarks being raised at Portsmouth 'made of sun-dried bricks and faggots [of wood] to serve for defence' and estimated that the fort there had a garrison of about two hundred men. But would the English Catholics rise up in support of an invasion?

> He replied that a large proportion of the country would join the Spaniards and King Philip.
>
> It was a common saying amongst the people that in this year 1588, by God's grace, England would be brought to obedience to the Roman Catholic Church and they were anxious to see the day.[55]

All potential invaders try to identify those citizens who would collaborate in their efforts to conquer the target country. They also build a list of enemy leaders who should be arrested on sight. Philip had two such lists delivered to him by Jacob Stuart, formerly employed by Mary Queen of Scots. The names of 'the heretics and schismatics' who faced a sticky end if Spain was victorious unsurprisingly included Leicester, his brother the Earl of Warwick and brother-in-law the Earl of Huntingdon; Burghley, 'Secretary Walsingham', the Earl of Bedford, Sir Christopher Hatton, and the queen's cousin, Lord Hunsdon. These, Philip read, were 'the principal devils that rule the court and are the leaders of the [Privy] Council'. Other names on this list included William Headon 'the principal man in Norfolk, a great enemy of his majesty'; Sir Thomas and Sir William Fairfax in Yorkshire 'and all the rest of the Council of York'.

Clearly Philip's informant was status conscious. The list of 'Catholics and friends of his majesty in England' was headed by 'the Earl of Surrey, son and heir of the Duke of Norfolk, now a prisoner in the Tower' and 'Lord Vaux of Harrowden, a good Catholic, a prisoner in the Fleet'.[56] One of the four names under the county of Norfolk was Sir Henry Bedingfield, 'formerly the guardian of Queen Elizabeth[57] the pretended queen of England, during the whole time that his majesty was in England'. The author added: 'I wish to God they had burnt her then, as she deserved, with the rest of the heretics who were justly executed. If this had been done we should be living now in peace and quietness.' The document reported that 'the greater part of Lancashire is Catholic, the common people particularly, with the exception of the Earl of Derby[58] and the town of Liverpool'. The counties of Westmorland and Northumberland remained 'really faithful to his majesty'.[59]

An assessment of Catholic loyalties in August 1586 estimated that five members of gentry could raise two thousand men in Lincolnshire, which was 'well affected to the Catholic religion'. Twelve gentlemen could raise three thousand soldiers in Norfolk, while Hampshire was 'full of Catholics. There are four gentlemen strongly Catholic and very powerful. The ports are good and victuals very abundant.' In Sussex 'there are six Catholics of good repute but I have been unable to discover their strength for fear of discovery'.[60]

At last, the 'most fortunate' Armada was ready for action.

It now comprised one hundred and twenty-nine vessels, displacing a grand total of more than 61,000 tons, of which thirty-five were major warships. Sixty-eight were armed merchantmen or cargo ships. Two had been converted into hospital ships with eighty-five staff embarked between them, including five physicians and the same number of doctors. There were also four Portuguese oar-propelled galleys. The fleet, divided into ten squadrons, was armed with 2,485 guns, of which 1,497 were cast in bronze, and it carried 123,790 cannonballs and 5,175 quintals[61] of gunpowder. Provisions, estimated to last six months, comprised 110,000 quintals of biscuit; 6,000 quintals of bacon; 3,433 of cheese, 8,000 quintals of various species of fish; 3,000 quintals of rice and 6,320 fanegas[62] of beans and chickpeas. For cooking, there were 11,398 arrobas[63] of oil and 23,870 of vinegar. The ships carried more wine than water for drinking: 14,170 pipes[64] of wine compared with 11,870 of water.

Warlike stores included 7,000 harquebuses, 1,000 muskets, 6,170 hand grenades, 11,128 pikes; 8,000 leather water bottles; 5,000 pairs of shoes and 11,000 pairs of sandals. The siege artillery train had twenty gun carriages; 3,500 cannonballs; wagons, limbers and harness for the forty mules that were to drag the guns.

There were 26,170 soldiers and sailors on board the ships, made up of 16,232 Spanish soldiers; 2,000 Portuguese and 124 volunteers, or 'gentlemen adventurers', motivated by religious fervour – or the alluring scent of plunder and riches – plus their 465 servants. The troops were organised into seven regiments, or tercios, of about twenty-five companies, each comprising one hundred men. Only about 10,000 were experienced soldiers – the remainder were recruited untrained from the countryside and were 'vine-growers, shepherds and farm labourers'.[65] The ships were manned by 7,700 sailors and the ordnance served by only 167 gunners. Medina Sidonia's personal staff and administrators totalled 158. For the spiritual comfort of the Armada, 180 preaching friars were embarked, plus Thomas Vitres, an Irish priest.[66]

There were also English, Irish and Dutch amongst the Armada crews. At least four of the 'gentlemen adventurers' appear to be English, and among the salaried officers there were eighteen who had English or Irish names such as Sir Maurice Geraldine, Edmond and William Stacey, Sir Charles O'Connor, Tristram Winslade, Richard Burley, Sir Peter Marley, Patrick Kinford, Robert and Edward Riford, Richard Seton, Sir Robert Daniell, Frederick Patrick and Henry Mitchell.[67]

Life on board lacked privacy and must have been noisy, apart from the frequent periods of prayer. There were no fixed sleeping quarters, except for the very high-ranking, and hammocks were rare. The upper deck, with its batteries of guns, was the favoured place to sleep and some nailed truckle beds to the deck and erected low partitions to stake their claim to places out of the prevailing wind. Before going into action, these would have to be thrown overboard. No wonder those on board the Armada ships prayed for good weather.[68]

Medina Sidonia, always a man for detail, laid down strict instructions governing the rations supplied to the Armada. Each man would receive one and a half pounds (680 grams) of bread per day (or two pounds on days when biscuit was served instead) and could drink the equivalent of a bottle of wine – sherry or Lisbon wine – except when the more alcoholic Candia wine from the island of Crete was dished out, when only a pint was supplied per man, diluted with water. The water ration itself was three pints a day for all purposes. On Sundays and Thursdays, six ounces (170.1 grams) of bacon and three ounces (85.1 grams) of rice were available and six ounces of Sardinian cheese and three ounces of beans or chickpeas on Mondays and Wednesdays. On 'fish days' – Wednesdays, Fridays and Saturdays – six ounces of tuna or cod per man were on the menu, or when these ran out, six ounces of squid or five sardines from Galicia and Andalusia with three ounces of Sicilian beans or chickpeas.

This was rather a meagre diet compared to that served up on the queen's ships. English sailors were allowed one pound (450 grams) of biscuit on fish days, together with a quarter of a 'stock-fish' or the eighth part of a ling, together with four ounces of cheese, two ounces of butter and a gallon (4.55 litres) of 'small', or low alcohol beer. This liquor, however, frequently soured. On 'flesh days' they had the same rations of beer and biscuit plus one pound of salt beef. Monday was 'bacon day' with a pound of bacon per man and a pint container of peas.[69]

In Flanders, Parma's army totalled 17,000 infantry and 1,000 cavalry, after being depleted by disease and desertion, but his cooks were still baking 50,000 loaves a day. He hurriedly levied more recruits so (in addition to the horsemen) his final expeditionary force amounted to 26,000 infantry, of whom 4,000 were Spanish, 1,000 Irish and Scottish,[70] 8,000 Walloons, 1,000 Burgundians, 3,000 Italians and 9,000 Germans.[71] Among them was an Englishman named Barnes.

Building the barges proved so problematic that the Spanish believed they were victims of deliberate sabotage. Green unseasoned timber was used, making the hulls unserviceable. In the end, most of the three hundred flat-bottomed vessels had to be commandeered or hired from owners of canal fleets, together with 'a great number of little galleys and skiffs' and thirty or forty hoys.[72]

On 5 April, Parma sent a somewhat barbed valedictory message about the start of naval operations to the king: 'Since God has been pleased to defer for so long the sailing of the Armada ... we are bound to conclude that it is for His greater glory and the more perfect success of the business, since the object is so exclusively for the promotion of His holy cause.' Then the duke returned to his fears that his plans were compromised: 'The enemy have been ... forewarned and acquainted with our plans and have made preparations for their defence. It is manifest that the enterprise, which at one time was so easy and safe, can only now be carried out with infinitely greater difficulty and at a much larger expenditure of blood and trouble.' Parma refused to be a hostage to fortune, as his next comment indicated:

> I am sure that your majesty will have adopted all necessary measures for the carrying out of the task of protecting my passage across, so that not the smallest hitch shall occur in a matter of such importance. Failing this, and the due cooperation of the duke with me, both before and during the actual landing ... I can hardly succeed as I desire in your majesty's service.[73]

On St Mark's Day (25 April) Medina Sidonia went piously to Lisbon Cathedral to receive the blessed standard of the Armada, which was laid up on the high altar. The banner was decorated with the arms of Spain, flanked by Christ crucified and the Blessed Virgin Mary and a scroll proclaiming: *Exurge, domine et vindica causam tuam* – 'Arise O Lord and give judgment on thy cause'. It was carried solemnly between lines of kneeling soldiers and sailors down to the harbour where the admiral boarded his flagship. Her mainsail bore another image of the Virgin Mary.

Pope Sixtus declared a special indulgence to all who sailed with the Armada and to those who prayed for its victory. In Spain, there were constant prayers for the success of the invasion of England, with processions on holy days and Sundays 'so that more people might attend'. In the Escorial Palace, the royal family shared their nation's supplications, organised in three-hour relays.[74] 'The king himself is on his knees two or three hours every day before the Sacrament,' reported Lippomano. 'Those in waiting on his majesty declare that he rises in the night to pray to God to grant him a happy issue out of this struggle.' The Venetian envoy was philosophical, if not stoic: 'Everyone hopes that the greater the difficulties, humanly speaking, the greater will be the favour of God.'[75]

Not everyone was so optimistic. The experienced admiral Martin de Bertendona, commander of the Levant squadron, warned a papal emissary in May that the English had 'faster and handier ships than ours and many more long-range guns'. They would avoid, at all costs, battling it out hull-to-hull with the Armada, but 'stand aloof and knock us to pieces with their culverins, without our being able to do them any serious hurt'. He added with more than a touch of sarcasm: 'We are sailing against England in the confident hope of a miracle.'[76]

In fighting such a holy war, the Armada was going to be a godly fleet. Medina Sidonia, in his sailing orders, emphasised that as the principal purpose of the mission was to 'serve God and to return to his church a great many of contrite souls that are oppressed by the heretics, enemies of our holy Catholic church', every soldier and sailor should be shriven and receive the Holy Sacrament before they departed. Furthermore, none should 'blaspheme or rage against God or Our Lady or any of the saints upon pain that he shall therefore sharply be corrected and very well chastened'. Each morning 'at the break of day' each ship's company 'shall give the good morrow to the mainmast'.[77] At nightfall, the ship's boys would sing the *Ave Maria*; some days the *Salve Regina* was added to the religious repertoire, along with the litany of Our Lady on Saturdays. Even the nominated passwords for each day of the week had sacred derivations. 'Jesus' was the chosen word for Sunday; 'Holy Ghost' on Monday; 'Holy Trinity' for Tuesday; 'Saint James' for Wednesday; 'The Angels' for Thursday; 'All Saints' for Friday; and 'Our Lady' for Saturday.

'Common women' – including prostitutes – were forbidden to sail with the Armada and the crews were warned that uttering oaths of 'less quality' would incur withdrawal of their wine allowance. What's more, gambling would be forbidden. Any 'quarrels, angers, defiances, and injuries that are and have been before this day, of all persons' were to be 'suppressed and suspended'; those who transgressed 'directly or indirectly, upon pain of disobedience' would be deemed guilty of treason 'and die therefore'. Soldiers and sailors should live together in the ships in 'confirmed friendship'. To ensure 'amity', Medina Sidonia prohibited the carrying of daggers as personal weapons.

Then the admiral turned to operational matters. His flagship *San Martin* would signal departure by firing a cannon, at which point the fleet 'shall follow without losing time', sounding their trumpets. Upon leaving Corunna, the Armada would set course for south of the Scilly Islands, off Cornwall; any stragglers should rejoin the fleet after rendezvousing in Mount's Bay, between Land's End and the Lizard peninsula. If Medina Sidonia wanted to summon his captains for a conference, he would fly a flag at the flagship's mizzen mast near its great lantern and fire a signal gun.

Each ship was to take particular care to douse its charcoal cooking fires 'before the sun goes down'. In the event that a vessel caught ablaze, its immediate neighbour would send its boats and skiffs to help in fire-fighting or to rescue the crew. The army colonels and captains were charged with ensuring that their soldiers 'always have their armour clean, ready and in order for time of necessity' and the equipment was to be cleaned twice a week.

The ships' gunners were to ensure that they had barrels of water mixed with vinegar standing by to extinguish any incendiary devices fired at their vessels. Every warship was to carry two boat-loads of stones for use as missiles to hurl from the mast tops at the enemy whilst boarding. No ship was to sail ahead of the flagship or astern of the vice-admiral at the rear, and every vessel should take care to trim its sails as it was important 'that all our navy do go as close as possible as they may and in this the captains, masters and pilots must have such great care'.

No one could plead ignorance of the admiral's instructions: his orders were to be read out loud by the pursers before departure and then, during the voyage to the English Channel, three times a week.[78]

In England, a remarkably accurate intelligence report of 7 May, quoting a captain 'of an Italian ship serving in the Spanish fleet', estimated its order of battle at between 125–130 ships, including 73 'great ships' which were ready to sail. Embarked on this Italian vessel was Don Alonso de Leyva, commander-in-chief of the cavalry of Milan, together with seven hundred infantry and five siege guns.[79]

It was to be expected that the king would issue some last-minute instructions to Medina Sidonia, emphasising the importance of maintaining close contact with Parma so that Spanish naval and land operations could be synchronised. Philip pointed out that the English fleet's aim would be to 'fight at long range, in consequence of his advantage in artillery', but the Armada should try to bring the enemy ships 'to close quarters and grapple with [them]'. Another document described how the queen's ships use their guns 'in order to deliver [their] fire low and sink [their] opponent's ships and you will take such precautions as you consider necessary in this respect'. After Parma had established a bridgehead in England, the Armada should station itself in the Thames estuary, with some squadrons guarding the passage between Kent and Flanders.

In this, the king failed to appreciate the importance of his navy having a safe harbour on or near the invasion beach, or the difficulties of capturing a convenient port. His only nod in this direction was contained in a separate set of secret instructions. These ordered Medina Sidonia to seize the Isle of Wight if Parma's invasion failed:

[The island] is apparently not so strong as to be able to resist and may be defended if we gain it. This would provide ... you with a safe port for shelter and will enable you to carry out such operations as may be rendered possible ... If you adopt this course, you will take notice that you should enter from the east side, which is wider than the west.

Finally the admiral received a sealed document which he was charged with delivering to Parma after the landing in England. This repeated the three objectives in any peace negotiations following the invasion in their order of importance: freedom to worship in the Catholic faith; return of the towns and cities captured by the English in the Low Countries; and financial compensation 'for the injury they have done to me, my dominions and my subjects. This would amount to an exceedingly large sum.'[80] Philip also appointed the cavalry commander, Don Alonso de Leyva, 'as a man of courage, quality and experience' as Armada captain-general in the event of Medina Sidonia being killed in action.[81]

On 21 May, Medina Sidonia wrote to Philip informing him that bad weather still detained the Armada at its moorings in Lisbon. Nine days later, when three leagues (nine nautical miles or 16.65 km) off the Portuguese coast, he reported the Armada was on its way to achieve the 'Enterprise of England'.

The king, always anxious to tie up any loose threads, wrote to Mendoza in Paris. He was worried that bad weather might force some of his vulnerable galleys and galleasses into French ports where they should 'enjoy the privileges accorded by the treaties of alliance between the Christian King [Henri III] and myself'. There was no mention, naturally, of Philip's financial and diplomatic assistance to the Duke of Guise and the Catholic League in France. Indeed, the ambassador was instructed to lie to the French king about the Armada's mission by explaining that 'the boldness of the English corsairs has forced me to endeavour to clear the seas of them this summer and I have consequently fitted out a fleet for that purpose and care will be taken that no damage or injury shall be done to his subjects'. The Spanish king wanted his French counterpart to understand this so that his ships should be 'treated in a manner cor-responding with the peace and kindness that exist between us. You should thus banish any suspicion on his own behalf and ingratiate him with the object in view.'[82]

Mendoza called a meeting of the English exiles in Paris and

promised the Earl of Westmorland that his attainted estates would be fully restored to him. They all toasted the prospects of returning home to a Catholic England at a celebration at Lord Charles Paget's house. Paget and his brother, who had purchased new uniforms from their tailor, then set off to join Parma's army for the invasion. They boasted that Philip would hear Mass in St Paul's Cathedral before October, but Stafford, the English ambassador, on hearing of this sneered that 'if Philip came there himself, he shall be hanged at Tyburn before that time'. Amid all this excitement, Westmorland began to feel some qualms about a Spanish invasion, telling Stafford 'his stomach is against a stranger setting foot in his country'.[83]

A rallying call to arms, written by the Jesuit Pedro de Ribadeneira in Lisbon, was issued to the Armada's officers and gentlemen adventurers to boost their morale. Ribadeneira urged them to sail forth 'to our glorious, honourable, necessary, profitable and not difficult undertaking'. God 'in Whose sacred cause we go, will lead us. With such a Captain we need not fear. The saints of heaven will go in our company and particularly the holy patrons of Spain and those of England itself who are persecuted by the heretics and cry aloud to God for vengeance.' English martyrs such as John Fisher, Cardinal-Bishop of Rochester and Sir Thomas More and 'innumerable holy Carthusians, Franciscans and other holy men, whose blood was cruelly shed by King Henry [VIII]' call out to God 'to avenge them from the land in which they died'. Those seminary priests 'whom Elizabeth has torn to pieces with atrocious cruelty and exquisite torments' would also help the new crusaders.

> With us too, will be the blessed and innocent Mary, Queen of Scotland, who, still fresh from her sacrifice, bears copious and abounding witness to the cruelty and impiety of this Elizabeth and directs her shafts against her.
>
> There also will await us the groans of countless imprisoned Catholics, the tears of widows who lost their husbands for the faith, the sobs of maidens who were forced to sacrifice their lives rather than destroy their souls, the tender children who suckled upon the poison of heresy, are doomed for perdition unless deliverance reaches them ... and finally, myriads of workers, citizens, knights, nobles and clergymen and all ranks of Catholics, who are oppressed

and downtrodden by the heretics and who are anxiously looking to us for their liberation ...

Courage! Steadfastness! Spanish bravery! With these, the victory is ours and we have nought to fear.[84]

Antonio Aquereis, one of the army captains, feared it would be no contest because the English would not fight 'as the force of the King is so great'. His cocksure confidence was reflected amongst his colleagues as the 'best gentlemen in Spain' cast lots over 'who shall have England'.[85]

FIRST SIGHTING

When land was first sighted from this galleon, I had hoisted to the maintop a standard with a crucifix and the Virgin and [Mary] Magdalene on either side of it. I also ordered three guns to be fired and that we should all offer up prayer in thanks for God's mercy in bringing us thus far.

Medina Sidonia to Philip II of Spain, *San Martin*,
off the Lizard peninsula, 30 July 1588.[1]

The Armada made heavy weather sailing north along the coasts of Portugal and Spain in the teeth of adverse winds. The speed of any convoy is determined by that of its slowest ship and Medina Sidonia's elderly transport hulks and the Mediterranean grain ships of Admiral Bertendona's Levant squadron made ponderous headway through the rolling Atlantic swell. Their slow progress exacerbated the fact that the Armada's soldiers and sailors were consuming food at an alarming rate. As some provisions had rotted and had to be thrown overboard, the Armada commander reduced meat rations and cut the issue of biscuit to one pound (454 grams) per man, per day.[2]

Eleven days into the mission, the hulk *David Chico*, loaded with biscuit, beans and peas, was dismasted and limped into Vivero in Galicia for repair[3] as the winds veered to the north-west. With these more favourable conditions, Medina Sidonia dispatched Captain Francisco Moresin in a *zabra*, or pinnace, to deliver his report to the Duke of Parma in Flanders. Given that the Armada had been managing only four knots or four nautical miles (7.4 km) per hour, he was more than a little optimistic in urging Parma to bring his invasion force out to sea to meet his ships as soon as Moresin arrived.

The captain-general also announced his intention, after rendez-vousing with Parma, to seek out an English port capable of sheltering 'so great a fleet as this'. He had consulted his 'pilots and practical seamen' who had unanimously selected the east coast harbours of Ipswich and Harwich (as well as Dover), as suitable havens. The prospect of having to besiege and capture them did not seem to figure in his thinking. Rejoicing that his men remained 'in good health and spirits, ready for the fight if the enemy face us', Medina Sidonia told Parma: 'I am equally anxious to have the joy of saluting your excellency soon because our junction must precede the execution of his majesty's plans.'⁴ This confidence proved premature.

On 13 June, off Cape Finisterre on the tip of north-west Spain, the beds and partitions on the upper decks were swept away as the Spanish fleet rehearsed their battle drills at sea for the first time. Henceforth, most would be sleeping under the stars with no protection from the elements – so the prayers for fair weather assumed even more fervency.

With headwinds continuing to impede progress, Medina Sidonia began to fret about his supplies of food and potable water, which had become dangerously low. Dysentery, contracted from the green, fetid water held in the unseasoned casks, was also approaching endemic proportions. The full impact of Drake's destruction of seasoned barrel staves the previous year was becoming evident. Four light galleys sent out from Corunna with fresh provisions for the Armada encountered two English reconnaissance ships heading south. After a brief struggle off Bayonne, the English vessels were captured and several Spaniards, acting as pilots, were discovered hiding on board. They were summarily executed and the English prisoners enslaved to man the galleys' oars.⁵ However, the galleys with their supplies failed to make contact with the Armada.

The captain-general considered putting into Corunna or Ferrol, but feared this would trigger mass desertion by the Armada's soldiers and sailors, adding glumly, 'as usual'. Eventually the growing provisions crisis forced him to steer for Corunna and by late evening on 19 June his flagship *San Martin* and thirty-five other warships were moored safely in its harbour. The remainder of the Armada, mainly the slower, more cumbersome vessels, anchored off the headland north of the port, below its second-century Roman lighthouse, La

Torre de Hercules, planning to enter Corunna after dawn the next morning.

That night south-westerly gales battered the fleet, scattering the squadrons outside the harbour. Mountainous waves tossed the ships around like corks: *La Concepción de Zubelzu,* of the Biscayan squadron, lost her mainmast and the rudder of one of the four Portuguese galleys was swept away. Some vessels sought shelter in ports in Biscay, Asturias and Galicia, such as de Leyva's badly damaged *Rata Santa María Encoronada* and *Santa Ana,* the flagship of the Guipúzcoan squadron, the latter minus its mainmast, yardarms and sails. A handful were driven northwards as far as the Scilly Isles. Medina Sidonia told the king on 21 June: 'The people of the country say that so violent a sea and wind, accompanied by fog and tempest, have never been seen. It is very fortunate that not all the Armada was caught outside, particularly the galleys which would certainly have been wrecked and the whole Armada endangered.'[6]

As the storm continued to rage over the next few days, the captain-general dispatched *zabras* to hunt for the lost ships and ensure they mustered at Corunna. At least fourteen galleons and galleasses had been seriously damaged and thirty-five ships were missing, together with his entire siege artillery train and 6,567 soldiers and 1,882 sailors. Ensign Esquivel, whose *zabra* arrived off St Michael's Bay and 'Cape Longnose' (the Lizard peninsula) in Cornwall four days after leaving Corunna, described the vessel's terrifying battle against the elements, 'with heavy squalls of rain and such a violent gale that during the night we had winds from every quarter of the compass'. The *zabra* shipped water at every wave and at four o'clock in the afternoon 'after we have already received several heavy seas, a wave passed clean over us and nearly swamped' the boat.

> We were flush with the water and almost lost but by a great effort of all hands, the water was bailed out and everything thrown overboard.
> We had previously thrown over a pipe of wine and two butts of water.

The next day they sighted six sails, three to the north and the remainder to the south-east: 'We ran between them ... and two ... gave us chase.' After some hours, the ships – probably English scouts – gave up their pursuit and later the Spanish came across an Armada straggler, 'lying to and repairing with only her lower sails set'.[7]

The *San Salvador*, vice-flagship of the squadron of hulks, together with twelve sister ships, had been blown near the Scillies and encountered six enemy ships sent 'to reconnoitre us' while 'signal lights were shown on land'. Three enemy vessels closed on the *San Pedro Menor* at the rear of the Spanish line and fired on her before heading back to the shore. Three days later, at dawn, the squadron sighted two ships near Lands End and the hulk *El Gato* attacked one of them, capturing it before it sank. *Paloma Blanca* opened fire on the other ship, damaging her main yardarm. 'The admiral [Don Juan Gómez de Medina] went on board the prize to make her fit for sailing but the sea was terribly rough and the admiral was only saved by a miracle, for he broke two of his ribs whilst leaving the prize.' It later sank in 'immensely high' seas.[8]

The weather was acknowledged to be astonishingly bad for June. Despondent, his faith in miracles thoroughly shaken, Medina Sidonia's original grave doubts about the wisdom of the expedition were reawakened. On 24 June he told Philip that he had reluctantly taken on the mission as:

> I recognised that we were attacking a kingdom so powerful and so warmly aided by its neighbours that we should need a much larger force than your majesty had collected at Lisbon. This was my reason for at first declining the command, seeing that the enterprise was being represented to our majesty as easier than it was known to be by those whose only aim was your majesty's service ...
>
> We have now arrived at this port scattered and maltreated in such a way that we are much inferior in strength to the enemy ... Many of our largest ships are still missing as well as two of the galleasses, whilst on the ships here there are many sick, whose number will increase in consequence of the bad provisions.

Because so much food had become putrid, there was only enough left for two months; 'by this your majesty may judge whether we can proceed on the voyage upon the success of which so much depends'. To make matters worse, many of those engaged in this 'Enterprise of England' were inexperienced:

I am bound to confess that I see very few, or hardly any, of those on the Armada with any knowledge or ability to perform the duties entrusted to them.

I have tested and watched this point very carefully and your majesty may believe me when I assure you that we are very weak.

Do not, your majesty, allow yourself to be deceived by anyone who may wish to persuade you otherwise ...

A moment of truth had arrived. The captain-general asked bluntly: 'Well, Sire, how do you think we can attack so great a country as England with such a force as ours is now?' While the Armada (or what was left of it), was being repaired in Corunna, would this not be the ideal opportunity to agree 'some honourable terms with the enemy'?[9]

Not surprisingly, this gloomy letter alarmed and depressed Philip, who spent all 'day and night in prayer, though suffering from the gout in his hand', according to the Venetian envoy, Lippomano. He had celebrated his sixty-second birthday on 21 May, and his anxieties over the Armada were taking a toll. Although reportedly in 'sound health', the king was known to be 'worn and tired' by the huge volume of paperwork crossing his desk. Outside the Escorial Palace, Spain was still staging innumerable religious processions and 'austerities, fasting and devotion' for the success of the Armada.

More disquieting news arrived from Flanders. On 22 June, Parma wrote to the king, worried that the captain-general had

persuaded himself that I may be able to go out and meet him with these boats. These things cannot be and in the interests of your majesty's service, I should be anxious if I thought [Medina Sidonia] were depending upon them ... He will plainly see that with these little flat boats, built for rivers not for the sea, I cannot diverge from the short direct passage which has been agreed upon ... If we came across any armed English or [Dutch] rebel ships, they could destroy us with the greatest ease.

An apprehensive Philip noted in the margin alongside this passage: 'God grant that no embarrassment may come from this.'[10]

Parma was also still short of cash with which to buy provisions and pay his troops. Don Juan de Idiáquez, one of Philip's secretaries, noted in a memorandum that invasion preparations in Flanders were proceeding well: 'Everything seems to be satisfactory except the question of money. I hope to God that the duke's tact and the prompt arrival of the Armada will have averted the threatened disorders on account of the lack of money,' he added.[11]

Parma had arranged for copies of a proclamation to be printed in Antwerp, ready for distribution once the Spanish landed in England. The broadsheet, signed by Cardinal Allen and almost certainly written by him, made clear that the Armada was merely executing Pope Sixtus's bull excommunicating Elizabeth, rather than being an act of naked aggression against England. It released her subjects from any obedience to her and called upon them to 'unite themselves to the Catholic army'. English Catholics were to be protected from pillage and looting by marauding Spanish soldiers and large rewards were offered for the capture of 'the said usurper or any of her accomplices'. Generous plenary indulgences would also be available to those penitents who helped capture and punish Elizabeth and her ungodly ministers. English heretics would face what today we would recognise as 'religious re-education'; they would not be punished 'until by conference with learned men and better consideration they may be informed of the truth'.[12] The dark shadow of the Spanish Inquisition had fallen over England.

In Rome, Philip's ambassador Olivares was filled with apprehension about the ominous silence from Madrid about the fleet's progress. 'As it is now thirty-nine days since the Armada sailed, I am extremely anxious that I have no news of it. If I recollect aright it was about this date that your majesty landed at Southampton,' he wrote to the king.[13] Sixtus V meanwhile remained 'firm in his determination not to disburse one crown until the news [of the landing] arrives and he is unyielding to the pressure I put upon him for money when he received the news that the Armada had sailed'. The parsimonious Pope was busy collecting money 'from all quarters so as not to be obliged to trench upon the sum in the Castel di Sant' Angelo. He is furiously angry with your majesty and with me.'[14]

Meanwhile in Corunna, despite five more vessels struggling back over three days, Medina Sidonia's doubts were as pressing as ever. Without waiting for his royal master's reply, he called a council of war of his commanders on 27 June on board the *San Martin*. He sought their views on whether the Armada should continue their advance up the English Channel without the twenty-eight ships still missing from its order of battle. Only the firebrand Admiral Don Pedro de Valdés, who commanded the Andalusian ships, voted for going on immediately. However, he had examined his own squadron's stores and found 'biscuit sufficient for three months' partly in bad condition, while 'the bacon, cheese, fish, sardines and vegetables were all rotten'. The Armada's inspector general, Don Jorge Manrique, confirmed that, with the exception of the bread and wine, 'everything was spoilt and rotten as it had been on board for so long'. Accordingly the commanders agreed that the provisions were 'insufficient for so large a force' and that this should be reported immediately to Philip.[15]

Unsurprisingly, Medina Sidonia received a barrage of letters from the Escorial Palace and officials in Madrid. The king, writing on 1 July, began in a forthright, if not acerbic, manner:

> From what I know of you, I believe that your bringing all these matters to my attention arises solely from your zeal to serve me and a desire to succeed in your command.
>
> The certainty that this is so prompts me to be franker with you than I should be with another.

God was still firmly on the side of Spain: 'If this was an unjust war, one could indeed take this storm as a sign from Our Lord to cease offending him. But being as just as it is, one cannot believe that He will disband it but will rather grant it more favour than we could hope.' He reminded Medina Sidonia that, were the Armada to remain in Corunna, there was a danger the English – although possessing inferior naval forces to those of Spain – could impose a blockade and trap it inside the harbour, while simultaneously attacking and looting Spain's treasure convoys or her coastal cities, in a repeat of Drake's shaming and damaging raid on Cadiz.

> We all know that every great enterprise is beset with difficulties and that the merit lies in overcoming them.
>
> Nor is the enemy's power so great that it could serve as a pretext for us to cease in our pursuit of him ...
>
> Of the enemy's ships, some are old, others small and inferior to

ours in strength and general excellence; if even the numerical superiority of our crews were overlooked and the advantage of long experience enjoyed by many of them.

When the tiros in the Armada are mingled with the practised hands, all may be considered as experienced.

The enemy's crews, on the other hand, consist of novices, drawn from the common people – a tumultuous crowd, lacking military discipline.

These were brave words, bordering on the foolhardy. Was Philip guilty of the grave error of underestimating his enemy? Was his judgement skewed by his own propaganda? Or was he merely trying to bolster the morale of a dispirited commander? More likely, his unyielding faith in God's favour for his personal and holy enterprise overrode any of Medina Sidonia's objections.

There was no place for misgivings in Philip's heart or mind. Neither would he accept any further argument: 'I have dedicated this enterprise to God ... Pull yourself together then and do your part!' he told Medina Sidonia imperiously. Equally peremptory statements were expressed by the royal advisers Don Cristobal de Moura ('Put on some weight and get some sleep') and Idiáquez, who repeated his monarch's heartfelt plea: 'Pull yourself together!'[16]

A second letter from Philip, dated four days later, was less mordant:

My intention is ... that when the forces are collected the voyage may be resumed. I hope that Our Lord will change these difficulties at the commencement [of the] triumph of His cause. Success largely depends upon fine weather and the season is now so advanced that not an hour should be lost. You must therefore exert every effort to make ready with all promptitude.

He brushed aside every one of the Armada's logistical problems. Food supplies were 'very considerable, besides what you may take on board at Corunna and the supplies that will be sent after you and provided for you in Flanders'. The king stressed: 'You must take great care that the stores are really preserved and not allow yourself to be deceived as you were before.' Medina Sidonia should be careful to 'keep all the officers well up to their duties' when loading adequate water supplies. As to the captain-general's complaints about the slow speed of the Levant ships: 'the expedition must not be abandoned on account of this difficulty which is not such a very great one after all'.[17]

Strangely, rather than increasing his forebodings of a mission impossible, these critical and pointed letters encouraged Medina Sidonia and stiffened his resolve. Perhaps he finally understood that he could not escape from his responsibilities. Thanking the king for his 'consolation', he pointed out, almost lyrically, that 'those that go down to the sea in ships are exposed to these vicissitudes and I am consoled in the idea that He who has this expedition in His hand designs to take this course with it in order to infuse even more zeal in your majesty and more care in your officers'. As if to prove this divine support, God 'has been pleased to send into this port today all the missing ships except two of the Levanters, the *San Juan de Sicilia* and the *Santa María el Visón* and two hulks, one of which is now in sight to leeward, the other being the *Casa de Paz Grande* which separated from the rest off Biscay as she was making a great deal of water'.

He promised Philip: 'The refitting of all these ships shall be taken in hand at once. It shall have my personal attention for I am more anxious than anyone to expedite matters and get away from here. Your majesty may rest assured that no efforts of mine shall be spared and when the ships are refitted I shall not fail to take advantage of the first fair wind to sail.'[18] Just to make sure of Medina Sidonia's resolve, the king appointed as principal naval adviser Don Diego Flores de Valdés, commander of the Castilian squadron, to serve on the flagship at the captain-general's elbow at all times.

While the Armada was being repaired and refitted, fresh food and water was loaded into its hulls and stores and munitions redistributed among the ships. A reinvigorated Medina Sidonia was not afraid of undertaking hard work himself to set an example in urging his men onward. On 10 July, he spent six hours in the dark and dirty depths of the *Santa María de la Rosa* hold, helping with the stepping of a replacement mainmast. He told Philip cheerfully: 'When it was finished, I thought we had not done badly.'[19]

The captain-general also established a hospital to look after the five hundred men still suffering from fever. These were 'progressing favourably under care and I hope, by God's help, that every man will embark on the Armada'. However, others had voted with their feet. Despite Medina Sidonia's precautions – he stationed a local infantry company on the quayside to picket the ships – and his pledges that he would 'not lose a single man', the Armada's military contingent continued to slowly seep away through desertion.[20]

The commander of the Biscayan squadron, Admiral Juan Martinez de Recalde, who was recovering from an attack of sciatica, knew that for all his commander's public display of energy and enthusiasm, the captain-general remained 'much vexed at having to hurry the departure'. Recalde, too, had misgivings about the king's naval strategy and believed it was imperative to locate a safe harbour to shelter the Armada after Parma had landed. He told Philip: 'If it were found possible to obtain anchorage ... in the river [Thames] itself, supported by the army, no other reinforcements will be needed, or at least those from Flanders will suffice.' Failing that, a West Country port such as Falmouth, Plymouth or Dartmouth, would prove convenient:

> especially as the highly necessary reinforcements of men and stores will have to be sent from Spain and isolated vessels will be exposed to much danger from the enemy higher up the [English] Channel ...
>
> In the case of our encountering and defeating the enemy, I feel sure that he will not suffer so much damage ... [and] at all events [have enough ships to] impede the passage of our reinforcements high up the Channel.
>
> But it will be difficult for him to do this if our Armada be stationed in [these] ports.
>
> If it were possible for the reinforcement to be sent in sufficient strength to attack these ports whilst the conquest is being effected higher up [in the English Channel], that will be the best course.
>
> After the army of Flanders has been taken across and strengthened, the Armada might return towards Ushant and meet the reinforcements with which it might enter one of the ports and then either push a force inland towards the Bristol Channel or form a junction with the other army.

Recalde was also worried about the problems of transporting Parma's army across the Straits of Dover: 'This will take some little time, as in the case of there being a cavalry force (as I understand there will be), it cannot be carried over in one passage and we shall be fortunate if it can be done in two.'[21]

On 13 July, the Armada finally mustered at Corunna, totalling one hundred and twenty-nine ships, with 7,700 sailors and 18,000 soldiers embarked, augmented by two companies from the city's garrison. Many replacement troops were raw and untried and Medina Sidonia ordered that selected veterans should be transferred into some units 'so that every vessel will have a proportion of old and new men' to stiffen their *esprit de corps.*

Other recruits appeared even less martial. Recalde despaired of the 'young fellows' who had been appointed captains simply because they were gentlemen. 'Very few of them are soldiers or know what to do,' he complained. The medical officer of the Andalusian flagship *Nuestra Señora del Rosario* reported that some of these adventurers, having landed in Corunna, 'would not go forward'.[22]

There was worse to come. Four hundred Galician soldiers sent by the Count of Lemos and some of the levies from Monterey were 'so useless that they are no good, even as pioneers', Medina Sidonia observed. A number of the troops were starving and appeared more dead than alive. None knew what a harquebus or musket was. 'They are nearly all married and have large families and are absolutely unserviceable old men. Their wives have been coming in with their troubles and lamentations to such an extent that it goes against my conscience to ship the men. I have thought it best to send them all away and they have gone to their homes.'[23]

Undeterred by all these problems, a confident captain-general told Philip two days later: 'With God's help, [I] hope to have everything ready for sailing by tomorrow or the day after, weather permitting.' His Castilian, Guipúzcoan and Andalusian squadrons had already been towed out of harbour, together with the auxiliary squadron of *pataches* and *zabras*, and the remainder would follow the next day. The Armada's departure depended merely on a fair wind blowing up.

Medina Sidonia ordered that tents and altars be erected on a small island in the harbour – where the Castillo San Antón was under construction – for friars to hear the confessions of his sailors and soldiers, who were landed ship by ship, company by company.[24] As a talisman, each man was given a pewter medallion with an image of Christ on the obverse and that of the Blessed Virgin Mary on the reverse. The act of shrivening the Armada assumed industrial proportions: already 8,000 had been granted absolution, and the captain-general proudly informed the king that 'this is such an inestimable treasure that I esteem it more highly than the most precious jewel I carry on the fleet'. Cynics, however, would have noted that celebrating the sacrament of absolution on an island at least served to prevent further desertions.

Frustratingly, bad weather continued to be a factor: a strong west-north-west wind and the big Atlantic seas running into Corunna bay delayed sailing. On 19 July the Armada commanders met in the duke's cabin in *San Martin* to discuss tactics. It was agreed that they should sail up the English Channel in the tried-and-tested crescent-shaped formation known as the *lunula*, which had flanking horns formed by heavy-gunned warships. Again, Don Pedro de Valdés was the one dissenting voice, urging the Armada to be divided equally into a vanguard and a rearguard with the slower transport and supply ships at its heart between the two lines of protecting vessels.[25]

Captain Antonio de Taso Aquereis wrote to his family in Andalusia: 'All things are embarked. [We are] only tarrying for wind; and [it] is commanded, upon pain of death, [that] no man [should] disembark himself.'[26]

On the morning of 21 July, the Armada finally departed Corunna, favoured by a light south-westerly breeze. It must have presented a brave, formidable display of Spanish naval might to the watching (and praying) crowds perched on the headland high above the harbour, with the ships' colours flying and the trumpets sounding raucous, piercing fanfares across the bay.

For a 'great and most fortunate navy' the Armada had, up to now, suffered more than its fair share of bad luck. Unfortunately, this day was to be no different.

At two o'clock, within nine nautical miles (16.65 km) of land, the wind died completely. The ships remained stationary in the flat calm, sails hanging limply from their yardarms, until three the next morning when a brisk south-easterly wind suddenly blew up. In hoisting her sail, the galley *Zúñiga* broke the socket holding her rudder and the fleet waited impatiently for this damage to be repaired. Almost twelve hours later, the Armada rounded Cape Ortegal, butting into the Bay of Biscay, and Medina Sidonia set course for England and dreams of glory.

Back in England, there was palpable tension in the air as final preparations to the defences of Elizabeth's realm were hurriedly scrambled. A number of armed merchantmen had been hired to augment her navy, along with ships supplied by coastal towns.[27] Howard had taken his twenty-strong fleet to join Drake, his vice-admiral, at Plymouth, leaving a squadron of fourteen queen's ships plus sixteen vessels drawn from various ports, under Sir Henry Seymour in *Rainbow*, to guard the Straits of Dover and to interdict any attempted crossing by Parma's army.[28]

Like their Spanish adversaries, the English navy was afflicted by a grievous shortage of food. On 28 May, the lord admiral wrote desperately to Burghley: 'My lord, we have here now but eighteen days' victual and there is none to be gotten in all this country.' The wind being favourable, it was likely the Armada was on its way and if the weather held, in 'six days they will knock at our door'. He added: 'God send us a wind to put us out, for go we will, though we starve.' At Plymouth, there were 'the gallantest company of captains, soldiers and mariners that I think ever was seen in England. It [is a] pity they should lack meat when they are so desirous to spend their lives in her majesty's service.'[29]

In the Low Countries, the English commander Lord Willoughby pointedly reminded the rebel States General of their agreement to 'equip certain ships at their own expense' to join forces with the English navy 'in case of any enterprise of the King of Spain against [Elizabeth]'. Moreover the queen had heard of planned enemy attacks on Bergen-op-Zoom and Ostend, a seaport 'very destitute of supplies and fortifications' and therefore urged the Dutch to repair the fortifications and reinforce their garrisons.[30]

Seemingly by a process of osmosis, Elizabeth's government had decreed that the Thames estuary, and more specifically the eastern county of Essex, was the most likely target for Parma's landing. This was where her army would stand and fight. But just in case this guesswork proved wrong, a decision was taken to build a bridge of boats across the river between Tilbury in Essex and Gravesend in Kent, to enable the army to quickly reinforce the south-east corner of her realm. Like many of Elizabeth's decisions, the go-ahead for the bridge came very late in the day. Surveying work only began on 27 July.

The fort at Tilbury (like the boom of ships' masts and chains stretched across the Thames) scarcely presented a credible defence against attack by a determined enemy – particularly if they were armed with the siege artillery carried by the Armada. Built in 1539 by Henry VIII,[31] the old two-storeyed, D-shaped blockhouse was now to be strengthened. Two encircling ditches (with drawbridges over) were excavated and a new counterscarp bank thrown up, topped by a timber palisade. The fort was designed to provide withering crossfire against any ships sailing up the river to attack London, in conjunction with a similar structure eight hundred yards (731.52 metres) across the Thames at New Tavern, Gravesend.[32] However, these defences were hastily constructed and had the appearance of fieldworks rather than permanent fortifications.

New batteries were also built or proposed at Northfleet, Erith and Greenhythe in Kent, but the Earl of Leicester, appointed the queen's general of land forces in July, found that there were no platforms there fit to mount guns. In addition, he deemed the blockhouses at Milton and Gravesend 'indefensible', having been built 'to the least purpose that I ever saw'.[33] Seymour suggested in the middle of June that twenty hoys from Harwich and Ipswich 'being nimble of sail and quick in turning to and fro' should be stationed in the Thames estuary to forestall any landing by Parma.[34] In the end, only the 90-ton *Brigandine* took up position at the Nore,[35] a sandbank where the estuary merged into the North Sea, to provide advance warning of a Spanish approach. William Borough, whose naval career was now miraculously rehabilitated after Drake's accusations at Cadiz, was given command of the 300-ton *Bonavolia,* the only large oared galley in the queen's navy, which acted as a guardship downstream from London 'lest invaders come at half tide'. It was a scant consolation prize for all Borough's travails.[36]

Walsingham, in bed 'awaiting the recurrence of a fit', was both angry and frustrated at Elizabeth's stubborn reluctance to commit her finances to the defence of her nation, and less than optimistic about England's chance of defeating a Spanish invasion. He told

Burghley that he was sorry to see 'so great a danger hanging over the realm so lightly regarded and so carelessly provided for. Would to God the enemy were no more careful to assail than we to defend.' His concerns were unconsciously echoed by Howard on 19 June: 'For the love of God let her majesty care not now for charges.'

There remained the question of Elizabeth's personal protection. On 2 June, the queen had ordered some of the nobility to 'speedily put the realm in a posture of defence to resist the attempts of Spain' and to hold themselves in readiness to 'attend upon her person with a ... convenient number of lances and light horse' at such time as the Privy Council ordered.[37] Her household servants had already been placed on alert, ready to move to a place of safety. A dozen of the principal recusants had been speedily arrested and sent to the Tower to prevent any chance of assassination.[38]

Burghley, having received a copy of Allen's venomous *Admonition to the Nobility and People of England* on 12 June from Sir Henry Killigrew in The Hague, sent this 'vile book' to Walsingham, adding with a touch of bravura: 'The Cardinal is deceived if he thinks that any nobleman or gentlemen of possessions will favour the invasion of the realm.'[39] Just to make sure, he issued a proclamation on 1 July threatening punishment, under martial law, to anyone possessing or distributing papal bulls, books or pamphlets.[40]

Spy fever gripped England. The mayor and jurats of Dover had arrested one Adrian Menneck, 'lately arrived with Calais' who they believed was an agent working for Parma. Suspiciously, he had been found with a 'map or charts of all the coasts of England, Scotland and Ireland'.

There was no up-to-date hard intelligence about the Armada's movements or intentions and if the turbulent weather had played cruel tricks on Medina Sidonia's ships, it had succeeded in frustrating the English navy too.

Drake reported on his reconnaissance in the Channel approaches in a letter to Burghley dated 6 June and written from 'her majesty's good ship *Revenge*' now safely back in Plymouth Sound. For seven days they had suffered 'a great storm', which the vice-admiral considered unusual weather for early summer. They met a hulk, returning to her home port of San Lúcar, which sixteen days before had encountered:

a great fleet of ships which came from Lisbon, having the wind
northerly and so coming to the westward ... The skipper and the
company ... saw so many as they could not number [count] them.

Either we shall hear of them very shortly or else they will go to
the Groyne [Corunna] and there assemble.

Drake concluded: 'I daily pray to God to bless her majesty and give us
grace to fear Him so shall we not need to doubt the enemy, although
they be many.'[41]

Three days later, Walsingham passed on to Howard Elizabeth's
firm instructions not to sail to Bayonne 'to watch the proceedings of
the Spanish fleet'. The queen feared that the Armada could slip past
her ships unnoticed and therefore recommended that her fleet 'ply up
and down between the English and Spanish coast so as you may be
able to answer any attempt that the fleet shall make either against
this realm, Ireland, or Scotland'.[42] Howard, still beset by storms,
argued that 'it was the opinion of all [his] most experienced commanders that they ought to proceed at once' to the Spanish coast.
Moreover, the delay in awaiting the Armada would consume all their
provisions. Nonetheless, he would obey orders.[43]

First news of the Armada came on Monday 23 June when a barque
from Mousehole, laden with a cargo of salt for France, 'encountered
nine sail of great ships between Scilly and Ushant, bearing north-
east' towards the Cornish coast – some of the Armada ships blown
north from Corunna.

Coming near unto them, he, not doubting they were Spaniards, kept
the wind of them. They ... began to give him chase ... three of them
followed him so near that the Englishman doubted hardly to escape.

At his first sight of them, there were two flags spread which were
suddenly taken in again ... Their sails were all crossed over with a
red cross. Each of the greater ships towed astern them either a great
boat or pinnace without a mast.[44]

The previous day, 'One Simmons of Exeter' declared 'that on Friday
last he was chased [by] a fleet of great ships, having some of his men
hurt with shot from them'. He escaped, landed in Cornwall, and hurried to Plymouth to inform the lord admiral.[45]

At the other end of the Channel, Seymour was alert for any sign of Parma's sortie out of Flanders. In late June he spent thirty hours off Gravelines, during which he spotted two small ships leaving Dunkirk.

> Two of our pinnaces chased them, with the discharging of some saker shot and yet [they] would not strike [their sails] till at last one of our shot struck down the mainmast of one of these vessels, being a French bottom [vessel] belonging to Calais.
>
> I demanded what he meant not to strike his sails and to come to the queen's ships, knowing us so well. He answered that he took us for the King of Navarre's fleet, making himself ignorant what to do.
>
> I replied that if the Duke of Parma or the Duke of Guise should do the like, I would sink them or they would distress me – adding further that my sovereign lady was able to defend her country against the Holy League, besides able to master any civil discord and so dismissed them with some little choler [anger].

The second fugitive ship ran aground and the crew fled, wading through the surf. 'My boat, which I manned with some [musketeers], came upon their skirts but a little too late. Yet there came very near a hundred men, horse and foot but dare not approach ...' But suddenly the wind rose, forcing Seymour to seek shelter from 'marvellous foul weather' for thirty hours in a Kent harbour.[46]

Howard now received hard intelligence that the Armada was regrouping at Corunna. Forgoing the loading of all his stores, he took advantage of a prosperous north-easterly wind to depart Plymouth with sixty ships on 4 July. He set course for Spain, hoping to give battle off Corunna, but again bad weather intervened, with storms and southerly gales off the Scillies and Ushant. The English fleet was driven back to Plymouth five days later, short of supplies and some of the ships leaking. Howard was quick to defend John Hawkins, one of his captains and Treasurer of the Navy:

> I have heard that there is in London some hard speeches against Mr Hawkins because the *Hope* came in [to] mend a leak that she had.
>
> I think there were never so many of the ships so long abroad and in such seas with such weather as these have had with so few leaks.

The *Hope*'s leak was so small 'that I would have dared to have gone with it to Venice', he added dismissively. Some of the hired merchantmen needed new spars and cordage and some ships reported sickness amongst their crews.[47]

In London, events had moved on and there were graver problems than a slight leak in one of her majesty's ships. A new crisis was confronting Elizabeth's government: they were almost bankrupt. In January 1588, she had extorted a forced loan from her richer subjects that had brought £75,000 into her hard-pressed exchequer. Three months later, the queen borrowed £30,000 from the City of London, repayable at 10 per cent. Now, that money was long gone.

On 19 July, Burghley, grievously afflicted with gastric pains, wrote to Walsingham describing his desperate straits in finding cash to keep the fleet at sea:

> I find my mind as much troubled to write as now I do as commonly my stomach is against purging but I cannot conceal from you the causes which will shortly bring forth desperate effects.

Burghley had paid out £6,000 that week for wages and foodstuffs for the ships, but then had received demands for more than £19,000 for naval pay up to 28 July. Old debts of £13,000 for provisions had been demanded too, but the treasurer had persuaded the creditors to take postponed, staged payments. 'I marvel that where so many are dead on the seas, the pay is not dead with them or with many of them,' Burghley wrote ruefully. On top of all this, costs of the army totalled nearly £11,000:

> I shall but fill my letter with more melancholy matter if I should remember what money must be [paid to] 5,000 footmen and 1,000 horsemen for defence of the enemy landing in Essex ...
>
> A man would wish if peace cannot be had, that the enemy would not longer delay but prove (as I trust) his evil fortune, for as these expectations do consume us, so I would hope by God's goodness upon their defect, we might have on half a year's time to provide for money.

He had talked with two London bankers, Sir Horatio Palavicino[48] and Richard Saltonstall, about a loan amounting to £40,000 or £50,000, repayable at 10 per cent interest, 'but I find no probability how to get money here in [gold] specie which is our lack but by exchanging to have it out of the parts beyond [the] sea which will not be done in a long time.' Burghley also had hopes that English merchants at Stade, on the River Elbe, near Hamburg,[49] might lend £20,000 or £30,000.[50]

Medina Sidonia had his own worries. Using Captain Don Rodrigo Tello de Guzmán as his courier, he had sent another message to Parma on Monday 25 July, reporting his progress. At dawn the following day there was a dead calm before heavy squalls forced the Portuguese galley *Diana* to head for a Spanish port after her oar-slaves mutinied and she began to take in water. These long narrow ships, designed to operate in calmer waters, could not cope with the long Atlantic rollers; under constant battering, the seams of the hull planking were beginning to spring apart. The other three galleys disappeared from sight and fresh storms on the 27th scattered the Armada yet again. The captain-general reported:

> The sea was so heavy that all the sailors agreed that they have never seen its equal in July.
>
> Not only did the waves mount to the skies but some seas broke clean over the ships and the stern gallery of Diego Flores' flagship [*San Cristobal*] was carried away.
>
> We were on watch all night, full of anxiety lest the Armada should suffer great damage but could do nothing more.
>
> It was the most cruel night ever seen.

Next day, when the seas were less rough and visibility had improved, Medina Sidonia looked out at his fleet and realised that forty ships were missing – all of Pedro de Valdés Andalusian squadron, all the hulks and some of the *pataches*. The captain-general had suffered his first casualties.

The galley *Bazana* was wrecked at the entrance to Bayonne harbour and her sister ship *Diana* beached.[51] The Biscayan flagship *Santa Ana* lost her mainmast and sought refuge in the French port of La Hogue on the Cherbourg peninsula; she later moved to Le Havre, where she was to spend the rest of the Armada campaign immobilised.[52] The galleass *San Lorenzo* had a damaged rudder; Medina Sidonia noted with just a touch of fatalism: 'These craft are really very fragile in heavy seas.' He had lost three of his ships before a shot had been fired.

Friday dawned fine but hazy, clearing later in the day. At four that afternoon the Lizard peninsula was sighted and the fleet shortened sail to allow the stragglers to catch up.

The following day Medina Sidonia offered up prayers in thanks for 'bringing us thus far'. 'God Almighty grant that the rest of our voyage may be performed as we and all Christendom hope it will be,' he told Philip in a letter.

– 6 –

ACTION THIS DAY

Sir, for the love of God and our country, let us have, with some speed, some great shot sent us of all bigness [sizes], for this service will continue long – and some powder with it.

Lord High Admiral Howard to Sir Francis Walsingham,
Ark Royal 'thwart Plymouth', 31 July 1588.[1]

Early on Saturday 30 July, as his fleet lay hove to within sight of the enemy coast, Medina Sidonia summoned a council of war on board his flagship *San Martin*.[2] While the admirals were saluted with proper naval ceremony, the lookouts atop the warship's main-mast could see the drifting smoke of the warning beacons on high points along the Cornish coast. Everyone in the battered, creaking ships of the Armada knew that, at last, action was imminent and their thoughts inevitably turned to divine protection. At prayers that morning, prompted by their ministering friars, the crews had knelt reverently upon the wet decks, 'beseeching Our Lord to give us victory against the enemies of His holy faith'.[3]

Their king, fretting and fussing in Madrid, would have heartily approved of their piety, had he but known. There was the rub. The lack of news on the Armada's fortunes had substantially increased his anxieties, and rumours abounded throughout Europe about the fate of his ships. One account, circulating in Antwerp, said the 'English and Spanish armadas have met on the English coast and the Spanish ... have been beaten'. The gossip in Turin, on the other hand, was that the Armada had sailed up the English Channel and successfully rendezvoused with Parma. A third version, in Prague, had the fleet sailing home to Corunna having been stricken by an outbreak of bubonic plague.[4] That report had reached the ears of King Henri III of France while he was dining in state at Rouen in late July. 'That is a fine story!' he sneered. 'It is only because they had seen the English fleet and were frightened.'[5]

How was the Armada going to triumph over the heretics of the English fleet? Much has been written about that morning's heated discussion as the Spanish fleet lay poised at the entrance to the English Channel. We know that afterwards the captain-general reported to Philip that it was decided to: 'proceed slowly ... as far as the Isle of Wight and no further until I receive [news from] the Duke of Parma informing me of the condition of his force'.

> All along the coast of Flanders there is no harbour or shelter for our ships [and] if I were to go from the Isle of Wight thither ... our vessels might be driven on to the shoals, where they would certainly be lost.
> In order to avoid so obvious a peril I have decided to stay off the Isle of Wight until I learn what the duke is doing as the plan is that at the moment of my arrival he should sally with his fleet without causing me to wait a minute.

Medina Sidonia was astonished to have heard nothing from Parma: 'During the whole course of our voyage we have not fallen in with a single vessel ... from whom we could obtain any information and we are consequently groping in the dark.'[6] Unbeknown to all those arguing around the table in the *San Martin* that morning, the vital co-ordination between the two arms of Spanish naval and military might – upon which the success of the 'Enterprise of England' hinged – was already fatally flawed. The bitter seeds of disaster had been sown and Spain would reap a lethal harvest in the days and weeks to come.

The polished courtly phrases of the captain-general's formal dispatch gave no hint of the impassioned debate that had taken place during the council of war. Some commanders – Recalde, Alonso de Leyva and Oquendo among them – had urged the captain-general to immediately attack or blockade Plymouth by deploying fireships, particularly if English ships were caught inside the harbour.[7]

Medina Sidonia, ever mindful of his royal master's instructions to protect Parma's amphibious landing, was still fretting about the lack of a safe haven for the Armada, particularly after the latest bout of storm damage to his fleet. But, like Borough before Drake's attack on Cadiz the previous year, the captain-general judged his admirals' plan to be too perilous. The entrance to Plymouth harbour was believed to be narrow and hazardous, only permitting entry by three ships sailing abreast. Moreover he feared the firepower of the defending shore batteries and was anxious to avoid further damage or loss of his ships before achieving his primary objective of safely escorting the Flanders army across the Dover Straits. His view was supported by Pedro de Valdés, commander of the Andalusian squadron.

Therefore, with the wind in the south-west, orders were issued to press on up the English Channel in a tight half-crescent formation, with Bertendona's Levantine ships in the vanguard, followed by the main force under Medina Sidonia, with the Guipúzcoan and Andalusian squadrons stationed on either wing. The slower transport hulks were protected in the centre of this *lunula* and the Biscayan ships formed a rearguard. A number of ships were also designated to form a *socorro*, a tactical battle group designed to be deployed to reinforce the formation wherever danger loomed.

Howard already knew of the Armada's arrival. Thomas Fleming, on board the barque *Golden Hinde*, was part of the screen of English ships positioned in the south-west approaches to provide early warning of the Spanish onslaught. Around three o'clock that Saturday afternoon, Fleming sailed into Plymouth with news of the enemy fleet off the Lizard.

His may have been the impudent and audacious English ship that had darted daringly between the warships in the Spanish vanguard before heading eastwards, defiantly pooping off one round from a cannon and ignoring the more powerful shots fired in reply by the Levanter *Rata Santa María Encoronada*. Worried by this incident, Medina Sidonia sent the English-speaking Ensign Juan Gil in his flagship's oared tender to gather intelligence on the whereabouts of the English fleet, which he confidently expected to be 250 miles (402.34 km) away, concentrated in the Dover Straits, ready to prey upon Parma's invasion barges. He also believed that the much-feared *El Draque* commanded only a small squadron off the Devon coast.

Legend has Howard and Drake enjoying a quiet game of bowls on Plymouth Hoe when the information they had been anxiously awaiting finally arrived via Captain Fleming.[8] This immortal incident was first recorded more than forty years later and the naval hero's calm, almost throwaway response – 'We have time to finish the game and beat the Spaniards too' – first appeared in print two centuries after the event.[9]

The story may be apocryphal, but there are facets of that afternoon's events that suggest it has some veracity. News of the Armada had been spread by Cornwall's beacon system and the warning pealing of church bells, calling the local militia to arms. The shore defences were alerted and such few batteries of guns as existed were manned and loaded. Faced with adverse winds and a flood tide running into Plymouth harbour, the English fleet were prevented from leaving their moorings until the tide began to ebb early that evening. Moreover, the enemy ships were too distant to take advantage of the flood to attack Plymouth, so the English mariners found themselves with a few precious hours in which to complete provisioning and arming their ships, or, with true English *sang froid,* to finish that game of bowls.

Howard and Drake spent the afternoon and evening gainfully by slowly and laboriously warping[10] their ships out of harbour and collecting them in the shelter of Rame Head, ready for battle at first light. They now mustered a powerful force: with the arrival of reinforcements, the English fleet numbered more than one hundred vessels.

Just after midnight, Ensign Gil returned to the Armada with a captured Falmouth fishing smack and its crew of four. Under interrogation, the Cornish prisoners disclosed the unwelcome news that not only had Howard and Drake joined forces, but their ships had departed Plymouth and were readying for action. Diego Flores Valdés, the fleet's naval adviser, cautioned Medina Sidonia that, given the Armada's current speed and course, he was liable to run on ahead of the enemy and risked being attacked from behind, as well as surrendering the tactical advantage of the weather gauge.[11] Accordingly, the Spanish ships spent the remainder of the night anchored in the lee of the 400-foot (120 metre) headland of Dodman Point, notched with its Iron Age earthen ramparts, near Mevagissey in Cornwall. It was to be a busy night for Captain Uceda, the officer charged with rowing out to each ship in the fleet to deliver detailed orders for battle on the morrow.

Dawn broke on Sunday 31 July with the sea shrouded in mist, soon dispersed by a west-north-westerly wind that freshened, bringing thick drizzly rain. Medina Sidonia was astounded, if not mortified, to see at least eighty-five English ships windward of him, five miles (8 km) west of the Eddystone Rock, his enemy having gained the weather gauge. More worrying still, a fifteen-strong enemy squadron was tacking close inshore between the Armada and the Cornish fishing village of Looe, with the clear intention of luring some Spaniards out of line, that they might easily be picked off. The captain-general fired a signal gun, ordering his fleet to take up battle stations, then he hoisted the royal standard to his maintop as a signal to engage the enemy.

The Spanish fleet smoothly fell into the *lunula* fighting formation, each vessel hoisting the personal colours of its captain or squadron commander to strident trumpet calls and the beating of drums. Guns were run out and nets stretched across the upper decks to prevent the enemy scrambling aboard. Leyva's squadron formed the vanguard or northerly horn of the crescent and Recalde's Biscayans the southerly, with Medina Sidonia's galleons stationed in the centre to guard the transport ships. From horn to horn, the width of the Armada *lunula* probably stretched about six miles (9.6 km).

With its garish multicoloured sails, ensigns and streamers, the *lunula* presented a daunting, if not deadly sight. To many, the slow-moving crescent resembled a dense infantry formation, the forest of masts like a mass of soldiers' pikes. The speed and precision of the manoeuvre and the sheer magnitude of the Armada in full battle array amazed and overawed all those on the decks of the closing English ships. Henry White, captain of the 200-ton armed merchantman *Barque Talbot*, commented: 'The majesty of the enemy's fleet, the good order they held and the private consideration of our own wants did cause, in my opinion, our first onset to be more coldly done than became the value of our nation and the credit of the English navy.' Another seaman described his astonishment more candidly: 'We never thought that they could ever have found, gathered and joined so great a force of puissant ships together and so well appointed them with their cannon, culverin and other great pieces of ordnance.'[12] An Italian eye-witness called Bentivollo was more graphic: 'You could hardly see the sea ... The masts and rigging, the towering sterns and prows which in height and number were so great that they dominated the whole naval concourse [and] caused horror, mixed with wonder.'[13]

In the twenty-first century, such diplomatic niceties as a formal declaration of war before hostilities commence appear to have fallen out of fashion.[14] At best, an enemy country might expect an ultimatum or a menacing United Nations' resolution before the shooting starts or the bombs begin to fall. Even the word 'war' is now shunned, hidden behind such bland euphemisms as 'conflict' – doubtless because somewhere down the line, lawyers and expensive litigation may become involved.

This is a far cry from the sixteenth century when war was more gentlemanly – but just as bloody. Howard felt compelled to observe the chivalrous etiquette then expected on such famous occasions as the meeting of two enemy fleets at sea, each one prepared to give battle. He therefore dispatched his own 80-ton barque *Disdain* to issue a formal challenge or 'defiance', as it was called, to the Spaniards. The little ship bravely sailed to within hailing distance of the tightly packed Spanish ships in the bulging centre of the *lunula* and fired a single, symbolic shot at de Leyva's *Rata Santa María Encoronada*, before beating a hasty retreat back to the safety of the English fleet.

This civility properly fulfilled, Howard gave the order to attack at around 9 a.m. Wary of the potentially deadly trap between the crab-like pincher claws of the flanking horns of the Armada, his preferred tactic was to harry the rear of the enemy centre while Drake's and John Hawkins' squadrons launched assaults on the more vulnerable tips of the crescent. As a precursor, Howard, in *Ark Royal*, led an attack on the Spanish southerly wing with the aim of engaging Medina Sidonia's flagship – in line with the gentlemanly code that dictated commanders should always fight someone of equal rank.

His ships swept across the Armada's rear, initially trading shots with Leyva's vanguard, and Howard opened fire on the *Rata Santa María Encoronada* at a range of four hundred yards (437 metres) in the mistaken belief that she was *San Martin,* the Armada flagship. After a flurry of cannonades, he then engaged Recalde's rearguard on the northern side of the crescent, in support of the attack by Drake's forty-strong squadron.

Pedro de Calderón, the chief purser of the Armada, witnessed this artillery duel from the 650-ton transport ship *San Salvador*, vice-flagship of the hulks squadron. He described how *Rata* tried to close on Drake's *Revenge*, 'which ... allowed herself to fall off towards [her] but they could not exchange cannon shots, because the enemy's ship, fearing that the *San Mateo* would bring her to close quarters, left the *Rata* and bombarded the *San Mateo*'.[15]

Naval battles carry their own brand of particular terror, especially for the inexperienced sailor. The jarring, deafening crashes of repeated cannonades. The sickening, heart-stopping thumps of enemy roundshot smashing into the timber hull of your ship amid the heat, smoke and confusion. The terrible wounds caused by wooden splinters flying through the air like deadly arrows. The piercing screams of the wounded, their limbs torn off by iron or stone cannonballs. The all-pervasive stench of copiously spilt blood, spent gunpowder and naked fear. The disorientation of sudden and unexpected changes in course as ships manoeuvre to press home an attack or avoid a devastating enemy salvo. Dominating all was the horror of fire breaking out – perhaps triggering the explosion of a magazine that would blow your ship out of the water, raining down debris and body parts into the waves. All these sights, sounds and smells constantly assailed every one of the senses. For those on board, driven almost out of their wits by the madness and pandemonium around them, there was nowhere to run to. In a ship fighting a close-quarter battle, there were no hiding places.

No surprise then that the ferocity of Drake's assault, which included the mighty *Triumph* and *Victory*, unnerved the Biscayan ships. Panic set in, causing some to break station and seek shelter within Medina Sidonia's centre. These were probably the vessels Calderón had in mind when he described ships 'basely' taking to flight 'until they were peremptorily ordered by the flagship to luff[16] and face the enemy'.

At around 10.30, Recalde, in the Armada's 1,050-ton vice-flagship *San Juan de Portugal*, shortened sail and turned his ship to bring all guns to bear on the attackers, receiving in turn concentrated fire from eight English ships that had closed to a range of 300 yards (274 metres). Recalde was clearly hoping to board one of his enemies, but the English, wary of his cannon and the well-armed soldiers on board, were content to stand off at a distance and pound his ship for about an hour.

Isolated from the remainder of the Spanish fleet and suffering continual damage, Recalde later estimated that in excess of three hundred rounds were fired at him 'damaging key parts of the rigging, including the mainmast stay'. One shot smashed through his foremast 'from one side to the other'.[17] But he had not yet sustained many casualties: only 'Captain Pedro de Ycaina and others were wounded', according to Calderón. These were patently gentlemen; the purser did not bother to mention the fifteen crew members who had been killed.

Realising the danger in Recalde's position, Medina Sidonia struck his flagship's foresail, slackened her sheets and put his helm hard over to steer for the threatening mêlée on his northern flank. Some of the Andalusian and Guipúzcoan ships in the *socorro* followed his lead, together with the Biscayan *El Gran Grin* and the four Neapolitan galleasses, *San Lorenzo, Napolitana, Zúñiga* and *Girona*. *San Martin* came under immediate attack by two of the English galleons.

The action continued furiously for another ninety minutes until shortly before one o'clock, when the English broke away, possibly because they were running low on ammunition and powder. Despite Medina Sidonia lowering his topsails as an invitation to continue the battle, the first day's action was now over. The former spy Nicholas Ousley, now aboard *Revenge,* acknowledged that the Spanish 'keep such excellent good order in their fight [and] if God do not miraculously work, we shall have to employ ourselves for some days'.[18] Medina Sidonia was surprised at the English tactics and the agility of their ships, noting in his diary how they fired cannon salvoes 'without attempting to grapple'.[19]

The Armada's threat to Plymouth may have been neutralised, but Howard and Drake nonetheless must have been left anxious. They had not been successful in penetrating and disrupting the Armada's defensive crescent, and their long-range bombardment had failed to inflict any real damage on their enemy. Worryingly, expenditure of cannon shot and gunpowder was greater than anticipated. (Captain Vanegas, the Spanish flagship's gunnery officer, estimated that the English had fired 2,000 rounds against just 750 from his own side.)[20] On a positive note, however, the English vessels had proved faster,

more nimble and manoeuvrable than the lumbering Spanish warships, and they had frustrated every enemy attempt to board them.

As the clearing acrid smoke rolled across the sea, Recalde moved
his battered ship into the protective centre of the crescent to undertake emergency repairs. The Armada continued slowly eastwards,
its progress interrupted by forays from harrying English ships, firing
occasional long-range shots.

Within minutes of the English breaking off the action came the first
of two calamitous accidents that were to cost Medina Sidonia two
of his major warships. Fearing that Recalde's stricken vessel would
'not be able to abide any new fight if it were offered the same day',
Admiral Don Pedro de Valdés in the *Nuestra Señora del Rosario*
was swiftly cutting through the water to assist when he collided with
one of the Biscayan ships, breaking the bowsprit and wrecking its
steering. Then at around two o'clock, a catastrophic explosion tore
through another ship, carrying the Armada's pay in gold. Calderón
takes up the story:

> The *San Salvador* of Oquendo's [Guipúzcoan] squadron blew up
> by reason of the powder which had been brought on deck for the
> fighting.
>
> It is said that Captain [Pedro] Priego had beaten a German artil-
> leryman who went below, saying that one of the pieces [guns] had
> got wet and would have to be discharged.
>
> He fired the piece and then threw the port fire [linstock] into a
> barrel of powder.
>
> Both of the after decks were blown up, killing over two hundred
> men, including Ensign Castañeda who was on watch and the ship
> was rent in the bows and stern.
>
> Many of the men jumped into the sea and were drowned.

With a bureaucrat's worry for a colleague and his responsibilities,
Calderón added that 'Paymaster Juan de Huerta, his staff papers and
some money in his charge were saved'.[21]

Sensational rumours swept the Spanish fleet. One suggested that
a Dutch master-gunner, rebuked for poor aiming or rate of fire, had
laid a powder trail to a barrel of explosives, coolly lit it, and then
jumped overboard. Another tale recounted how the gunner had been
reproved for smoking on the quarter-deck by the captain and had

calmly knocked out his clay pipe into the ubiquitous barrel of gun-powder. A third version said the master-gunner was a German who had been struck by a Spanish officer with a stick as a punishment for neglecting his duty.[22]

A more florid report, written some time after the event by the Florentine Petruccio Ubaldino, concerned a gunner who had been cuckolded by a Spanish army officer and had taken his own, devastating revenge:

> The captain of the soldiers ... having small regard of an orderly and civil life, did insolently beat a Flemish gunner. What cause he had, I know not, whether upon occasion of words touching his charge [responsibilities] or by means of the gunner's wife whom he had abused, according to the custom of that nation. Whereupon the perplexed man, seeing himself among such a kind of people as not only made him serve their turns but disgraced him in as vile manner, as if he were a slave, despairing of life, wife and his young daughter and perchance rather moved with the dishonour of them ... set himself on fire in a barrel of gunpowder, procuring thereby ... a cruel revenge of his injuries.[23]

Some support for this exciting story of lust, despair and terrible revenge is provided by an English report that a German woman was discovered among the survivors from the 958-ton *San Salvador*.[24] So much for Medina Sidonia's ban on women accompanying the Armada.

The explosion blew apart the ship's stern castle and destroyed the two aft upper decks as well as damaging her rudder. The captain-general halted the Armada and sent *pataches* to pick up survivors from the burning hull and the surrounding sea, beginning with 'the principal persons' – those of high rank. Calderón received thirty-five casualties on his ship, mostly suffering from terrible burns, including the *San Salvador*'s captain, Don Pedro Priego. Directing operations from the *San Martin*'s poop deck, Medina Sidonia ordered boats to transfer the *San Salvador*'s treasure to other ships and help turn her battered stern away from the wind to prevent the fire that was raging amidships from blowing further forward. Forming human chains to pass buckets, the remaining crew, aided by volunteers, eventually managed to extinguish the blaze. They were only just in time: the fire was edging dangerously close to the magazine beneath the forecastle, holding seven tons of gunpowder. Two galleasses took the stricken ship in tow, its badly burned survivors still on board, and the Armada continued its stately progress up the Channel.[25]

The day had not gone well for Medina Sidonia. Standing on *San Martin*'s poop deck, high above the waves, he probably reflected that although the Armada had survived the first English attack, it was galling that the most serious damage to his ships had been caused by avoidable accidents rather than by enemy action. He had eaten nothing all day but some bread and Sardinian cheese, brought to him in rare moments of quiet. If his cup of despair and disappointment had been full before, it now flowed over.

The wind turned squally, whipping up increasingly choppy waves. The damaged *Rosario* began losing steerage and at five o'clock she was involved in a second collision – this time with her sister Andalusian galleon, the 730-ton *Santa Catalina*. Her foremast snapped off at its base and came crashing down on to the mainmast, reducing the upper deck to a tangled mass of fallen timber and rigging. Pedro de Valdés' ship was now uncontrollable and he fired a signal gun for assistance.

The *San Martin* came up alongside and her captain, Captain Marolín de Juan (also the Armada's sailing master), ordered that the *Rosario* should be taken in tow. But the sea had risen still further and within minutes of the tow being secured, the hawser parted. Medina Sidonia's naval adviser Diego Flores de Valdés urged him to abandon the damaged ship as any delay could jeopardise both the Armada's mission and the fleet itself. This was a painful decision for Medina Sidonia. He was probably aware that there was no love lost between his naval adviser and the *Rosario*'s commander – the two were estranged cousins who nursed resentment over ancient personal slights. Later he acknowledged ruefully: 'If I could have remedied the situation with my blood I would have gladly done so.'[26]

In stark naval tactical terms, the decision to abandon the *Rosario* was probably correct, although it damaged morale in the Armada. Word quickly spread that 'no ship should take any risks for if a ship had not received any relief who would rescue the rest from any danger in which they might place themselves?'[27] Two *pataches* were sent to take off the *Rosario*'s crew, but Pedro de Valdés rejected any aid, stubbornly refusing to abandon his ship with the enemy so close. In addition to the admiral, those on board included Captain Vicente Alvarez, the owner of the ship, and 228 sailors, along with a military contingent comprising Captain Alonso de Zayas and 122 soldiers of Antonio de Heria's company, plus twenty more from Juan de Ibarra's unit. The hold contained 50,000 gold ducats belonging to Philip II; curiously, Medina Sidonia, who must have been aware of its existence, made no attempt to remove it.

There were seven other names on the *Rosario*'s manifest: English Catholic exiles who had joined the Armada to help depose Elizabeth.

As darkness fell, while survivors said their evening prayers on the heaving deck, the flagship departed to rejoin the Armada, which was now two hours' sailing time ahead. Admiral Agustín de Ojeda, commander of the auxiliary squadron, in his flagship *Nuestra Señora de Pilar de Zaragoza,* was detailed to stay with the helpless *Rosario,* together with four pinnaces. A few hours later, the sound of cannon shots echoed across the waves.

Valdés was furious at being abandoned in the face of the enemy. Although his commander was 'near enough to me and saw in what case I was and might easily have relieved me, yet he would not do it'. He was left 'comfortless in the sight of the whole fleet, the enemy being but a quarter of a league from me'.[28]

That night, Howard wrote to Walsingham from the *Ark Royal,* off Plymouth, describing the first day's action:

> I will not trouble you with any long letter – we are at present otherwise occupied than with writing ...
>
> At nine of the [clock] we gave them fight, which continued until one. [In this] fight we made some of them bear room to stop their leaks. Notwithstanding, we dare not adventure to put in among them their fleet being so strong.
>
> But there shall be nothing either neglected or unhazarded that may work their overthrow.
>
> Sir, the captains in her majesty's ships have behaved themselves most bravely ... and I doubt not will continue to their great commendation.

In a hurried postscript, Howard referred to his earlier aborted reconnaissance mission – 'The southerly wind that brought back from the coast of Spain brought them out' – and revisited his fears of missing the Armada with the comment: 'God blessed us with turning back.'[29] The lord admiral also added an urgent and impassioned plea for more cannon shot and gunpowder.

Drake, in a terse letter to Henry Seymour, still guarding the narrow seas off Flanders, recounted how 'we had them in chase and so coming up to them, there ... passed some cannon shot between some of our fleet and some of them and as far as we perceive, they are determined to sell their lives with blows'. He warned Seymour to put his ships 'into the best and strongest manner you may and [be] ready to assist his lordship [Howard] for the better encountering of them in those parts where you are now'. He estimated the Armada to be 'above one hundred sails, many great ships but truly, I think not half of them men-of-war'.[30]

Howard called a council of war aboard the *Ark Royal*. The day's events were discussed, including the problems they had encountered in penetrating the Armada's defences. Drake in *Revenge* was ordered to be lead ship of the English fleet tailing the Armada during the night, with a large lantern displayed at his stern so the remainder of the pursuing ships could safely judge their distance from the enemy. This was an eminently sensible order by Howard, given Drake's experience, navigational skills, and superlative seamanship. But he had not reckoned with his maverick vice-admiral's greed in the face of the enemy.

Medina Sidonia, in another letter to Parma, reported:

> This morning the enemy's fleet came out and having got the wind of us, attacked our rear.
>
> During their exchange of cannon fire with the Armada, my flagship became so closely engaged that it was necessary for us to attack the enemy in force, whereupon they retired, although they still continue within sight of the Armada with the object, apparently, of delaying and impeding our voyage.
>
> If their object had been to fight they had good opportunity of doing so today.

Reiterating his intention 'with God's help, to continue my voyage without allowing anything to divert me until I received from your excellency instructions as to what I am to do', the captain-general requested Parma to supply pilots for the Flanders coast 'as without them I am ignorant of the places where I can find shelter for ships so large as these in case I am overtaken by the slightest storm'.[31] The message was entrusted to the redoubtable Ensign Gil, but continuing rough seas delayed the departure of his pinnace until the following day.

Westwards, the *Rosario* continued to wallow helplessly, dead in the water. At around nine o'clock, the leading ship of the shadowing English fleet, the 210-ton *Margaret and John*, a privateer financed by the City of London, scenting the rich sweet smell of prize money, closed on the stricken Spaniard. At the English fleet's approach, Ojeda's galleon and four guardship pinnaces promptly abandoned their charge and headed back to the main body of the Armada, now south of Start Point in Devon. The disabled ship was showing no lights nor any sign of life. John Fisher, the *Margaret and John*'s captain, cautiously brought his ship close in and fired several volleys of musket fire into the *Rosario*'s stern gallery. It must have seemed like disturbing a hornets' nest, for Valdés immediately fired off two cannon shots. The English vessel replied with its own salvo and, discretion being the better part of valour, withdrew a short distance to await events.

Overnight there was a light breeze, probably with banks of fog hugging close to the surface of the sea. Howard, in *Ark Royal*, accompanied by two great ships, Lord Edmund Sheffield's 1,000-ton *Bear* and Edmund Fenton's 600-ton *Marie Rose*, led the fleet as it followed Drake's stern lantern.

Sometime in the early hours, the light disappeared.

Most ships prudently hove to. The admiral was summoned from his cabin, but his fears were soon eased by the lookout's call that a light could be seen again dead ahead. It was further away than expected, but it must be Drake's lantern. In Howard's anxious haste to catch up, most of the English fleet were left behind and scattered. Dawn on Monday 1 August revealed them only as topmasts low on the western horizon, beating before a moderate westerly wind.[32]

More worryingly, there was no sign of Drake's *Revenge*.

Instead, *Ark Royal* and her two companion ships found themselves hard up against the rearguard of the Armada, now approaching

Berry Head, near Brixham in Devon. The light they had been following was not Drake's but a lantern mounted on the poop deck of an enemy warship.

Immediately recognising *Ark Royal* as the English flagship, Admiral Hugo de Moncada, commander of the Neapolitan squadron of four galleasses, begged Medina Sidonia to allow him to engage the three isolated English ships. His oar-powered ships, with powerful guns mounted in the bows, could ignore the vagaries of the wind and achieve considerable speeds for short distances. These, he argued forcibly, were the best vessels to attack the English warships, cut off any chance of their escape, and blow them out of the water. But for some reason, 'this liberty the duke thought not good to permit unto him'. What was the captain-general's motivation? Was he, like Howard, convinced that only admirals should fight admirals? Or was he yet again obeying Philip's instructions to avoid battle if possible?

While this debate was raging in the Spanish fleet, Howard and his two ships heeled round and escaped.

The lord admiral's great fear now was that the enemy intended to land in nearby Torbay. It would be many hours before the remainder of the English fleet could catch up, leaving the Devon coast vulnerable and unprotected.

Where was Drake? As dawn broke, *Revenge* was spotted hove to near the damaged Spanish squadron flagship *Rosario*, in company with Captain Jacob Whitton's 300-ton Plymouth privateer *Roebuck*[33] and two of Drake's pinnaces.

Sometime during the night five of those seven English Catholics on board the Spaniard had slipped away by boat, only too cognisant of their fate if captured by the queen's navy.

Valdés initially rejected Drake's call to surrender. Later, flattered by the reputation of his adversary, he agreed to come aboard *Revenge* to discuss the terms of capitulation. These were generous. He was granted time to consider the offer alone, after which he yielded. His ship became Drake's prize, but Valdés was royally entertained to dinner as Drake's guest and his men treated as prisoners of war, possibly to be exchanged at a future date. Valdés reported afterwards: 'He gave us his hand and word of a gentleman and promised he would use us better than any others who would come to his hands.'[34]

Drake could not believe his good fortune when he discovered the

50,000 gold ducats, which were immediately transferred in canvas bags to *Revenge*. With them went a box of jewel-hilted swords that Philip had sent as gifts to England's noble Catholic families.[35] Whitton towed the prize into Dartmouth and the ship was stripped of its ordnance, munitions and gunpowder to help alleviate the shortages in the English fleet. Most of the four hundred prisoners were sent to rot in prison. The two English captives were taken by a Captain Cely to the Tower of London as 'rebels and traitors to their country'. One, named as Tristram Winslade, was handed to Walsingham's officers, who were told to interrogate him 'using torture ... at their pleasure'.[36] Forty Spaniards were held in the Bridewell gaol, 'there to be entertained with such diet as English prisoners have in Spain'.[37]

On rejoining the fleet, Drake soon bluffed his way out of what could have been an awkward situation. His disingenuous version of events was quite straightforward: shortly after midnight, sighting strange sails to starboard and believing them to be Spanish, he doused his lantern and set off in hot pursuit. Later he discovered they were merely German *Hansa* merchant hulks and *Revenge* was set back on a course to rejoin the lord admiral as soon as possible. Imagine Drake's surprise when, at dawn, he found himself 'within two or three cables of the *Rosario*'.

Doubtless Howard deemed it impolitic to court-martial one of England's naval heroes at a time of national emergency – even though, through his actions, the English fleet had lost both time and distance in chasing the Armada. Had the Spanish successfully landed in Torbay, the fault would have been entirely down to Drake and his lust for ducats.

Most of Drake's contemporaries seemed more inclined to envy him than castigate his dereliction of duty, with the exception of Martin Frobisher, captain of the *Triumph*, who seethed: '[Drake's] light we looked for but there was no light to be seen ... like a coward [Drake had] kept by her [the *Rosario*] all night because he would have the spoil. He thinks to cozen [cheat] us out of our share of 50,000 ducats. But we will have our shares or I will make him spend the best blood in his belly.'[38]

A second, less valuable prize fell into English hands sometime after one o'clock that day. Believing the *San Salvador*, crippled in the previous day's explosion, to be in danger of sinking, Medina Sidonia gave the order for her surviving crewmen to abandon ship. Within her forward magazine were 130 barrels of gunpowder and her hold contained 2,246 rounds of cannon shot; a naval commander of more experience would have ordered her to be scuttled to prevent these munitions falling into enemy hands, but the captain-general merely cast her adrift.

Late that evening, the English fleet found the *San Salvador* still afloat. Howard dispatched his cousin Lord Thomas Howard in *Lion* and John Hawkins in *Victory* to claim her as a prize. On boarding the wreck, they discovered

> a very pitiful sight, the deck of the ship fallen down, the steerage broken, the stern blown out and about fifty poor creatures burnt with powder in the most miserable [way]. The stink in the ship was so unsavoury and the sight within, that Lord Thomas Howard and John Hawkins shortly departed.

Captain Fleming, who had brought news of the Armada's arrival to Howard, was deputed to tow the *San Salvador* into Weymouth on the Dorset coast. There she was stripped of her gunpowder and munitions, which were ferried to the English ships out at sea by a fleet of small coasters.

Some of the Cornish militia, ordered to march eastwards to reinforce the neighbouring counties, thought they had done more than enough to serve their queen. The Spanish fleet had passed their coast and now it was someone else's problem. Their minds were on the harvest back home and these reluctant soldiers decided to slink away from their commanders and their colours.[39]

FIRESTORM

It was devised to put [the Armada] from their anchor and [eight] ships were allotted to the fire to perform the enter-prise; among them the ship I had in charge, the Barque Talbot ... So now I rest like one that had his house burnt and one of these days I must come to your honour for a commission to go a-begging.

Henry White to Sir Francis Walsingham,
Margate, Kent, 8 August 1588.[1]

On 23 July 1588, the Privy Council instructed the lords lieuten-ants of the English counties to mobilise their forces and, within six days, to send those earmarked to repel the invasion to Stratford by Bow in Essex as 'the Spanish fleet has now of late been discov-ered again on the seas'. In addition, a further six thousand men were based in Kent, facing Parma's threatening forces in Flanders. As English military planners remained uncertain exactly where the invaders might splash ashore, the remaining local militia should be ready 'upon the firing of the beacons to ... impeach such attempt as the enemy may make to land his forces in any place'. In addition, the lieutenants were told to ensure good order in every town and 'to stay and apprehend all vagabonds, rogues and suspected persons that are like to plod up and down to [cause] disorders and if any such be found ... tending to stir trouble or rebellion, to cause such to be executed by martial law'.[2]

During that month filled with apprehension and anxiety, Leicester was commissioned lieutenant and captain-general of Elizabeth's armies 'in the south parts' to fight not only the invaders but any 'rebels and traitors and other offenders and their adherents attempt-ing anything against us, our crown and dignity' and to 'repress and subdue, slay or kill and put to death by all ways and means' any such insurgents 'for the conservation of our person and peace'.³ A Captain Cripps was appointed provost marshal to execute these draconian legal sanctions. To avoid the danger of the militia having fifth-columnist recusants in their ranks, each officer and soldier had to swear an oath of loyalty to Elizabeth before their muster-masters.⁴ The nightmare spectre of large-scale Catholic support for a Spanish invasion was still seen as a clear and present danger to the English throne.

Richard Rogers, pastor of the parish of Westerfield, near Ipswich in Suffolk, recorded in his diary: 'We are now in peril of goods, liberty [and] life by our enemies the Spaniards and at home, papists in multitudes ready to come upon us [as] usurpers.' His parishioners marked the departure of their local militia by fasting for their success.⁵

A proclamation warned against the 'wicked and traitorous lies' that suggested the Spanish were merely trying to defend English Catholics. The truth, according to the English government, was that a defeated England would be 'subject to the Pope's will and the crown ... translated to ... a foreign potentate as he shall name ...' There would be 'a tyrannical conquest ... by depriving of her majesty and by slaughter of all her subjects, both noble and others, as shall, for their conscience towards Almighty God, persist in the true profession of Christian religion ... and their allegiance towards her majesty'. This 'crown, kingdom, country and ancient liberty, wherein it has remained and been inhabited with kings and people of ... English blood more than this five hundred years' was now facing its gravest threat.⁶

The Tudor propaganda machine grew more strident as the Spanish fleet appeared on England's southern doorstep, delivering a terrifying message of genocide and ethnic cleansing to stiffen a fearful population's resistance. Mendoza's spies reported that Elizabeth's ministers, 'being in great alarm, made the people believe that the Spaniards [are] bringing a shipload of halters in the Armada to hang all Englishmen and another shipload of scourges to whip women, with 3,000 or 4,000 wet nurses to suckle the infants. It is said that all children between the ages of seven and twelve would be branded in the face so that they might always be known. These and other things of the same sort greatly irritated the people.' A rumour at court claimed 'the Spaniards have orders from their king to slaughter all English people, men and women, over the age of seven years' – a story that later spread throughout London. 'We know that the only object of this is to incense the people against the Spaniards,' one spy commented.[7]

While the Armada sailed up the English Channel, all foreigners were forbidden to leave their houses and their shops were closed up.[8] If all of this was less than subtle misinformation, it served to fuel existing rampant xenophobia, always a prominent attribute of the English character during the Tudor period (if not now, more than four centuries later).[9] Petruccio Ubaldini, chronicler of the Armada campaign, was continually harassed in the London streets and asserted ruefully that it was easier 'to find flocks of white crows than one Englishman who loves a foreigner'.[10]

There were indications that the prospect of a Spanish invasion aroused unexpected patriotism even among the most hardened recusants. Some of those interned in Wisbech Castle petitioned Burghley to be allowed to fight as ordinary soldiers alongside their Protestant countrymen. Their offer was politely rebuffed by the lord treasurer, who pointed out that shutting them up would be more helpful to the queen 'than the help of many hands'.[11]

Such loyalty did not always burn brightly in the hearts of Elizabeth's untrained and ill-armed soldiers. Later, as the Armada anchored off Calais, the four thousand militia based in frontline Dover deserted in large numbers, possibly because of their lack of pay, but more probably through abject fear at what was happening immediately across the English Channel. Philip's agents observed that they could only muster twenty-two companies of one hundred men each and were 'in very poor condition'.[12] The port's defences were stiffened by importing a contingent of eight hundred Dutch musketeers.[13] There were also disquieting uncertainties about the faithfulness of the inhabitants of Kent. Walsingham's omnipresent informers reported that some publicly rejoiced 'when any report was [made] of [the Spaniards'] good success and sorrowed for the contrary' whilst others contended that the Spanish 'were better than the people of this land'.[14]

Ministers were meeting in almost permanent and frenetic session at Richmond Palace, upriver from London, as the running battle

unfolded off the south coast. Previous sins of omission and procrastination over expenditure were dreadfully revealed. Defensive
works which should have been finished weeks ago had to be rushed
through. Sir Robert Constable, lieutenant of the ordnance, was
ordered to send 'as many wheelbarrows as he can conveniently provide, or in lieu, twenty dozen baskets or more' to the uncompleted
fort at Gravesend, to enable the sweating labour force to complete
its earth and timber fortifications.[15] Lord Buckhurst was urged not
to dismiss his forces in Sussex just yet 'though their lordships do not
think the Spanish Navy will or dare attempt to land on that coast,
being followed by the lord admiral'. Five lasts of gunpowder were
dispatched to Portsmouth for Howard's fleet and a similar amount
to Brentwood in Essex, for Leicester's army.

Elizabeth's ministers were also forced to intervene in the exasperating quarrel between the still warring Earl of Sussex and Marquis
of Winchester in Hampshire, politely emphasising that it was the
queen's pleasure 'that they should dispose of themselves to better
agreement, [it] being requisite that in this troublesome time that no
unkindness should arise'. Patiently, they explained that a thousand
men 'might suffice to defend Portsmouth until her majesty's navy
might come to give them succour if occasion served'. Sir John Norris's
orders for its defence 'should be observed and not altered for breeding inconvenience and contention'.[16]

Sir Henry Seymour, awaiting Parma's departure, was desperate
for gunpowder, 'humbly praying' the council to send supplies for
which he had begged 'diverse times' previously. The following day,
his appeals were answered: ten lasts were sent to Kent for his ships,
'five by carriage over land and five by sea ... with all expedition'. But
Elizabeth had allowed the former monastic building of the Maison
Dieu (God's House) in Dover to fall out of use as a victualling estab-
lishment, so provisions for Seymour's squadron had to be sent by
water from Rochester and London. Richard Barry, lieutenant of
Dover, was instructed 'to cause such provision of beer to be brewed
... in Dover, Sandwich or other [of] the Cinque Ports ... for the use
of her majesty's navy'.[17] War at sea was a thirsty business.

In the first week of August, four thousand Essex militia arrived
at West Tilbury, on the northern shore of the Thames estuary,
'upon very good ground ... for the defence of this coast' as Leicester

reported to Walsingham. 'They [are] forward men and [are] all will-ing to meet with the enemy as ever I saw.' Such was the hustle in concentrating the army, that they carried no food with them 'so that at their arrival here, there was not a barrel of beer or a loaf of bread for them. Enough after twenty-mile (32.19 km) march to have been discouraged and to have mutinied, but all with one voice … said they would abide more hunger than this to serve her majesty and the country,' Leicester noted approvingly. He had sought one hundred tuns (large barrels) of beer to await their arrival but these had not been delivered, so he delayed the march of a further thousand men from London 'till we may provide for them here'. Food and drink for the army was going to be a problem, as Leicester had discovered.

> I did two whole days before the coming of these make proclamation in all market towns for victuallers to come to the place where the soldiers … encamp and to receive ready money for it but there is not one victualler come in to this hour.[18]

Reading the letters and dispatches written during those days of national peril, one senses something approaching a barely controlled panic gripping Elizabeth's government. Walsingham writes of 'more travail than ever I was in before' and was horrified when he heard of sailors deserting from Howard's and Seymour's ships. The spymaster had also received reports that Parma 'is looked to issue out presently' and for security, 'has suffered no stranger this seven or eight days to come to him or to see his army and ships, but he has blindfolded them'.[19]

Henry Carey, First Lord Hunsdon, lord chamberlain and the queen's cousin, had also been appointed lieutenant general com-manding the army to protect her person. This force, totalling almost 29,000 infantry and 4,400 cavalry, was to concentrate at St James, on the western edge of London. The counties would also contrib-ute a further 10,000 reinforcements to be mustered in London by 7 August.[20]

Abroad, the Dutch parliament had answered Elizabeth's appeals for assistance and had stationed their admiral, Justin of Navarre, with twenty-four ships to blockade the Flemish coast to stop Parma's force crossing the Dover Straits. Another thrity-two vessels were off Sluys and 135 were patrolling outside Antwerp. But some Dutch leaders suspected that Spanish troops would attack Holland and Zeeland rather than England and had stopped any reinforcements being sent to Nassau's squadron. Seymour, in the Downs off Kent, observed wryly: 'The Hollanders are not with us and ... I think [the Dutch] desire more to regard their coast more than ours.'[21]

King James VI of Scotland proved a stauncher ally, at least on paper. He wrote to Elizabeth – 'Madam and dearest sister' – promising everything at his command to assist the fifty-four-year-old childless queen to defend her country. A cynic would suspect he already had his eye firmly fixed on the succession to the English crown, as he affirmed that 'in times of straits, true friends are best tried' and he counted himself such a friend to Elizabeth and her subjects:

> This time must move me to utter my zeal to the [Protestant] religion and how near a kinsman and neighbour I find myself to you and your country.
>
> I ... hereby offer unto you my forces, my person and all that I may command to be employed against [...] strangers in whatsoever fashion and by whatsoever means as may best serve for the defence of your country wherein I promise to behave myself not as a stranger and foreign prince but as your natural son and compatriot in all respects.

He prayed that Elizabeth could resolve the crisis 'with all possible speed' and wished her 'a success convenient to those that are invaded by God's professed enemies'. James concluded: 'I commit, madam and dearest sister, your person, estate and country to the blessed protection of the Almighty.'[22]

Meanwhile in the Channel, west of the Portland Bill isthmus in Dorset, Medina Sidonia had changed the shape of the Armada following another council of war late in the afternoon of Monday 1 August. Worried about the prospect of a simultaneous frontal attack by Seymour's ships in the east and an assault from the rear by Howard's squadrons, he divided his warships into two flotillas to protect his hulks, travelling at only two or three knots in the centre of the formation. The larger rearguard of forty-three ships was commanded by Don Alonso de Leyva and included the Portuguese galleons *San Mateo, San Luis* and *San Francisco de Florencia* and the Biscayan *Santiago*, together with the galleasses. The duke himself led the smaller vanguard of about twenty galleons.[23] With the memories of the Biscayan galleons fleeing during the previous day's fighting still raw in the captain-general's mind, his written orders warned grimly that the commander of any ship that quit its station would be hanged immediately. Provost marshals and hangmen accompanied the orders when they were delivered by *pataches*, to reinforce the import of his message.[24]

Howard wrote to Walsingham requesting urgent reinforcements: 'I pray [you send] out to me all such ships as you have ready [for sea at] Portsmouth with all possible speed. They shall find us steering east-north-east after the fleet. We mean so to course the enemy as that they shall have no leisure to land.'[25]

That night the wind dropped. Both combatant fleets found themselves becalmed in Lyme Bay, off the Dorset coast. Dawn at five o'clock on Tuesday 2 August brought a light north-easterly breeze which later veered to the south-east. The Armada had Portland Bill almost abeam to port and the wind direction provided them with the weather gauge for the first time since they had passed the Eddystone Rock. Medina Sidonia ordered Hugo de Moncada to attack the leading English ships with his Neapolitan galleasses, but possibly because of his rebuffed plea to attack Howard and his isolated ships twenty-four hours earlier, he huffily declined. The English took advantage of this hiatus, with the lord admiral's ship heading a line of galleons, sailing close to the wind, to pass the Spanish left or northern flank inshore and win back the weather gauge. But Medina Sidonia led his squadron to cut him off, forcing the English ships to come about and head south-east. Martin de Bertendona's Levantine flagship *Ragazona* tried to board one ship, possibly *Ark Royal,* but she deftly turned seaward and quickly opened the range between them, pursued by the *San Marcos, San Luis, San Mateo, Rata Santa María Encoronada* and other vessels of the *socorro.*

By nine o'clock, the engagement was four miles (6.44 km) off Portland and had developed into a confused series of skirmishes with Howard's agile ships still out-manoeuvring any attempts to board them. A separate English squadron of five armed merchantmen (*Centurion, Merchant Royal, Margaret and John, Marie Rose* and *Golden Lion*) led by Martin Frobisher's mighty 1,100-ton *Triumph,* found itself becalmed just south of Portland Bill and the captain-general, seeing a possibly decisive naval coup, ordered Moncada's red-and-gold-painted galleasses to attack the group.

Frobisher's ships were not as helpless as they seemed. They may well have been stationed as a trap, to take advantage of the notorious seven-knot tidal race that passes immediately south of Portland Bill, caused by 'The Shambles', a shingle and shell bank just to the south-east. With Moncada's *San Lorenzo* in the lead, the galleasses opened fire with their powerful bow guns on Frobisher and a smaller ship which soon seemed to be in trouble, as her crew were seen jumping into their boats. But as much as the galleasses tried to close on *Triumph,* using their oars as well as sails, they were swept back, the turbulent waters of the Portland Race threatening to swamp them. The English gunfire had been directed at the rowers and some had been cut to ribbons, their oars becoming hopelessly entangled as they slumped lifeless on their benches. An officer in the *Zúñiga* said that while they were attacking Frobisher and two other ships

> five of the enemy's galleons bore down on the galleasses, the wind at this time [one o'clock] having suddenly shifted [to the south] so that the enemy had it astern while we had it against us.
>
> Consequently none of our ships could come to our aid. The galleasses therefore had to run and join the rest of the Armada.[26]

Medina Sidonia was unsympathetic at their plight. He sent a senior officer to Moncada to 'say aloud to Don Hugo ... certain words which were not to his honour'[27] and that night sent a note to him that declared harshly: 'A fine day this has been! If the galleasses had come up as I expected, it would have gone badly for the enemy.'[28]

The change in wind direction once more handed the weather gauge to the grateful English and Drake's squadron attacked the rearguard forming the southerly flank of the Armada with Recalde's *San Juan* coming first under fire from a dozen English ships. Other Spanish ships gave way in the face of the galling cannonades and Recalde complained indignantly of this lack of assistance 'from any other ship in the fleet because they all seemed to want to take refuge one behind the other, so that they fled from the action and collided together. It is a disgrace to mention it.'[29] Eventually, fourteen large Spanish galleons were ordered to assist Recalde.

The English fleet switched its main attack on to Medina Sidonia's now isolated flagship, *San Martin*, firing at her as each vessel, *Ark, Elizabeth Jonas, Leicester, Golden Lion, Victory, Marie Rose, Dreadnought* and the *Swallow* swept past. Calderón, in the hulk *San Salvador*, reported that the duke's ship replied with more than eighty shots from its forty-eight guns, but the enemy had fired 'at least five hundred cannonballs, some of which struck his hull and others his rigging, carrying away his flagstaff and one of the stays of his mainmast'.[30] The holy banner was rent in two and the flagship began to take in water from roundshot holes in the hull which were swiftly plugged by battle-damage teams. *San Martin* was so enveloped in gun-smoke that observers on other Armada ships could not see her for more than an hour. Spanish vessels crowded around their flagship as the last of Drake's squadron came up, shielding it from the English barrages, and the *San Martin* safely rejoined the Armada. During this engagement, William Coxe, captain of the 50-ton pinnace *Delight*, 'showed himself most valiant in the face of his enemies at the hottest of the encounter', Howard reported. 'At which assault, after a wonderful sharp conflict, the Spaniards were forced to give way and flock together like sheep.'[31]

An English (probably official) account of the action said the fight 'was very nobly continued from morning to evening, the lord admiral being always [in] the hottest [part] of the encounter'.

> It may well be said there was never a more terrible value of great shot, nor more hot fight than this was for although the musketeers and harquebusiers of crock[32] were then infinite, yet could they not be discerned nor heard that the great ordnance came so thick that a man would have judged it to have been a hot skirmish of small shot, being all the fight long within half a musket shot of the enemy.[33]

Another narrative, by a sailor who spent two days with the Spanish fleet and later landed in Brielle, on the mouth of the New Maas in south Holland, confirmed these descriptions of the furious artillery duel off Portland, claiming that the English 'fired four shots to every one of the Spaniards'. He also reported some of the Armada ships in flames: 'When he left them and as long as they were in sight, there were great fires, as if several ships were burning.' However, this is the only account of Spanish ships ablaze and he may have been misled by the thick billowing smoke of gunfire.[34]

At around five o'clock, Howard broke off the attack, probably again because of his crippling shortage of gunpowder. After almost twelve hours of confused fighting, no side could honestly claim victory, nor indeed had suffered anything approaching a defeat. Frustratingly for the belligerents, the stalemate at sea was continuing. Warships on both sides had been damaged, but no killer blow had been landed on any vessel. Most of the English guns had been fired at ranges beyond that of the heaviest Spanish cannon and at those distances, there was little chance of causing any substantial harm to enemy targets. Conversely, whether through inexperience, excitement or panic, the Spanish were also firing too early – long before the English came into lethal range of their own cannon. Around fifty Spanish had been killed and another sixty wounded, but the English butcher's bill was unknown.

In tactical terms, Medina Sidonia may have cut Howard's fleet in two, but he threw away any advantage gained by chasing the lord admiral's squadron as it briefly moved seaward, away from the battle. Had he concentrated his vanguard's firepower on Frobisher's six supposedly stranded ships, Medina Sidonia would have forced Howard to turn and fight on Spanish terms – or be obliged to abandon Frobisher to a grim fate. As far as Howard was concerned, the English fleet had been fragmented into three uncoordinated divisions which had acted independently, paying little regard to events elsewhere in the engagement.[35]

As the Armada plodded on slowly eastwards, Howard sent 'diverse barques and pinnaces on to the shore for more cannon shot and gunpowder'.[36] Fresh supplies were ferried out from Lyme, Weymouth and Portsmouth, but Elizabeth's government provided barely enough for any new engagement. Without the 220 barrels of powder and 3,600 roundshot salvaged from the captured *Rosario* and *San Salvador*, some of Howard's guns could have fallen silent.[37] John Hawkins, in his precise and neat handwriting, later told Walsingham: 'We had a sharp and long fight with them, wherein we spent a great part of our powder and shot so it was not thought good to deal with them any more, till that [shortage] was relieved.'[38]

That night, in his note to Moncada, Medina Sidonia emphasised that 'the important thing for us is to proceed with our voyage, for these people [the English ships] do not mean fighting but only to

delay our progress'. Accordingly, the captain-general had again tink-
ered with the Armada's formation, this time adopting a simple block
of ships with a vanguard and rearguard, commanded respectively
by Recalde and Leyva. This was the very same tactical formation
proposed weeks before by Don Pedro de Valdés during the Corunna
council of war. The captain-general, recalling the events of the
day, ended his letter to Moncada on a barbed note: 'You with your
flagship and two other galleasses will join the rearguard ... whilst
Captain Peruchio with his galleass *Patrona* [apparently an alternative name for the *Zúñiga*] will go in the vanguard with me. You will
keep the three galleasses well together and be ready to proceed without further orders to any point where they may be needed.'[39] With
his king's instructions still in the forefront of his mind, he might well
have added: 'I have dedicated this enterprise to God ... Pull yourself
together then and do your part!'

Medina Sidonia must have considered seizing a secure anchorage at Spithead[40] or elsewhere in the Solent (the sheltered sea strait
between the Isle of Wight and the English mainland), having agreed
at the onset of his passage up the Channel to pause at the island
to await news of Parma. Worryingly, the captain-general still had
heard nothing from the Spanish general and he was growing ever
more uneasy about awaiting the invasion barges off Margate on the
Kent coast. Here, he reasoned, the Armada could easily become a
sitting duck to attacks from both east and west by elements of the
English fleet. Better to hold a defensible anchorage, protected from
the weather at Spithead or the Solent – which, as his pilots would
have told him, enjoys a double tide, a phenomenon that brings longer
periods of high water. Here he would also have the chance to capture
and hold a beachhead on the northern coast of the Isle of Wight,
where he could replenish his water and forage for fresh food.[41]

Dawn on Wednesday 3 August revealed another problem for
Medina Sidonia. During the night, the 650-ton *El Gran Grifón*, flagship of the hulks squadron, had fallen behind the Armada rearguard
on its seaward flank. As the sun rose, Drake in *Revenge* was naturally the first among the shadowing English ships to close on the
hapless Spaniard. Clapping on as much sail as possible to exploit the
light south-south-westerly wind, the English vice-admiral came up
alongside, fired a rippling broadside at his wallowing target; came

about to fire a second and then swept past the stern, raking her with both cannon and musket shots. At least forty cannonballs hit the hulk, killing around sixty on her upper decks and wounding a further seventy. Flemish deserters claimed later that Drake's gunfire had miraculously killed only the English and Dutch exiles that were sailing with the Armada.[42]

Once again Recalde's *San Juan* was first on the scene, together with the Armada's flagship, and a series of fierce barrages were fired by both sides, perhaps upwards of 5,000 rounds. The mainmast of *Revenge* received a direct hit (bringing down the mainsail boom), from the stern guns of Moncada's galleasses, while a sister ship successfully took the *Gran Grifón* in tow.

The light breeze died away in the early afternoon, leaving both fleets drifting slowly eastwards towards The Needles, the line of white chalk sea stacks off the western tip of the Isle of Wight.[43]

Howard, only too well aware of the dangers posed by a Spanish occupation of the island or the seizure of an anchorage, called another council of war in *Ark Royal* to discuss how to block their entry into the Solent. He decided to reshape his fleet's tactical fighting formation into four independent squadrons of twenty-five ships apiece, commanded by himself, Drake, Frobisher and Hawkins. In addition, he ordered that six armed merchantmen from each squadron should 'set upon the Spanish fleet in sundry places at one instant in the night time to keep the enemy waking'.[44] Such plans to deny sleep to those in the Armada had to be cancelled that night because all ships were becalmed.

Thursday 4 August saw no return of the wind and the two fleets merely drifted on the current, with a speed more appropriate to that of a rowing boat than a galleon. It was St Dominic's Day, seen as auspicious by the Spanish because it celebrated Medina Sidonia's personal patron saint.

It always seemed improbable that the Armada would try to enter the Solent from the west as the narrow and shoaled tidal race between The Needles and the mainland would deny them sea room and they would be forced within range of the guns of Hurst Castle, on the end of a long hook-shaped shingle spit jutting into the channel from the mainland.[45] If the Spanish wanted a Solent anchorage, they would have to pass the southern cliffs of the Isle of Wight and enter from

the east, via St Helen's Roads.[46] Time and tide were firmly against
them as the flood would allow entry into the Solent only between
seven o'clock and noon that morning. Afterwards the current would
work against the Armada.[47]

Medina Sidonia wrote to Parma, informing him of his change of
plan: he would now steer for the coast of Flanders, rather than awaiting him off the North Foreland, near Margate. He also brought the
land commander up to date with the frustrations of his repeated
skirmishes with the English fleet:

> We have made but slow headway, owing to the calms that have beset
> us and the most I have been able to do is to arrive off the Isle of
> Wight.
>
> The enemy's ships have continued to bombard us and we were
> obliged to turn and face them so that the firing continued on most
> days from dawn to dusk ...
>
> The enemy has resolutely avoided coming to close quarters with
> our ships although I have tried my hardest to make him do so.
>
> I have given him so many opportunities that sometimes some of
> our vessels have been in the very midst of the enemy's fleet to induce
> one of his ships to grapple and begin the fight, but all to no purpose
> as his ships are very light and mine very heavy and he has plenty of
> men and stores.

The captain-general was also running low on munitions and asked
Parma 'to load speedily a couple of ships with powder and balls[48]
and to despatch them to me without the least delay'. He emphasised:

> It will also be advisable for [you] to make ready to put out at once
> to meet me, because, by God's grace, if the wind serves, I expect to
> be on the Flemish coast very soon.[49]

More fighting now confronted the Armada as Howard sought to
drive the Spanish safely past Selsey Bill, on the western tip of the
Sussex coast, far distant from any hope of gaining a Solent anchorage. He also nurtured hopes that some enemy ships would founder
on the Owers and Mixon reefs that lie off the low peninsula.

Early that morning, there were two more stragglers astern of the
Armada: the Portuguese vice-flagship *San Luis de Portugal* and
the Andalusian *Duquesa Santa Ana*. Were they laggards or bait in

another elaborate trap? The westerly wind was still very light, barely a breeze. The nearest English squadron was led by John Hawkins and because of the lack of headway he was forced to lower his boats to tow his flagship *Victory* into attack against the two Spanish vessels. Almost immediately, *San Lorenzo, Napolitana* and *Girona,* Moncada's three galleasses, recently attached to the rearguard, came up, their oars providing rapid propulsion in the flat calm. One towed the *Rata* into the fray to provide additional firepower. The jaws of this carefully laid ambush were about to snap shut.

Lord Thomas Howard's *Golden Lion* and Howard's *Ark Royal,* hampered by the same lack of wind, also had to resort to tows by their ship's tenders, and slowly moving into range on Hawkins' port side, opened fire on the galleasses. One began to list, another's prow or ram was damaged, and the third had its stern lantern shot away. The official English account was unusually vivid:

> Three of the galleasses and an armado[50] issued out of the Spanish fleet with whom the lord admiral and the Lord Thomas Howard fought a long time and much damaged them, that one ... was fain to be carried away upon the careen with another, by a shot from the *Ark* lost her lantern, which came swimming by, and the third his nose.
>
> There were many good shots made by the *Ark* and the *Lion* at the galleasses in the sight of both fleets, which looked on and could not approach, it being calm.[51]

It claimed that the oared vessels were so beaten about 'that the galleasses were never seen in fight any more', but their damage was plainly not too serious as they managed to tow away the two decoy galleons.

It was now around nine o'clock and the two fleets were south of the Isle of Wight's Dunnose Point, with Frobisher's ships close in to its yellow and red sandstone cliffs, riding the one-knot easterly current in an attempt to slip past the northern flank of the Armada. A brisk south-westerly had blown up and the fighting continued in the rear of the Armada with Howard and his squadron attacking the *San Martin*. Medina Sidonia described the fighting:

> They came closer than on the previous day, firing off their heaviest

guns from the lowest deck, cutting the trice [halyard] of our main-mast and killing some of our soldiers.

The *San Luis* came to the rescue and the enemy was also faced by Recalde, the *San Juan* [*Bautista*] of Diego Flores' squadron and [Miguel de] Oquendo, who placed himself before our flagship, as the current made it impossible for him to stand alongside ...[52]

Frobisher was unexpectedly becalmed as he exchanged shots with the *San Martin* and the galleass *San Lorenzo*, dutifully keeping station on her flagship. He lowered his ensign briefly and fired three signal guns to summon assistance. Eleven ship's boats from his squadron were sent to tow him to safety as the ships on the northern flank of the Armada attacked. Two of Howard's galleons, *Bear* and *Elizabeth Jonas*, swept in to delay the Spanish sortie. Then the wind suddenly freshened, *Triumph*'s sails were filled, and Frobisher rejoined his squadron. Calderón described how he made off so swiftly 'that [although] the galleon *San Juan* and another quick ship – the speediest vessels in the Armada – gave chase, [they] seemed ... to be standing still'.[53]

Medina Sidonia, again thwarted of a tactical victory and anxious about his low remaining stocks of munitions, fired a signal cannon to re-form the Armada in his new defensive 'roundel' (as the English called it) to continue on eastwards. Recalde had been closing on *Triumph* and was beside himself with fury at her escape and that the battle had ended suddenly and so inconclusively:

> As we were ... harassing the enemy and pressing home our victory, our flagship fired a signal gun to call us back, so we could resume our voyage.
>
> In my opinion, we should not have desisted as our flagship did, until we had either made them run aground or else followed them into a port.
>
> Nor was it wise to sail ... beyond that anchorage, near to the Isle of Wight, until we had heard from the Prince of Parma, because it was the best anchorage in the whole Channel.[54]

The Armada moved slowly forward, safely skirting the hazardous Owers reef six miles (10.16 km) south-east of Selsey Bill. Another fifty had been killed and seventy wounded in the day's fighting. The official Spanish casualty list for the three actions since they entered the English Channel totalled 167 dead and 241 wounded. This must be a dramatic understatement, given the losses when the *San Salvador* blew up, and may have been driven not only by the desire to put the best gloss on events, but more cynically, to allow commanders to claim the pay of those killed but not yet reported dead. The practice was prevalent in both fleets, as Burghley noted grimly: 'The men are dead but not the pay.' On the English side, Thomas Fenner, captain of the *Nonpareil* also played down his fleet's losses, writing to Walsingham:

> God has mightily protected her majesty's forces with the least losses that ever have been heard of, being in the compass of so great volleys of shot, both great and small.
>
> I verily believe there is not three score men lost of her majesty's forces.
>
> God make us all majesty's good subjects to render hearty praise and thanks to the Lord of Lords therefore.[55]

The fighting had been watched anxiously from the cliffs as the Wight's small force of defenders prepared to repel any landing. Its governor, Sir George Carey, had only three thousand men to protect the strategically important island and he must have worried what the day would bring. He sent his eye-witness account to London, which echoed others' earlier impressions of the intensity of the fighting:

> This morning began a great fight betwixt both fleets south of this island six leagues[56] which continued from five of the clock until ten with so great an expense of powder and bullet that during the said time the shot continued so thick together that it might have been judged a skirmish with small shot on land than a fight with great shot on sea in which conflict, thanks be to God, there has been [only] two of our men hurt.
>
> The news in the fleet [is] that my Lord Harry Seymour is hardly laid unto by the Dunkirkers and that Scilly is taken by the French or Spanish.

(Neither of these rumours was true: Seymour had not been attacked by Spanish forces based in Dunkirk and the Scilly Islands had not been captured.) The two embattled fleets had sailed out of sight by three that afternoon.[57]

Both sides had fired a further four thousand rounds during the day's fighting and Howard, like his enemy, was still short of gunpowder and shot.

> For as much as our powder and shot was well wasted [used], the lord admiral thought it was not good in policy to assail them any more until their coming near unto Dover, where he should find the fleet under ... Lord Henry Seymour and Sir William Wynter, whereby our fleet should be much strengthened and in the meantime, better store of munition might be provided from the shore.

Walsingham, in response, ordered 'twenty-three last [to be] sent unto him with a proportion of bullet accordingly'.[58]

That day the Privy Council also wrote to Howard promising more musketeers:

> Her highness, being very careful that your lordship be supplied with all the provisions that may be had, has [ordered] that in the county of Kent, a good number of the best and choicest shot of the trained bands ... should be forthwith sent to the seaside ... that they may be brought to you to double man the ships that are both with your lordship and the Lord Henry Seymour.[59]

A battle at close quarters was now a priority in Howard's tactical plan.

Further east in the Channel, Seymour was agitated about the weakness of his squadron. He told the Privy Council: 'I have besides to signify to your Lordships that our fleet being from the first promised to be seventy-eight sail, there was never yet when the same was [at] most thirty-six and now we have not above twenty.' Of these, just eight were queen's ships, apart from pinnaces. 'I am driven to write this much because in my former letters, your lordships, having many matters, do forget them.'[60] Eight more armed merchantmen, hired in London, were sent 'into the narrow seas' under the command of Nicholas Gorges: *Susan Anne Parnell, Solomon, George Bonaventure, Anne Frances, Vineyard, Violet, Samuel* and *Jane Bonaventure*.

Seymour was right to be concerned; Sir Edward Norris reported from Ostend that Parma 'is looked for at Dunkirk now this full moon to see the shipping and the heights of the water. All the cavalry that they can possibly make do march towards Dunkirk. The voyage [to] England now is spoken more assuredly than ever.'[61]

In London, the incarcerated Philip Howard, Earl of Arundel, in his room in the Tower, allegedly secretly celebrated Masses for the success of the Armada. Information about these services came from John Snowden, the other Englishman captured in the *Rosario*, who sought to save himself from a horrible traitor's death on the Tyburn scaffold. He filched a missal and sent it to Walsingham as proof of his changed loyalties. William Bennet, the old priest who purportedly said the Masses, was moved to another gaol, the Counter in Wood Street (one of the sheriff's prisons in the City of London), and questioned there. His confession, 'written with his own hand' but hardly freely given, was damning:

> The Earl of Arundel [had] said: 'Let us pray now, for we have more need to pray now than at any time. If it pleases God, the Catholic faith shall flourish. Now is the time at hand of our delivery.'
>
> Moreover, the earl said that he would make me dean [of St Paul's Cathedral] if the Catholic enterprise took hold.
>
> I call to mind that when the said earl [heard] of the discovery of the Spanish fleet, he desired me in the presence of Sir Thomas Gerard[62] to say Mass of the Holy Ghost that it would please God to send them good success.
>
> So I said Mass to his lordship and he did help me say the same. At which Mass, Sir Thomas Gerard and Hammond,[63] servant unto the earl, were present.[64]

A confession was also extracted from Gerard who admitted:

> [the earl] told us that the Spanish fleet was seen in the narrow seas, like unto a huge forest [of masts] and our fleet was not able to deal with them ...
>
> The queen and the council were greatly afraid of their approach and then [he] sorrowfully said: 'God save my brother Thomas [who had volunteered to serve in the English fleet] ... and I hope,' said the earl, 'ere long ... to say Mass openly and to see the Catholic faith flourish again.'

Arundel had also asked the other priests imprisoned in the Tower to pray 'for the advance of the Catholic enterprise all the twenty-four hours of the day'.[65]

When the earl was questioned on these allegations, Lord Hunsdon, one of his interrogators, was enraged by his calmness and composure, calling him a 'beast and traitor and said rather than he should not be hanged within four days, that he himself would hang him'. Arundel's impeachment for high treason was unavoidable.[66]

Not all members of the Catholic nobility were so militant in their faith. A prominent papist, the sixty-two-year-old Anthony Browne, First Viscount Montague, had been thrown off the Privy Council on Elizabeth's accession and removed as lieutenant of Sussex in 1585 because of the invasion threat. Now one of his brothers was serving with the Armada. But on 2 August, Browne, having heard of the firing of the beacon on Portsdown Hill above Portsmouth, volunteered himself and his retainers in Elizabeth's defence, complaining that he 'had not received letters as others have done for attendance of her majesty's person'.[67] His willingness to serve against the Spanish was an enormous propaganda coup for the English government.

Back in the Channel, Friday 5 August, coasters replenished Howard with munitions, as both fleets lay becalmed off the Sussex coast and undertook emergency repairs. That evening, as the wind freshened, the lord admiral summoned another council of war and it was decided not to fight the Armada again until they reached the Dover Straits. Howard took advantage of the occasion to exercise his prerogative as a commander and knighted Hawkins, Frobisher, Lord Thomas Howard, Lord Sheffield and the eighty-year-old captain of *Dreadnought,* George Beeston.

The wind continued to increase during the night and, with more speed, the Armada sighted the French coast at ten o'clock that Saturday morning. Medina Sidonia's pilots had cautioned him to anchor in the Calais Roads if he did not want to be swept into the North Sea by the strong currents. Accordingly, at about four o'clock that afternoon, the Spanish fleet dropped anchor 4 miles (6.44 km) off the French port of Calais and 24 miles (38.62 km) along the coast from Parma's nearest embarkation port of Dunkirk. Howard's shadowing English fleet anchored in Whitsand Bay, just outside cannon range, and Seymour's thirty-five ships arrived a few hours later. To leeward lay shallow waters full of sandbanks, known as the 'banks of Flanders', which had been made still more perilous by the Dutch deliberately removing the buoys and navigation marks.[68]

Although the French were officially neutral, boats were seen going back and forth between the *San Martin* and Calais castle, head-quarters of the town's governor, de Gourdan. He had earlier lost a leg fighting the English so it was no surprise that Medina Sidonia's envoy, a Captain Heredia, returned with 'friendly assurances and promises of service'. The captain-general wrote to Parma, announcing his arrival off Calais but not hiding his exasperation at the continuing silence from Flanders.

> I have constantly written ... giving you information as to my where-abouts with the Armada and not only have I received no reply to my letters but no acknowledgement of their receipt ...
>
> I am extremely anxious at this as [you] may imagine and to free myself of the doubt as to any of the messengers have reached you safely, I am now despatching this flyboat.

The enemy remained on his flank and was 'able to bombard me, whilst I am not in a position to do him much harm'. Forty or fifty small ships from Parma's fleet were needed to augment the Armada's defences in such shallow waters. When he finally sailed 'we can go together and take some port where this Armada may enter in safety'.[69]

Reports of the Spanish fleet's progress had not yet reached Flanders, judging by the reaction of the English negotiators at the Bourbourg peace talks. At three o'clock that afternoon, the English delegation received news of the first engagement off Plymouth six days before. They promptly packed their baggage and departed after making a voluble protest.[70] Parma, in ignorance of the news, initially believed this was merely a negotiating ploy. 'My efforts to induce them to continue the negotiations, notwithstanding the presence of the Armada, were unavailing,' he told the king.[71]

Medina Sidonia at last received a reply from Parma at dawn the following day. Don Rodrigo Tello's pinnace was fired upon by some of the Armada ships, who mistakenly believed it an English vessel, but after showing its colours, it delivered its message, which had been written three days before. Its contents must have stunned Medina Sidonia into dumbfounded silence.

Parma was not ready to sail. He had not even embarked 'a barrel of beer, still less a soldier'. He would not be able to join forces with the Armada until the following Friday, 12 August.

Worse, a subsequent message warned that embarkation could take fifteen days.[72]

The delays were spawned by Parma's attempts to hoodwink the Dutch, who were watching his every movement. His troops were held back from the embarkation ports to fool them into believing his plan was to invade Holland or Zeeland. To create uncertainty about his port of embarkation, the invasion fleet was split between Sluis, Dunkirk, Nieuport and Antwerp, where there were seventy ships, including Parma's flagship and a large oared galley, which had been built on site. Pioneers had excavated a new canal, ten yards (9.14 metres) wide, to take the flat-bottomed barges from Sluis to Nieuport. One hundred and seventy-three barges were at Nieuport, together with seven armed merchantmen, which would join almost one hundred transport vessels at Dunkirk for the crossing.[73] Parma had 15,300 men waiting at Dunkirk and a further 5,000 at Nieuport, with other units moving towards the harbours.

In a dispatch to Philip, Parma said his boats were

> in a proper condition for the task they have to effect, namely to take the men across, although we have not so many seamen as we ought to have ...
>
> The boats are so small that it is impossible to keep the troops on board for long. There is no room to turn round and they would certainly fall ill, rot and die.
>
> The putting of the men on board of these low, small boats is done in a very short time and I am confident there will be no shortcoming in your majesty's service.

It grieved him to learn of Medina Sidonia's position 'without a place of safety in case of necessity, whilst the winds that have prevailed for so long still continue. The wind will prevent our boats coming out, even if the sea were clear of the enemy's ships. But I trust in God that He will aid us in everything and allow us shortly to send your majesty the good news we wish for.'[74]

The next day, Sunday 7 August, while fresh water and food were being loaded into his ships (and some of his crews seized the opportunity to desert), Medina Sidonia sent his inspector general, Don Jorge Manrique, to Parma to explain his predicament. His current position was dangerous

> in consequence of the lack of shelter and the strong currents which will force me to clear away at the least sign of bad weather. I therefore beg you to hasten your coming out before the spring tides end. The general opinion is that it will be inadvisable for the Armada to go beyond this place.

Yet, he could not stay much longer anchored off Calais and it was 'impossible to continue cruising' as the size of the Spanish ships, 'cause [them] to be always to the leeward of the enemy ... It is impossible to do any damage to him, hard as we may try.' Later, Don Jorge became involved in a fierce quarrel with Parma over his lack of readiness and the general 'was only restrained from laying violent hands' on him by those around him.[75]

Nearly 2,500 yards (2,286 metres) away, Howard sat discussing future tactics with his commanders in the stern cabin of *Ark Royal*. The pressing need remained disrupting and dispersing the densely packed Armada, so they could be picked off, ship by ship, by the now numerically stronger English fleet. Furthermore, some enemy ships could founder on the shoals immediately to the north.

The effective answer was fireships. Local conditions favoured such an attack: that night fortuitous spring tides and a freshening westerly breeze would ensure the blazing vessels were swept into the heart of the Armada, riding helplessly at anchor. The stratagem was a powerful weapon of destruction but also a potent means of attacking enemy morale. The Spanish remembered all too well the 'hell-burners of Antwerp' during their siege of the Dutch city in April 1585 when the Italian Fedrigo Giambelli had loaded vessels with explosives and launched them against a Spanish pontoon bridge, killing over eight hundred of their troops and flinging wreckage over more than a square mile (259 hectares). The Spanish knew that Giambelli was in England but they were not aware he was only occupied in building an ineffective defensive boom across the Thames.

A pinnace was dispatched to Dover, where Walsingham had

ordered fireships to be made ready. But these would not arrive in time to exploit the favourable wind and tide, so Howard ordered eight vessels from his fleet, all displacing between 90 and 200 tons, to be converted. Drake and Hawkins immediately volunteered two of their own ships, the *Thomas Drake* and the *Barque Bond* respectively. The remainder, Henry White's *Barque Talbot,* William Hart's *Hope Hawkins,* the *Bear Yonge, Elizabeth of Lowestoft* and another vessel, only identified as 'Cure's Ship', were all armed merchantmen, chartered for the campaign. The final designated fireship was a volunteer, the *Angel* of Southampton. They were anchored in the midst of the fleet to hide the preparations and work began packing them with pitch, rags and old timber as combustibles and the masts and rigging were painted with tar.

Medina Sidonia had recognised the danger and during the afternoon he stationed a screen of pinnaces outside his perimeter, equipped with grappling irons, to tow off any attacking fireships. In the event of such an attack, he ordered his fleet to slip their anchors and stand out to sea while the fireships harmlessly burnt out.

That night Parma began to embark his men on the barges in Dunkirk and Nieuport.[76]

Off Calais, Medina Sidonia saw lights moving up and down the lines of English ships and, worried what the *edemoniada gente* – the 'infernal devils' – might be up to, ordered a sharp lookout on his ships.

The tide turned at eleven o'clock. The English launched their attack soon after midnight, double-shotting the fireships' saker cannon (to be set off by the heat of the blaze), to increase panic in the Armada. The ships were commanded by a Devon man, Captain John Young (of the *Bear Yonge*), with the Cornish Captain Prouse as his deputy. They and their skeleton volunteer crews steered the ships in a perfect line abreast towards their target and with about fifteen minutes before the first Spanish ship was reached, lit the fires and then escaped in five boats towed behind the vessels. Because of the shortage of gunpowder, there were no explosives on board.

Two fireships, well ablaze, with fountains of sparks flying up against the moonless sky, were successfully grappled by Medina Sidonia's pinnaces and towed into the shallows but six came on, driven by the strong westerly wind, their guns firing roundshot in the blood-red heat. The hoped-for terror spread like a deadly contagion among the Spanish ships.

Vice-Admiral Sir William Wynter, in *Vanguard*, watched the attack with great gratification:

> This matter did put such terror among the Spanish [fleet] that they were fain to let slip their cables and anchors and did work, as it appear, great mischief among them by reason of the suddenness of it. We might perceive that there were two great fires more than ours and far greater and huger than any of our vessels that we fired could make.[77]

Calderón was woken by the shouts of alarm:

> The enemy set adrift, with their sails set and the tide in their favour, eight ships with artificial machines on board which came towards us all in flames, burning furiously in the bows, with the mainsails and foresails set and the rudders lashed. [A] galle[ass] which was near the duke's flagship, fired a shot warning [to] our ships to avoid them and the duke ordered our cables cut, the Armada then sailing in a northerly direction.[78]

In fact, it was Diego Flores de Valdés, panic-stricken like many in the Armada, who ordered the cables to be cut.

Medina Sidonia saw the six ships penetrating his defensive screen and, fearing that the fireships 'might contain fire machines or mines' ordered the *San Martin* to let go her anchor cables. He had sent the Prince of Asculi[79] out in a *felucca* to ensure that the ships had buoyed their anchors and, with an extraordinary sense of bad timing, to summon his captains to a council of war. Recalde, in *San Juan* was having none of that. He shouted down that 'this was no time for him to leave his ship and [anyway] his advice counted for nothing'. The prince called back that 'his vote did not count' either.[80]

One after the other, the Armada ships ran before the wind, scattering in Calais Roads in a confused mêlée, some swept northwards by the current towards the sandbanks off the Flemish coast.

Moncada's flagship *San Lorenzo* had been tardy in cutting her anchor and once under way, collided with her sister galleass *Girona* before crashing her stern into the *Rata Encoronada*. Moncada's poop deck was smashed and his rudder gear broken by becoming entangled in the anchor cable of the Neapolitan, leaving him with no steering. As the fireships sailed nearer, the soldiers on board escaped by climbing ropes thrown over the side of the *Rata*. The *San Lorenzo*'s convict oarsmen 'began to cry out pitifully and to hammer at their chains and fetters in the hope of escaping by jumping in the sea, preferring to die by water than by fire'.[81] Moncada tried ineffectively to repair his rudder and dismissed offers by two French pinnaces to take him in tow. Perhaps their price was too high.

The galleass squadron commander eventually paid a higher one. His drifting ship grounded on a sandbank just off the mouth of Calais harbour and was left marooned in the heavy surf. Her deck heeled over at an increasing angle to landward as the tide fell with her port battery pointing skywards. The oars were a tangled mess. Howard sent a hundred-strong boarding party in eleven ship's boats and a pinnace to capture her, and a sharp fight ensued. The Italian sailors and artillerymen were the first to flee ashore and fewer than fifty crew 'stood by the captain to defend the ship'. Moncada fell, a bullet between the eyes, in fierce hand-to-hand fighting with needle-sharp half-pikes, swords and pistols. The *Margaret and John*, always on a quest for plunder, joined the assault to capture the galleass, running aground in her eagerness to be in at the kill.

In their habitual fashion, the English immediately began to pillage the galleass but were interrupted by French troops, sent out from Calais to assist the *San Lorenzo*. Fearing loss of their loot, they fought the rescuers and the brawl only ended when the English heard that, unless they immediately withdrew, the shore batteries would blow them and the stricken galleass into smithereens. Some cannon shots were fired to reinforce the message.

Richard Tomson, lieutenant of the *Margaret and John*, was one of the English boarders:

> We continued a pretty skirmish with our small shot against theirs, they being ensconced within their ship and very high over us; we in our open pinnaces and far under them, having nothing to shroud and cover us; they being three hundred soldiers [sic], besides four hundred and fifty slaves.
>
> Within half an hour, it pleased God, by killing the captain with a musket shot, to give us victory above all hope or expectation, for

the soldiers leaped overboard by heaps on the other side and fled [to] the shore, swimming and wading.

Some escaped with being wet, some and that very many, were drowned ...

Hereupon we entered with much difficulty by reason of her height above us and possessed us of her by the space of an hour and a half ... each man seeking his benefit of pillage until the flood came that we might haul her off ... and bring her away.

After the French rescue party arrived, 'some of our rude men fell to spoiling [them], taking away their rings and jewels as from enemies. Whereupon [the French] going ashore and complaining, all the bulwarks and [gun] ports were bent against us and shot so vehemently that we received sundry shot very dangerously through us.' The *San Lorenzo* was armed with many brass cannon, two hundred barrels of powder and 'of all other things great provision and plenty but very little or no treasure that I can learn to be in her', Tomson added ruefully.[82]

About fifty English and a similar number of Spanish and slaves 'who made a terrible outcry' were killed in three hours of fighting. William Coxe, master of the *Delight*, was the first to board the galleass and the first to die.[83]

As dawn broke on Monday 8 August, the Armada was scattered far out to sea. The blackened ribs of six fireships still smouldered near the entrance to Calais harbour.

At last, Howard had his chance to destroy his enemy.

– 8 –

FLEEING FOR HOME

Their force is wonderful great and strong and yet we pluck their feathers, little by little. I pray to God that forces on the land [are] strong enough to answer so puissant a force.

Lord Admiral Howard to Sir Francis Walsingham,
Ark Royal, 8 August 1588.[1]

At dawn on Monday 8 August, Medina Sidonia's *San Martin* was one mile (1.61 km) north of the English fleet, her sea anchors struggling to hold her position against the strong current in rapidly worsening seas. Howard, fatally distracted by the abortive seizure of the stricken *San Lorenzo*, unwittingly provided the captain-general with two hours of grace to collect his ships and rebuild his defences against the coming onslaught. Lying just astern of the Spanish flagship were the Portuguese galleons *San Marcos, San Mateo, San Felipe* and Recalde's *San Juan*. Medina Sidonia sent pinnaces to collect the Armada, now scattered seven miles (11.85 km) beyond Gravelines, instructing his ships to revert, as soon as possible, to the horned *lunula* as a protective formation. The wind was blowing south-south-west and, anxious to avoid the treacherous shoals and sandbanks off Dunkirk, he set a northerly course and prepared to fight a desperate rearguard action to allow time for the Armada to regroup.

Howard meanwhile brought his one-hundred-and-thirty-six-strong fleet, still anchored off the Calais cliffs, to battle stations. The previous day's council of war had agreed that he would lead the next attack, followed by Drake's squadron and then Seymour's ships. This could be their last chance to defeat the Armada and it was decided that the English ships should close on their adversaries and open fire at point-blank range. Today, the wind and tide were in their favour.

First light brought a rude shock for the Prince of Asculi, still hud-dled on board his *felucca* with a companion, Captain Marco:

> I found myself in the midst of the enemy fleet and the Armada too far away for us to reach it. Whilst I was in this position, I saw a small pinnace ... [that] had been sent to carry orders through the Armada for the ships to put themselves in fighting trim. I therefore went on board ... with the full intention of making for the [flagship] and we clapped on all sail with that object. Both wind and tide were against us and the enemy were engaged with our fleet so I was cut off and in the rear of both fleets.[2]

In the event, it was Drake in *Revenge* with Thomas Fenner in *Nonpareil* who first joined battle at about six o'clock that morning, leading the four queen's ships in his squadron, closely supported by Frobisher's flotilla. Medina Sidonia probably had half a dozen war-ships gathered around *San Martin* and Drake held his fire until he came within one hundred yards (91.43 metres) of the enemy flagship, first bombarding her with his bow guns, then coming around to loose off a rippling salvo from his port battery, a tactic repeated by his ships, struggling in the now heavy seas. But the Armada could still bare its teeth: *Revenge* was hit by more than forty cannonballs[3] during this short engagement and Drake led his squadron off to the north-east.

Was he cravenly fleeing to safety? Had he departed on another chase for plunder and prizes? Perhaps he had turned away to attack enemy ships that were standing off the shoals, waiting to safely form up on their flagship in deeper water. His unexplained and premature departure from the main action incensed the always hot-tempered Sir Martin Frobisher, coming up in *Triumph*. Later, during a heated argument ashore in Harwich, Essex, he could not stifle an angry outburst about his vice-admiral's conduct off Gravelines:

> Drake reports that no man has done any good service but he, but he shall well understand that others have done good service as he – and better too. He came bragging up at the first ... and gave them his prow and his broadside and then kept his luff and was glad that he was gone again, like a cowardly knave or traitor – I rest doubtful but the one I will swear ...

He lies in his teeth. There are others that have done as good as he and better too.[4]

Back in the action off the Flemish coast, Frobisher loosed off cannonade after cannonade at the *San Martin*, while other ships of his squadron fired as they cut across her stern and bows. As *San Marcos* joined the fray around the embattled flagship, Hawkins' squadron, headed by his flagship *Victory,* swept into attack, followed by *Marie Rose, Dreadnought* and *Swallow*, which broke through to the middle of the gathering Spanish fleet. Forty Spanish soldiers had been killed in *San Martin*, their bodies piled up on the upper deck. A 50-pound (22.68 kg) shot had also holed her below the waterline, through the seven planks' thickness of timber of her lower hull. The Armada's chief purser, Pedro Calderón watched anxiously:

> So tremendous was the fire that over two hundred balls struck the sails and hull of the flagship on the starboard side, killing and wounding many men, disabling and dismounting three guns and destroying much rigging.
>
> The holes made in the hull between wind and water caused so great a leakage that two divers had as much as they could do to stop them up with tow[5] and lead plates, working all day.[6]

For the first time in this inconclusive campaign, the Spanish ships were suffering serious damage and the fight between the two fleets was becoming a bloodbath. *San Felipe* and *San Mateo*, which brought up the rear of the Armada, were engaged by up to seventeen English ships which were coming so close, according to Calderón, that the 'muskets and harquebuses of the galleon were brought into service, killing a large number of men on the enemy's ships'. The English fire shattered the *San Felipe*'s foremast, disabled its rudder and blew five of her starboard cannon off their carriages as well as killing 260 of its crew and soldiers. Although his upper deck had been smashed, the ship's pumps broken, and his command 'almost a wreck', the *San Felipe*'s captain Don Francisco de Toledo, ordered the grappling hooks to be readied and dared the nearest English ship[7] to come to close quarters with him.

They summoned him to surrender in fair fight and one Englishman, standing in the maintop with his sword and buckler[8] called out:

'Good soldiers that you are, surrender to the fair terms we offer you.'

But the only answer that he got was a gunshot which brought him down in sight of everyone and the ... muskets and harquebuses were [ordered] to be brought into action.

The enemy thereupon retired, whilst our men shouted out to them that they were cowards and, with opprobrious words, reproached them for their want of spirit, calling them Lutheran hens and desiring them to return to the fight.

The *San Felipe* was rescued by the *socorro* battle group of *San Luis*, *San Mateo* and the *La Trinidad Valencera*. *San Mateo* came under heavy fire from both Sir William Wynter's *Vanguard* and Seymour's *Rainbow*, which had closed on the enemy vessel 'and an Englishman jumped on board but our men cut him to bits instantly'.[9] Calderón's ship, the transport hulk *San Salvador*, also endeavoured to help the *San Felipe* but paid a penalty for such gallantry.

Her bows, side and half her poop being exposed for four hours to the enemy's fire, during which time she received no aid. She had a number of men killed and wounded and her sails and rigging, so much damaged that she was obliged to change her mainsail. She leaked greatly through the shot holes and finally the *Rata Santa María Encoronada* came to her assistance.[10]

The majority of these ships, Medina Sidonia explained afterwards, 'were so much damaged as to be unable to offer further resistance, most of them not having a round of shot to fire'.[11]

On board the *San Marcos*, Pedro Estrada had lost one of his comrades in the fierce enemy fire: 'This day was slain Don Felipe de Córdoba with a bullet [roundshot] that struck off his head and splashed [out] his brains. [He was] the greatest friend ... and twenty-four men that were with us trimming our foresail [also died].'[12] The upper deck of Bertendona's *Ragazona* in the Armada rearguard was running with blood from her dead and wounded and her main battery guns had been blown off their mountings. She bravely fought on, with musketeers firing from high up in her maintops or from the deck, using the heaps of casualties as protective cover.

Skirmishing around the Spanish flagship continued for about two

Princess Elizabeth as a young teenager. She was less enthusiastic about the Catholic faith, complaining 'loudly all the way to the church' and 'wore a suffering air' during Mass.

Mary I painted by Hans Eworth in 1554. She hated Elizabeth with a dark sibling passion and feared her half-sister as an ever-present threat to her throne.

Mary Queen of Scots by François Clouet, c.1558-60. In 1564, during a visit by the Scots Ambassador, Elizabeth is said to have picked up this miniature and kissed it. She changed her mind about her cousin four years later when Mary Queen of Scots fled to England. With Mary's viable claim to the crown of England, she became an inveterate conspirator against Elizabeth.

Philip II of Spain, painted by an unknown artist, after 1580. Deposing
Elizabeth and the conquest of heretic England became a holy crusade.

Don Alonso Pérez de Guzmán, Seventh Duke of Medina Sidonia, was the reluctant commander of the Armada following the death of Santa Cruz from typhus in February 1588.

Alessandro Farnese, Duke of Parma, was to bring the Spanish invasion forces across from Flanders in narrow, flat-bottom barges. He never sailed.

Pope Sixtus V. Always counting his ducats, he reluctantly agreed to subsidise the Armada, but stipulated that not a penny should be paid before the first Spanish soldier set foot on English soil. He was also a great admirer of Elizabeth I, much to everyone's discomfort.

Elizabeth's new 'race built' warships had sleek lines which enabled greater manoeuvrability during naval battles, emphasised here by the superimposed image of a fish.

Howard's flagship *Ark Royal*, purchased from Sir Walter Raleigh to clear some of his debts to the crown.

Sir Francis Walsingham, Elizabeth's secretary of state and spymaster, who dismissed early reports of preparations for the Armada as mere 'Spanish brag'.

BELOW:
Dorset warning beacons, showing their construction.

Sir William Cecil, Lord Burghley, Elizabeth's lord treasurer, who struggled to find the money to pay for England's defence.

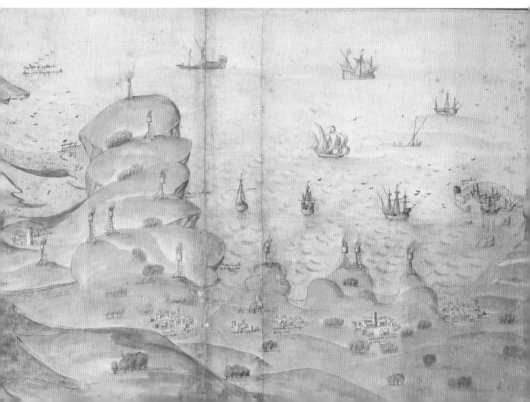

Charles Howard, Second Baron Effingham. He was one of Mary Queen of Scots' judges at Fotheringay and two years later, as Lord High Admiral, pursued the Spanish Armada up the English Channel and fought them in the Battle of Gravelines on 8 August 1588.

Sir Francis Drake. The vice-admiral of the English fleet was a maverick and endangered Howard's campaign against the Armada by leaving his station to pursue mystery ships, the next morning, claiming the stricken Spanish ship *Rosario* as a prize.

hours whilst the Armada ships were rounded up by Don Alonso de Leyva in the *Rata*. On board *San Martin*, Friar Bernardo de Gongora (a refugee from the earlier casualty *Rosario*), was bewildered and terrified by the thunder of battle:

> It was the greatest war and confusion that there has been in the world, in respect of the great amount of fire and smoke ...
>
> There were many ships that went on fighting in eight cubits of water.[13]
>
> All this day, we had been holding ourselves with the bowline held against the weather so as not to run aground on the banks and thus our ships could not ply their artillery as they wished.
>
> Some of the people died in our ship but none of quality and it was a miracle the duke escaped.[14]

His fellow friar, Padre La Torre, also on board the flagship, said the hail of shot was so great 'it was cut to pieces below and aloft. In the end, I saw myself in such sore straits that it was a miracle of God we escaped, for since the ships were so scattered and could not help one another, the enemy's galleons came together and charged us in such numbers that they gave us no time for breath.'[15]

But by ten o'clock, the Armada ships were grouped in the familiar horned crescent formation, bearing north-north-east as Wynter, in *Vanguard*, observed:

> They went into a proportion of a half-moon. Their admiral and vice-admiral ... went into the midst ... and there went on each side, in the wings, their galleasses, in the whole to the number of sixteen in a wing.[16]

Wynter attacked the starboard or easterly horn and his fire drove some Spanish ships into the main body, with four 'entangling themselves one aboard the other'. The Levantine *San Juan de Sicilia* had lost half her crew and her gun 'port holes were all full of blood'. Another ship, Pedro de Ugarte's 665-ton *María Juan*, of the Biscayan squadron, was badly damaged by Captain Robert Crosse's *Hope* and while in 'speech of yielding unto the captain before they could agree on certain conditions', she sank – so quickly that only one boat with eighty survivors on board was picked up by the *San Martin*. Others who clung desperately to the upper spars and rigging went down with her and, in all, 188 crew were lost.[17] She became the first casualty of English cannon fire.

The battle continued until six that afternoon with Howard leading the *Bear*, *Bonaventure* and the *Lion* to attack the centre of the rearguard in close-quarter fighting. *Vanguard* had fired five hundred roundshot from her demi-cannon, culverin and demi-culverin at close range and when Wynter (who had been injured by the recoil of one of his cannon) 'was furthest off in discharging any of the pieces, I was not out of the shot of their harquebus and most times within speech one of another'. He was certain the 'slaughter and hurt they received was very great'.[18]

The weather now changed for the worse with a succession of fierce squalls and heavy rain blowing in from the west-north-west, reducing visibility dramatically. The English fleet broke off the action and kept their distance, shadowing the Armada as it limped north-eastwards. The crew of *Santa Ana*, Oquendo's flagship, had to man the pumps constantly to prevent her sinking. The Castilian *San Pedro* was also very badly holed. The dead were heaved over the side and the wounded tended as emergency repairs were undertaken by the exhausted Armada crews. For the Spanish, there still remained the imminent danger of shipwreck on the shoals off the Flanders coast. Padre Geronimo reported that 'Hardly a man slept that night. We went along all wondering when we should strike one of those [sand] banks.'[19] He was busy hearing confessions and there were constant appeals to the Blessed Virgin Mary for their survival against now seemingly impossible odds.

Howard signalled his fleet to re-form and to remain on the Armada's weather quarter. Weary from battle, he wrote to Walsingham bemoaning London's bureaucratic requests that he should supply estimates of how much powder and shot he needed. His lack of munitions was as acute as ever with some of the smaller English guns firing scrap metal such as broken plough shares as makeshift antipersonnel munitions. 'I have received your letter wherein you desire a proportion of shot and powder to be ... sent to you, which for reason of the uncertainty of the service, no man can do. Therefore I pray you to send with all speed as much as you can.' He then reported on that day's fighting:

We have chased them in fight until this evening late and distressed them much but their fleet consists of mighty ships and great strength. Yet we doubt not, by God's good assistance, to oppress them.[20]

Drake was more ebullient, if not cheerful:

God has given us so good a day in forcing the enemy so far to lee-ward as I hope in God the Prince of Parma and the Duke of Sidonia shall not shake hands this few days. Whensoever they shall meet, I believe neither of them will greatly rejoice of this day's service ... [which] has much appalled the enemy and no doubt but [it has] encouraged our [fleet].[21]

Fenner, in *Nonpareil,* self-righteously believed that God Himself had 'mightily protected her majesty's forces with the least losses that ever have been heard of, being within the compass of such great volleys of shot, both great and small. I verily believe there is not three score men lost.' He felt assured that God 'will defend his [own] from the raging enemy who goes about to beat down His word and devour His people' and this would be 'a just plague for their wickedness and idolatry'.[22]

Hawkins told Walsingham more soberly:

All that day we followed the Spaniards with a long and great fight wherein there was great valour shown generally by our company in this battle ...

So the wind began to grow westerly, a fresh gale, and the Spaniards put themselves somewhat to the north, where we follow and keep company with them.

In this fight there was some hurt done among the Spaniards.

Our ships, God be thanked, have received little hurt.

Now their fleet is here and very forcible, it must be waited upon with all our force, which is little enough.

There should be an infinite quantity of powder and shot provided and continually sent aboard without which, great hazard may grow to our country for this is the greatest and strongest combination ... that was ever gathered in Christendom ...

The men have been long unpaid and need relief. I pray your lord-ship that the money which should have gone to Plymouth may now be sent to Dover.[23]

Hawkins was right to be cautious about the true import of the Battle of Gravelines. The English fleet might have severely mauled the Armada but it had not defeated it.

As darkness fell, the worst damaged of the Armada ships began to fall behind the protective crescent. *San Mateo* was fast flooding with seawater, not just from shot holes but also because her seams had sprung open through the shocks of the repeated recoil of her guns.[24] That evening she had to be beached on a sandbank between Ostend and Sluis. Dutch sailors from the hoys attached to Justin of Nassau's blockading fleet attacked her, but her crew fought them off for two hours before her captain, Don Diego Pimentel, requested surrender terms. He and his five officers were taken prisoner but the others were callously thrown overboard to drown or were hanged later. Among them was William Browne, a 'gentleman adventurer' and brother of the Catholic Viscount Montague, and 'another Englishman' who were both killed on the ship.[25] The local commissioner for the States of Zeeland reported that this second man was 'very rich who left William as his heir ... There were other Englishmen who usually messed with Pimentel. One was called Robert, another Raphael, once servant to the ... mayor of London, Thomas Tostal, or some such name. We do not know their surnames.'[26]

The *San Mateo*'s sister ship, Don Francisco de Toledo's *San Felipe*, had been secured alongside the *Doncella*, the 500-ton Guipúzcoan *urca*, to evacuate her crew after firing cannon shots to indicate her distress. Three hundred were taken off before it was feared that the *Doncella* was also sinking, so the warship was forced to cast off, but not before some rejoined the wallowing, damaged warship. 'Captain Juan Poza ... said that the hulk was going down. [Toledo] replied that if that were the case, they had better be drowned in the galleon than in the hulk and they both went back to her.'[27] *San Felipe* was later also beached between Ostend and Sluis, minus her mainmast and with her sails torn to shreds. After another fight with the Dutch, Toledo and 'most of the other gentlemen' escaped by boat to Nieuport, but only 127 'poor mangled souls' from her complement of 640 were saved from the surf. After botched Dutch attempts to refloat her, the *San Felipe* sank before she could be brought into Flushing the next morning. A third ship, an unnamed *patache*, probably the *San Antonio de Padua* from Diego Flores' Castile squadron, also sank off the castle and town of Rammekins in Zeeland.

The Spanish ships had been badly battered, losing four vessels in addition to the *San Lorenzo* off Calais harbour. Their casualty lists totalled more than a thousand killed and around eight hundred wounded. Understandably, amid the screams of the injured and the moans of the dying below decks, morale on the ships slumped that night, even though the damaged fleet remained a formidable fighting force and still represented a potent, fearsome threat to England.

Early the following day, Tuesday 9 August, the extent of similar disillusionment amongst the Armada's high command became apparent. There was traitorous talk of surrender amongst Medina Sidonia's immediate subordinates, but the friar Padre La Torre, in *San Martin,* reported there was 'no pinnace available [to communicate with Howard] which was a particular favour from God and in any case, the duke did not want to follow this course, preferring to die like a knight'.[28] Caught between the English fleet and the coast, the Armada was in peril of wrecking itself on the Flanders Banks, a fear magnified by the leadsmen's continual calls of ever shallower water lying beneath the keels as they squatted in each ship's bows, taking soundings. Luis de Miranda, a member of the captain-general's staff, admitted: 'We saw ourselves lost or taken by the enemy or the whole armada drowned upon the banks. It was the most fearful day in the world, for the whole company had lost all hope of success and looked only for death.'[29]

San Martin remained in the rear of the Spanish fleet, with the galleons *San Marcos* and Diego Flores' *San Juan,* together with the galleasses. Their enemy, numbering 109 ships, followed astern at only half a league's (2.78 km) distance. At one stage it seemed the English intended to attack, but the galleasses swept around to protect their flagship and the enemy ships retired, perhaps believing that the Spanish ships were doomed anyway, as the line of white crested surf breaking on the deadly sandbanks was now visible to all in the Armada.

With the depth at seven fathoms (12.8 m.), Medina Sidonia hailed one of his veteran commanders, Miguel de Oquendo, whose *Santa Ana* was coming up fast alongside the flagship: 'Señor Oquendo, what shall we do, for we are lost?' he called across the sweeping rush of the sea between the ships. He shouted back: 'Let Diego Flores answer that' – an indication of just how unpopular the naval adviser had become in the Armada. 'As for me,' Oquendo continued, 'I am going to fight and die like a man. Send me a supply of shot.'[30]

Medina Sidonia fired two cannon to signal the Armada to regroup and sent *pataches* to order his vessels to keep their heads close to the wind. His pilots warned him grimly that 'it was impossible to save a single ship ... as they must inevitably be driven by the north-west wind on to the banks of Zeeland'. He believed that 'God alone could rescue them'.[31]

God indeed did save them.

The wind suddenly veered to the south-west, enabling the Armada to immediately steer a northerly course away from the coast and safely into the North Sea.

Howard summoned his commanders to *Ark Royal*. His perennial shortage of gunpowder and shot made it impossible to attack as they had at Gravelines. As one of his captains, Henry White, complained later: 'Our parsimony at home has bereaved us of the [most famous] victory that ever our navy might have had at sea.'[32] They decided unanimously to pursue the Armada 'until we have cleared our own coast and brought the Firth [of Forth in Scotland] west of us and then to return back again, as well as to revictual our ships (which stand in extreme scarcity) [but] also to guard and defend our coast at home ...'[33] The danger of Parma's army remained, so Howard left a reinforced squadron under Seymour to guard the Dover Straits, some of which could restock with provisions and munitions at Harwich. Seymour, still hungry for action, obeyed the order very much against his will. Unbeknown to him and Howard, Parma had heard the cannonades of the previous day's battle and had completed the embarkation of his 16,000 men.

That evening Medina Sidonia called his own council of war. Don Diego Flores argued strongly for a return to Calais, but they all resolved to return to the English Channel only 'if the weather would allow of it but if not, then they should obey the wind and sail to Spain by the North Sea, bearing in mind that the Armada was lacking all necessary things and that the ships, which had resisted hitherto, were badly crippled'.[34] Chief Purser Calderón had misgivings about the wisdom of sailing around the north of Scotland, west of Ireland and then out into the Atlantic. He warned them they would have to sail seven hundred and fifty leagues (4,167 km) 'through stormy seas, almost unknown to us, before we could reach Corunna'. Ever efficient, Calderón then investigated the Armada's dwindling stock of provisions and water supplies. It would not be a bountiful voyage.

Superficially, there was some sense in the selection of this course. Even though the voyage would take between a month to five weeks to complete, the commanders could reasonably expect the season's weather to be settled. They could be almost home in Spain by the time that the regular late September gales would blow up around the autumn equinox.

Thirty leagues (166.68 km) east of Newcastle, Medina Sidonia ordered that the horses and the forty artillery mules be thrown overboard as there was no more water for them.

In London, the tension and anxieties of the past month were beginning to recede. Earlier the Privy Council had sent a letter to John Whitgift, Archbishop of Canterbury, seeking public prayers to be said against the success of the Armada.[35] As the London citizens were so alarmed, Spanish prisoners, including Don Pedro de Valdés of the *Rosario,* detained after the first engagement, were paraded in carts through the streets 'so that people might see that some prisoners had been captured'.[36] Under questioning, Valdés said that none of the English exiles serving with the Armada were 'privy to the secrets of the enterprise' and denied any knowledge of promises made by recusants to take up arms in support of invasion. Burghley, with a shrewd eye for telling propaganda, had dictated the questions to be put to prisoners during interrogation. How would 'the spoils of London and other towns be [divided]? What profit should be reserved for the king? Was it intended to impose ransoms [for English prisoners of noble birth]?' Valdés, however, maintained there was no permission granted for pillaging or looting once Spanish forces had landed.[37]

Although the bonfires burned in celebration in London after news of Gravelines arrived, the Armada was still perceived as an imminent threat by Elizabeth's government. On 9 August George Talbot, Sixth Earl of Shrewsbury, the lord lieutenant of Derbyshire, Nottinghamshire and Staffordshire, emphasised the vital need for constant vigilance, ordering: 'All those who have the custody of recusants must detain them close prisoners.'[38] He also offered his services to the queen to resist the invasion: 'though I be old, yet her quarrel shall make me young again; though lame in body, yet lusty in heart to lend her greatest enemy one blow and to live and die in her service'.[39] As late as 18 August, Sir Thomas Morgan warned the Earl of Leicester that Parma 'has in readiness 30,000 or 40,000 men and intends with the next spring tide to put out his forces for England, hoping to meet the king's fleet[40] and the following day, Sir Thomas Scott told Leicester that Drake had warned him 'that the Spanish army did intend to land at Dungeness, near Lydd [Kent] and there to entrench themselves and to be supplied from time to time out of France with victuals and all necessaries'.[41]

There were mounting fears among her advisers and military and naval commanders that Elizabeth's perpetually straitened finances and her natural parsimony would lower England's guard before it was safe to do so. Howard warned Walsingham: 'Let not her majesty be too hasty in dissolving her forces by sea and land and I pray you send me with speed what [news] you have of Dunkirk for I long to do some exploit on their shipping.[42] Drake was also worried that 'some may advise the queen not to continue her forces' and he dared not 'advise her to hazard her kingdom for the saving of a little charge'.[43]

Meanwhile the Armada was slowly heading northwards, watched by a reduced number of English ships. Medina Sidonia had some unpleasant business to settle. He had fired cannon three times to summon his commanders but his signal was ignored. Eventually his boats collected the captains and Padre La Torre recounted their welcome on board *San Martin*. A furious captain-general asked them: 'Did you not hear the gun?' and they admitted they had. 'Then why did you not rally?' he asked and was enraged by their reply: 'We thought your flagship was sinking and that we should all hasten away to safety.' There was a long silence. 'Hang the traitors,' ordered Medina Sidonia.[44]

There were other crimes to punish. On Thursday 11 August, twenty navy and army captains were arraigned for cowardice at Gravelines. Francisco de Cuéllar, captain of the Castilian *San Pedro,* appeared before Don Francisco de Bobadilla, the Armada's senior military commander, in *San Martin*[45] accused of not keeping station with the fleet.

He ordered me to be taken to the [judge advocate general's] ship [*Lavia*] for his sentence to be carried out. There I repaired, and though he was a severe judge, the fiscal heard my case and took testimony concerning me.

He heard that I served his majesty as a good soldier and therefore became unwilling to execute the orders he had received.

He wrote to the duke about it, saying that unless he received a direct order written by the duke and signed with his own hand, he would not comply with his orders.[46]

Cuéllar was reprieved. But Don Cristobal de Avila, captain of the hulk *Santa Barbara,* 'a gentleman of renown' was 'hanged with great cruelty and dishonour' – strung up from the masthead of a pinnace and his body paraded through the ranks of the Armada as a dreadful warning. Others were condemned to the galleys or reduced in rank. Calderón noted: 'It is said that this was because on the day of the battle, they allowed themselves to drift out of the fight.'[47]

On the afternoon of Friday 12 August both fleets reached the Firth of Forth with the wind blowing from the south-south-west. Howard was worried that the Spanish might attempt a landing in Scotland in support of Catholics wishing to depose James VI of Scotland. As the Armada continued north, he left two pinnaces to shadow it until they passed the Orkney and Shetland islands, and at two o'clock he gratefully steered a course for home and much-needed food and water. He told Walsingham: 'We are persuaded that either they [will] pass about Ireland and so do what they can to recover their own coast or else they are gone for some part of Denmark.'[48]

Medina Sidonia recorded in his diary: 'The enemy's fleet was quite close to us but as they saw we were well together and that the rear-guard had been reinforced, the enemy fell astern and sailed towards England until we lost sight of him. Since then we have continued sailing with the same wind ... and it has been impossible for us to return to the English Channel.'[49] The following day he ordered tighter rations with only eight ounces (226.8 grams) of bread and half a pint (0.28 litre) of wine plus a pint of water each day. Rather desperately perhaps, he offered 2,000 ducats to a French pilot 'if he would conduct him to a Spanish port'.[50]

In Rome, Philip's ambassador Olivares was still facing an uphill struggle to extract any money from Sixtus V, despite him saying daily Masses for the success of the Armada. On 7 August he stood uncomfortably before the Pope and made a long speech seeking, yet again, an advance on the promised subsidy for the invasion. He reminded the diffident and restless pontiff that it was he himself who had persuaded Philip to undertake the heavy task of the 'Enterprise of England':

> His majesty trusts that the Pope's postponement of the payments, which he could easily make, may, by God's grace, not result in some reverse, which would be a great injury to the cause of our Lord and the glory of his Holiness. The Pope would never cease to grieve if he had been the cause of such a disaster and all subsequent efforts he might make to repair it would be unavailing; whilst what is asked of him now he can do with the greatest of ease.

These slightly intimidating words of persuasion failed to sway the Pope. Sixtus merely shrugged his shoulders for, as Olivares commented, 'when it comes to getting money out of him, it is like squeezing his lifeblood. [All] our efforts availed nothing.'

Eleven days later the envoy reported again on his hopeless mission. When the question of the cash was raised

> the only effect is that the moment my back is turned, he babbles the most ridiculous nonsense at table as ... would not be said by a baby of two years old.
>
> He possesses no sort of charity, kindliness or consideration and his behaviour attributed by everyone to the repulsion and chagrin that he feels as the hour approaches to drag this money from his heart.

Sixtus insisted on the strict letter of the agreement: no landing, no money. Then he tried some brazen bluster, alleging

> that the Armada business is nothing but a trick and that your majesty has not raised the fleet for the English enterprise at all, but for brag and to frighten the Queen of England into making peace ... He shows reports he has received to this effect ... however unlikely a report may be, it matters not to his Holiness if it serves his purpose.[51]

As if to antagonise Philip even further, Sixtus, not famous for his empathy with the Spanish king, remained besotted with Elizabeth. He told an open-mouthed Giovanni Gritti, the Venetian ambassador to the Holy See, that the king 'goes trifling with this Armada of his, but the queen acts in earnest. Were she a Catholic, she would be our best beloved, for she is of great worth.'

Just look at Drake! Who is he? What forces has he? Yet he burned twenty-five of the king's ships ... and as many again at Lisbon. He had robbed the flotilla and sacked San Domingo. His reputation is so great that his countrymen flock to him to share his booty.

We are sorry to say it, but we have a poor opinion of this Spanish Armada and fear some disaster.

The king should have sailed when we told him, in September of last year.

What can the king do? He has no money and has borrowed 300,000 ducats from Mantua and 200,000 from the Archbishop of Toledo.

Twenty thousand of his troops have been lost through this delay, some dead, some killed.

The queen has had time to arm.[52]

If the Vatican was an unreliable source of loans, there were always bankers. That August, Philip borrowed 'one million of gold' from Genoa at nearly 25 per cent interest, having already pawned his wife's jewellery.

First reports from any conflict frequently contain misleading information as a consequence of slow communications, wishful thinking, or just the impenetrable fog of war. The ever-optimistic Mendoza in Paris excitedly informed Philip on 9 August of a great victory over the English fleet the week before, enclosing a letter from Isoardo Capello from Rouen claiming that the Armada had 'sunk fifteen of the enemy's ships, including the flagship' and that the survivors had retreated towards Dover. The king replied: 'As you consider the news to be true, I am hopeful that it will prove to be so, particularly as the author claims to have been an eye witness.' He wrote to Medina Sidonia:

This news is asserted in France to be true ... I hope to God that it may be so and that you have known how to follow up the victory and make the most of it, pursuing the enemy actively without giving him the opportunity of reforming and pushing on until you join hands with my nephew, the duke [of Parma]. This being done, it may be hoped that with God's help, the enemy's fear of us and our men's courage, other victories will have followed.

Philip ended his letter: 'I confidently look for God's favour in a cause so entirely His own and expect your valour and activity will have accomplished all I could desire. I anxiously await news.'[53]

Hieronimo Lippomano, Venetian envoy to Spain, was all too familiar with Mendoza's unbridled optimism. 'The report is so confused and that ambassador so accustomed to deceive himself that they are awaiting confirmation of the news. No public rejoicings have taken place, nor have the ambassadors congratulated the king.' Philip had 'exclaimed that he trusted God would favour his cause to the full, for he was moved by no desire to increase his possessions, but only to increase the faith and the Catholic religion'. The king added rather sorrowfully, 'Even if I conquered England I would not in many years recover the expenses of the Armada for a single day.'[54]

In Paris, Stafford, the English ambassador, spent five crowns on printing four hundred copies of a pamphlet denying Spanish claims of the Armada's success which had been 'cried so lively around the town'. Mendoza said the Catholic Parisians would not allow 'this fancy news to be sold, saying it is all lies. One of the ambassador's secretaries began to read in the [royal] palace [an account] ... sent from England but the people were so enraged that he was obliged to fly for his life.' The Spanish ambassador, now half blind, still stuck to his guns, insisting that reports from Rouen indicated that 'the English lost heavily in the engagement' and were 'very sad as it was said that Drake had been wounded in the legs by a cannonball'.[55]

There were further optimistic reports from Spanish sources. Juan de Gamarra, in Rouen, had heard that the English fleet had lost forty ships in a battle off Newcastle: 'Our Armada attacked them so stoutly that we sank twenty of their ships and captured twenty-six in perfectly good condition. The rest of the English fleet, seeing only ruin before them, escaped with great damage and their ships are now all in bits and without crews.' The Armada then entered the port of Newcastle 'where they are very well, as all affirm'. He concluded: 'The English here are very sulky.'[56] Other rumours had the English panic-stricken at their naval losses. Drake had been captured trying to board the *San Martin* (news of this emboldened Mendoza to light a celebratory bonfire in front of his house in Paris); Elizabeth's government had prohibited the publication of any news about the fate of the English fleet and fears were growing daily of a dangerous uprising by English Catholics.

Then a *Hansa* ship's captain reported sailing through a sea filled with swimming mules and horses.[57]

On 15 August a delighted Leicester wrote to the queen, having heard that she planned to visit her army in its 'Camp Royal' atop the steep hill at West Tilbury, Essex. The troops were now ready 'to die for her. Good sweet queen! Alter not your purpose if God give you good health. Your usher[58] likes the lodging prepared for you. It is a properly sweet clean house within a little mile' of his encampment 'and your person will be as sure as at St James'.[59] It was about time that Leicester had received good news. He had found it difficult to muster his men; their equipment was poor, and cavalry and dray horses were hard to find. Sir Henry Cocke and Sir Philip Boteler had 'dealt with the gentlemen of Hertfordshire, suspected of having acting fraudulently and undutifully with her majesty in retaining back their best horses and sending inferior horses to the camp'.[60]

Detailed arrangements had been made to feed and house Leicester's 16,000 infantry and 2,000 cavalry, with provisions merchants within 20 miles (32.19 km) of Tilbury threatened with 'the most grievous imprisonment or fine' if they withheld or hid 'any grain or other victuals'. Prices were fixed for sixty-three items of food for the troops, regulated by clerks at the markets: twenty shillings was the price for a quarter (28 pounds or 12.7 kg) of 'best wheat, clean and sweet'; three pennies (1.67 pence) for a pound (0.45 kg) of butter 'sweet and new, the best in the market'; one penny for a pound 'of good Essex cheese' and one shilling (5 pence) for a stone (6.35 kg) of 'the best beef at the butchers'.[61] Even so there were cheats and profiteers.

Leicester wrote to the queen fussing about her planned route – warning her to avoid the coast where her sacred person could be captured by a marauding Spanish landing party:

This far, if it please, you may dare – to draw yourself to your house at Havering [Essex] and your army being about London ... [there] shall be always a defence.

If it please you, spend two or three days to see both the camp and the forts. It is not about thirteen miles [20.92 km] from Havering and a very convenient place for your majesty to lye in by the way and rest you at the camp.

I trust you will be pleased by your lieutenant's cabin[62] and within a mile there is a gentleman's house where your majesty may lye.

Thus far but no further can I consent to adventure your person and, by the grace of God, there can be no danger in this.[63]

Howard arrived back with his ships and starving crews at Harwich and Margate Roads early on Thursday 18 August.

That same morning, Elizabeth joined her royal barge at Westminster for the journey to Tilbury. Her gentlemen pensioners, bravely kitted out in brightly polished half-armours and gaily feathered morion helmets, escorted her in nine oared boats as the royal procession slipped down the Thames on the ebb tide, to the sweet sound of silver trumpets. She arrived at Tilbury, greeted by joyous peals of bells from nearby church towers. The tented camp, enclosing around five acres (2.02 hectares) was surrounded by hastily excavated defensive earthworks. A raised causeway ran from the river across flat marshland up to the hill.

Elizabeth was met by an escort of two thousand infantry and one thousand cavalry under the command of Sir Roger Williams. With Leicester at her side, the red-haired queen, wearing a plumed hat, rode onwards, pausing only when some soldiers fell to their knees at the roadside, crying out their blessings upon her. So says the official account, but one suspects they may also have been seeking their pay arrears from the queen. Certainly, Elizabeth felt it necessary to send messengers ahead to modestly bid the soldiers 'not to pay her such idolatrous reverence'.[64]

The queen spent that night, not in her 'lieutenant's cabin', but in 'Mr Ritchie's house'[65] – probably Arderne House, on Horndon-on-the-Hill – the building surrounded by a bodyguard of two thousand men. She returned to the 'Camp Royal' the following morning, carrying a marshal's baton (or 'truncheon') and rather incongruously wearing a man's breastplate and backplate over her gown as 'armed Pallas'. She then reviewed her troops, four footmen walking each side of her horse, her ladies behind, with her bodyguard riding at the rear. Her army, with colours flying and drums beating, marched past in gallant array. Thomas Deloney described the scene in a loyal ballad:

> Then came the Queen on prancing steed
>   attired like an angel bright
> And eight brave footmen at her feet
>   whose jerkins were most rich in sight
> Her ladies, likewise of great honour
>   most sumptuously did wait upon her
> With pearls and diamonds brave adorned
>   and in costly cauls of gold
> Her guards, in scarlet, then rode after,
>   with bows and arrows, stout and bold.[66]

Still mounted on her plump white gelding, Elizabeth delivered the speech of her life, her words noted down by Leicester's chaplain, Dr Lionel Sharpe.[67]

My loving people: I have been persuaded by some that are careful of my safety to take heed I committed myself to armed multitudes, for fear of treachery.

But I tell you that I would not desire to live to distrust my faithful and loving people.

Let tyrants fear! I have always so behaved myself that under God I have placed my chiefest strength and safeguard in the loyal hearts and goodwill of my subjects.

Wherefore I am come among you at this time not for my recreation and pleasure, but being resolved in the midst and heat of battle to live and die amongst you all to lay down, for my God and for my kingdom and for my people, my honour and my blood even in the dust.

I know I have the body but of a weak and feeble woman but I have the heart and stomach of a king. And of a king of England too – and take foul scorn that Parma or any prince of Europe should dare to invade the borders of my realm.

To the which, rather than any dishonour shall grow by me, I myself will venture my royal blood; I myself shall be your general, judge and rewarder of every one of your virtues in the field.

I know that already, for your forwardness, you have deserved rewards and crowns and I assure you in the word of a prince, you shall not fail of them.

In the meantime, my lieutenant general shall be in my stead, than whom never prince commanded a more noble or worthy subject.

Not doubting but by your concord in the camp and valour in the field and your obedience to myself and my general, we shall shortly have a famous victory over these enemies of my God and of my kingdom.[68]

The troops responded 'all at once [with] a mighty shout or cry' – a patriotic 'huzza' – and Leicester believed that her speech had 'so inflamed the hearts of her good subjects as I think the weakest person among them is able to match the proudest Spaniard that dared to land in England'.[69]

Afterwards, the queen received favoured visitors in Leicester's tent. One was Sir Edward Radcliffe, who described the scene for his kinsman, the ill-tempered Earl of Sussex:

Her majesty has honoured our camp with her presence and comforted many of us with her most gracious usage.

It pleased her to send for me into my lord general's tent and to make me kiss her hand, giving me many thanks for my forwardness in the service, telling me I showed from what house I descended with many gracious words of your lordship's good service, assuring me that before it wear long, she would make me better able to serve her.

But while she was dining with Leicester, 'there came a post [which] brought intelligence that the duke [of Parma] with all his forces was embarked for England and that he would be here with as much speed as possibly he could'.

The news was published throughout the camp, to what end I know not, but no preparation is made for the sending of more men, which makes us think the news untrue.[70]

Leicester urged her to return to St James' Palace for her safety but the queen was enjoying her taste of martial glory and refused to leave: she 'would not think of deserting her army at a time of danger'. Another memorable quotation for posterity! It was only when night had fallen that Elizabeth was graciously pleased to quit the Tilbury fortifications.

The next day her troops kept a public fast for victory.

Fortified by the Armada's flight, the queen found time to reply to James VI of Scotland's kind offer of assistance:

> Now may appear, my dear brother, how malice joined with might strives to make a shameful end of a villainous beginning.
>
> For by God's singular favour, having this fleet well beaten in our narrow seas and press with all violence to achieve some watering place to continue their pretended invasions, the wind has carried them to your coasts where, I doubt not, they shall receive small succour and less welcome . . .
>
> You may assure yourself that I doubt [not] but all this tyrannical proud and brainsick attempt will be the beginning, though not the end, of the ruin of that king [Philip] . . .
>
> He had procured my greatest glory that meant my furthest wrack and has dimmed the light of his sunshine.[71]

With the cost of her forces in Essex and Kent amounting to £783 14s 8d per day, the queen ordered an immediate demobilisation.[72]

As the Armada rounded the north of Scotland, an Italian friend of Lippomano's, serving in a Spanish ship, wrote him a letter brimming with despair. 'Our route outside Scotland is long – pray God we come safe home. I am very hungry and thirsty for no one has more than half a pint of wine and a whole one of water each day. The water you cannot drink for it smells worse than musk; it is more than ten days since I drank any. They say we are to go straight to Corunna.'[73]

Many hundreds of Spanish sailors and soldiers would never see their homes again, their dreams of return blown away by Atlantic storms.

– 9 –

SHIPWRECKED UPON AN
ALIEN SHORE

I numbered on one strand [of Sligo] *of less than five miles in length, above 1,100 dead corpses of men which the sea had driven upon the shore ... and as the country people told me, the like was in other places, though not of like number.*

Geoffrey Fenton, secretary of the Irish Council,
to Lord Burghley, Dublin, 28 October 1588.[1]

Unwittingly, Medina Sidonia's sailing orders to the Armada for its voyage, via Cape Finisterre, to its home ports of Corunna or Ferrol, became darkly prophetic. His laconic instructions, written on a quarter of a sheet of paper, were distributed on 13 August as the fleet laboured through a bewildering mix of weather – squalls, rain, fog and heavy seas – in the northern reaches of the North Sea. His directions warned his captains 'to take great heed lest you fall upon the island of Ireland, for fear of the harm that may happen unto you upon that coast'.[2]

The battle damage sustained by the Armada at Gravelines was still taking its toll on progress and two days later, despite Recalde's voluble protests, the captain-general ordered the fleet to put on full sail. Coldly rational, he had decided that those ships whose damage slowed them down would be left to make shift for themselves, as he had with the *Rosario* at the start of the long fight up the English Channel. After the dank drizzle cleared to reveal the grey horizon on the morning of 19 August, Don Diego Enriquez Tellez's Levanter *San Juan de Sicilia*, with barely serviceable sails, was missing. That night, thirteen slower vessels also disappeared from sight, reducing Medina Sidonia's fleet to only 110 ships. One, the 600-ton hulk *Santiago* (the so-called 'ship of the women'), was wrecked on the Norwegian coast and thirty-two survivors, soldiers and their wives, ended up in Hamburg. A second ship may also have been lost on the same shore.[3]

In the absence of any sea charts of Scotland and Ireland, both chief purser Calderón and his French pilot urged Medina Sidonia to 'give a wide berth to the coast of Ireland' but the naval adviser Diego Flores opposed this view and his fateful advice was adopted.[4] One of the consequential navigation errors proved particularly lethal: confusion between Cape Clear on Ireland's southern coast and numerous headlands on its western seaboard, such as Erris Head.

The captain-general wrote to Philip on 21 August in an anxious attempt to explain the failure of his mission:

> The Armada was so completely crippled and scattered that my first duty to your majesty seemed to [be to] save it, even at the risk which we are running in undertaking this voyage which is so long and in such high latitudes.
>
> Ammunition and the best of our vessels were lacking and experience had shown how little we could depend upon the ships that remained, the queen's fleet being so superior to ours in this sort of fighting, in consequence of the strength of their artillery and the fast sailing of their ships.

What followed in his letter was surprising: 'Your majesty's ships depended entirely on harquebuses and musketry which were of little service unless we could come to close quarters.'

> With the concurrence of the officers ... appointed as counsellors, and the generals, we have adopted the course we are now following ... rendered necessary by the weather, the wind having continued to blow from the south and south-west.
>
> We have therefore run through the Norwegian Channel and between the Scottish islands [Orkney and Shetland] so as to make the voyage as short as possible.
>
> Our provisions are so scanty that in order to make them and the water last a month the rations of every person, without exception, have been reduced.[5]
>
> Your majesty may well imagine what suffering this entails ... we

have consequently over three thousand sick, without counting the wounded (who are numerous) in the fleet.

God send us fair weather, so that we may soon reach port, for upon that depends the salvation of this army and navy.

Somewhat lamely, Medina Sidonia expressed his fervent hope that 'during your majesty's time [I may] yet see your holy plans completed successfully to the greater glory of almighty God'.[6] He gave the letter to one of his staff, Don Balthazar de Zúñiga, before landing him at Scalloway, on the Atlantic coast of 'mainland' Shetland,[7] with orders to sail to Spain and to arrange for provisions to await the Armada's return to Galicia.[8] Fish and fresh water were also seized from Scottish and Dutch fishing boats to augment the fleet's ever-declining stocks and pilots engaged 'to carry them for the coast of Ireland and so into Spain'.[9]

From 24 August to 4 September, the Spanish fleet struggled around the north of Scotland, beset by fogs, storms and squalls.[10] Given the difficult weather conditions and the poor repair of the ships, contact was unavoidably lost with a number of vessels. Calderón's hulk, *San Salvador,* last saw the Armada on the twenty-fourth and found herself alone near a large island on Ireland's west coast.

The sea [was] running strongly towards the land, to the great danger of the [ship]. The purser ordered her to tack to the north-west which took her thirty leagues (166.68 km) distant and it is believed that the rest of the Armada would have done the same. If not, they would certainly have lost some of the ships, as the coast is rough, the sea heavy and the winds strong from seaward.[11]

His forebodings were wholly warranted. At least twenty-seven Spanish ships came to be wrecked in what became the graveyard of the Armada (and Philip's grandiose military ambitions) off the west coasts of Ireland and Scotland.[12]

The transport squadron's flagship, the 650-ton *El Gran Grifón;* her sister hulks *Barca de Amberg* and *Castillo Negro* and Don Alonso de Luzón's 1,100-ton Levanter *La Trinidad Valencera* were four which became separated from the Armada. They sailed south-west in company for almost two weeks before the *Barca* began to founder on 1 September. Her surviving crew, numbering 256, were transferred to the *Valencera* and *Grifón* before the *Barca* disappeared beneath the waves.

The converted Venetian grain ship *Valencera* carried siege guns – weighing two and a half tonnes apiece and firing 40-pound (18.14 kg) roundshot as cargo – in addition to her own battery of forty-two guns. She had sailed from Corunna with 335 soldiers and 75 crew, but sickness and enemy action had depleted their numbers. Though some battle damage had been patched up, her pumps could not cope with the leaks in her hull. With his water and food stocks being consumed by the additional men from the *Barca* and with one hundred sick on board, Don Alonso de Luzón decided to head for land to seek fresh sustenance. On 16 September, *Valencera* suddenly grounded on a reef a short distance off the shingle beach at the western end of Kinnagoe Bay, Co. Donegal, between Malin Head and Lough Foyle.

Luzón and four officers landed and were confronted by more than twenty 'savage people'. Alarmed, they drew their rapiers in self-defence but were surprised to be courteously helped out of their boat. A larger crowd forcibly stripped them of their weapons, gold buttons, clothing and around 7,300 gold ducats in cash.[13] Eventually, after some haggling, the local Irish magnate Sir John O'Docherty supplied boats in exchange for 200 ducats, and the ship's complement began to be ferried ashore. Over the next two days more than four hundred Spaniards, Greeks and Italians were rescued, despite one boat sinking and the Irish being distracted by their enthusiastic plundering of the wreck. The Spanish purchased horsemeat and butter to provide the first fresh meal they had eaten in weeks. The *Valencera* eventually broke in two, drowning forty-five sick and wounded before they could be taken off.[14] More than thirty Irish looters were also lost as the wreck disappeared beneath the waves.

Luzón and his men were now stranded in a hostile country.

They decided to march the 20 miles (32.19 km) south across the boggy Inishowen peninsula to Illagh Castle, home of Connor O'Devenny, Bishop of Down and Connor,[15] en route to the west coast where Luzón hoped to find ships to take them to Spain. However, they were surprised by Major John Kelly with a force of Irish mercenaries in English service based at Castle Burt, comprising two hundred cavalry and three companies of 'footmen, harquebusiers and bowmen'. After some perfunctory skirmishing to satisfy both sides' honour, Luzón agreed to surrender and be taken to Dublin.

The forty-seven Spanish officers, thought likely to draw sizeable ransoms, were separated from their men and surrounded by a menacing square of soldiers. The 'other ranks' were led into a nearby field and, after being stripped naked, were cut down by volleys fired by the harquebusiers. Others were speared by the lances of the cavalry as they tried to flee. Juan Lázaro, the ship's helmsman, described how they were forced to sit on the ground and two horsemen, with long white beards,[16] signalled to the soldiers to open fire.[17] About three hundred were killed and a further one hundred injured were left to die on the bloodstained turf.

The walking wounded managed to struggle across a peat bog to Illagh Castle. Some were robbed by Irish peasants, but other locals treated the fugitives well, providing food and accommodation along the way.[18] Most survivors escaped to Scotland with the help of the charmingly named Irish chieftain Sorley Boy McDonnell of Dunluce, who ignored threats from Dublin 'not to ship any more on pain of death and confiscation of all his property'.[19] McDonnell pledged that he would 'rather lose his life and goods and those of his wife and children than barter Christian blood. He had dedicated his sword to the defence of the Catholic faith and despite the governor, the queen and all England he would embark the rest of the Spaniards.'[20]

The captured officers and gentlemen were taken on a forced march to Drogheda, 30 miles (48.28 km) north of Dublin, but only Luzón and Don Rodrigo Lasso survived the terrible privations of the journey. Both were later taken to London before being repatriated in an exchange of prisoners in March 1591.[21]

Further south, off Valentia Island, south Kerry, the Castilian galleon *La Trinidad*, 872 tons, disappeared on 12 September, having kept station with *San Juan Bautista* since 27 August. The large *zabra,* or two-masted pinnace, *Nuestra Señora de Castro*, 75 tons, anchored in Tralee Bay off the little town of Fenit on 15 September, her hull leaking badly, eighteen days after last seeing the flagship *San Martin*. Three of the twenty-four crew on board swam to shore and surrendered themselves to Lady Margaret Denny, the dour wife of Sir Edward Denny, at Tralee Castle.

Unfortunately, fate had dealt them an ill-starred card.

Denny had been given Colonel Sebastiano di San Giuseppe, the Italian commander of the Dún an Óir ('Fort of Gold') at nearby Smerwick, for ransom after the 1579–80 papal incursion into Ireland, but he had inconveniently escaped,[22] leaving Denny not only humiliated but out of pocket too. That day, eight years before, he had sworn that, henceforth, he would kill any Spaniard he could lay his hands on, and here was his unexpected chance to fulfil that bloody vow. The crew were detained and, during less than gentle interrogation, admitted that the Armada now numbered only seventy ships. They also disclosed there was an Englishman called 'Don William', described as 'of a reasonable stature [and] bald', on board Medina Sidonia's ship.[23] Denny promptly strung up seventeen of the Spanish sailors at Dingle, but three 'offered ransoms for their lives, promising that they should find friends in Waterford to redeem them'. They could not name these guarantors, so they were summarily executed as well.[24]

Seen through sixteenth-century eyes, these judicial killings and massacres would seem entirely reasonable, if not normal. There was no Geneva Convention then to protect captured combatants. Prisoners of war enjoyed no special rights, particularly those with no hope of bringing their captors bountiful ransoms. Moreover, the English in Ireland could manage only precarious governance over the restive Irish chieftains and the unruly Catholic population. Memories were still fresh of the Desmond rebellion and the papacy's ill-advised military adventure on the Dingle peninsula. No wonder then that reports of Spanish ships landing troops galvanised the English government in Dublin, who suspected this was yet another foreign invasion of Ireland.

Sir Richard Bingham, the ruthless governor of Connacht, told of 'further news of strange ships. Whether they are of the dispersed fleet which are fled from the supposed overthrow in the Narrow Seas, or new forces come from Spain directly, no man is able to [tell] otherwise by guess.' Bingham believed that as many ships were on the west coast, they must have sailed from Spain. 'I look this night for my horses to be here and on receipt of further intelligence, I will make towards the sea coast, either upwards to Thomond or downwards to Sligo.'[25]

Sir William Fitzwilliam, lord deputy of Ireland, warned of 'so ticklish and dangerous a time' for 'this poor realm'[26] and emphasised to Elizabeth's Privy Council that he had less than seven hundred and fifty trained soldiers with which to defend Ireland. The Irish government looked 'rather to be overrun by the Spaniards than otherwise', he warned. With so few soldiers on hand to defeat a Spanish incursion, he ordered his officers on the west coast 'to apprehend and execute all Spaniards found of whatever quality. Torture may be used in prosecuting this policy.'[27] George Fenton, secretary to the Irish Council, was more sanguine about the chances of any Irish rebellion supported by the surviving Spaniards: 'The Irish [are] more greedy of spoil than apt to hearken after other things.'[28]

Francisco de Cuéllar, whom we met earlier, narrowly escaping execution in the Armada, was shipwrecked in Co. Mayo. He has left us a vivid description of the inhabitants he encountered:

> These savages live like beasts in the mountains … in thatched cabins and are all big men, handsome and well-built and fleet as the roe-deer. They dress … [in] short loose coats of very coarse goat's hair [and] wrap up in blankets and wear their hair down to their eyes.
>
> They are continually at war with the English … they don't let them into their lands which are all flooded and marshy.
>
> What these people are most inclined to is thieving and robbing one another so that not a day passes between them without a call to arms, because as soon as the people in the next village find out … that there are cattle or anything else, they come armed at night and all hell breaks loose and they slaughter one another.
>
> In short; in this kingdom there is neither justice or reason, so that everyone does as he pleases.[29]

History has judged these Irish severely, criticising their enthusiasm for plunder and their apparently callous indifference to the hundreds of Spanish who drowned on their coast. It is true there were few recorded attempts to rescue the wretched crews as their ships went down one after the other, but hardly any Irish could swim in the sixteenth century. Their culture also apparently maintained that it was downright unlucky to save a man from the sea. If they did, they, or one of their kin, would one day be drowned instead.[30]

The sea, they believed, would always claim its victims.

Compared to the scale of the English slaughter, relatively few survivors were killed by the Irish, aside from stories that on one beach Melaghlin M'Cabb, a giant gallowglass, hacked eighty helpless men to death with his battle axe.[31] Indeed, some of the Irish rebel chiefs risked their lives and property to protect Spanish survivors from English retribution; one of them, called O'Rourke, hid one refugee throughout the following winter and when Fitzwilliam demanded that he be handed over to the government, he steadfastly refused. O'Rourke's two sons were hanged in reprisal.[32]

Opportunities for booty for the Irish were growing as Armada ships were now being driven ashore in greater numbers by a fortnight of fierce storms.

Twenty-four hours after the *Nuestra Señora de Castro* surrendered, Boetius Clancy, the sheriff of Clare, informed Bingham that 'last night two ships were seen about the islands of Arran and it is thought more sails were seen westwards from the islands'. One ship was currently

> anchored in an unusual harbour, about one mile (1.6 km) west of Sir Turlough O'Brien's house called Liscannor.
>
> The said ship had two cockboats [and] ... one landed and is not like our English cockboats. It would carry twenty men at least and it is painted red with [a] red anchor with an earthen vessel like an oil crock.
>
> They offered to land the last night in one of the cockboats which they could not by reason of the weather and the harbour.
>
> I watch here with the most part of the inhabitants of the barony.[33]

Four days afterwards, the ship, Don Felipe de Córdoba's 736-ton Guipúzcoan warship *San Esteban,* was washed ashore on the white strand near Doonbeg, north of Kilrush. Two hundred men were drowned and sixty captured as they struggled out of the waves. Six miles (10.14 km) to the north, another Armada ship, probably the *San Marcos*, was wrecked the same day between Mutton Island[34] and Lurga Point, with only four survivors. Clancy hanged them, with those from the *San Esteban*, on a low hill thereafter called Cnoc na Crocaire (or Gallows Hill) and they were buried in one pit near Killilagh church.[35]

It was an ill day for the Armada. The Levanter *Anunciada*, 703 tons, was set on fire and scuttled in Scattery Roads, off Kilrush on the north bank of the River Shannon estuary. She had anchored there a week before with five *zabra*s, her leaks threatening to sink her. Twenty-four hours after *Anunciada*'s arrival, the little group of ships was joined by the tub-bellied hulk *Barca de Danzig*, 450 tons, also badly battered by the weather. Ragusan carpenters managed to repair the transport's hull, but their own *Anunciada* was beyond help. After her crew, artillery and what remained of her provisions and water were shipped over to the *Barca de Danzig* she was burnt near Scattery Island.[36]

Off Ireland's south-west coast, in Co. Kerry, some ships survived. Marcos de Aramburu's galleon *San Juan de Castilla* anchored in Blasket Sound, at the entrance to Dingle Bay, for repairs. (She managed to reach Santander on 14 October.) The same day Recalde's *San Juan de Portugal* (1,050 tons), with more than one hundred seriously sick on board, joined Aramburu in the Sound. Recalde had twenty-five pipes of wine but no drinkable water; what remained had been loaded in Spain and 'stinketh marvellously'.

Both ships replenished their water from a spring on Great Blasket Island. At noon on 21 September, they were joined by the Guipúzcoan vice-flagship *Santa María de la Rosa*, 945 tons, her sails in shreds. She dropped anchor and then, shortly after two o'clock, suddenly sank having struck the submerged Stromboli pinnacle of rock. All three hundred hands were lost, save Giovanni de Manona, son of the Genovese pilot, who managed to float ashore on a wooden plank. Captured by the English, he described how one of the ship's officers had accused his father of treason in deliberately wrecking the ship and had killed him in a moment of fury. The ship had gone down almost in seconds – so that the officers had no time to launch their boat. He also claimed that the Prince of Asculi, Philip's illegitimate son, had been on board and had not survived, but as the prince was in Flanders and subsequently served in Italy, this was patently untrue. Manona was executed by his English captors.[37]

Fernando Horra's *San Juan Bautista* arrived on 23 September, without her mainmast and clearly damaged beyond any hope of repair. Her crew were transferred to the *San Juan de Castilla* and *San Juan de Portugal* and she was burnt to the waterline. Recalde and his ship reached Bilbao on 7 October but he died two days after-wards from exhaustion in a monastery.

Between 16 and 21 September, three ships were wrecked on the coast of Co. Mayo – the Levanter *San Nicholas Prodaneli* (834 tons) and the two *urcas*, *Santiago* (600 tons) and *Ciervo Volante* (400 tons). Their crews, possibly numbering as many as five hundred men, were drowned or executed, either soon after coming ashore or later while held in Galway gaol by Sir Richard Bingham.[38] A fourth vessel may have come ashore in Tirawley, probably in Killala Bay.

Don Alonso de Leyva's *Rata Santa María Encoronada* sailed into Blacksod Bay, an area of sea inlets enclosed by the Mullet Peninsula and Achill Island.[39] On board was Maurice Fitzmaurice, son of the Irish rebel James Fitzmaurice Fitzgerald. Despite deploying sea anchors, she ran aground on Fahy Strand, near Ballycroy, on 21 September, a victim of the vicious local rip-tides. Fitzgerald died on board and was solemnly consigned to the waves in a large cypress chest.

Leyva burnt the ship and moved his men and remaining provi-sions into Doona Castle, overlooking the bay. The Andalusian hulk *Duquesa Santa Ana* had meanwhile anchored safely in Elly harbour, 10 miles (16.9 km) across the bay and six miles (9 km) south of Belmullet. Leyva marched his men 25 miles (40.23 km) around the bay to her and took command, intending to sail the *Duquesa* to neu-tral Scotland, with the seven hundred and fifty men he now had on board. Ill luck dogged him, however, and another storm drove the 900-ton ship ashore in Loughros Mor Bay at Rossbeg, Co. Donegal, during the night of 25–26 September, when Leyva was injured in the leg by a spinning capstan bar as he quit the ship. Undaunted, he took over an old fort just off the coast on O'Boyle's Island in Lough Kiltooris, and positioned a light gun from the wreck in the ruins. The galleass *Girona* was then reported at Killybegs, 19 miles (30.58 km) to the south and, carried in a rough-and-ready chair, built by the ship's carpenters, de Leyva led his men down the road from Ardara to join her.

The next two weeks were spent repairing the *Girona*, using mate-rials salvaged from another Spanish ship that had been stranded off Camtullagh Head at the mouth of Killybegs harbour. Some Irish begged Leyva to stay and lead them against the English heretics, but he argued that his commission prevented him from doing that.[40]

Having heard that Lord Deputy Fitzwilliam was leading an English force towards them, Leyva 'put himself aboard her, having for his pilot three Irishmen and a Scot'.⁴¹ At last, on 26 October, the galleass departed for Scotland with more than a thousand Spanish on board, three hundred of them galley slaves.⁴² Two hundred had to be left behind – one of them James Machary 'of the Cross within the county of Tipperary'. The lord deputy had 'good will to hang him, [as] he is a subject of her majesty's' but spared him to allow the Privy Council in London to question him.⁴³

Two days later the *Girona* was wrecked at midnight in a storm at the base of towering Lacada Point in Co. Antrim, the ship breaking in two on the rocks. Only nine survivors managed to climb the cliffs to seek shelter in Dunluce Castle⁴⁴ and eventually arrived in Scotland. Sorley Boy McDonnell recovered 'certain wine' washed up on the shore but at least gave the two hundred and sixty bodies pulled from the sea a decent burial in the local cemetery.⁴⁵ The loss of the galleass brought mourning to a number of the great noble houses of Spain and Italy: 'The gentlemen were so many that a list of their names would fill a quire of paper,' according to one Spanish source.

For months, there were high hopes in Madrid that Leyva and his force were miraculously still alive and were fighting the English, in alliance with Irish rebel leaders. One report in January 1589 talks of him capturing the town of Dundalk with 'three Irish knights', having joined up with 'O'Neill and McDonnell who are great gentlemen and enemies of the Lutheran queen'. Irish merchants the same month passed on rumours that Leyva had fortified a port in Co. Sligo, which was 'well-entrenched' and armed with 'artillery and ammunition of the vessels that had gone aground'. His Irish allies, O'Rourke and O'Connor, were 'well content since they had joined with him and were not afraid of the power of the English'.⁴⁶

But such optimism was groundless: brave and determined Leyva had died in the single greatest loss of life suffered by an Armada ship. He was described as 'long-bearded, tall and slender, of a flaxen and smooth hair, of behaviour mild and temperate, of speech good and deliberate, greatly reverenced not only of his own men but generally of the whole company'.⁴⁷ Philip said later that he mourned his loss more than that of his Armada.

So the slaughter went on. On 22 September, the Biscayan vice flag-ship *El Gran Grin* (1,160 tons) was wrecked on a reef off Clare Island at the western edge of Co. Mayo's Clew Bay, drowning more than two hundred of her crew. Her captain, Pedro de Mendoza, managed to reach the island with one hundred survivors but when they tried to escape by stealing fishing boats the local chieftain, Dawdarra Roe O'Malley, killed sixty-four, including Mendoza.[48] Only one Spaniard and an Irishman from Wexford were spared.[49]

Three days later three Levantine armed merchantmen sank off the two mile (3.22 km) wide sands of Streedagh Strand, in Donegal Bay, north of Sligo: *Juliana* (860 tons), *Santa María de Visón* (660 tons) and the squadron vice-flagship *Lavia* (728 tons). The ships went aground some distance from the shore and broke up within the hour, drowning almost one thousand men. Some three hundred survivors were killed by Sir Richard Bingham's soldiers. One of those who escaped was Francisco de Cuéllar, who was in the Venetian *Lavia* after being relieved from command of *San Pedro*. He described her shipwreck:

> A huge gale hit us broadside on, with the waves reaching the sky ... the [anchor] cables could not hold and the sails were no use, so that we found ourselves hurtling ashore with all three ships on to a beach of very fine sand, hemmed in at either side by tremendous rocks.

A colonel, Don Diego Enríquez, 'the hunchback', had loaded his ship's boat with 16,000 ducats in jewels and gold coins. It had a deck, and four men sheltered below, ordering the hatch to be closed and caulked above them. Suddenly, more than seventy men who were left on the wreck jumped down into the boat and 'an enormous wave' submerged her, sweeping away the crew and washing it ashore, leaving it upside down on the beach.

> In this sorry plight, the gentlemen who had gone below died.
> When the boat had been a day and a half on the shore, some savages reached her and turned her over ... Breaking open the deck, they pulled out the dead and Don Diego Enríquez who finally expired in their hands.
> Then they stripped them and took their jewellery and money, dumping the bodies around without burying them.

Cuéllar was on the *Lavia*'s poop deck, watching with horror as many drowned inside the ships, whilst others jumped into the water 'never to come up again';

> others were shrieking inside the ships, calling on God for help. The captains were throwing their gold chains and gold coins into the sea. I could see ... the beach full of enemies, dancing and skipping about with glee at our misfortune. When any of our men reached the shore, two hundred savages and other enemies went up to him and took everything he was wearing until he was left stark naked ... Survivors were pitilessly beaten up and wounded.

Cuéllar, who could not swim, looked around for some debris he could cling to as he struggled for the shore. Suddenly, Martin de Aranda, the judge advocate general who had reprieved him, was alongside him on the *Lavia*'s poop deck. He was 'extremely tearful and dejected' and could hardly stand as he was weighed down with gold ducats he had sewn into his doublet. Cuéllar, clutching a wooden hatch cover for buoyancy, jumped into the water. Aranda scrambled on top of the flotsam but was swept away by an enormous wave, piteously appealing to God as he drifted out of reach to drown. Covered in blood from injuries to both legs, Cuéllar managed to reach the beach, and hid that night. The next morning he found a deserted monastery that had been torched by the English. Inside the church there were twelve Spaniards hanging from the iron bars of the window gratings. On the beach were six hundred corpses, being eaten by scavenging dogs and ravens.[50]

Much later Lord Deputy Fitzwilliam visited Streedagh Strand:

> I went to see the bay where some of those ships wrecked and where, as I heard, lay not long before, 1,200 or 1,300 of the dead bodies.
>
> I rode along that strand near two miles and then turned off from that shore, leaving before me [more than a] mile's riding in which places ... there lay a great store of the timber of the wrecked ships ... being in mine opinion more than would have built five of the great ships that ever I saw, besides mighty great boats, cables and other cordage ... and some masts for bigness and length as in mine own judgement I never saw any two could make the like.[51]

Fitzwilliam had sent David Gwyn (who had escaped from one of the Armada galleys wrecked earlier off Bayonne) to take charge of salvaging the treasure and guns from the ships at Streedagh Strand and to question Spanish prisoners in Drogheda. Unfortunately, Gwyn fled to La Rochelle in France with £160 in coins, gold chains and jewels, stolen from the survivors. Back in Dublin, he was the subject of scurrilous allegations that, while serving on the galleys, he had boasted that Walsingham 'was for the Spaniards and would deliver her majesty's person into their hands'. Incensed, the lord deputy swore he would defend Walsingham's loyalty with the loss of his own blood.[52]

Cuéllar later met two armed men, an Englishman and a Frenchman and 'a most extremely beautiful girl' of about twenty who prevented her companions from killing him but not from stripping him of his clothes and a gold chain and the forty-five ducats sewn up in his doublet – two months' pay received before he left Corunna. His doublet was returned, but not his shirt, which 'the savage damsel hung round her neck, saying, by signs, that she meant to keep it and that she was a Christian, being as much like one as Mohammed was', the Spaniard recounted. Eventually Cuéllar escaped to Scotland and sailed on to Dunkirk where this unlucky man was shipwrecked again, and saw two hundred and seventy of his companions put to the sword by the Dutch at the harbour's mouth. It was not until 4 October 1589 that he reached the safety of the Spanish-held city of Antwerp in the Low Countries.[53]

Back in Ireland, the hulk *Falcon Blanco Mediano*, 300 tons, ran ashore near Inishbofin island, Galway, on 25 September. The eighty-strong crew were fed and hidden by the O'Flahertys of Connemara, until the governor issued a proclamation ordering that anyone who harboured Spaniards for more than four hours would be hanged as traitors, at which point the O'Flahertys surrendered their guests to Sir Richard Bingham.[54] Even Bingham, who had boasted of killing eleven hundred survivors from the wrecks off Connaught, was perhaps tiring of the slaughter for he spared them – or was he thinking more of the ransom? However, they were later executed on Fitzwilliam's own orders. Another ship, the 418-ton Biscayan *Concepción de Juan de Cano* came ashore further south at Ard Bay, near Carna, more than 18 miles (30 km) west of Galway city, after being lured to shore by the bonfires of a party of wreckers.[55]

There were two more identified Armada wrecks – this time in Scotland.

After parting company with the ill-fated *La Trinidad Valencera* on 4 September, the 650-ton flagship hulk *El Gran Grifón* had been blown backwards and forwards by errant winds off Scotland's west coast. On 27 September, she sighted Fair Isle, between Orkney and Shetland, and was beached at dawn in a narrow inlet beneath the towering cliff of Stromshellier.[56] Seven died as the crew scrambled ashore and the three hundred survivors (some of whom came from the *Barca de Amberg*) were well treated by the handful of crofter families on the island.

They must have wondered at the strange world that fate had brought them to. The inhabitants were all bald, 'not a hair between them and heaven' – an affliction they ascribed to 'excessive toiling in rowing through impetuous tides'.[57] A senior Spanish officer, retaining some pride amongst all this privation, asked a local chieftain, Malcolm Sinclair of Owendale, if he had ever seen 'such a man as he'. There was a pause and then the islander replied: 'Fair in the face ... [but] I have seen many [a] prettier man hanging in the Burrow Moor.'[58] After months of neglect, some fifty Spanish died from wounds or disease and were buried at the south end of Fair Isle on a spot still marked as 'Spainnarts' graves'.[59] The others were so weak that two of them were easily pushed off the cliff by the islanders. The survivors were taken to Anstruther, on the Scottish mainland, in hired ships, landing on 6 December, and two hundred and fifty were repatriated to Spain in March 1589.

The 800-ton Ragusan warship *San Juan de Sicilia,* with a crew of more than three hundred, became the second Armada casualty in Scotland, but not through the effects of bad weather. Don Diego Tellez Enríquez had dropped anchor on 25 September in Tobermory Bay, at the north-east tip of the island of Mull, off the west coast. For more than four weeks, she remained there, repairing her damage and taking on fresh supplies, ready for the voyage home. In return for allowing her safe anchorage, the local landowner, Lachlan MacLean of Duart, employed around one hundred Spanish soldiers as mercenaries to sort out some of his local clan feuds. The Spanish plundered the nearby islands of Rum and Eigg, belonging to the MacDonalds of Clanranald, and also Canna and Muck, owned by the Macleans of Ardamurchan.

On 5 November, the ship unexpectedly blew up, leaving just fifteen survivors from those aboard.[60] MacLean kept on a force of fifty remaining Spaniards for another year before they were returned home.

In Ireland, Fitzwilliam believed that a Frenchman who had been condemned for 'embezzling treasure and jewels' had lit some gunpowder and blown up the ship.[61] But it was Sir Francis Walsingham's secret service that destroyed the enemy ship. His agent, John Smollett of Dumbarton, was one of the Scottish merchants who were selling foodstuffs to the Spanish. He took advantage of a heaven-sent opportunity when, unwisely, the crew were drying gunpowder on the foredeck. After dropping a piece of smouldering cloth nearby, he swiftly left the ship and headed for shore. Moments later, the huge explosion followed.[62]

The scattered remains of the San Juan de Sicilia lie in eleven fathoms (20.12 metres) of water, around five hundred and fifty yards (500 metres) from the shore.[63] In 1730 a cannon bearing the arms of Francis I of France was recovered – probably captured by the Spanish at the Battle of St Quentin in 1557. It is now at Inverary Castle. Despite persistent rumours to the contrary, she was not a treasure ship, although a silver plate eleven inches (27.94 cm) in diameter was brought to the surface in 1906.

In London, Walsingham had heard reports by 8 September that the Spanish 'had lost a great number of their ships towards the back side of Ireland in the last storm' and three weeks later the English government had sufficient information to prepare a 'printed book' that provided details of the Armada losses.[64] He wrote to Sir Edward Stafford, Elizabeth's ambassador in Paris: 'We do look shortly to hear … of other ships to fall into the like distress for the south-west winds have blown so hard as, in the judgement of our seamen, it has not be possible for them to return to Spain.'[65]

Reports of Spanish soldiers roaming the wild wastes of Ireland alarmed Elizabeth, who ordered the lords lieutenant of England's western counties to put their militia 'into readiness to march for Ireland with an hour's warning'. Fitzwilliam asked for 'five or six ships from Bristol' to be stationed off the Irish coast 'to destroy the forty sea-beaten vessels returning into Spain'.[66]

In the event, no army was needed as the supposed Spanish military threat just melted away. Of the survivors, some soldiers entered the service of Hugh O'Neill, Earl of Tyrone. Eight years later, there were eight still working for him, including Pedro Blanco, who had escaped from the *Juliana* shipwreck to become the earl's bodyguard.

About one hundred 'ransomable' well-born Spaniards were reprieved by Fitzwilliam, of whom sixty-one were sent to England. Thirty others managed to escape en route between Dublin and Chester in the last months of 1588. They were put into the *Swallow*, a pinnace owned by Christopher Carleill, constable of Carrickfergus in Northern Ireland (and Walsingham's stepson by his first marriage), as she was anchored in Dublin Bay. Afterwards, when he claimed compensation for his stolen vessel, Carleill reported that his eight-man crew and the one gentleman on board were overcome by the prisoners who 'forcibly ... carried both pinnace and men away'. They arrived at Corunna safely and the pinnace was seen there in August or September 1589. Luke Plunkett reported that *Swallow* and another vessel, which had rescued some Italians from the Armada, were preying on shipping along the Irish coast. Three 'sailors from Ireland' – presumably members of her original crew – had been executed by the Spanish by December 1589.[67]

Estimates of the number of Spanish who perished off Scotland and the west coast of Ireland or were subsequently slaughtered vary greatly. Beltrán del Salton, in his report to Philip in April 1589, believed that 3,428 drowned and 1,016 were executed by the English.[68] He listed only thirteen wrecks, however, with one hundred and six survivors and if the casualties from the ships lost but not known to Beltrán are included, the total number who died rises to 6,751 – fairly close to earlier official Spanish totals of about 6,161.[69] George Fenton noted sixteen shipwrecks and 5,394 killed.[70] More recent documentary research suggests that 3,750 drowned or died from hunger and disease after coming ashore; 1,500 were killed by the English or Irish; and there were 750 survivors.[71]

As Fitzwilliam told Burghley on 26 September: 'God has fought by shipwrecks, savages and famine for her majesty against these proud Spaniards.'[72] He did not think it relevant to mention the English massacre of the survivors.

Unfortunately, the Armada had not yet suffered its last ship losses.

On 4 October, the 600-ton Neapolitan galleass *Zúñiga* was driven by gales into the French port of Le Havre and her purser, Pedro de Igueldo, told Mendoza in Paris that she had to be re-masted, careened and her seams re-caulked with pitch to make her hull seaworthy. Rations were at meagre levels and it is unsurprising therefore that, almost immediately, sixteen Frenchmen and twelve Italians and Spanish deserted. 'It is the greatest trouble in the world to guard them on board and none is allowed on shore,' said Igueldo.

> Two convicts escaped this morning and I reported to the [French] governor that the guard at the town gate had aided them to get away.
>
> He at once went in person and gave the corporal of the guard twenty blows with his crutch and would have put him in chains in the convicts' place if I had not begged for mercy for him.
>
> He then sent the corporal to seek out the convicts and he was so smart about it that he brought them both back this afternoon, finely tricked out in French clothes.[73]

The three-hundred-strong crew were marooned in France for almost a year until *Zúñiga*'s repairs were completed and paid for. She became the last Armada ship to return home.

The 550-ton hospital ship *San Pedro el Mayor* was lost when, having successfully skirted the dangers of the Irish west coast, on 6 November she ended up stranded on Bolt Tail, a rugged headland in South Devon. Her one hundred and sixty-eight survivors were eventually sent to France; together with the three hundred from the Biscayan *Santa Ana* which lost her mainmast on 27 July and sought refuge in the French port of Le Havre; they were back in Spain by the end of the year.

Parma finally abandoned his plans for an invasion on 31 August, standing down his fleet and dispersing his army for attacks on Dutch objectives.

On 3 September the first hints of the disaster that had befallen the 'Enterprise of England' reached the Escorial Palace via a dispatch from France that reported the defeat off Gravelines and the Armada's flight northwards to Scotland.

After some delay, Philip's private secretary Mateo Vázquez chose to break the news obliquely to his master by passing on to the king a letter from another official, Pedro Nuñez, written late the previous day. Among its courtly phrases came a hard-edged sentence that warned of imminent grim news by citing 'the case of Louis IX of France, who was a saint and was engaged in a saintly enterprise[74] and yet saw his army die of plague, with himself defeated and captured'. It added pointedly: 'We certainly cannot fail to fear greatly for the success of our Armada.' Vázquez suggested in a separate note that further prayers should be offered up for the safety of the mighty Spanish fleet. Philip, taken aback, scribbled in the margin: 'I hope that God has not permitted so much evil for everything has been done for His service.'[75]

Medina Sidonia arrived in Santander on the north Spanish coast on 21 September. It was not a joyous homecoming.

He anchored off Point Enoja 'as the tide was against us [in our] intention of entering the harbour by the morning tide'. The captain-general was very ill after twenty-five days of fever and dysentery 'which have grievously weakened me' and described himself as 'almost at my last gasp'. He was lowered into a pilot boat to come ashore, leaving the *San Martin* to be towed in by pinnaces.

But the weather that afflicted him so sorely throughout the 'Enterprise of England' still had the last word. A south-westerly wind was blowing so strongly that the flagship had to run for Laredo, where she was anchored with the galleass *Napolitana*. Three hawsers were wrapped around her hull, because her sprung seams were letting in so much seawater.

'Eight ships have entered this port and five or six others have run for the Biscay coast,' the captain-general reported to Philip.

> There are also six or seven more cruising off this port so that I hope to God that they will all come in, one after the other.
>
> The troubles and miseries we have suffered cannot be described. They have been greater than have ever been seen in any voyage before and on board some of the ships, there was not one drop of water to drink for a fortnight.
>
> On the flagship, one hundred and eighty men died of sickness, three out of the four pilots on board having succumbed and all the rest of the people on the ship are ill, many of typhus and other contagious maladies.

> All the men of my household, to the number of sixty, have either
> died or fallen sick and only two have remained to serve me.

'God be praised for all He has ordained,' the captain-general added, without any trace of irony or bitterness. He then returned to his sick bed 'unable to attend anything, however much I might wish to do so'.[76]

Miguel de Oquendo brought five of his ships back to Guipúzcoa. Almost immediately, his flagship was ravaged by fire after a magazine blew up, killing one hundred of her crew. Oquendo, whose wife and children lived in Santander, refused to see them. He turned his face to the wall and died, probably from typhus.

In Rome, the cardinals supporting Spain's cause complained that the promised money had not been paid – 'for it is not the king's fault if no landing was effected. If things have not gone well,' they added with masterly understatement, 'that is a reason for consoling, not for further harassing of his majesty.'[77]

Before he died, Recalde sent Philip his journal of the Armada campaign. 'I have read it all,' the king noted in his aide-memoire, 'although I would rather not have done, because it hurts so much.'

– 10 –

'GOD BE PRAISED FOR
ALL HIS WORKS'

My dear countrymen (and well-beloved in the Lord) …
the trial of your valiant courage and proof of your war-
like furnitures was prevented by the great mercy of God
and the provident foresight of her excellent majesty, so as
God Himself has stricken the stroke …

Anthony Marten, *An Exhortation to Stir up the Minds*
of all her majesty's Faithful Subjects … 1588.[1]

Ship by ship, the battered survivors of the *Grande y Felicísima Armada*, the 'Great and Most Fortunate Navy', limped gratefully into ports along Spain's northern coast that September and October. The depleted roll call of the returning vessels and their dreadful condition was an eloquent testimony to the nightmare conditions of their voyage home. Of the 129 ships that finally departed Corunna on 21 July, a minimum of fifty (or 39 per cent) did not come back. Other estimates suggest that as many as sixty-four vessels were lost, including a number of the smaller and more vulnerable *patache*s and *zabra*s.[2] Only thirty-four great galleons returned, some so badly damaged that they were condemned as unseaworthy. These Armada losses represented 'the greatest disaster to strike Spain in over six hundred years'[3] as Friar José de Sigüenza, a monk at the Escorial Palace, acknowledged miserably shortly afterwards.

In contrast, the English lost just the eight vessels employed as fire-ships off Calais and lost a total of perhaps 150 killed in action.

Despite the triumphant claims by Elizabeth's government, this was not a crushing defeat inflicted by the queen's ships through over-whelming naval tactics or much vaunted racial superiority. Apart from the four ships destroyed in the Battle of Gravelines, all the

Spanish casualties were lost in accidents or in the fierce storms that raged after the Armada had sailed north to Scotland. Philip, recognising that most lethal of enemies, complained: 'I sent my fleet against men, not against the wind and the waves.'

The Armada's run of appalling bad luck did not end with its ignominious and inglorious homecoming. After de Oquendo's mighty 1,200-ton *Santa Ana* blew up in Santander harbour, another ship ran aground at Laredo simply because it had too few men left to lower the sails or drop the anchor. A third, awash with seawater from the leaking seams in her hull, sank beneath the waves after safely mooring.

Its losses in manpower were just as horrendous as those in its order of battle. The Armada returned with fewer than 4,000 from its complement of 7,707 sailors and only 9,500 of its 18,703 soldiers, a casualty rate of just over 49 per cent. These totals do not include the fatalities amongst the wretched slaves in the Neapolitan squadron or the Portuguese galleys whose losses were thought to be not worth counting by Spanish bureaucrats. Again, enemy action – even those cruel massacres and executions on the Irish west coast – accounted for only a small percentage. The majority of deaths were brought about by a scandalous litany of causes: the putrid food and contaminated water; inadequate medical care of the wounded; the ravages of disease; the unaccustomed cold of the North Atlantic; all compounded by poor navigation and pilotage. Many casualties were thus wholly avoidable. Indeed, 'a great mortality' from typhus, scurvy and influenza continued to rage amongst the hapless survivors on their return home.

Soon after the first ships arrived, Garcia de Villejo informed the secretary for war, Andres de Prada, in Madrid that there were 'over one thousand sick and if the men be all disembarked at once, the hospital would be overcrowded ... It is impossible to attend to so many sick and the men are bound to fall ill if they sleep in the ships full of stench and wretchedness.'

With an accountant's stern eye, Villejo warned of a 'great deal of rotten foodstuffs [still] in the ships and I beg you to order that it be thrown overboard. If this is not done, someone will be sure to buy it to grind it up to mix it with the new biscuit, which will be enough to poison all the armadas afloat.'[4] The sick list soon grew to well over four thousand. Other survivors, already thin and wasted from reduced rations, finally died from starvation in port as the Spanish commissariat, overwhelmed by demand, could not provide sufficient provisions to feed them. What the English had signally failed to achieve, Spanish incompetence accomplished instead. The collapse of Medina Sidonia's much-vaunted administrative arrangements, Philip's impatience to sail as soon as possible and his flawed campaign strategy, fatally combined to destroy Spain's invincible Armada.

Officials in Guipúzcoa estimated that 502 men from their province had died in the Spanish fleet – 128 from the port of San Sebastián alone. Just over a hundred of them had died in Ireland, but 221 had succumbed to disease in Lisbon before the Armada had even made its abortive first departure on 30 May. Only twenty-three Guipúzcoans were killed in action.[5] This appalling death toll was mirrored in other areas of northern Spain: 'The like lamentation was never in any country as in Biscay and Asturia,' reported one traveller.[6]

The impact on thousands of families, both rich and poor, was too dreadful to bear. For some, entire male lines had been wiped out: for example, nine cousins of Martin de Aranda, the fleet's judge advocate general (who drowned at Streedagh Strand) did not return home.[7] The new papal nuncio to Spain, Annibale de Grassi, who arrived in November, met so many people wearing mourning that (rather unfeelingly) he inquired the reason and was told they were related to those killed in the Armada.[8] If the stress and pain of bereavement was immense, the inconsolable agony of not knowing what had happened to a father, brother or son was even more insupportable. Three months later, families were still desperately trailing along Spain's northern coast, trying to establish the fate of their missing menfolk, their fading hopes regularly and cruelly raised by sightings of each new ship that straggled back over the horizon.

In late October, Philip wrote to the Archbishop of Toledo, presenting a brave public face to the catastrophe.

> Seeing that it is our duty to thank God for all it has pleased Him to do, I have returned Him thanks for this and for the pity He has shown to all, for owing to the violent storm that attacked the fleet, a much worse issue might reasonably have been looked for and I

attribute this favour to the devout and incessant prayers which have been raised to Him.

But the time for supplication was over: 'I consider that the prayers and public orations have done their work for the present and may now cease,' he ordered.[9]

The shock of the Armada's defeat was all the more devastating because hopes of its success had been raised by false rumours. One of Walsingham's secret informants, Edward Palmer, an English Catholic priest in Spain, related how news reached San Sebastián of Howard and Drake being captured; Plymouth and the Isle of Wight taken; and that Parma's army was expected in London within a few days. 'Upon the news, the towns made great feasts all that day, running the streets on horseback [in] rich apparel and crying out that the great dog Drake was a prisoner in chains and fetters. At night, [they] made bonfires and reviled her majesty and broke all my windows with stones.' But after the Armada returned, 'they all hang down their heads like cur-dogs and are ashamed of all they did. The king keeps in the Escorial and no one dares speak to him for all the world laughs [at] him in scorn.'[10]

So the king turned his face away from the world, locking himself up in his quarters at San Lorenzo as the scale of the disaster became obvious, even to a man with an unshakeable faith in God's power to work miracles.

The daily business of government ground to an abrupt halt as Philip mourned his Armada and his lost hopes of victory in such a holy cause. Lippomano, the Venetian ambassador to Spain, observed that 'the king gives no audience and does not dispatch business. No one is paid [and] the cry of his people goes up to heaven.' A royal chaplain, Padre Marian Azzaro, told Philip that although his prayers and processions 'were very good things, yet it was certain that God gave ear to other voices before his'. When the king asked him: 'What voices?' Father Marian replied: 'Those of the poor oppressed who stay about the court in pain, without being paid and without having their business attended to.'[11]

There was also no redress for the owners of vessels lost in the campaign. Lippomano reported that

some of the owners whose ships have been cast away or burned have applied to the King for pay ... Those owners have been told quite frankly that the King is under no obligation, any more than a private individual who hired a ship ... The contention that the ships were taken by force is of no weight against the privilege of the King.[12]

Stubborn denial turned to bleak despair in the Escorial Palace that November. Now ill with recurrent fevers and a return of the painful gout, the king wrote an anguished, desolate letter to his secretary Mateo Vázquez:

> Very soon we shall find ourselves in such a state that we shall wish that we had never been born.
>
> If God does not send a miracle (which is what I hope from Him) I hope to die and go to Him before all this happens ... which is what I pray for, so as not to see so much ill-fortune and disgrace.
>
> Please God, let me be mistaken, but I do not think it is so.
>
> Rather, we shall have to witness ... what we so much fear, if God does not return to fight for His cause.

Philip emphasised: 'All this is for your eyes alone.'[13] He confided to his chaplain: 'God does not return to fight for His cause. [This] would not have been permitted except to punish us for our sins.'

Medina Sidonia tried to feed and care for the survivors but it was a daunting task, given the huge numbers of sick and starving and the lack of food available in the surrounding countryside. One wonders what good the sugar, raisins and almond preserves that he ordered could have achieved.

Predictably, the captain-general faced harsh criticism in Spain for his conduct of the campaign. Lippomano reported that 'what is heard on all sides is the bad generalship and timidity of the duke ... and everyone lays the blame [for] all these misfortunes upon his inexperience and lack of valour'.[14] Medina Sidonia begged royal leave to return to his home amid the orange groves of San Lúcar to recover, rather than go immediately to Madrid to explain why his mission had so totally failed. Philip, with a surprising generosity of spirit and compassion, told him to 'attend to his health and to vex himself about nothing [and] when he is better to go and see his wife as there will always be plenty of time for him to come to court'.[15]

On 5 October, with his back-pay of 7,810 gold ducats in his saddlebags, Medina Sidonia 'apparelled himself and his gentlemen all in black and like mourners' set off for home across the mountains in a curtained horse-drawn litter[16] leading a column of eleven mules and seventeen bearers carrying his baggage. On his arrival nineteen days later, Padre Victoria observed that he 'had gone to sea without grey hairs and had come back grey'. He retained his rank as captain-general of the ocean and that of the coast of Andalusia, responsible for the region's defence, as well as the governorship of Cadiz.[17]

In Rome, prayers for the Armada's success were stopped at the end of October.[18] Any remaining hopes of Spain ever seeing one penny of the papal subsidy for the 'Enterprise of England' vanished like a puff of Vatican incense. Olivares told Philip: 'I am greatly afraid that we shall get nothing from the Pope. It is impossible to imagine how openly he has shown his selfishness and bad disposition on this occasion.'[19] Sixtus V instructed one of his cardinals to write to the king to console him on the Armada losses and to encourage him to launch a new expedition against England. He refrained from writing himself as he feared that Philip 'might make it a pretext for asking him for money'.[20]

In those long silent and solitary hours in the Escorial Palace, the king mentally revisited every facet of the Armada expedition and slowly, his organised mind rationalised the disaster and reinforced his steely determination to destroy England.

Accordingly, he came out fighting. The Venetian ambassador believed that Philip

> made up his mind that the late disasters are to be attributed, not to the ability of the enemy, nor to the unfavourable weather but rather to the want of courage shown by his officers.
>
> He declares that if they had lost, as they have, fighting instead of flying – for one must call it flying when they showed no heart for the fight – he would have considered all his expenses and labour as well invested.
>
> Above all, he feels the stain on the Spanish name and declares that with a prudent and valorous commander, they can still recover the honour they have lost.

Philip could not countenance talk that the Queen of England 'may possibly be able to defend herself against his forces'. He stalwartly maintained that she was weak, weary, short of money and her miserable people were 'downtrodden, some by the burden of taxes, others on the score of religion'. Lippomano added:

> In short, his majesty outwardly displays a fixed resolve to try his fortune once again next year ... Whatever decision is taken, everyone is agreed that prayers for the life of the king are needed, for though he maintains the contrary, he is really deeply wounded by these disasters.[21]

The king decided to send a revitalised, re-armed and rebuilt Armada to assail Elizabeth's realm. In November, representatives of the *Cortes*, the Spanish Parliament, met Philip and 'secretly told him they would vote four to five million [of gold], their sons and all they possess so that he may chastise that woman and wipe out the stain which has fallen upon the Spanish nation'.[22]

But the astute Venetian envoy warned of the dangers of a new attack on Spanish ports by a triumphant Drake:

> No small trouble would arise now if Drake should take to the sea and ... make a descent on the shores of Spain, where he would find no obstacle to his depredations and might even burn a part of the ships that have come back, for they are lying scattered in various places along the coast without any troops to guard them, as all the soldiers reached home sick and in bad plight, besides which some of these ships are in harbours which have no forts.[23]

Meanwhile in Flanders, there had been baseless reports that Parma had attempted to break out with his invasion barges on 13 August but was driven back with the loss of two Spanish ships off Dunkirk.[24] Two days later the duke had written to Medina Sidonia, urging him to return with the Armada to escort his army across the narrow seas. His letter was too late and he knew, in his heart, it was just an empty gesture, although vaingloriously 'he protested [that] he would go on with the attempt and would die in the pursuit of it'.[25]

On 31 August, Parma stood down his invasion fleet and redeployed his army to resume campaigning against the Dutch rebels, despite growing dissension in his ranks. His Spanish soldiers 'bitterly railed' against him for not invading and his Walloon troops 'demanded their pay very rudely' but were bluntly told it was still in the Armada pay-chests.[26] Paying no heed to this discord, Parma besieged the town of Bergen-op-Zoom, but after six weeks of indecisive fighting abandoned his fieldworks and marched away. Elizabeth cheerfully observed that his ignominious failure was a further blow to Spain's military reputation and represented 'no less [a] blemish by land, than by sea'.

Naturally, it was time for recriminations in Spain.

Lippomano reported 'serious differences' between Medina Sidonia and Parma – 'each one trying to throw the blame on the other'. His fellow ambassador in France reported 'charges of gross negligence' levelled against Parma by his enemies, whilst his supporters claimed he had been 'ready to embark and that he had already begun to do so but that Medina Sidonia, though he sailed by Parma, did so in his flight from the fireships'.[27]

Count Nicolo Cesis, one of Parma's dependants, arrived in Rome and went to great lengths with the Pope and cardinals to

> justify the duke, his master's conduct, by showing ... that he had not failed to carry out the king's orders. He had embarked 14,000 men and being unable, through stress of weather, to join [Medina Sidonia], he awaited the [Armada] in a place where it was quite easy for the [fleet] to put in but Medina Sidonia had not chosen to effect the junction and Parma could do nothing.[28]

Parma's pleas were not well received and many believed 'that in exculpating himself ... [he has] been [found] wanting in respect to his majesty by making his excuses for his attacks on Medina Sidonia to any other than his sovereign'.[29] Far from being persuaded of the justice of Parma's case, the Vatican cast 'much of the blame on [him] and they say that the Duke of Medina Sidonia should lose his head' according to Olivares.[30] In Turin, Jusepe de Acuña, the Spanish ambassador, passed on the Duke of Savoy's offer to take command of Philip's forces in Flanders, in place of Parma. They had heard accounts 'of how badly Parma has carried out his orders (whether through malice or carelessness) to be ready to aid Medina Sidonia [and] it seems impossible to the duke that your majesty can leave him in the Netherlands'.[31]

The campaign's key strategic failures were the Armada's lack of a sheltering port and Parma's inability to embark the Spanish invasion force in time for Medina Sidonia's arrival off Calais. The great vulnerability of Philip's plans for the subjugation of England had always been the vital timing of the rendezvous between his land and naval forces, and this, not unexpectedly, was exposed by a series of mishaps. Unreliable and (in modern terms) snail-like communications by sea had prevented any coordination between the two commanders. Parma, trying to disguise his tactical intentions from the blockading Dutch, could not keep his heavily armed soldiers on the flimsy, crowded invasion barges whilst impatiently awaiting the arrival of the Armada. Medina Sidonia, beset by the harrying English ships, had nowhere safe to go where he could await the embarkation of the Spanish troops. He also felt unable to risk taking on the combined Anglo-Dutch fleets in the dangerous shoaled waters off Dunkirk in order to clear the narrow seas for the invasion to be mounted.

However, if Parma's troops had landed in Kent and had been able to deploy the siege artillery carried by the Armada, the prospects for Elizabeth's government would have looked very bleak indeed. The ill-trained and poorly armed levies and partially completed defences are likely to have been easily overcome by the duke's seasoned veterans. Judging by Parma's progress in 1592, when his 22,000 troops covered 65 miles (104.61 km) in just six days after invading Normandy, he could have been in the streets of London within a week of coming ashore.[32] But amphibious landings are the most risky of any military operation, with so much dependent on favourable weather and tides and still more on good fortune. Parma would have been the luckiest of generals not to have lost hundreds of men in the hazardous transit of the narrow seas in their vulnerable flat-bottomed barges.

Parma was questioned by officials in Madrid about 'the real truth as to the date when this army could have been ready to sail, if weather had permitted and the Armada had performed its task'. On 30 December, he wrote to Don Juan de Idiáquez from Brussels:

> I will reply frankly and freely to your question. Notwithstanding all that has been said or may be said by ignorant people or those who maliciously raise doubts where none should exist, I will say that on 7 August ... I saw already embarked at Nieuport 16,000 foot soldiers and when I arrived in Dunkirk on Tuesday the eighth before

dawn, the men who were to be shipped there had arrived and their embarkation was commenced.

They would all have been on board with the stores ... as everything was ready and the shipping was going on very rapidly if the embarkation had not been suspended in consequence of the intelligence received of the Armada.

But for that, they might well have begun to get out of port that night and have joined those from Nieuport during [the] next day, so that together they could have fulfilled their task, as nothing necessary was lacking.

It is true that, in consequence of the number of infantry having increased, there was little room for the cavalry, there being only twenty rafts for them, unless the Armada could aid us with accommodation for the rest.

Even if this had been impossible, we should have tried to send the rest of the cavalry over in the other boats and no time would have been lost in the principal task and in taking a port for the Armada in the channel of London.

Parma felt secure against any criticism of his conduct. He offered to supply certificates and sworn depositions by his commanders and local magistrates about the readiness of provisions and stores, adding: 'You may truly believe that when I told [Medina Sidonia] that only three days would be required for the embarkation and the sailing, I did not speak lightly and I should have effected it in less time than I [predicted], with God's help.'[33]

There were other tactical causes for the Armada's failure – some of them institutional or cultural. Despite Medina Sidonia's late pleas to Parma for more small-calibre roundshot, ample stocks of all sizes of cannonballs have been discovered in the Armada wrecks so far excavated. The reason for this surfeit was their very slow, almost pedestrian, process of loading, aiming and firing the large-calibre guns on board each ship. The twenty-one cannon in the battery of the *San Francisco* fired just 242 rounds and her sister, *Santa Catalina*, 300 from her twenty-three guns, creating an average firing rate of three shots per gun per day. *Santa Barbara* managed a maximum of 8.37 rounds per gun during the Battle of Gravelines, but in earlier engagements she only achieved rates of between 1.1 and 2.35 rounds fired by each gun. None of this amounts to a deadly ship-smashing barrage. Of two hundred 10 lb (4.54 kg) cannonballs issued to the *El Gran Grifón*, ninety-seven have so far been recovered from her wreck site off Fair Isle, demonstrating just how few rounds were fired from her main armament.

Cargo manifests, drawn up by diligent Spanish clerks, provide another strand of evidence that confirms the low firing rates achieved by the Armada. The Levantine *Trinidad de Escala* left Corunna with 10,808 lbs (4,902.4 kg) of gunpowder but fired only one hundred and four rounds in anger, expending 2,027 lbs (919.4 kg) of propellant, compared with the 2,527 lbs (1,100.74 kg) used for ceremonial salutes or distress signals.[34]

In addition, poor casting by the gun-founders in Spain and Portugal, constantly chivvied for faster deliveries, resulted in some faulty guns being delivered to the ships; for example, one Italian saker recovered from the wreck of the *Juliana* off Streedagh Strand had suffered a catastrophic barrel explosion during firing, probably causing the loss of its crew.[35]

Finally the Armada was armed with smaller calibre cannon, creating an overall effective firepower one-third less than Howard's ships. The Spanish vessels had 138 guns of sixteen-pound (7.26 kg) calibre or above, compared with the English fleet's 251.[36] Hull for hull, the Spanish lacked punch in their broadsides compared with the queen's ships.

Unlike the English, whose guns were mounted on four-wheeled truckle carriages, the Spanish muzzle-loading cannon relied on awkward large-wheeled mountings with long trails, more suitable for operations on land than in the cramped conditions of a pitching ship's deck. The size of these carriages required them to be pulled back and reloaded in a diagonal position, a difficult and inconvenient manoeuvre on a narrow, crowded gun deck. The only alternative would be to sponge out the cannon, reload, and ram down the charge and shot, while sitting precariously astride the barrel as it projected outboard, beyond the protective gun port in the side of the ship. As shot and musket bullets flew thick and fast in the height of battle, it would take a brave man to repeatedly undertake this task in such an exposed position.

Furthermore, each gun had to be manhandled and served by six soldiers drawn from those detailed to fire muskets or harquebuses from the mast-tops or the main deck. Once the gun was ready to fire, they would return to their sniper duties, only to be recalled to reload their cannon. Inevitably this was a sluggish process and the consequential slow rate of fire was unlikely to sink, let alone seriously damage, an enemy ship. Medina Sidonia's sailing orders laid down that guns should always be loaded; after that first shot was fired, many guns in the Armada probably only managed one further round whatever the heat of battle.[37] Whether through inexperience or undisciplined panic, Spanish crews also tended to fire at extreme ranges, again reducing the efficacy of their barrage. However, the smaller, breech-loading guns, with an anti-personnel role, achieved much higher rates of fire because they were more easily served.

Spanish cannonades therefore failed to inflict serious injury on the queen's ships, as demonstrated by evidence that the cost of repairs to the queen's ships *before* the fighting far exceeded government expenditure afterwards. A survey of the fleet by master shipwrights at Chatham in September 1588 reveals a preoccupation with decay – caused by the weather and natural wear and tear – rather than battle damage.

Drake's *Revenge* did need a new mainmast 'being decayed and perished with shot'; *Nonpareil*'s 'foremast, bowsprit with the main mizzen mast are all to be made new' and *Victory* also required a new bowsprit and mizzen. Of the others, the hulls of the *White Bear, Hope, Marie Rose, Dreadnought* and *Tiger*, were all reported to be leaking, possibly caused by the shocks of their broadsides starting the caulked seams. Several ships' boats were replaced; some of which may have been smashed by enemy fire while secured on the upper decks.[38] More information is provided by Sir John Hawkins' accounts for 1588 as navy treasurer. A total of just £3,500 was spent on structural repairs after the Armada campaign, out of a total of £92,000 for the year. Five hundred feet (152.4 metres) of four-inch (101.6 mm) planking and one thousand treenails used for hulls were required, suggesting only superficial damage from cannon shot. Most of the planking purchased was narrower and therefore only suitable for superstructures and internal decking, some of it to replace the decayed timbers identified by the shipwrights' survey.[39]

The better-trained English gunners, with a greater number of heavy cannon than the Spanish, were able to inflict grievous damage on their enemy through firing low and by exploiting their ships' position to windward of the Armada to attack the lower area of the Spanish hulls as they heeled away. Had it not been for the English ships' continuing and chronic shortage of gunpowder and ammunition, they would have destroyed more enemy ships.[40]

Few heads rolled for this Spanish national disaster.

The main casualties were the unpopular Armada naval adviser Diego Flores de Valdés, who was thrown in gaol in Burgos for eighteen months; several profiteering bakers, who were hanged for supplying biscuit bulked out with inedible lime; and the master of ordnance in Naples, who was found guilty of sending a boat 'full of powder and other munitions to the Queen of England on the pretext of forwarding it to Spain', and sentenced 'to be torn asunder by four galleys' rowing in opposite directions.[41] There were also reports that 'sundry officers of the victualling department had been executed'.[42] Medina Sidonia was harangued by angry youths in Valladolid where he stopped overnight on his way home. Outside his lodgings, they chanted unkind taunts of 'Drake, Drake, Drake' and dubbed him *el duque de gallina* – 'the chicken duke'.[43]

In Paris, Mendoza paid a bitter price for his earlier optimism about the Armada's success. He scarcely dared show his face outside his ambassadorial residence as street urchins would mock him mercilessly as he rode along the city's thoroughfares on his mule, crying out '*Victoria! Victoria!*' – in a snide reference to his premature celebration of Medina Sidonia's triumph.[44] Hearing whispers that Philip was 'little satisfied with his conduct and especially for the false reports which he scattered about', Mendoza 'asked leave to retire' citing his blindness as a reason.[45] The king, however, retained his diplomatic services in Paris until 1590 when Mendoza's loss of sight became total.

Abroad, Henri III praised 'the valour, spirit and prudence of the queen of England, aided, as she was, by marvellous good fortune'. With a flustered Mendoza listening uncomfortably, the king added that what Elizabeth had achieved 'would compare with the greatest feats of the most illustrious men of past times, for she had ventured, alone and unaided, to await the attack of so puissant a force as Spain, and to fight it'.[46] Giovanni Mocenigo, Venetian ambassador in France, was brimful of admiration for English naval prowess: '[They] have shown that they are the skilled mariners which rumour reported them to be ... for they have not lost a single ship.' Unaware of Elizabeth's havering and unwillingness to spend money on defence, Mocenigo reserved his special praise for England's *Gloriana*:

> Nor has the queen ... lost her presence of mind for a single moment, nor neglected aught that was necessary ... Her acuteness in resolving on her action, her courage in carrying it out, show her high-spirited desire of glory and her resolve to save her country and herself.[47]

In Lutheran Germany, woodcut caricatures were published in broadsheets, with this succinct description of the Armada's tribulations: 'She came. She Saw. She fled' – a cutting, sarcastic nod in the direction of Julius Caesar's immortal *Veni, Vidi, Vici*; 'I came. I saw. I conquered.[48]

The Dutch rebels struck a number of commemorative medals to celebrate the defeat of the Armada. One, just over two inches (52 mm) in diameter, with an image of the terrestrial globe slipping from the hands of the Spanish king on the obverse,[49] has an inscription that symbolises the Protestant belief that God was firmly on their side in this battle against popery. The words echo the thanksgiving sung by Moses and the Children of Israel after their escape across the Red Sea: '*Flavit Jehovah et dissipate sunt*' or 'God breathed [the wind] and they were scattered'.

The great battle ensign of the *San Mateo* was hung as a war trophy in the choir of St Peter's church, Leiden, for all to see and admire. Amid this euphoria, the States of Zeeland wrote to Elizabeth claiming that the blockade of Parma's embarkation ports by Justin of Nassau's ships was the 'chief cause of the enemy's failure. The defeat of the Armada was entirely due to [Parma's] inability to succour and strengthen it with his forces.'[50] One can imagine the queen's scornful reaction.

In England, twenty-four hours after the triumph of her Tilbury speech, Elizabeth ordered her army to be disbanded (despite her advisers' grave misgivings), initially to six thousand men and then to 1,500 a week later.[51] This was not merely a question of reducing the drain on her hard-pressed exchequer; after several years of famine, the levies were required at home to bring in the harvest. Five days later, the camp at Tilbury was dissolved.

Many of Elizabeth's bucolic would-be heroes went home unpaid and resorted to selling their weapons and armour to raise money. A proclamation promised miscreants that they would suffer her 'heavy displeasure' and face imprisonment if caught, or if they 'most falsely and slanderously give out that they had received no pay'. Purchase of military equipment was declared illegal and anyone attempting to sell their armour was liable to be detained, delivered into the hands 'of the nearest constable' and imprisoned.[52]

She also began to stand down her navy, discharging the hired ships and laying up others. The pitiful condition of the Spanish survivors was replicated among the 15,599 sailors in the English fleet. Howard told the queen on 31 August: 'with great grief, I must write to you in what state I find your fleet. The infection is grown very great and in many ships is now very dangerous. Those that come in fresh are soonest infected – they sicken the one day and die the next.' He reported to the Privy Council 'that the most part of the fleet is grievously infected and [men] die daily, falling sick in the ships by numbers and that the ships of themselves be so infectious and corrupted as it is thought a very plague ... Many of the ships have hardly men enough to weigh their anchors.' Furthermore, those still well were greatly discontented because 'after this so good service' they hoped to receive all their pay, but this comes 'scantly unto them' breeding 'a marvellous alteration amongst them'.[53]

In Plymouth, of the *Elizabeth Bonaventure*'s original five hundred crew, two hundred had died. Sir Roger Townsend, of *Elizabeth Jonas*, had just one man living from the crew he had sailed with. Howard told Burghley: 'It is a most pitiful sight to see, here at Margate, how the men, having no place to receive them, die in the streets.' He had come ashore to help provide roofs over their heads: 'the best I can get is barns and such outhouses. It would grieve any man's heart to see them that have served so valiantly die so miserably.'[54] The lord admiral sold some of his silver to provide money for his men and pleaded to 'open the queen's purse [for money] ... to salve them' as it 'were too pitiful to have men starve after such a service. I know her majesty would not.' After being so long at sea, many of the sailors had little clothing: 'There [should] be a thousand pounds' worth ...

of hose, doublets, shirts, shoes and such like sent down ... or else in very short time, I look to see most of the mariners go naked.'⁵⁵

Howard's hopes of charity from Elizabeth's government were soon dashed. With the coldness of a lord treasurer constantly surrounded by urgent demands for money, Burghley responded that 'by death, by discharging of sick men and such like, there may be spared something in the general pay'.⁵⁶

The men, like their Spanish counterparts, were dying from typhus and scurvy, but in those medically unenlightened times, Howard and his captains believed the cause was the sailors' beer: 'There was some great fault in the brewer [who] excused it by the want of hops.' He added: 'For my own part I know not which way to deal with the mariners to make them rest contented with sour beer, for nothing doth displease them more.' Fresh beer was then brewed in Dover 'as good as was brewed in London'.⁵⁷

A total of £80 was finally paid out to the wounded sailors from the exchequer, and if that seems parsimonious, consider the total of £5 that was shared among the hundred seamen who manned the fireships off Calais.⁵⁸

Howard resorted to issuing printed licences authorising his maimed sailors to beg for sustenance. One signed by him and addressed to vice-admirals, justices of the peace, sheriffs, bailiffs, constables and churchwardens, authorised William Browne 'of London, gunner' to beg in all churches for the space of one year. He had 'lately served in her majesty's service against the Spaniards in the barque [*Hazard*] of Faversham' who 'in that service was shot through his body and grievously wounded in sundry places and by means of the same maimed for ever'.⁵⁹

Far from the stench of death in the ports and the misery of the sick sailors, the English also struck a number of Armada victory medals, dated 1588, with arrogant words redolent of the achievement of a crushing triumph over their enemies. On the obverse of a one-inch (25 mm) diameter medal is the year, a family of four praying and the words: HOMO · PROPONIT · DEVS · DISPONIT – 'Man proposes, God disposes'. On the obverse is the image of a sailing ship breaking up, with the inscription: + HISPANI · FVGIV'T · ET · PEREV'T · NEMINE · SEQVETE – 'The Spaniards are put to flight and perish with no man in pursuit'.

Another, designed by the Dutchman Gerard van Bijlaer, is a pointed attack on England's enemies. The reverse shows a cabal of Sixtus V, a collection of Catholic bishops, Philip II of Spain, Henri III of France and the Duke of Guise seated in a room plotting against Elizabeth. They are blindfolded and the floor beneath them is studded with pointed spikes. The inscription reads: DVREM EST CONTRA STIMVLOS CALCITRARE or 'It is hard to kick against the pricks' taken from the Biblical Acts of the Apostles 9:5, 'And [Saul, later St Paul] said: "Who art thou Lord?" And the Lord said: "I am Jesus whom thou persecutest: it is hard for thee to kick against the pricks."'[60] The medal's reverse shows the Armada driven on to rocks with sailors being hurled into the sea with the legend, taken from Psalm 86, v.10: 'TV DEVS MAGNVS ET MAGNA FACIS TV SOLVS DEVS' – 'Thou God art great and doest wondrous things; thou art God alone'.[61]

The Privy Council went to St Paul's Cathedral on 20 August to give thanks for the English victory and Dr Alexander Nowell, the dean of the cathedral, delivered a sermon of thanksgiving at the preaching cross in the churchyard. The queen was supposed to attend but at the last moment declined to go. Six days later a celebratory review of troops was held by Leicester, watched by Elizabeth and her general from the windows of a nearby house. The Genovese Marco Antonia Messia, who was spying for Spain, saw a parade by a company of sixty musketeers, the same number of harquebusiers and two hundred light horse, smartly dressed in orange uniforms with facings of white silk. The dragoons bore a proud ensign with the word 'Hazard'[62] embroidered upon it and the light cavalry carried one of red damask, 'with a veil worked with gold on top, which, no doubt, was a lady's favour'. There was jousting and a mock cavalry skirmish, pitting 'one squadron against the other, lowering their swords as they approached, so as not to wound'.[63]

The next day, fifty-five-year-old Leicester, who had been suffering poor health, departed for the restorative spa at Buxton in Derbyshire, making the journey in easy stages, stopping first at Rycote, near Reading. There he wrote to Elizabeth asking after her health and 'what ease of her late pains she finds, being the chiefest thing in the world I do pray for, for her to have good health and a long life'. The queen had given him some medicine, which he found 'amend much better than any other thing that has been given to me'. Leicester ended: 'With the continuance of my wonted prayer for our majesty's preservation, I humbly kiss your foot' and added the postscript: 'I received your majesty's token from young Tracey' (a messenger).[64]

He stopped again at a 'gentleman's house' at Cornbury, near Woodstock in Oxfordshire. Messia reported that he 'supped heavily and being troubled with a distress in the stomach during the night, he forced himself to vomit'. Leicester then went down with malaria and died at ten o'clock on the morning of 4 September,[65] leaving debts of '£20,000 more than his goods and chattels are worth' and still owing £3,169 to the crown for exceeding his allowance as lieutenant general of English forces in the Netherlands.[66]

Elizabeth was grief-stricken at the loss of her long-time favourite (whom she nicknamed 'Eyes'), shutting herself up in her chamber for some days to mourn alone 'until the treasurer and other councillors had the doors broken open and entered to see her'.[67] Until the end of her life she kept his note from Rycote in the personal treasure box by her bed, inscribing upon it the words: 'HIS LAST LETTER'. Her anguish was only momentarily lifted by news of the Armada wrecks in Ireland, which she received 'with tears of joy in her eyes, as if it were the final liberation from this [Spanish] attack'.[68]

Another service of thanksgiving was held at St Paul's on 8 September, when the captured Spanish battle standards were proudly displayed, including one pennant 'wherein was an image of Our Lady, with her son in her arms which was held in a man's hand over the pulpit'. The following day, the banners were hung in Cheapside and at the Southwark end of London Bridge.[69] The Privy Council wrote to the bishops of Salisbury and Lincoln, passing on Elizabeth's desire that 'certain sermons should be made of thanksgiving to God for the late victory it has pleased Him to give her ... against the forces of the Spanish king'.[70] A specially written prayer thanked God for 'turning our enemies from us and that dreadful execution which they intended towards us, into a fatherly and most merciful admonition of us ... and to execute justice upon our cruel enemies, turning the destruction that they intended against us upon their own heads'. It pledged perpetual memory in England for 'thy merciful protection and deliverance of us from the malice, force, fraud and cruelty of our enemies'.[71]

Elsewhere there was similar jubilation at the defeat of the Armada. The parishioners of the church of St Faith's at Gaywood, near King's Lynn, Norfolk, patriotically commissioned an oil painting on a diptych panel for the wall of the south aisle showing Elizabeth arriving at Tilbury and the Spanish fleet in flames. Its inscription proclaimed: 'Blessed by the great God of my salvation'.

Others celebrated more noisily and exuberantly: churchwardens' accounts detail expenditure for bell-ringing or firing guns on 19 November, appointed as the national day of thanksgiving for deliverance from the Spanish. At All Saints church, Hastings, in the former front-line county of Sussex, 2s 2d was paid out for 'meat and drink at the ringing day for the Spaniards'[72] and at Lewes two barrels of gunpowder were expended 'by the whole consent of the fellowship in shooting of the great pieces in the castle at the rejoicing day for the overthrow of the Spanish navy'.[73] An allegorical play about the defeat of the Armada, *The Three Lords and Three Ladies of London,* cast the villainous Spaniards as Pride, Shame, Ambition, Treachery, Tyranny and Terror, and ended with their being routed by a bunch of English schoolboys.[74]

Pamphleteers had a field day, prompting Burghley to comment: 'Friends and enemies on either side, according to their own humours, do feed the world with diversity of reports agreeable to their own affections and passions ... yet there is only one truth whereby the reports ought to be ruled and reformed.'[75] This is a passable definition of propaganda, which was a talent in which Tudor governments throughout the sixteenth century excelled.

The author of a pamphlet with the rather prolix title *A Skeltonical Salutation or condigne gratulation and just vexation of the Spanish Nation* devoted ten pages of doggerel verse in blackletter type to such matters as whether the fish that ate the flesh of drowned Spaniards would become infected by their venereal diseases, inquiring whether this year

> it were not best to forebear
> On such fish to feed
> Which our coast doth breed
> Because they are fed
> With carcase dead

> Here and there in the rocks
> That were full of the pox ...
> [As] our Cods and Conger
> Have filled their hunger
> With the heads and feet
> Of the Spanish fleet
> Which to them were as sweet
> As a goose to a fox
> And seeing the pox
> Possessed each carcase
> From the slave to the marquis
> No man can avoid
> But he may be annoyed.

But god-fearing fish-eating Englishmen need not fear, for all would be well if the fish were 'well dressed' ...

> And your stomachs not oppressed
> You need them not detest
> Howsoever they are fed
> Or where so ever they are bred
> Be no more afraid
> Of sea fish to feed
> If them thou love or need.[76]

The polemicist Thomas Deloney, whom we met at Tilbury, penned a trenchant ballad celebrating the capture of Pedro de Valdés' ship *Nuestra Señora del Rosario,* sung to the French tune *Almain.* Its title, *A Joyful new Ballad,* is something of a misnomer, as it makes grim reading. The loss of Moncada's flagship *San Lorenzo* at Calais saw many Spanish drown: 'There might you see / the salt and foaming flood / Dyed and stained like scarlet red / with store of Spanish blood.' Working himself up into a patriotic fervour, Deloney's next verses leave no stone unturned to describe Spanish perfidy:

> They do intend by deadly war,
>   to make both poor and bare,
> Our towns and cities,
>   to rack and sack likewise

> To kill and murder man and wife
>> As malice doth arise
> And to deflower
>> our virgins in our sight;
> And in the cradle cruelly
>> the tender babe to smite
> GOD'S HOLY TRUTH
>> they mean to cast down
> And to deprive our noble Queen
>> Both of her life and crown.
>
> Our wealth and riches,
>> which we enjoyed long;
> They do appoint their prey and spoil
>> by cruelty and wrong
> To set our houses
>> a fire on our heads
> And cursedly to cut our throats
>> As we lie in our beds
> Our children's brains
>> to dash against the ground
> And from the earth our memory
>> for ever to confound.

Then he raised the horrid spectre of the Armada's consignment of those infamous Spanish scourges:

> One sort of whips they had for men,
>> so smarting, fierce and fell
> As like could never be devised
>> by any devil in hell:
> The strings whereof with wiry knots,
>> like rowels[77] they did frame.
> That every stroke might tear the flesh,
>> they laid on with the same.

Women were not to be spared:

> And for our silly women,
>> their hearts with grief to clog;

> They made such whips, wherewith no man
> would seem to strike a dog.
> So strengthened with brazen tags
> and filed so rough and thin
> That they would force at every lash,
> the blood abroad to spin.[78]

A long tract, written at Burghley's behest, was more measured but the message was just as powerful. *The Copy of a Letter to Don Bernardin[o] Mendoza* was said to have been found 'in the chamber of one Richard Leigh,[79] a seminary priest who was lately executed for high treason', whose identity was conveniently stolen for propaganda purposes. The pamphlet claimed that after the defeat of the army, many English Catholics were appalled by this forcible attempt to return England to Rome's authority:

> I do find that many good and wise men, which of long time have secretly continued in most earnest devotion to the Pope's authority, begin now to stagger in their minds ... and to conceive that this way of Reformation intended by the Pope's Holiness is not allowable in the sight of God ... to put [the temporal sword] into a monarch's hand to invade this realm with force and arms, yes, to destroy the queen ... and all her people addicted to her, which are in very truth now seen, by great proof this year, to be in a sort infinite and invincible so as some begin to say that this purpose by violence, by blood, by slaughter, by conquest, agrees not with Christ's doctrine.

The truths of English naval supremacy or the omnipotence of the Protestant God were undeniable. 'The Spaniards did never take or sink any English ship or boat or break any mast or took any one man prisoner', which amazed the Spanish prisoners in London who exclaimed that 'in all these fights, Christ showed himself a Lutheran'.

Medina Sidonia attracted special vilification: he spent much of his time 'lodged in the bottom of his ship for his safety'. The propaganda tract concluded with this scornful and contemptuous phrase: 'So ends this account of the misfortunes of the Spanish Armada which they used to call INVINCIBLE.'[80]

But the most lasting propaganda image of the Armada's misfortunes is a giant picture painted with oils on a wooden panel now at

Woburn Abbey. The 'Armada Portrait' of Elizabeth, measuring 52.4 by 41.3 inches (133 by 105 cm) shows her in a gown covered with suns, with a large pearl, symbolising chastity, suspended from her bodice. Her right hand rests upon a globe with her fingers pointing to the New World; her left elbow is alongside an imperial crown on a table. In the background, English fireships threaten the Spanish fleet on the left, and on the opposite side enemy ships are being driven ashore by God's Own Breath. The figure of a mermaid is carved on the arm of her chair, representing the power of feminine wiles luring unwary sailors to their death.[81]

Elizabeth finally celebrated her victory over Spain at another service of thanksgiving at St Paul's on Sunday 24 November. She was drawn from Somerset House in the Strand in a chariot with a canopy topped by a crown with two pillars in front bearing the figures of a lion and dragon, supporters of the heraldic arms of England at that time.[82]

The campaign to defend her realm had cost her exchequer around £167,000 (£463,000,000 in 2013 spending power). Of this only £180 had been spent on government 'rewards to the injured'.

The queen was closely guarded. Not only were there continuing fears that she may be endangered by an assassin's attack, there was also concern that the large number of discharged and disgruntled soldiers and sailors in London might attempt some kind of angry protest.[83] They had good reason for discontent. Not only were they unpaid, but more than half of those who had fought the Armada were now dead from disease and starvation.

Many did not know it, but these surviving veterans were soon to face their old enemy once again in combat.

But this time the fighting would be on Spanish soil.

THE ENGLISH ARMADA

*In our march towards Lisbon, the King and the Prince of
Portugal ... looked for the nobility and chief of the country to come ... But none came, save only ... poor peasants without stockings or shoes and one gentlewoman
who presented the king with a basket of cherries.*

William Fenner to Anthony Bacon, Plymouth, 1589.[1]

After the Armada's humiliating retreat, Queen Elizabeth was
haunted by two worrying and pressing issues. Firstly, the
Spanish fleet was far from vanquished. Her spies suggested it could
return to threaten England's shores once again, with Parma's unde-
feated veterans in Flanders still available as a formidable invading
army. Next time, assuming the Spanish high command could learn
from their disastrous mistakes, the land and naval forces might link
up successfully. Secondly, Elizabeth's exchequer was uncommonly
and uncomfortably bare. Her continuing paucity of cash threatened
to jeopardise not only the defence of her realm but also her continued payments to the Dutch for the war against the Spanish in
the Netherlands and to Spain's enemies in France. Lord Treasurer
Burghley had been driven to distraction to find the money to con-
front the Armada and was forced to borrow at exorbitant, if not
punitive, interest rates, including arranging a £30,000 loan from the
City of London in July 1588. There was a real danger that the sweet
savour of victory could soon be transformed into the sour taste of
defeat in all the queen had striven for at home and overseas.

The queen's regular annual income amounted to £250,000
and Parliamentary subsidies had brought in £215,000 in 1585–8.
Additional contingency funding totalling £245,000 had been drawn
from the exchequer's £300,000 reserves – her 'chested treasure'

– accumulated through Burghley's far-sighted management of her budget over the previous decade. This money had disappeared at an alarming rate. Elizabeth's financial support to the Dutch rebels had totalled more than £400,000 over the last three years, despite cynical attempts to economise by only part-paying her seven thousand troops based in the Low Countries. After deducting the £167,000 cost of defence against the Spanish threat, by early October 1588 there was just £55,000 left in the exchequer. Even at peacetime rates of spending, this would barely last eight months.[2]

It would take time to collect any new income voted to her by Parliament and her ministers were increasingly worried by mounting popular resistance to new taxation. Burghley had warned Walsingham in July of 'a general murmur of the people and malcontented people will increase ... the comfort of the enemy'.[3] Notwithstanding these fears, the counties were instructed to impose an enforced loan on the gentry totalling about £50,000 in December, and in February 1589 the merchant adventurer William Milward was sent to Germany to arrange a huge credit of £100,000. He was ordered to disguise the identity of the debtor (lest the lenders be tempted to demand exorbitant interest rates) and, under no circumstances, to agree to anything higher than 10 per cent. But his mission proved fruitless: no one would advance him a penny, not even the Fuggers, who had lent money so willingly to the queen's father, Henry VIII, almost five decades before.[4] Elizabeth was therefore forced to adopt what she called the 'vicious policy' of selling off her properties – an anathema to a Tudor monarch, forever rapacious for wealth and always conscious of status.

Throughout those worrying days, Burghley may have reminded her how Henry had bankrupted England by his runaway expenditure on wars with France and Scotland in the 1540s, leaving himself with no option but to debase the coinage, generating rampant inflation and wreaking havoc with the economy of the realm for more than a decade afterwards. That fiscal policy could not be repeated.

Given all these bleak financial realities, it is unsurprising that Elizabeth was enthused by a new strategy that could resolve both her monetary and defence quandaries at a stroke. Sir John Hawkins and Walsingham had long been its advocates, and even the cautious Burghley was now an eager supporter. It was simple, relatively safe

and, with its successful conclusion, the queen could enjoy the satis-
faction of revenge on Philip of Spain.

By attacking Philip's annual convoy carrying silver bullion from
the New World colonies to Cadiz, Elizabeth stood to reap several
million pounds' worth of plundered ingots, which would fall like
ripe plums into her welcoming and thankful exchequer. Moreover,
this sequestering of the king's revenues would leave him unable to
meet the cost of a new Armada, fund his armies in Flanders and subsidise the Catholic League in France. Who knows? The threat, real
or implied, of repeated interdiction of his treasure fleets, or the loss
of even part of one shipment, might coerce Philip to sue for peace
so that Elizabeth's cripplingly expensive war could at last be ended.

There was just one snag, as there always is with any simple plan
offering alluring benefits.

The queen's ships, after being at sea on active service for up to
eight months, required refurbishment, a process that would take
many weeks to complete. When the time required to sail to the
Azores to intercept the treasure fleet was factored into the operational planning, it became obvious the English vessels would arrive
on station too late to seize the ponderous Spanish ships. Quite liter-
ally, Elizabeth had missed the boat. And her financial and defence
imperatives dictated that she did not have the luxury of waiting until
the 1589 bullion convoy crossed the Atlantic from Havana in Cuba.

All was not lost, though. On 19 September, Sir John Norris proposed a modified plan with three objectives. First, English ships
should attack any Armada vessels under repair in the northern
Spanish ports. Second, an English army, supported by the queen's
ships, should capture Lisbon and set Dom Antonio, the Portuguese
pretender, on the throne. Third, the fleet and its troops should sail on
to the Azores and capture the islands, which would allow plenty of
time before the Spanish treasure fleet was due to arrive there.

Sir Francis Drake was a fervent supporter of Norris's strategy and
both men – these 'warriors of the Lord' – were comforted by the
corporate opinion of a group of London Puritan ministers, who after
protracted and tedious disputation, decided that there was no incon-
gruity in restoring a Catholic pretender to the Portuguese throne if
it would grievously damage God's greater enemy, Philip II of Spain.[5]

Elizabeth, in her fiscally embarrassed state, could not fund the expedition and was anyway distracted by the expense of having to hastily organise the defences of Ireland to round up the Spanish shipwreck survivors. So it was decided to follow the example of Drake's financially successful raid on Cadiz and make it a private enterprise operation, with the queen providing only £20,000 towards the costs. Backers in the City of London and other 'adventurers' would provide funding of £43,000 and pay the operating costs of six 'second-class' queen's ships (*Revenge, Nonpareil, Dreadnought, Swiftsure, Foresight, Aid*) and two pinnaces (*Advice* and *Merlin*), as well as providing armed merchantmen. Her commissioners would raise eight thousand troops and one thousand pioneers for the army. Half the soldiers would be volunteers and the rest would be armed only with swords and daggers to save money. Elizabeth would supply two captured Spanish prizes, ten siege cannon and six field guns, together with twenty lasts of gunpowder and tools for the pioneers. The Dutch rebels would be asked to contribute four thousand harquebusiers and to provide the weapons for the troops: a thousand halberds, three thousand muskets, four thousand calivers, two thousand breastplates, six siege guns and forty lasts of powder. Food and other provisions, enough for four months, would also be supplied from Holland. The Dutch contribution would amount to £10,000 in kind. It looked, initially at least, a cut-price invasion.

The queen did not demur even when Norris asked for £5,000 in advance, promising that they would not ask for the remainder until the full £43,000 of private cash was raised.[6] On 11 October at Westminster, she issued a commission to Drake and Norris, granting them authority for the 'whole charge and direction' of the enterprise; allowing them to choose their officers and levy troops 'to invade and destroy the powers and forces of all such persons as have this last year, with their hostile powers and armadas, sought and attempted the invasion of the realm of England'.[7] They also obtained royal permission for any person to volunteer for the expedition.

It had taken just over three weeks for the plan to be formulated, discussed and approved – an astonishing achievement, given Elizabeth's habitual procrastination and havering. Was she being uncharacteristically bold – or was she desperate to find some solution to her worries?

In Paris, Mendoza was quick to pick up rumours of the expedition.

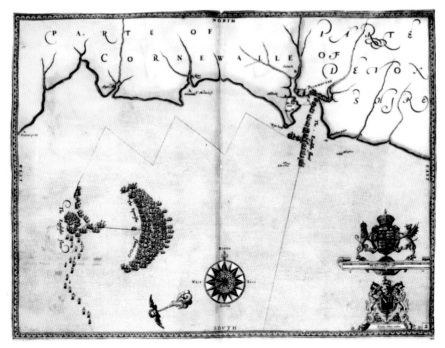

The action off Plymouth on 31 July 1588. Howard's pinnace *Disdain* is shown firing her 'defiance' at the middle of the Armada's *lunula*, or crescent formation, off Dodman Point, Cornwall. This detail is from an engraving, one of a set by Augustin Ryther in 1590 to illustrate Petruccio Ubaldino's account of the naval battles.

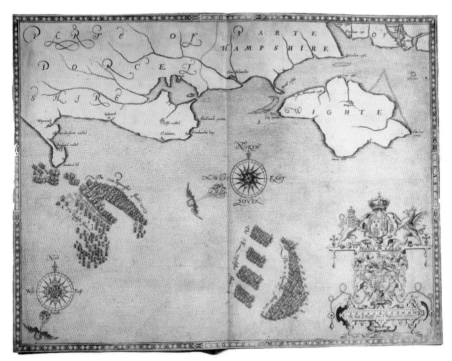

Fighting off Portland and the Isle of Wight on 2 August 1588. Detail showing the Spanish galleasses attacking Frobisher's squadron, seemingly becalmed off Portland Bill.

Howard sends eight fireships in an attack on the anchored Armada off Calais, 7 August 1588 (Aert Anthonisz, 1590). In the left foreground, a Spanish squadron flagship is engaged with an English ship, which has a galleass astern of her. In reality, the English fleet did not follow up the fireship attack, as shown by this painting.

The Battle of Gravelines, 8 August 1588.

An English chart by Augustin Ryther, 1588, showing the course home
taken by the Spanish Armada.

Map of Northern Ireland, 1589, with the positions of four Armada
wrecks marked with the word 'Spanish'. One is unidentified.

OPPOSITE:
Left-hand panel of a triptych in St Faith's Church,
Gaywood, Norfolk, showing Elizabeth's arrival at Tilbury
and inscribed: 'Blessed be the great God of my salvation'.

'Armada Portrait' of Elizabeth I, showing behind her the attack of her fireships
on the Armada and the Spanish ships being wrecked by the 'Protestant Wind'.

OPPOSITE:
Licence to William Browne, gunner in the barque
Hazard of Faversham, Kent, allowing him to
beg in all churches for one year, signed by Lord
High Admiral Howard.

.Deo.Draco.   .Eliza: Victrix Anglia.   1588.

Harles Lord Howard, Baron of Effingham Knight of the Noble order of the Garter, Lord high Admirall of England, Ireland, and Wales, and the dominions and Iles of the same, of the towne of Callis and marches therof, of Normandy, Gascoyne, and Guynes, and Captaine Generall of her Maiesties Seas and Nauy Royall. To all and singuler Vizeadmiralls, Iustices of Peace, Maiors, Sherisfes, Bayliffes, Constables, Customers, Comptrowlers, Ministers, Parsons, Vicars, Curats, Churchwardens, Collectors for the pore, and all other her Maiesties Officers, Ministers, and louing subiects, aswell within the Citie of London, as the dominions of her Maiesties Realme of England, and to euery of them greeting. Wheras this bearer William Browne, of London gunner, lately serued in her Maiesties seruice against the Spaniards, in the Barke of Feuersham, and in that seruice was shot through his bodie, and grauously wounded in sundry places, and by meanes of the same maimed for euer: In consideration wherof and for that I vnderstand he is greatly indebted to his Surgeons, in the curing of his wounds and otherwise brought to extreame pouertie thereby. I haue thought good to graunt him these presents, and by authority hereof, in her Maiesties name do require and earnestly entreate you and euery of you, throughout the said Citie of London and the dominions of her Maiesties Realme of England, to haue a Christian and pitifull regard of the said William Browne and his extreame want and miserie gotten in the seruice of our gracious Prince, and defence of this our Countrey, and to helpe and relieue him with your charitable beneuolence and almes, towards the supplying of their great want, and to permit, suffer and assist them, to gather and aske the same in all Churches and Chappels, and of all well disposed people within the said Citie of London, and her Maiesties said dominions, without any let, trouble, molestation, or incumbrance whatsoeuer, wherin you shall do a dede very acceptable in the sight of God, and greatly comfortable to him, his said wife and children in this extremitie, wherin we require you not to fayle. This presents to indure for the space of twelue moneths, from the date hereof. Giuen at London in her Maiesties highe Court of Th'admiralty, vnder the great seale thereof, the seuenteenth of August, 1590. And in the two and thirtieth yeare of the raigne of our soueraigne Lady Elizabeth by the grace of God Queene of England, Fraunce and Ireland, defender of the faith, &c.   Hareward.

C. Howard.

God saue the Queene.

The Somerset House conference on 19 August 1604 that produced the
Treaty of London, ending the nineteen-year Anglo-Spanish war.

One of his spies in London, Manuel de Andrada, codenamed 'David', was a handily placed member of Dom Antonio's household. His reports led the ambassador to believe there were plans 'of sending forty or fifty sail' to assist the pretender, 'but no preparations to that effect are visible'.[8] Two weeks later, Mendoza was convinced that the pretender would sail for Portugal, but considered this merely a diversionary tactic, as the real target was the Azores: 'Fifty ships [are] being fitted out [and] are now being hurried forward furiously. A great number of bullocks have been slaughtered to provision them. Most of them are being fitted out by private persons in the hope of gain, as they see that the many ships that go out to pillage come back laden with booty.'[9] In early November, he reported Elizabeth's tart riposte when she heard that the Spanish king was repairing and reinforcing his fleet: 'I will give Philip plenty to do before he can repair damages or turn round [the ships].'

Parma had begun to besiege Bergen-op-Zoom on 12 September and on 20 October. Norris, who had taken across an extra 1,500 English troops to help relieve the town, laid the plans before the rebel Dutch Council of States.[10] Two months later, they agreed to most of the English requests for the expedition. They would provide ten warships for five months, plus 1,500 infantry, and Norris would be allowed to purchase weapons, armour, ammunition and provisions free of any tax or customs duty.

The paramount need for the expedition was underlined by intelligence that around forty Armada ships remained at Santander and another twelve at San Sebastián. There were few sailors to man these warships and repairs were proceeding slowly because of a shortage of dockyard workers. The soldiers were in winter quarters 20 miles (32.19 km) inland.[11] Walsingham warned Stafford in Paris that Elizabeth was determined 'to use advantage of the late victory ... by keeping the King of Spain unable to redress and set up [again] the like forces to the disquiet of his neighbours'. Therefore Stafford should urge Henri III to ban all exports of cereals and naval stores from France.[12] The German *Hansa* merchants were also warned that their ships would be stopped on the high seas and if their cargoes were found to be provisions or munitions destined for Spain, these would be seized.[13]

In February 1589, the queen issued orders to Drake and Norris, emphasising that their mission had two overriding objectives: 'the one to distress the King of Spain's ships, the other to win possession of the islands of Azores thereby to intercept the convoys of treasure that yearly pass that way to and from the West and East Indies'. Only after the destruction of the surviving Armada ships could they move on to restore Dom Antonio to the Portuguese throne. But this phase carried the stern proviso that 'nothing can be attempted without very great hazard' should local Spanish forces prove too strong. If popular support for the pretender was overwhelming, the English army should stay long enough merely to ensure that Dom Antonio's frontiers with Spain were protected and the English army's costs of the operation repaid by the new king.[14] Her orders could not have been clearer or more insistent.

Elizabeth demanded that Drake and Norris swore solemn oaths, promising to obey these operational priorities. If they failed to fulfil their vows, they fully acknowledged they would be 'reputed as traitors'. The queen must have suffered nagging doubts that Drake would resort to his old tricks and become distracted by the prospects of lucrative plunder. She decided to send a 'trusty servant of her own', Anthony Ashley, one of the clerks of the Privy Council, to be her 'eyes and ears' on the expedition. He was granted authority 'for the observation of their actions and for writing of their common letters ... and to assist them with good counsel and advice'. He was also told to 'keep a true journal in writing of all public actions and proceedings'.[15]

Many of the discharged soldiers were swept up in this new call to arms against Spain. Other recruits were found among the much-despised vagabonds, 'the scum and dregs' of English society, and the Privy Council noted with alarm the 'ragged condition and debauched condition' of many volunteers. The Spanish spy codenamed 'David' reported they were recruited 'under the impression that they have only to land and load themselves with gold and silver ... They also say that they have been promised by Dom Antonio the sack of all towns which do not submit to him and that when they enter Castile they shall sack every place and carry war with blood and fire through the country.'[16]

War is not always such fun. Some recruits were seriously wounded during training when they fired gunpowder contaminated by 'small hailshot' either put in the mix by 'the lewdness of those who sold the same [to make it heavier] or by other negligence'.[17] In Southampton, justices and 'other gentlemen dwelling near the sea coast' were instructed to issue proclamations to enrol all 'mariners and fishermen to the end there may be a good choice had of apt and sufficient men for her majesty's service'.[18]

Periods of national crisis often throw up the more eccentric among us. John Trew wrote to the queen in December offering his services for 'her preservation and salvation ... Though an old man, I desire to be employed in the wars.' Like those unfortunates who, in later centuries, scurry between newspaper offices carrying tattered brown paper packages containing incontrovertible evidence of a world secretly governed by aliens, Trew's fixation soon became apparent in his letter: 'I have an invention which would do as much service as five thousand men in times of extremity and also an engine which can be driven before men to defend them from the shot of the enemy,' he boasted. Like others of his ilk, his offer was politely declined and we shall never know whether John Trew was the earliest inventor of the main battle tank.[19]

Predictably the expedition's plans soon went awry and the costs began to climb, rendering the original budget set by the commanders hopelessly inadequate. Promises were not kept. There was no siege train of artillery. No Dutch warships ever hove into sight. Around half of the military stores which Norris bought in the Netherlands never arrived. No cavalry came from the Low Countries and only twelve experienced infantry companies were sent over from Flanders – 1,800 trained men rather than the 3,500 expected. The *Minion* of Fowey, laden with biscuit, beef and beer, sank within Dover harbour during a storm, but was later raised.[20] There were too few ships to transport what had become a 19,000-strong army gathering there in March 1589.

Then, over the horizon, sailed a rare piece of good fortune. Sixty Dutch flyboats displacing 150–200 tons each, passed through the Straits in ballast, en route for France to collect cargoes of sea salt. Drake immediately commandeered every one, citing the passports from Parma found in some of the vessels as justification for this act of war.[21]

The fleet sailed on to Plymouth but were delayed there by 'unusually stormy' weather, with the 'wind continuing contrary'. Finding provisions for the fleet proved increasingly problematic. William Hawkins, mayor of Plymouth, could not purchase more than twelve tons of oil 'and by reason it is now seed time, we cannot both in peas and beans furnish above four hundred quarters' [5,080.24 kg]. No more than two thousand new landed fish could be bought from the fishermen, but beef supplies were abundant and there was plenty of butter and cheese 'which the country yielded readily'.[22]

The expedition was turning into a financial disaster before it had even sailed. Stuck in harbour for longer than planned, they had no option but to raid the provisions earmarked for the voyage to feed the army as well as the four thousand sailors in the fleet. Drake and Norris had already spent in excess of £96,000 – 18 per cent more than their latest budget for the entire expedition. After the fleet was forced back to Plymouth by adverse winds on 17 April, Norris told Burghley the next day:

> We are utterly unable to supply ourselves and, the voyage breaking, we cannot think what to do with the army.
>
> Upon failing of the voyage, every man will call for pay from her majesty, being levied by her highness's commission.
>
> And if they have it not, the country will be utterly spoiled, robberies and outrages committed in every place, the arms and furnitures[23] lost, beside the dishonour of the matter.[24]

Burghley saw through this piece of thinly disguised blackmail, but the project had progressed too far to pull back now. The Council authorised the mayor of Plymouth to victual the fleet for one month more. The sum of £10,000 was to be sent down in carts from London and a further £4,000 supplied by Cornwall and Somerset tax collectors. In the event, there were economies imposed by sleight of hand: fish and peas were substituted for beef, and there were no supplies of beer, saving nearly £7,000 in the cost of provisions. Moreover, the final cost to the exchequer of this latest contribution was £11,000 rather than the £14,000 promised, as not all the money left London.[25]

Elizabeth's new court favourite was the red-haired Robert Devereux, Second Earl of Essex, Leicester's twenty-two-year-old stepson. This tall, handsome, vain and quarrelsome young man had first come to court four years earlier, burdened with the huge debts inherited from his imprudent father's abortive attempts to subdue the Irish province of Ulster. The son's wilful and extravagant lifestyle soon augmented his army of creditors. Faced with massive debts amounting to £23,000 (£70,000,000 at 2013 spending power), Essex became disenchanted with the fripperies of court life and decided to seek military glory (and profitable plunder) from the expedition to Spain and Portugal, both to brighten his aimless life and appease his twitchy creditors. Without the queen's permission, he recklessly left St James' Palace late on the afternoon of 13 April and headed off to the West Country.

He wrote to the Privy Council from Plymouth, itching to fight but seeking pardon 'of her majesty'. He appealed to 'your lordships to mediate ... for me, [as] I was carried with this zeal so fast that I forgot those reverend forms which I should have used. Yet I had rather have had my heart cut out of my body than this zeal out of my heart.'[26] In another letter, he was frank about his need to earn some cash:

> My debts [are] at the least two or three and twenty thousand pounds. Her majesty's goodness has been so great as I could not ask more of her. [There is] no way left to repair myself but my own adventure which I had much rather undertake than offend her majesty with suits [requests for money] as I have done heretofore. If I speed well, I will adventure to be rich. If not, I will not see the end of my poverty.[27]

Elizabeth was incensed at his unauthorised absence and concerned that his life would be endangered by this foreign military adventure. The next day she sent off his uncle, Sir Francis Knollys, to find Essex and bring him back to court like a naughty schoolboy truant.

It was too late. Essex sneaked on board Henry Noel's *Swiftsure* and hid there until that evening, when she departed Plymouth. A panting and dishevelled Knollys was given use of a pinnace by Drake and Norris to pursue the errant favourite, but the vessel could not clear nearby Rame Head before the wind veered southerly and he was forced back into harbour.

The actions triggered by the queen's infatuation with the unruly earl were fast assuming the comedy, chaos and confusion of a Keystone Cops' chase. The Earl of Huntingdon was dispatched to Plymouth hard on Knollys's heels with fresh commands from Elizabeth, so the expedition commanders sent Knollys off again in another pinnace. Unknown to all, the change in wind direction had forced *Swiftsure* back into port – at Falmouth, 60 miles (96.56 km) west of Plymouth – and there Essex remained for more than ten days, spending his time carousing with army officers, particularly 'my faithful friend' Sir Roger Williams, colonel general of the infantry. Drake told Burghley: 'The matter of the Earl of Essex has been a great trouble to us but we have as yet been unable to discover him.'[28] Despite his blandishment, there seems little doubt that Drake colluded in his escapade.

The expedition finally sailed on 28 April 1589. It numbered around one hundred ships, formed into five squadrons, including eleven hired armed merchantmen, some of them veterans of the Armada campaign – *Merchant Royal, Edward Bonaventure, Toby, Centurion, Golden Noble, Tiger* and *Vineyard*. Essex was in *Swiftsure* when she departed Falmouth the same day.

Instead of making for Santander and the damaged Armada ships, Drake steered for Corunna, blaming contrary winds. Besides, in a strange echo of those phantom *Hansa* ships that unwittingly led him to the plunder of the *Rosario*, he and Norris claimed to have received reports of two hundred ships 'of diverse nations at The Groyne [Corunna] and other ports of Galicia and Portugal with a store of munition, masts, cables and other provisions for the enemy'. As the queen rightly feared, the lure of plunder aplenty had distracted Drake from his agreed tactical objectives before a shot had even been fired.

The English fleet anchored a mile (1.61 km) off Corunna at three o'clock on the afternoon of 4 May. Their arrival took the Spanish completely by surprise. The new Venetian ambassador to Madrid, Tomaso Contarini, reported:

> The [marqués of Seralva] governor of Galicia was attending to private matters. The courts were sitting. The soldiers had left their quarters and their arms and were scattered all over the country.
>
> Everyone was so far from expecting an attack that they had no time to turn the useless out of the town or put their dearest possessions in safety.

[The governor's] wife and daughter fled in their terror six miles [9.66 km] on foot.

The marqués did all that he was able and the troops performed their duty but the forces of the enemy, their sudden arrival, the weakness of the fortress and the want of proper munitions, place the city in danger of falling.[29]

There was no sign of Drake's two hundred ships. The only vessels within the quiet harbour were the battered *San Juan*, a 600-ton Flemish hulk, another ship loaded with pikes and firearms, and two oared galleys.

Despite the wet and stormy weather, seven thousand soldiers were landed within three hours on the narrow isthmus that connects Corunna to the mainland and their fire drove back the few enemy forces to shelter behind the walls of the lower or 'base town'. Norris landed two demi-culverins on 5 May and opened fire on the two galleys (which promptly rowed off to the safety of Ferrol) and the *San Juan*, silencing her few remaining operational guns.

Another two thousand English soldiers landed before dawn on 6 May and attacked the lower suburbs of Corunna, swiftly winning control of the streets. The *San Juan* was set ablaze by the defenders and the two hulks abandoned to the English who set about looting the town. Many soldiers were soon lying insensible from drinking the copious supplies of wine they had 'liberated'. The alcohol certainly did not help, but epidemics further decimated the troops, possibly caused by typhus picked up from 'the old clothes and baggage of those which returned with the Duke of Medina Sidonia', as Sir Roger Williams suggested.[30] During the subsequent interrogation of prisoners, Norris and Drake heard there was a 'good store of munitions and victuals' within the upper part of Corunna. Rather than consuming their own stores, they decided on its capture. After a four-day siege of the upper city, they reported:

With great difficulty a little breach was made [in the walls] and at another, a mine which threw [down] a round tower near adjoining.

An assault was attempted but the gentlemen and leaders, very suddenly and valiantly mounting on top of the breach, some walls ... overthrew those that went upon it and [the] fall buried such as were at the foot of it.

[This] unfortunate and unlooked for accident was the cause the town has not been entered and taken.[31]

Conveniently forgetting the target of Santander, they determined to sail onwards to Lisbon, but this decision may have been influenced by their inability to stop the galleys re-supplying the garrison and the news that twelve more were on their way with substantial enemy reinforcements.

Although they failed to capture the citadel of Corunna, English raiding parties had been able to roam with impunity in the surrounding countryside, happily pillaging and looting. 'Black Jack' Norris defeated a hastily gathered 8,500-strong Spanish force of raw levies at Puente de Burgos, killing up to 1,500 of them before they fled. Returning in triumph with a captured Spanish royal standard as a trophy, he urged Burghley to persuade Elizabeth to send out more artillery, powder and munitions and thirty companies of trained soldiers from the Low Countries, 'which would serve to continue this war here all this year which was a more safe and profitable course than to attend an enemy at home'.[32]

Drake may have committed a cardinal tactical error in quitting Corunna so soon. The Spanish feared that, if he held the port, he could be reinforced and provisioned from England, enabling much more damaging punitive operations both inland and along the coast. The Venetian envoy observed:

The naval forces of Spain are not such as to allow them to face the enemy on the open sea.

Owing to the want of ships and men, they are extremely weak ... From want of soldiers they have adopted a plan which may prove more hurtful than helpful. They have enrolled Portuguese and have so armed the very people whom they have cause to fear.[33]

In London, the queen was greatly angered by the disobedience of the expedition commanders. After receiving news of the inconclusive action at Corunna – 'a place of no importance and very hazardous in the attempt' – she insisted they 'had not performed that which they promised ... They had two places where they should have done greater service in taking and burning the ships.' When Thomas Windebank, one of the clerks of the signet, suggested that

Drake and Norris would never do anything but 'the best service for her majesty and her realm', Elizabeth observed acerbically that 'they went to places more for profit than for service'. She ordered them to attack the Armada shipping at Santander, which should be accomplished 'before your return ... you have [not] given us cause to be satisfied with you'.[34]

It would be many days before Drake and Norris could taste the queen's indignation, so the fleet sailed on for Lisbon, apparently in the mistaken, if not disingenuous, belief that the 'better part of the king's fleet' was within that city's harbour. The fleet, now joined by Essex in *Swiftsure,* landed a vanguard of two thousand troops at Peniche, 45 miles (74.4 km) north of Lisbon, on 26 May, beneath the walls of the castle.[35] True to form, the earl was the first ashore, splashing through the surf, before he killed a Spaniard in hand-to-hand fighting – one of a force of five thousand stationed to oppose the landing on the cliffs above. An English soldier, Ralph Lane, described the skirmish that followed on a sandy plateau overlooking the beach:

> The Earl of Essex and the colonel general [Sir Roger Williams] took their first landing ... and made fight with the enemy almost two hours before the general could make land by reason of the huge billows and most dangerous rocks that split diverse of our boats and [cast] many of our men away in landing.
>
> Very brave charges the enemy made and made two retreats and in the third were clean repulsed and quitted the field ...
>
> The earl lost a brave captain, a man of his own, Captain Pew, was slain by a push of the pike and some others of meaner account.
>
> But the Spaniard did abide it even to the very pike.[36]

Two days later Norris, with Essex in tow, marched off towards Lisbon at the head of six thousand men (the force heavily depleted by disease), arriving in the city's western suburbs on 2 June. The siege was ineffectual. Norris had no artillery, little gunpowder and only small quantities of match, used for firing the infantry's shoulder arms. Dom Antonio's promises of a popular uprising in his support came to nothing. After desultory skirmishing and more casualties, the English broke away on 4 June, but only after Essex vented his frustration by sticking his pike into the city's wooden gates and challenging all comers to personal combat to defend the honour of Elizabeth's name. None of the defenders, observing this martial tantrum from the city walls above, decided to take up his kind offer.

Dom Antonio was scathing about the attempted invasion:

> We disembarked at Peniche where the strong wines of the country increased the sickness of the men. When we arrived before Lisbon, there were not enough fit men to attack a boat and our host [army] was far more fit to die than to fight.

But he had nothing but praise for Drake and Norris or the fighting qualities of the English soldier – when he was not drunk or sick: 'This I can assure you, that four thousand Englishmen are equal to eight thousand Spaniards and whenever I can embark with them I shall gladly do so, especially if Sir John Norris and Sir Francis Drake be amongst them for, by my faith, they are gallant gentlemen.'[37]

Meanwhile, instead of supporting the English army by sailing up the River Tagus, Drake was amusing himself capturing sixty *Hansa* merchantmen which were heading into Lisbon with supplies for Spain.

Norris was forced to retreat along the estuary to Cascaes, troubled by intermittent cannon fire from Spanish galleys that 'struck off a gentleman's leg and killed the sergeant-major's mule' from under him as they passed the town of St Julian. In spite of the reverse at Lisbon, Sir Roger Williams still believed that Spain and Portugal were soft targets, bragging to Walsingham that with '12,000 footmen and 1,000 lancers, her majesty might march' through the two countries 'and dictate terms of peace'. He added contemptuously: 'The Portuguese are the greatest cowards ever seen.'[38]

A friar then reported that the enemy had followed them as far as St Julian and were boasting they had driven the English from the gates of Lisbon. Affronted by this slight on his honour, Norris immediately formally offered battle, under flag of truce and trumpet. Essex, not to be outdone in the chivalry stakes, offered to fight the best man the Spanish could offer, or, he could test their mettle, six against six, or ten to ten, or any other number they cared to name.[39] The earl declared that he would be in the front rank of the English vanguard and could be easily identified, wearing a large plume of feathers in his morion and a red scarf on his left arm.

The next morning, there was only a deserted camp: the Spanish had gone.

It was the end of any military adventure for Essex. A few days later, a letter arrived from Elizabeth which left Drake and Norris in no doubt about what would happen if the earl was not returned to the safety of England immediately:

> If Essex be now come into [your company], you will cause him to be safely sent hither forthwith. If you do not, you shall look to answer for the same to your smart, for these be no childish actions, nor matters wherein you are to deal by cunning devices to seek evasions as the custom of lawyers is. Therefore, consider well your doings.[40]

Ashley, in his report home, adroitly observed that the landing at Corunna was 'judged to have been the special hindrance of good success here, the enemy upon knowledge thereof having in the meanwhile assembled great strength for the city and defeated Dom Antonio by all possible means of any favour or aid in these parts'.[41]

The English troops re-embarked and the fleet sailed out, intending at least to fulfil the expedition's final objective: the occupation of the Azores. This now looked impossible, given the poor condition of the troops and their reduced numbers. Perhaps Drake hoped to snatch glory out of ignominy by repeating the success of his Cadiz raid and capture a face-saving Spanish ship or two. But after burning the city of Vigo on 29 June, his plans were stymied by a fierce storm. *Revenge* sprang a serious leak so he was forced to sail home, arriving on 10 July with 'twenty or thirty ships'.

The expedition was a disaster. By 1 September, one hundred and two ships had returned, but of the 23,000 who had sailed with the fleet, only 3,722 were fit and well. The rest had been cut down by disease, and between 8,000 and 11,000 had died.[42] In one ship, only 114 were left out of a crew of 300, and just eight were in a fit state to work the ship as she approached Plymouth.

After spending at least £100,000, none of the three objectives of the expedition was achieved. Parallels with the Armada's fate were both ironic and mortifying. Beyond private loot, the plunder was limited to one hundred and fifty brass cannon captured at Corunna and £30,000 prize money for the cargoes in the *Hansa* ships captured by Drake. The German vessels had to be returned to their owners.

The Spanish spy codenamed 'David' reported that 'Dom Antonio and his people arrived in Plymouth in a wretched state' and that the Portuguese were now more unpopular in England than the Spaniards. 'The English hold Dom Antonio in no respect whatever and the only name they can find for him and his people is "dog". They openly insult [him] to his face without being punished.'[43]

On 4 or 5 July, Essex arrived at Plymouth with seven ships and cravenly sent his brother Walter ahead to the queen to abjectly seek her pardon for his absconding.

Once again, an English army was discharged, largely without pay.

At the end of the month, 'certain mariners and other lewd fellows' gathered 'in mutinous sort' outside the Royal Exchange in the City of London, trying to sell illegally their weapons and armour. The lord mayor was ordered to apprehend them and 'lay by the heels' any that 'persisted in any such tumultuous sort'. In this he failed signally, and 'all the mariners and soldiers remained about the city in contemptuous behaviour'. On 16 August the Privy Council wrote to Lord Cobham about the 'great disorders' committed by soldiers from Sir Edward Norris's and Anthony Wingfield's companies in Maidstone, Kent, demanding that the miscreants be captured and gaoled.[44] Night watches were set up to prevent soldiers from gathering because 'some of late have offered violence to persons they met on the highway and have taken money by force'. In the end, these hard-done-by heroes were treated like vagrants and posted back to their home counties.[45]

It was not only ordinary soldiers who suffered. In October, twenty-five army captains 'having acquainted the [Privy Council] with their great charges in raising their companies and maintaining their offices before the voyage and since coming home, without any consideration [recompense], pray their lordships they may be employed in her majesty's service'.[46]

Elizabeth was also fearful about the diseases the unemployed rude soldiery might be spreading on their return to England. A proclamation of 22 July banned anyone who had served with the fleet to come 'within the Court's gates' on pain of arrest by the queen's knight marshal and committal to the Marshalsea prison without bail.[47]

The private backers were also out of pocket. Thomas Cordell, one of the London merchants who invested in the enterprise, found, like his colleagues, 'upon the sudden return of the generals and the army' with a surfeit of provisions on their hands 'to their great loss'. A sympathetic Privy Council wrote to Burghley seeking a licence for him and his partners to export 1,200 quarters (15,240.71 kg) of corn and 50 fothers[48] of lead to Greece without customs charges as a reward for the 'good disposition and forwardness they did show in making them provision at their own charges which, if the voyage had gone forward, might have served to good purpose'.[49]

Despite the queen's public admiration for Drake's and Norris's 'valour and good conduct', once the scale of the losses in men and money became apparent, the two men faced a court of inquiry into the expedition in October 1589. The queen declared that if Drake had 'gone to Santander as he went to The Groyne, he [would have] done such service as never subject had done'.

> With twelve sail of his ships he might have destroyed all the forces which the Spaniards had there, which was the whole strength of the country by sea.
>
> There they did ride all unrigged and their ordnance on the shore and some twenty men only in a ship to keep them.
>
> It was far overseen that he had not gone thither first.[50]

Both commanders fell from Elizabeth's good grace. Norris was not granted another military command for two years, while Drake remained out of favour until 1595. Greed had undone him. England's naval talisman had lost some of his magic.

Philip pressed ahead with rebuilding his Armada, with twelve million in gold to spend. The Spanish boasted that, a year hence, they would have a 'fleet and an army to sack England and take a just and accumulated vengeance on their enemies'.[51]

EPILOGUE

The war with England is beginning now and the end must be either that the King of Spain becomes King of England too, or that the Queen of England becomes Queen of Spain. Peace we shall never make and she has not one shore only to defend ... we have learned that her armada is not invincible.

Bernardo Mendoza, Spanish ambassador to France, November, 1588.[1]

For all the assignment of blame and frenetic finger-pointing in Madrid after Medina Sidonia's return with the tattered remains of the Armada, one single factor stands out as a significant influence on the outcome of the 1588 campaign: the storms.

A weather cycle, characterised by very wet summers, began in north-west Europe in the late third century and continued for almost fifteen hundred years, with a brief interlude of drier conditions in the fourteenth century. By the middle of the sixteenth century, the pattern had reverted to soggy, unsettled summers, stormy autumns and colder winters – the so-called 'Little Ice Age'. We have anecdotal evidence to support this contention. The River Thames was not infrequently frozen over in London, indicated by accounts of fairs sometimes staged on the ice. A Venetian diplomat complained in the early sixteenth century that in England, the 'rain falls almost every day during the months of June, July and August. They never have any spring here.'[2] Then we have the oft-repeated refrain 'For the rain it raineth every day' in the fool's song from act five, scene one of William Shakespeare's *Twelfth Night*, written in 1601 and known to have been performed at a lawyers' feast in the Middle Temple, London, the following February. The line resonated so much with Shakespeare's audience that he used it again in *King Lear*, act three, scene two, written between 1603 and 1606. Doubtless it resonates still among the bedraggled British today.

On top of this high rainfall, the shift to unsettled summers and stormy autumns occurred during the lifetimes of those who fought in the ships of the English fleet, but the change evolved so subtly that it had not yet become part of the canon of seafarer's weather lore. Walsingham, however, may have been aware of it when his uncannily prophetic black propaganda predicting disaster for the Armada was compiled. The prolonged period of very stormy weather in August–September 1588 was probably caused by the cold air of the Atlantic Polar Front drifting southerly to an almost permanent position very close to Ireland and Scotland. The subsequent series of intense depressions, 310–620 miles (500–1000 km) wide, may have been deepened by warm and moist air from across the Atlantic, possibly exacerbated yet more by a decaying tropical cyclone moving northwards. All this would not have been understood or foreseen by the Spanish, who were unfamiliar with such changes in weather patterns in the more northerly latitudes.[3]

The Spaniards' first taste of their unfortunate fate came on 26–27 July when the Armada ran into a full north-westerly gale, with wind speeds gusting above forty knots, as a number of depressions passed over their route as they were leaving the Bay of Biscay and entering the south-west approaches. On 6 August, an anticyclone with light winds that had dominated the weather during the fighting up the English Channel moved south-east into France, permitting another batch of depressions to push in from the Atlantic. These brought the strong north-westerlies that swept the Armada so close to the sandbanks off Zeeland on 8 August, but the arrival of a ridge of high pressure caused the wind to suddenly veer through ninety degrees, allowing the Spanish to narrowly escape shipwreck and pass into the North Sea. By the time the Armada had sailed around Scotland and down into the North Atlantic, a succession of vigorous depressions swept in, bringing gales on 12–13 and 15–16 September. One deepened dramatically, triggering storm-force north-westerly winds that ravaged the west coast of Ireland five days later. This storm of 21 September took the heaviest toll of the Armada ships, followed by strong south-easterly winds on 25 September.[4]

On the evidence of this forensic reconstruction of the weather patterns during those crucial ten weeks by the UK Meteorological Office and the Climatic Research Unit at the University of East Anglia,[5] it seems very plausible that it was climate change that defeated the unlucky Armada rather than the popular misconception that the triumph was brought about by Drake's derring-do or the plucky 'little' ships of the English fleet.

Many of the Spanish prisoners captured by the English and Dutch suffered a terrible fate. Some of less exalted rank were thrown into London's Bridewell gaol and left to rot. In September 1588, a Spanish spy reported that 'last week there died Alonso de Serna and there are many of them ill. They suffer much, especially as winter is coming on and they have not enough clothes to cover their nakedness. My heart aches for them but I have not the power to help them.'[6] Six days later, another of Madrid's agents, Marco Antonio Messia, said the Italians in London 'have given them alms freely, but there are so many of them that a very small sum falls to each one'. He had visited the prisoners and found that a Sardinian and an Andalusian[7] had been released after converting to Protestantism. 'Those who refused to listen to the preaching of a Sicilian they have there, are not allowed any share in the alms.'[8] 'David', another spy, managed, doubtless through bribery, to rescue nine imprisoned Spaniards and Italians. He provided them with false passports and, in July 1589, shipped them from 'a rough beach near Plymouth' to land later on the Brittany coast from whence they made their way home.[9]

Eventually, in May 1589, Elizabeth's government accepted ransoms of £10 a head from the Duke of Parma for five hundred prisoners. The same deal was struck to release those held by the Dutch. For those of real status, the ransoms naturally came much higher – lending a sinister new meaning to the saying 'every man has his price'. Vasco de Mendoza and Alonso de Zayas were freed on payments of £900 apiece; Alonso de Luzón, captain of the ill-fated Levantine *La Trinidad Valencera* (lost on the reef in Kinnagoe Bay, Northern Ireland) and Diego Pimentel of the Portugal squadron's *San Mateo* (which had been captured by the Dutch after running aground off Nieuport) attracted ransoms of £1,650 each in March 1591.[10]

In contrast, Pedro de Valdés was treated well, even though he was disliked by his English captors because of his habitual haughty and arrogant speech and manner. Elizabeth wanted him imprisoned in the Tower. Drake managed to prevent this as the admiral was his personal prisoner, if not his own trophy of war. Valdés was not released until 1593, when his freedom was secured by payment of £1,500. In happier times, he succeeded to the estates owned by his despised cousin, Diego Flores Valdés, and died in 1615, aged seventy, leaving four bastard children and one legitimate heir.[11]

For the poor sailors of both fleets, there was no such happy ending. More than half who had sailed with Howard and Medina Sidonia were dead from disease or starvation by the end of 1588.

But attitudes to the sailors' role in Tudor society were slowly changing. In 1590, Howard, Hawkins and Drake established the so-called 'Chatham Chest' as a mutual benefit fund for seamen suffering poverty after being disabled on active service. This was funded by deducting six pennies per month from the pay of each seaman serving in the royal ships.[12] Four years later, Hawkins was licensed to build a hospital for 'the relief of ten or more poor mariners and shipwrights'. (The Hawkins Hospital still exists today in Chatham's High Street, providing eight flats for needy or disabled men or women who have served in the Royal Navy or Royal Marines – the oldest surviving naval charity.) Elizabeth's government continued to shy away from taking any responsibility for caring for those injured in her service. In 1595, her council directed the mayor and corporation of Bristol to enforce the collection of dues from ships because of 'the great number of mariners who of late have been maimed in her majesty's service ... who may have relief there'.[13]

In Madrid, after the initial devastating shock over the disaster that befell his Armada, Philip overcame his crisis of confidence and refused to be diverted from his personal crusade against the heretics who governed England. On 12 November 1588, his council of state unanimously recommended that the war with Elizabeth should continue, and so the long, painful process of rebuilding a new fleet began. That same month, four cities from the northern province of Asturias loyally offered the king ten galleasses displacing 120 tons apiece and six ships of between 400 and 500 tons. Similarly, neighbouring Biscay offered him the lease of fourteen galleons and Guipúzcoa, fourteen or fifteen 'great ships' with a *zabra* attached to each vessel. The Venetian envoy reported: 'This fleet is to be ready by April 1589 or May at the latest, fully fitted out except for bronze cannon.'[14] His prediction, no doubt based on the king's own deadlines, was hopelessly optimistic.

Twelve new 1,000-ton warships, nicknamed the 'Twelve Apostles', were laid down in the shipyards of Cantabria and money was spent on refitting those Armada ships judged still capable of active service.

In June 1596, a forty-eight-strong English fleet under Howard and Essex attacked Cadiz again, sinking two of the new 'Twelve Apostles', the *San Felipe* and *San Tomas*,[15] and capturing *San Andrea* and *San Mateo*. They also held the city for two weeks before leaving it ruinous. Medina Sidonia, as local governor, faced criticism for his slow military response to the assault, which allowed time for the city to be sacked.[16] He still had some supporters. One drew attention to his years of loyalty to the Spanish crown, 'much to his cost and those occasions that have met with misfortune have been the heaviest burden for him because of the care he has always put into royal service'.[17] In 1606, Medina Sidonia's obstinacy caused the loss of a Spanish squadron of ships in an action against the Dutch fleet off Gibraltar. He died in 1615 at San Lúcar, his reputation tarnished beyond repair.

Philip's new Armada sailed against the West Country or Ireland in October 1596, armed with an edict pledging that he was answering the 'universal demand of the oppressed Catholics' and was seeking 'to release them from the yoke that oppresses them without punishing the great majority of the [English] people whose innocence he recognises'. Times had clearly changed. The Spanish king promised that he had 'no quarrel with the English people as a whole and will punish with the utmost severity any man in the Catholic army who molests, injures or attacks the lands or people of the country, other than those who resist'.[18]

But his fleet of one hundred and twenty ships, commanded by Don Martin de Padilla Manrique, were caught in a fierce storm off the Galician coast which sank thirty. The remainder headed back for their home ports.

Philip tried his luck again a year later, while the English fleet was preoccupied off the Azores. A total of 136 ships, with nine thousand soldiers embarked, sailed with the objective of establishing a bridgehead at Falmouth, seizing Pendennis Castle, and marching on Plymouth. Nine days into the voyage, a three-day north-easterly storm sank twenty-eight vessels when they were only 30 miles (50.7 km) south-west of the Cornish port and Padilla reluctantly ordered a return to northern Spain. It was *déjà vu*: the 'Protestant Wind' had come to England's rescue yet again.

But the Spanish did manage to land twice in Elizabeth's dominions.

In July 1595, four galleys – *Capitana, Patrona, Peregrina* and *Bazana* – sailed from southern Brittany under the command of Carlos de Amésquita, with four hundred harquebusiers embarked. Richard Burley of Weymouth, a Catholic exile and salaried officer with the Armada in 1588, acted as their guide. The ships arrived at dawn on 23 July off the Cornish fishing village of Mousehole and landed two hundred troops who torched the settlement and the parish church of St Paul before the flotilla set off again. The galleys then sailed two miles (3.2 km) to Newlyn, near Penzance, and landed four hundred men. A small force of the Cornish militia fled in blind panic at their first sight of the Spanish troops and Penzance was then bombarded, destroying houses and sinking three ships in its harbour. Newlyn was also burnt. Fear of the imminent arrival of a fleet commanded by Drake and Hawkins forced the Spaniards to depart on 4 August – but not before a Catholic Mass was celebrated openly on English soil. Three Cornishmen were killed during the raid.[19]

The second landing came in 1601, when three thousand Spanish troops disembarked at Kinsale in south-west Ireland, in support of another Irish rebellion, this time by Hugh O'Neill, Earl of Tyrone. However, English forces eventually defeated Tyrone's followers and forced a Spanish surrender.

The English privateers continued the war against Spain. In the decade after the Armada, English ships made 236 attacks on Spanish ships in Caribbean or Atlantic waters. An attempt to ambush treasure ships in August 1591 ended in disaster when a small English squadron was attacked by fifteen warships under Don Pedro Alonso de Bazán. Five ships escaped, but Sir Richard Grenville in *Revenge* (Drake's old flagship) fought on alone off Flores in the Azores for twelve hours before finally surrendering with most of her crew dead. A week-long storm later sank fifteen of the Spanish ships and the captured *Revenge* off the island of Terceira.

Although the feared Catholic uprising in support of the Armada never happened, the continued threat of invasion ensured that government pressure was maintained on the recusant community and the seminary priests sent secretly to support them.

The number of priests smuggled into England declined after the defeat of the Armada, perhaps in response to the high proportion (possibly as high as 62 per cent) that were apprehended by Elizabeth's pursuivants throughout her reign. But the numbers secretly entering her realm stepped up again after 1591.[20] That year, a network of commissioners was set up in every county, town and port, to hunt down suspects, and in 1592 obdurate recusants were ordered to be imprisoned once more.[21] Yet, strong anti-Spanish feelings remained amongst English Catholics, as nationalism slowly became a more compelling force than religion. The Jesuit Robert Southwell declared her Catholic subjects' loyalty to the queen and assured her 'that whatever army ... should come against you, we would rather yield our breasts to be broached by our country's swords than use our own swords to the effusion of our country's blood'. Another priest, Anthony Copley, warned pruriently that if the Jesuits were allowed to establish Spanish influence over the realm, Englishmen could expect 'the rape of your daughter, the buggery of your son or the sodomising of your sow'.[22]

Yet Catholics still suffered for their faith. We last met Philip Howard, Earl of Arundel, allegedly praying for the success of the Armada while imprisoned in the Tower. He was found guilty of high treason by his peers in a trial in Westminster Hall on 14 April 1589.[23] Although attainted and condemned to death, Elizabeth never signed his execution warrant and Arundel lingered on for six years in the Tower, the sword of death always hanging over his head. He grew sick and malnourished and appealed to the queen to be permitted to see his wife and children. Elizabeth was resolute:

> [If Arundel] will but once go to the [established] church, his request shall not only be granted but he shall moreover be restored to his honour and estates with as much favour as I can show.

The earl's response was equally determined: 'On such condition, I cannot accept her majesty's offer. If that be the cause in which I am to perish, sorry am I that I have but one life to lose.' He died on 19 October 1595 (some say by poison) and was buried in the church of

St Peter ad Vincula within the walls of the fortress, in the same grave as his father, the Duke of Norfolk, was buried twenty-three years before. Arundel's funeral was designed to vilify him and his faith. The Minister humbly beseeched God

> as Thou has hitherto very gloriously and in great mercy preserved Thy servant, our Queen Elizabeth [and] to preserve her despite of all her enemies, who either secretly or openly go about to bring her to the grave, [her] glory to the dust.
>
> Confound still all Thine enemies and or convert them.

The earl was canonised as a saint by Pope Paul VI as a witness of Christ and an example of the Roman Catholic Church on 25 October 1970. The following year, his remains were placed in a shrine in the Catholic cathedral in Arundel, West Sussex.[24]

That other Howard, the lord admiral, was of course, a Protestant of unquestionable loyalty, and was created Earl of Nottingham – the second peer of the realm – on 22 October 1597. Two years later, he was appointed 'lieutenant general of all England' but finally retired from public life in January 1619, aged eighty-three. One of his favourite pastimes was hunting with dogs – he was a leading breeder of spaniels – and he continued to hunt enthusiastically right up to his final illness. He died on 14 December 1624 and was buried in the Effingham family vault at Reigate in Surrey.

Francis Drake spent some years labouring under the disgrace of his failures on the Portuguese expedition. Times were changing and he may have sensed that the glory days of his buccaneering exploits were drawing to a close, especially once the Spanish introduced a convoy system which, with improved intelligence, increasingly frustrated English privateer attacks on their treasure fleets from the New World. Perhaps deciding it was better to go out with a bang than a whimper, Drake joined Sir John Hawkins in embarking on a punitive expedition to the West Indies, intending to prey upon Spanish settlements. Hawkins, old, tired and sick, succumbed to dysentery at sea off Puerto Rico on 12 January 1596.

Drake had heard alluring talk of treasure hulks anchored in the harbour of Puerto Bello, on the coast of Panama, but after a fortnight of sickness, he died aged fifty-five, also from dysentery, at four in the morning of 28 January 1596. His body was dressed in his armour, encased in a lead coffin, and buried at sea, three nautical miles (5.56 km) off Puerto Bello, amidst salvoes fired in salute from the ships of his fleet. A foreigner who had met him at court had been captivated by his character, describing him as 'perceptive and intelligent ... his practical ability astonishing, his memory acute; his skill in managing a fleet virtually unique; his general manner moderate and restrained so that individuals are won over and gripped by affection for him'.[25] Despite his charm, his career marked him out as little more than a pirate.

In 1594, Spanish forces landed in France at Blavet, opposite Lorient in Brittany, in support of their Catholic League allies. They went on to capture and fortify Crozon, a rocky promontory dominating Brest harbour. Fearing that Spain would now capture a Channel port, the English mounted an expedition that November under a rehabilitated Sir John Norris and one of the last of Elizabeth's Armada sea-dogs, Sir Martin Frobisher, to expel the Spaniards. Frobisher was shot in the thigh as he gallantly led his sailors up a scaling ladder in an assault on the fort's walls. He was wounded at close range: the wadding used to tamp down the bullet in the musket barrel was trapped in his wound and he died from blood poisoning two days later on 15 November.[26]

We have seen how Elizabeth subsidised the Protestant forces in France's bloody religious wars. After the Duke of Guise, leader of the Catholic League, forced Henri III to flee Paris, he was appointed lieutenant general of France. Guise was summoned to attend the king at the Château de Blois on 23 December 1588 and he was assassinated there, crying out 'Treachery' as the royal guards thrust their daggers into his body. There is an apocryphal story that Henri looked down at the body of his slain opponent and commented: 'How tall he is! I had not thought he was so tall. He is even taller dead than alive.'[27] The bloodshed at the château was not over. Guise's brother, Cardinal Louis, was killed by pike thrusts from the king's bodyguard the next day.

Henri himself was assassinated on 1 August 1589 at Saint Cloud, Hauts-de-Seine. Jacques Clément, a Dominican friar, stabbed him with a dagger before being killed by the king's guards. The king lingered on until the next morning and died after naming the Protestant Henri of Navarre as his successor. The religious wars continued but the new king realised that he would need to convert to Catholicism if he were to have any chance of holding Paris. Accordingly, King Henri IV was received into the Catholic Church in 1593 and entered the French capital in March the following year. France's tragic civil wars of almost four decades were only resolved by the Edict of Nantes in 1598, which granted substantial rights to Protestants, as well opening up a path towards secularism and tolerance.

Parma also became involved in the French religious wars. In September 1590, he attempted to relieve Paris, besieged by Huguenot and royalist forces. Two years later he invaded Normandy but was wounded in the hand. He returned to Flanders only to be removed from the governorship. He died in Arras, France, aged forty-seven.

Philip was the first of the two warring monarchs to die. He had spent the winter of 1598 in Madrid but, when spring arrived, he had become so ill with gout and fever that his doctors refused to allow him to be moved. That June, he insisted on returning to the Escorial Palace so that he could die in peace 'to lay down my bones in my own house'.

It took six agonising days to carry him by litter the 28 miles (45 km) to the palace. The Spanish king had four suppurating sores on the fingers of his right hand, another on one foot and an abscess on his right knee. He could not eat or sleep and his stomach was agonisingly distended by dropsy. His pain from diabetic gangrene was so intense that it became impossible to move him and so for fifty-two days he remained unwashed, lying in his own excrement on his bed. Holes were cut in his mattress to drain his urine. Both his doctor and his daughter fled the sick-room because of the stench. As Philip lay wretchedly in constant humble prayer, he stoically told his son: 'Look at me! This is what the world and all kingdoms amount to in the end.' He died at dawn on 13 September 1598, aged seventy-one, clutching a crucifix in his hands, and was succeeded by Philip III, his son by his fourth wife, Anne of Austria.[28]

Elizabeth was scornful of the new Spanish monarch: 'I am not afraid of a King of Spain who has been up to the age of twelve learning his alphabet,' she declared. This was not just her curmudgeonly nature speaking: old age was creeping up on Gloriana and she became increasingly depressed by the loss, through death, of those she was accustomed to have around her.

Walsingham, her 'dark Moor', had died, heavily in debt, in the early hours of 6 April 1590, probably from testicular cancer.[29] Burghley, her loyal minister of four decades, was taken ill two years later, possibly from a stroke or heart attack. The queen spent hours sitting at his bedside, tenderly nursing him and feeding him with a horn spoon.[30] In a rare moment of sentiment, she told him that she would not wish to outlive him – a statement that brought tears to her old minister's eyes – and that she gave 'hourly thanks' for his services. She urged him to 'use all the rest possible you may, that you may be able to serve me at the time that cometh'. Although still suffering from decayed teeth and gout in his legs, Burghley did recover enough to regularly attend her council right up his last illness in 1598. He died at his London home, Cecil House in Covent Garden, at seven o'clock on the morning of 4 August, after declaring in his agony: 'Oh what a heart have I that I will not die.' He was succeeded as Elizabeth's chief adviser by his son Robert (by his second wife), whom Elizabeth had nicknamed 'her little pygmy'.

On top of all this, she had lost her favourite, Essex, who was clumsily beheaded with three strokes of the axe in February 1601, following a typically botched attempted *coup d'état* in London. Treason was an unforgivable offence to a Tudor monarch and overwhelmed even her affection for this ambitious and spendthrift courtier.

The queen spent the melancholy Christmas and New Year of 1602 at the Palace of Whitehall, but soon caught a severe cold and developed a painful boil on her face, which damaged both her rampant vanity and her regal dignity. On 21 January the court travelled to Richmond Palace in dank, cold and wet weather and Elizabeth fell ill again, experiencing difficulty in swallowing, possibly through the severe dental sepsis she was suffering from.

Almost exactly two months later she collapsed as she was processing into chapel and was carried, limp and barely conscious, into her bedchamber. She refused to be put to bed but sat on a spread of cushions on the floor, silent and brooding, one finger in her mouth, while her attendants watched anxiously, fearing to disturb her. More by force than by persuasion, the queen was finally got into bed. Despite her refusal to take nourishment, Howard, her cousin, brought her a small bowl of soup. She complained to him that she was tied with an iron collar about her neck. He tried to reason with her, but she replied firmly: 'No, I am tied, and the case is altered with me.'

Soon afterwards, she entirely lost the power of speech. On the evening of 23 March 1603 Archbishop Whitgift sat with her, praying at the bedside until she fell asleep. She died about three o'clock the following morning, aged sixty-nine, probably from bronchopneumonia brought on by oral sepsis and suppurative parotitis.[31] A Londoner with friends at court reported Elizabeth's death:

> This morning Her Majesty departed this life, mildly like a lamb, easily like a ripe apple from the tree, *cum leve quadam fibre, abseque gemitu* (with a slight shiver, without a groan). I doubt not but she is amongst the royal saints in Heaven in eternal joys.[32]

At ten that morning, James VI of Scotland was proclaimed her successor, becoming James I of England. On the night of 23 April, Elizabeth's corpse was taken downriver in a black-draped barge lit by flaring torches to Westminster. She was buried in the Abbey five days later and in one of history's little ironies, she rests side by side with her half-sister Mary in a tomb paid for by the new king. An inscription reads: REGNO CONSORTES ET VRNA, HIC OBDORMIMUS ELIZA-BETHA ET MARIA SORORES IN SPE RESVRRECTIONIS: 'Consorts in realm and tomb, here we sleep, Elizabeth and Mary, sisters in hope of resurrection.' They were unlikely friends in life and are equally so in death.

Nearby, on the south aisle of Henry VII's chapel, is the tomb of Mary Queen of Scots, erected there in 1613 by her son, James I. Its iconography includes the figure of Victory.

James I moved quickly to end the cripplingly expensive nineteen-year-old war with Spain. Burghley's son, Sir Robert Cecil and Howard were among the English negotiators hammering out a peace treaty with the Spanish and Habsburg delegations, the latter representatives of the rulers of the Habsburg Netherlands. The Treaty of London, signed on 28 August 1604, finally ended the conflict, ironically granting the Spanish much of what Philip II had demanded if only partial conquest of England had been achieved by the Armada. England ended its support of the Dutch rebellion and renounced its privateers' attacks on Spanish shipping.[33] On Spain's part, the treaty acknowledged that its hopes of restoring Catholicism in England were over for ever.

The accession of James I had marked a change in official policy towards Catholics. The new king seemed more moderate, promising not to persecute any 'that will be quiet and give an outward obedience to the law'.

At last some measure of religious tolerance had arrived in England, but not sufficient or speedily enough for some. Around midnight on 4 November 1605, a search of the undercroft below the House of Lords revealed Guy Fawkes guarding thirty-six barrels of gunpowder, hidden under piles of firewood and coal. He was waiting to blow up James, his nobility and his Parliament during the state opening ceremony the next day as a precursor to a revolt by Catholic gentry in the Midlands.

They planned to kidnap the king's nine-year-old daughter Elizabeth and put her on the throne as a Catholic queen.

APPENDIX I

ORDER OF BATTLE OF
ENGLISH FLEET

1 – The Queen's Ships: the 'Navy Royall'

Ship	Commander	Built/refit	Displacement (tons)	Guns	Crew	Troops	Total	Eventual fate/Comments
Ark Royal, (ex-Ark Raleigh)	Lord Admiral Howard (Flagship)	1587.	800	32	304	126	430	'Great ship', Plymouth sqdn. Bought from Sir Walter Raleigh for £5,000. Rebuilt in 1603, as *Anne Royal*. Sank in River Thames, April 1636.
Triumph	Sir Martin Frobisher	1562. Rebuilt 1578.	1,100	42	340	160	500	'Great ship', Plymouth sqdn. Rebuilt 1595–6. Sold 1618.
Bear (White Bear, ex-Great Barque)	Lord Edmund Sheffield	1538. Rebuilt 1564, 1578.	1,000	56	350	150	500	'Great ship', Plymouth sqdn. Rebuilt 1599.
Elizabeth Jonas (Elizabeth Jones, ex-Peter Pomegranate)	Sir Robert Southwell	1559. Rebuilt 1598.	900	50	350	150	500	'Great ship', Plymouth sqdn.
Victory	Sir John Hawkins	1562. Rebuilt as galleon 1586.	800	36	304	126	430	'Great ship', Plymouth sqdn. Rebuilt 1610 to displace 1,200 tons as *Prince Royal*. During interregnum, renamed *Resolution* but *Prince Royal* again after the Restoration. Flagship in 'Four Days' Fight' in the Dutch war but grounded on Galloper Shoal on 3 June 1666 and surrendered. Burnt by Dutch.

Elizabeth Bonaventure	Earl of Cumberland, later George Raymond	1567. Rebuilt 1581.	600	30	174	76	250	'Great ship', Plymouth sqdn. Bought in 1567 from Hull merchant. Broken up c.1611.
Marie Rose	Edward Fenton Esq.	1556.	600	28	174	76	250	'Great ship', Plymouth sqdn. Rebuilt 1589. Used as wharf at Chatham, 1618.
Hope	Robert Crosse, gent.	1558. Rebuilt as galleass, 1584.	600	36	174	76	250	Western sqdn. Rebuilt 1603 as *Assurance*.
Rainbow (Channel sqdn flagship)	Sir Henry Seymour	1586. Deptford.	500	26	174	76	250	Channel sqdn. Refitted 1602. Rebuilt with greater displacement 1617.
Lion (Golden Lion)	Lord Thomas Howard	1557. Rebuilt 1582.	500	30	174	76	250	Galleon, Plymouth sqdn. Broken up 1609.
Vanguard (Vauntguard)	Sir William Wynter	1586. Woolwich.	500	37	174	76	250	Galleon, Channel sqdn. Rebuilt 1615 and again in 1630 with greater displacement.
Revenge (Western sqdn flagship)	Sir Francis Drake	1577.	500	34	174	76	250	Galleon. Western sqdn. Captured off Azores by Spanish 1 September 1591 and sank five days later.
Nonpareil (ex-Philip & Mary)	Thomas Fenner, gent.	1556. Rebuilt 1584.	500	30	174	76	250	Galleon, Western sqdn. Rebuilt 1603 and renamed *Nonsuch*.
Antelope	Sir Henry Palmer	1546. Rebuilt 1581.	400	24	130	30	160	Galleon, Channel sqdn. Rebuilt as larger ship 1618.

Dreadnought	Sir George Beeston	1573.	400	24	160	40	200	'Great ship', Plymouth sqdn. Rebuilt 1592 and 1613. Sold c. 1644.
Swiftsure	Edward Fenner, gent.	1573.	400	26	140	40	180	'Great ship', Western sqdn. Rebuilt 1592.
Swallow	Richard Hawkins, gent.	1540. Rebuilt 1580.	360	20	130	30	160	Galleass. Plymouth sqdn. Condemned as unseaworthy 1603.
Foresight	Christopher Baker, gent.	1570.	300	24	130	30	160	Galleon, Plymouth sqdn. Condemned as unseaworthy 1604.
Bonavolia (ex-Galley Ellinor)	William Borough Esq.	1563. Rebuilt 1584.	300	5?	N/K	N/K	250	Oared galley. Confiscated from French Huguenots. Guardship in Thames Estuary under Seymour. Disposed of c.1603.
Aid	William Fenner, gent.	1562. Rebuilt 1580.	250	19	106	14	120	Galleon, Western sqdn. Deleted c.1599. Condemned as unseaworthy 1603.
Bull	Jeremy Turner, gent.	1546. Rebuilt 1570.	200	17	92	8	100	Galleass rebuilt as Galleon, Channel sqdn. Condemned as unseaworthy 1594.
Tiger (ex-Sea Dragon)	John Bostocke, gent.	1570. Private ship, exchanged c.1584.	200	19	92	8	100	Galleass, Channel sqdn. Hulk, c.1600; condemned as unseaworthy 1605.
Tramontana (Tremontain)	Luke Ward, gent.	1586.	150	22	63	7	70	Galleon, Channel sqdn. Broken up 1618.
White Lion	Charles Howard Esq.	N/K	140	18	N/K	N/K	50	Galleon, Plymouth sqdn. Owned by Lord Admiral Howard.

Name	Owner/Captain	Date						Notes
Scout	Henry Ashley Esq.	1577.	120	18	63	7	70	Barque, Channel sqdn. Remained at Portsmouth and took no part in hostilities. Declared a hulk c.1600 and condemned as unseaworthy 1604.
George	Richard Hodges	N/K	120	N/K	20	4	24	Hoy, Plymouth sqdn.
Achates	Gregory Riggs, gent.	1573.	100	16	53	7	60	Barque. Used as hulk c.1600. Condemned as unseaworthy 1604.
Brigandine	Thomas Scott	1584.	90	N/K	N/K	N/K	36	Small oared galley, stationed in Thames estuary. Deleted c.1589.
Disdain	Jonas Bradbury, gent.	N/K	80	N/K	N/K	N/K	40	Pinnace.
Popinjay	N/K	Purchased 1587.	80	N/K	N/K	N/K	50	Pinnace.
Charles	John Roberts, gent.	1586.	70	12	40	0	40	Pinnace. Sold 1616.
Moon	Alexander Clifford, gent.	1586.	60	9	40	0	40	Pinnace. Rebuilt 1602.
Advice	John Harris, gent.	1586.	50	10	40	0	40	Pinnace. Deleted c.1607.
Merlin (Marlyn)	Walter Gower, gent.	1579.	50	8	35	0	35	Pinnace. Deleted c.1599.
Spy	Ambrose Ward, gent.	1586.	50	7	34	5	39	Pinnace, Channel sqdn. Deleted c.1613.
Fancy	John Paul	N/K	50	N/K	N/K	N/K	20	Privateer pinnace on loan, Channel sqdn.

Ship	Owner/Captain	Year	Tons	Guns	Crew	Troops	Complement	Notes
Sun	Richard Buckley	1586.	40	3	30	0	30	Pinnace, Channel sqdn. Deleted c.1599.
Cygnet	John Sheriff	1585.	30	N/K	N/K	N/K	20	Pinnace, Channel sqdn. Disposed of c.1599.
Totals								
Thirty-eight ships			12,990 tons displacement	c.768 guns	4,438 crew	1,550 troops	c.6,454 total complement	No war casualties.

2 – Merchant ships hired for active service

Ship	Owner/Captain	Year	Tons	Guns	Crew	Troops	Complement	Notes
Susan Anne Parnell (London)	Nicholas Gorges Esq.	N/K	220	N/K	N/K	N/K	80	Reinforcement for Channel sqdn. Owned by the Levant Company. Received Bounty payment 1592.
Violet (London)	Martin Hawkins	N/K	220	N/K	N/K	N/K	70	Reinforcement for Channel sqdn.
Solomon (London)	Edmund Musgrave	N/K	200	N/K	N/K	N/K	80	Reinforcement for Channel sqdn.
Edward of Maldon	William Pierce	N/K	186	N/K	N/K	N/K	30	Plymouth sqdn.
Anne Frances (London)	Charles Lister	N/K	180	N/K	N/K	N/K	90	Reinforcement for Channel sqdn.
Vineyard (London)	Benjamin Cooke	N/K	160	N/K	N/K	N/K	60	Reinforcement for Channel sqdn.
George Bonaventure (London)	Eleazar Hickman	N/K	150	N/K	N/K	N/K	80	Reinforcement for Channel sqdn. Owned by the Levant Company.
Samuel	John Vassall	N/K	140	N/K	N/K	N/K	50	Channel sqdn.
Nightingale	John Date	N/K	120	N/K	N/K	N/K	60	Plymouth sqdn.

Ship	Captain	Built	Tons				Complement	Notes
Jane Bonaventure (London)	N/K		100	N/K	N/K	N/K	50	Reinforcement for Channel sqdn.
Lark	Thomas Hallwood		50	N/K	N/K	N/K	30	N/K
Fantasy (Fancy)	[Thomas] Chichester, gent.		50	N/K	N/K	N/K	50	N/K
Marigold	John Pawle	N/K	30	N/K	N/K	N/K	40	N/K
Black Dog	William Newton		20	N/K	N/K	N/K	10	Owned by Sir George Bond, Lord Mayor of London 1587–8.
Katherine	John Davis		20	N/K	N/K	N/K	10	N/K
Pippin	N/K	N/K	20	N/K	N/K	N/K	8	N/K
Totals								
Sixteen ships			1,866 tons displacement	N/K	N/K	N/K	798 total complement	No war casualties.

3 – Merchant ships on active service with Drake's Western squadron

Ship	Captain	Built	Tons				Complement	Notes
Galleon Leicester (ex-Galleon Ughtred, ex-Bear)	George Fenner, gent.	1578.	400	42	N/K	N/K	160	Owned by the Earl of Leicester. Ship in which the navigator Sir Thomas Cavendish died in South Atlantic in 1591.
Merchant Royal	Robert Feake or Flick	1576.	400	N/K	N/K	N/K	140	Owned by Levant Company. Received Royal Bounty 1573.
Roebuck	Jacob Whitton		300	N/K	N/K	N/K	120	Owned by Sir Walter Raleigh.

Ship	Captain	Date						Notes
Edward Bonaventure	James Lancaster	1574.	300	40	N/K	N/K	120	Owned by Earl of Oxford. Built to same design as *Foresight*. First English ship to voyage to India.
Golden Noble	Adam Seager, gent.	1567?	250	N/K	N/K	N/K	110	Owned by London merchant John Burd.
Hope Wean (Hope Well)	John Marchant	N/K	200	N/K	N/K	N/K	100	
Griffin	William Hawkins, gent.	N/K	200	N/K	N/K	N/K	100	
Spark	William Spark	N/K	200	N/K	N/K	N/K	80	
Minion (London)	William Wynter, gent.	1579?	200	N/K	N/K	N/K	80	
Barque Talbot	Henry White, gent.	N/K	200	N/K	N/K	N/K	80	Fireship. Burnt off Calais 28–29 July.
Thomas Drake (Thomas)	Henry Spindelow	N/K	200	N/K	N/K	N/K	80	Owned by Sir Francis Drake. Fireship. Burnt off Calais 28–29 July.
Virgin, God Save Her	John Grenville or Greenfield	N/K	200	N/K	N/K	N/K	70	Owned by Sir Richard Grenville.
Barque Bond	William Poole	N/K	200	N/K	N/K	N/K	70	Owned by Sir John Hawkins. Fireship. Burnt off Calais 28–29 July.
Hope Hawkins (Plymouth)	John Rivers	N/K	180	N/K	N/K	N/K	80	Owned by William Hart. Fireship. Burnt off Calais 28–29 July.
Barque St Leger	John St Leger, gent.	N/K	160	N/K	N/K	N/K	80	

Barque Mornington (aka Mannington), (Foy, Cornwall)	Ambrose Mannington, gent.	N/K	160	N/K	N/K	N/K	80	
Barque Hawkins (Plymouth)	William Snell	1560.	150	N/K	N/K	N/K	70	Received Royal Bounty 1560.
Barque Bonner	Charles Caesar	1574.	150	N/K	N/K	N/K	70	Received Royal Bounty 1574.
'Cure's Ship'	?Cure	N/K	150	N/K	N/K	N/K/	N/K	Fireship. Burnt off Calais, 28/29 July.
Bear Yonge	John Young, gent.	N/K	140	19	N/K	N/K	70	Fireship. Burnt off Calais, 28/29 July.
Angel (Southampton)	N/K	N/K	120	N/K	N/K/	N/K	N/K	Volunteer ship. Fireship. Burnt off Calais, 28/29 July.
Elizabeth of Lowestoft	N/K	N/K	90	N/K	N/K	N/K	N/K	Fireship. Burnt off Calais, 28/29 July.
Barque Buggins	John Langford, gent.	N/K	80	N/K	N/K	N/K	50	
Unity	Humphrey Sydenham, gent.	N/K	80	N/K	N/K	N/K	40	
Elizabeth Fowes	Roger Grant	N/K	80	N/K	N/K	N/K	60	
Elizabeth Drake	Thomas Cely or Seely	N/K	60	N/K	N/K	N/K	30	
Makeshift (Millbrook)	Piers Leyman	N/K	60	N/K	N/K	N/K	40	Privateer pinnace.
Chance	James Fowes	N/K	60	N/K	N/K	N/K	40	

Speedwell (Dartmouth)	Hugh Harding	N/K	60	N/K	N/K	N/K	40	
Diamond (Dartmouth)	Robert Holland	N/K	60	N/K	N/K	N/K	40	
Golden Hinde (Barque Fleming)	Thomas Fleming	N/K	50	N/K	N/K	N/K	30	
Delight	William Cox	N/K	50	N/K	N/K	N/K	30	Owned by Sir William Wynter.
Flyboat Yonge	Nicholas Webb	N/K	50	N/K	N/K	N/K	30	
Heartsease	Hannibal Sharpham	N/K	50	N/K	N/K	N/K	24	
Nightingale	John Grisling	N/K	40	N/K	N/K	N/K	24	
Unnamed Caravel	N/K	N/K	30	N/K	N/K	N/K	24	
Totals								
Thirty-six ships			5,360 tons displacement	N/K	N/K	N/K	2,262 total complement	Eight fireships destroyed off Calais. No other war casualties.

4 – Other armed merchantmen financed by the City of London

Hercules (London)	George Barnes, gent.	N/K	300	N/K	N/K	N/K	130	Plymouth sqdn. Received Royal Bounty 1588.
Toby (London)	Robert Cuttle	N/K	250	N/K	N/K	N/K	100	Plymouth sqdn. Merchant Adventurer.
Centurion (London)	Samuel Foxcraft	N/K	250	N/K	N/K	N/K	100	Plymouth sqdn.
Minion (Bristol)	John Seckfield	N/K	230	N/K	N/K	N/K	90	Plymouth sqdn. Received Royal Bounty 1579.

Margaret and John	John Fisher	N/K	210	N/K	N/K	N/K	90	Plymouth sqdn. Owned by John Watts.
Primrose (Harwich)	Robert Bringborne	N/K	200	N/K	N/K	N/K	90	Plymouth sqdn.
Tyger	William Caesar	N/K	200	N/K	N/K	N/K	80	
Red Lion	Jervis Wilde	N/K	200	N/K	N/K	N/K	70	Plymouth sqdn.
Ascension	John Bacon	N/K	200	N/K	N/K	N/K	150	Plymouth sqdn.
Mayflower (Lynn)	Edward Bancks	N/K	200	N/K	N/K	N/K	90	Channel sqdn.
Gift of God (Lowestoft)	Thomas Lentlowe	N/K	180	N/K	N/K	N/K	80	At Portsmouth. Did not fight.
Barque Burr	John Serocold	N/K	160	N/K	N/K	N/K	70	Plymouth sqdn.
Brave	William Funtlow	N/K	160	N/K	N/K	N/K	90	Plymouth sqdn.
Royal Defence (London)	John Chester	N/K	160	N/K	N/K	N/K	80	Plymouth sqdn.
Thomas Bonaventure	William Aldridge	N/K	150	N/K	N/K	N/K	70	Plymouth sqdn. Owned by the Levant Company.
Golden Lion	Robert Wilcox	N/K	140	N/K	N/K	N/K	70	Plymouth sqdn.
George Noble	Richard Harper	N/K	120	14	N/K	N/K	80	Reinforcement for Channel sqdn.
Toby	Christopher Pigot	N/K	120	18.	N/K	N/K	70	Reinforcement for Channel sqdn. Merchant Adventurer.
Antelope (London)	Abraham Bonner	N/K	120	15.	N/K	N/K	60	Reinforcement for Channel sqdn. Merchant Adventurer.

Ship	Captain		Tons	Guns			Complement	Notes
Prudence (Leigh)	Richard Chester	N/K	120	16	N/K	N/K	60	Reinforcement for Channel sqdn.
Salamander (Leigh)	William Goodlad	N/K	120	16	N/K	N/K	60	Reinforcement for Channel sqdn. Merchant Adventurer.
Jewel (Leigh)	Henry Rowell	N/K	110	17	N/K	N/K	60	Reinforcement for Channel sqdn. Merchant Adventurer.
Dolphin (Leigh)	William Hare	N/K	110	15	N/K	N/K	70	Reinforcement for Channel sqdn. Merchant Adventurer.
Rose Lion (Leigh)	Barnaby Acton	N/K	110	10	N/K	N/K	50	Reinforcement for Channel sqdn. Merchant Adventurer.
Anthony	Richard Dove	N/K	110	14	N/K	N/K	60	Reinforcement for Channel Sqdn. Merchant Adventurer.
Pansy (Pawnses) (London)	William Butler	N/K	100	14	N/K	N/K	70	Reinforcement for Channel sqdn. Merchant Adventurer.
Diana	Edward Cock	N/K	80	N/K	N/K	N/K	40	
Passport	Christopher Colthurst	N/K	80	N/K	N/K	N/K	40	
Release	John King	N/K	60	N/K	N/K	N/K	30	
Moonshine	John Borough	N/K	60	N/K	N/K	N/K	30	
Totals								
Thirty ships			4,610 tons displacement	N/K	N/K	N/K	2,230 total complement	No war casualties.

5 – Hired supply ships for Western squadron

Ship	Captain		Tons				Complement	
Mary Rose (London)	Francis Burnell	N/K	180	N/K	N/K	N/K	70	
Solomon	George Street	N/K	160	N/K	N/K	N/K	60	

White Hind	Richard Browne	N/K	130	N/K	N/K	N/K	40	
Elizabeth Bonaventure	Richard Start	N/K	120	N/K	N/K	N/K	60	
Richard Duffield	William Adams	N/K	120	N/K	N/K	N/K	70	
Elizabeth of Leigh	William Bower	N/K	115	N/K	N/K	N/K	60	Received Royal Bounty 1575.
Jonas (Aldborough)	Edward Bell	N/K	115	N/K	N/K	N/K	50	Received Royal Bounty 1575.
Pearl	Lawrence Moore	N/K	114	N/K	N/K	N/K	50	
Pelican	John Clarke	N/K	112	N/K	N/K	N/K	50	
Bearsabe	Edward Bryan	N/K	110	N/K	N/K	N/K	60	
Unity	John Moore	N/K	110	N/K	N/K	N/K	40	
John of London	Richard Rose	N/K	100	N/K	N/K	N/K	70	
Hope	John Skinner	N/K	107	N/K	N/K	N/K	40	
Marigold	Robert Bowers	N/K	80	N/K	N/K	N/K	50	
Total								
Fourteen ships		N/K	1,673 tons displacement	N/K	N/K	N/K	770 total complement	No war casualties.

6 – Volunteer ships with Lord Admiral Howard's Plymouth squadron

Sampson	John Wingfield	N/K	300	N/K	N/K	N/K	110	Owned by the Earl of Cumberland.

Ship	Captain		Tons			Men	Notes
Samaritan (Dartmouth)	N/K	N/K	300	N/K	N/K	150	
Galleon Dudley	John Erisay	N/K	250	N/K	N/K	100	Spanish prize owned by Sir Richard Grenville.
Barque Potts	Anthony Potts	N/K	180	N/K	N/K	80	
Crescent (Dartmouth)	N/K	N/K	160	N/K	N/K	75	
John Trelawney (Saltash and Tavistock)	Thomas Meek	N/K	150	N/K	N/K	70	
Frances of Fowey	John Rashleigh	N/K	140	N/K	N/K	60	
Golden Ryall (Weymouth)	N/K	N/K	140	N/K	N/K	60	
Bartholomew (Topsham)	Nicholas Wright	N/K	130	N/K	N/K	70	
Unicorn (Bristol)	James Langton	N/K	130	N/K	N/K	65	Received Royal Bounty 1593.
Command	N/K	N/K	120	N/K	N/K	80	
William (Plymouth)	N/K	N/K	120	N/K	N/K	60	
Ruben (Robin) (Sandwich)	William Cripes	N/K	110	N/K	N/K	65	Cinque Port ship. Channel sqdn.
Grace (Topsham)	Walter Edney	N/K	100	N/K	N/K	50	
Galleon of Weymouth	Richard Wheeler	N/K	100	N/K	N/K	50	
John of Barnstaple	N/K	N/K	100	N/K	N/K	65	

Name (Port)								Notes
Charity (Plymouth)	N/K	N/K	N/K	100	N/K	N/K	N/K	N/K	
Rat (Iow)	Gilbert Lee	N/K	80	N/K	N/K	N/K	40	Barque.
Heathen (Weymouth)	N/K	N/K	80	N/K	N/K	N/K	40	
Barque Sutton (Weymouth)	Hugh Preston	N/K	80	N/K	N/K	N/K	40	
Unicorn (Dartmouth)	N/K	N/K	76	N/K	N/K	N/K	30	
Phoenix (Dartmouth)	N/K	N/K	70	N/K	N/K	N/K	50	Barque.
Barque Halsey	Grinfeld Halsey	N/K	60	N/K	N/K	N/K	40	
Thomas Bonaventure (Lyme)	John Pentire	N/K	60	N/K	N/K	N/K	30	
Katherine (Weymouth)	N/K	N/K	60	N/K	N/K	N/K	30	
Margaret	William Hubbard	N/K	60	N/K	N/K	N/K	30	
Flyboat (IoW)	Thomas Clyffe	N/K	60	N/K	N/K	N/K	4	Owned by Sir George Carew. Based Portsmouth.
Dragon	N/K	N/K	N/K	N/K	N/K	N/K	N/K	Owned by Earl of Cumberland.
Carouse (Weymouth)	N/K		60				30	
Blessing	N/K	N/K	N/K	N/K	N/K	N/K	N/K	Discharged.
Elizabeth (IoW)	Adrian Gilbert		40		N/K	N/K	30	Owned by Sir George Carew.
Chance	N/K	N/K	N/K	N/K	N/K	N/K	N/K	Pinnace.

Galliego (Plymouth)	N/K	N/K	30	N/K	N/K	N/K	20	Barque.
Total								
Thirty-three ships			3,446 tons displacement	N/K	N/K	N/K	1,624 total complement	No war casualties.

7 – Coastal vessels with Lord Admiral Howard's Plymouth squadron

Handmaid (Bristol)	Christopher Pitt	N/K	N/K	N/K	N/K	N/K	N/K
Aid (Bristol)	N/K	N/K	N/K	N/K	N/K	N/K	N/K
Lytle John (Plymouth)	Lawrence Clayton	N/K	100	N/K	N/K	N/K	65
Barque Webbe	Nicholas Webbe	N/K	N/K	N/K	N/K	N/K	N/K
Anne Hart	John Wynnal	N/K	N/K	N/K	N/K	N/K	30
Rose (Topsham)	Thomas Sandy	N/K	N/K	N/K	N/K	N/K	50
Gift (Topsham)	N/K	N/K	N/K	N/K	N/K	N/K	21
Revenge (Lyme)	Richard Bedscodge	N/K	N/K	N/K	N/K	N/K	30
Jacob (Lyme)	N/K	N/K	N/K	N/K	N/K	N/K	50
William (Bridgewater)	John Smith	N/K	80	N/K	N/K	N/K	40
Mychael St Leger	N/K	N/K	N/K	N/K	N/K	N/K	N/K
Harte (Dartmouth)	John Haughton	N/K	60	N/K	N/K	N/K	32
Ralfe	N/K	N/K	N/K	N/K	N/K	N/K	N/K

Ship	Master		Tonnage					Complement	Notes
Raphael (IoW)	N/K	N/K	N/K	N/K	N/K	N/K	N/K	30	Owned by Sir George Carew.
Greyhound	N/K	N/K	N/K	N/K	N/K	N/K	N/K	N/K	
Total									
Fifteen ships			N/K	N/K	N/K	N/K	N/K	More than 348 total complement	No war casualties.

8 – Coastal ships forming Seymour's auxiliary squadron in Channel

Ship	Master		Tonnage					Complement	Notes
Daniel (Newcastle)	Robert Johnson	N/K	160	N/K	N/K	N/K	N/K	70	Discharged for 'wasting cloth trade'.
Galleon Hutchens (Newcastle)	Thomas Tucker	N/K	150	N/K	N/K	N/K	N/K	70	Discharged for 'wasting cloth trade'.
Barque Lamb (Newcastle)	Leonard Harvell	N/K	150	N/K	N/K	N/K	N/K	70	Discharged for 'wasting cloth trade'.
Marigold (Aldborough)	Francis Johnson	N/K	150	N/K	N/K	N/K	N/K	70	Discharged for 'want of victuals' 13 July.
Grace (Yarmouth)	William Musgrave	N/K	150	N/K	N/K	N/K	N/K	70	
William (Ipswich)	Barnaby Lowe	N/K	140	N/K	N/K	N/K	N/K	50	Hoy.
William of Brightingsea (Colchester)	Thomas Lambert	N/K	140	N/K	N/K	N/K	N/K	50	
Katherine (Ipswich)	Thomas Grymble	N/K	128	N/K	N/K	N/K	N/K	50	

Ship	Captain							Notes
Primrose (Harwich)	John Cordwell	N/K	120	N/K	N/K	N/K	40	Hoy.
Elizabeth (Ellen Nathan) (Dover)	John Litgen	N/K	120	N/K	N/K	N/K	70	Cinque Port ship.
William of Bricklesey	Thomas Lambert	N/K	100				50	
John (Chichester)	John Young	N/K	80	N/K	N/K	N/K	45	/
William (Rye)	William Coxon	N/K	80	N/K	N/K	N/K	60	Cinque Port ship.
The Frigote	— Grant	N/K	80	N/K	N/K	N/K	40	
Fortune (Aldborough)	N/K	N/K	N/K	N/K	N/K	N/K	N/K	
Handmaid (Hull)	John Gattenbury	N/K	75	N/K	N/K	N/K	38	Discharged for 'want of victuals' 17 June.
Griffin (Hull)	John Thompson	N/K	70	N/K	N/K	N/K	35	Discharged for 'want of victuals' 17 June.
Anne Bonaventure (Hastings)	John Conny	N/K	60	N/K	N/K	N/K	50	Cinque Port ship.
John Young (Romney)	Reynold Veazy	N/K	N/K	N/K	N/K	N/K	N/K	Cinque Port ship.
Fancy (Newcastle)	Richard Fearne	N/K	60	N/K	N/K	N/K	50	Discharged for 'wasting cloth trade'.
Little Hare (Hull)	Matthew Railston	N/K	50	N/K	N/K	N/K	25	Discharged 'for want of victuals' 17 June.
Grace of God (Hythe)	William Fordred	N/K	50	N/K	N/K	N/K	30	Pinnace. Cinque Port ship.

Ship	Captain		Tonnage				Complement	Notes
Minion of Fowey	N/K	N/K	N/K	N/K	N/K	N/K	N/K	Supply ship sank in storm alongside pier at Dover, 1589. Later raised.
Susan (Lynn)	John Musgrove	N/K	40	N/K	N/K	N/K	20	Discharged for 'want of victuals' 3 July.
Hazard (Faversham)	Nicholas Turner	N/K	38	N/K	N/K	N/K	34	Pinnace. Cinque Port ship.
Mathew (Lowestoft)	Richard Mitchell	N/K	35	N/K	N/K	N/K	26	Discharged for 'want of victuals' 13 June.
Total								
Twenty-six ships			More than 2,226 tons displacement	N/K	N/K	N/K	More than 1,113 total complement	No war casualties.

KEY

IoW = Isle of Wight; N/K = Not known; Sqdn = Squadron

TOTAL								
208 ships			More than 32,000 tons				More than 15,599	Eight fireships destroyed.

Sources

BL Egerton MS 2,541, f.1; Hatfield House CP 166/83; TNA AOI/1686/23–4; E 351/225; SP 12/213/34; SP 12/213/14. Laughton, *Defeat of the Spanish Armada*, vol. 1, 255, 315, 339; vol. 2, 179–82, 185, 210–12, 324–331; Dietz, 'The Royal Bounty...' *MM*, vol. 77 (1991), 5–20.

APPENDIX II

ORDER OF BATTLE OF
SPANISH FLEET

1 – Portugal Squadron (Admiral of the Ocean, Alonso Pérez de Guzmán, Duke of Medina Sidonia)

Ship	Commander	Built/ refit	Displace-ment (tons)	Guns	Crew	Troops	Total	Eventual fate/Comments
San Martin (Flagship of Fleet)	Marolín de Juan	1570s. Portugal.	1,000	48	177	300	477	Returned.
San Juan de Portugal (Vice-flagship)	Juan Martinez de Recalde	1586. Cantabria.	1,050	50	156	387	543	Returned.
San Francisco de Florencia	Gaspar de Sousa	1570s. Tuscany.	961	52	89	295	384	Returned; badly damaged.
San Luis	Don Agustín Mexia	1585. Cantabria.	830	38	116	376	492	Returned.
San Felipe	Don Francisco de Toledo	1583. Cantabria.	800	40	108	532	640	Captured by Dutch after running aground off Sluys 8 August.
San Marcos	Marqués of Peñafiel	1585. Cantabria.	790	33	117	292	409	?Lost off Mutton Island, Co. Clare, Ireland 20 September.
San Mateo	Don Diego Pimentel	1570s. Portugal.	750	34	120	275	395	Captured by Dutch after running aground off Nieuport 8 August.
Santiago	Antonio de Pereira	1585. Cantabria.	520	24	93	293	386	Returned.
San Cristobal	N/K	1570s. Portugal.	352	20	80	125	205	Returned.
San Bernardo	N/K	1586. Cantabria.	352	21	70	170	240	Returned.

		displacement (tons)	guns	crew	troops	total complement	
Augusta (*zabra*)	N/K	1585. Cantabria.	166	13	57	55	112	Returned.
Julia (*zabra*)	N/K	1585. Cantabria.	166	14	48	39	87	Returned.
Totals								
Twelve ships			7,737 tons displacement	387 guns	1,231 crew	3,139 troops	4,370 total complement	Nine ships (75%) survived.

2 – Castile Squadron (Admiral Diego Flores de Valdés)

San Cristobal (Squadron flagship)	Gregorio de las Alas	1583. Cantabria.	700	36	120	205	325	Returned.
San Juan de Castilla (Squadron vice-flagship)	Marcos de Aramburu	1585. Cantabria.	750	24	90	250	340	Returned.
La Santa Catalina	N/K	?1586. ?Cantabria.	882	24	140	193	333	Returned.
La Trinidad	N/K	?1586. ?Cantabria.	872	24	122	173	295	Lost off Valentia Island, Co. Kerry, Ireland 12 September.
Nuestra Señora de Begoña	Juan Gutiérre de Garibay	?1585. Location N/K.	750	24	80	175	255	Returned.
San Juan Bautista	Fernando Horra	1585. Cantabria.	650	24	60	180	240	Badly damaged, and burned in Blasket Sound 23 September.
San Pedro	Don Francisco de Cuéllar	1584. Cantabria.	530	24	90	185	275	Returned?

Ship	Commander	Built	Tons displacement	Guns	Crew	Troops	Total complement	Notes
San Juan	Diego Enriquez	1584. Cantabria.	530	24	80	165	245	Lost off Ireland.
Santiago el Mayor	N/K	1584. Cantabria.	530	24	105	180	285	Returned.
San Felipe y Santiago	N/K	1584. Cantabria.	530	24	80	160	240	Returned.
La Asunción	N/K	1584. Cantabria.	530	24	80	170	250	Returned.
Nuestra Señora de Barrio	N/K	1583. Cantabria.	530	24	80	180	260	Returned.
San Medel y San Celédón	N/K	1584. Cantabria.	530	24	75	170	245	Returned.
Santa Ana	N/K	?1581. France.	250	24	55	90	145	Returned.
Nuestra Señora del Rosario (*patache*)		1586. Cantabria.	75	14	25	20	45	?
San Antonio de Padua (*patache*)	N/K	1586. Cantabria.	75	12	25	20	45	Sank off Rammekin, on Flanders coast after battle of Gravelines 8 August.
Totals								
Sixteen ships			8,714 tons displacement	374 guns	1,307 crew	2,516 troops	3,823 total complement	Eleven ships (68.75%) survived.

3 – Biscay Squadron (Admiral Juan Martínez de Recalde)

Ship	Commander	Built	Tons displacement	Guns	Crew	Troops	Total complement	Notes
Santa Ana (Squadron flagship)	Juan Perez de Mucio	1586. Cantabria.	768	30	310	100	410	Lost a mast 27 July and sought refuge in French port of Le Havre. Abandoned.

Ship	Captain	Built	Tons					Fate
El Gran Grin (Vice-flagship)	Don Pedro de Mendoza	N/K	1,160	28	73	261	334	Ran aground off Clare Island, Co. Mayo, Ireland, 100 survivors, of whom 64 killed by Irish 22 September.
Santiago	N/K	1585. Cantabria.	666	25	105	205	310	Returned.
Santa María de Montemayor	N/K	?Ragusa.	707	18	48	158	206	Returned.
María Juan	Pedro de Ugarte	1585. Cantabria.	665	24	93	175	268	Sunk in battle of Gravelines 8 August.
La Magdalena	N/K	1585. Cantabria.	530	18	60	183	243	Returned.
Manuela	N/K	N/K	520	12	48	124	172	Returned.
La Concepción de Zubelzu	N/K	1585. Pasaje.	468	16	70	150	220	Lost her mainmast in storm off Corunna. Returned.
Concepción de Juan del Cano	Juan del Cano	1585. Cantabria.	418	18	58	160	218	Lost Galway Bay, Ireland late September.
San Juan	N/K	1585. Cantabria.	350	21	50	141	191	Returned.
María de Aguirre (patache)	N/K	1585. Cantabria.	70	6	25	19	44	N/K
Isabela (patache)	N/K	1585. Cantabria.	71	10	29	24	53	Returned.
María de Miguel Suso (patache)	N/K	1585. Cantabria.	96	6	25	20	45	N/K
San Estaban (patache)	N/K	1585. Cantabria.	78	6	25	10	35	Returned.

Totals

		6,567 tons displace-ment	238 guns	1,019 crew	1,730 troops	2,749 total comple-ment	
Fourteen ships							At least eight ships (57.2%) survived.

4 – Guipúzcoa Squadron (Admiral Miguel de Oquendo)

Santa Ana (Squadron flagship)	N/K	1586. San Sebastián.	1,200	47	82	303	385	Basque merchantman. Lost main-mast, sails and yardarms in storm off Corunna. Returned safely but powder magazine blew up at San Sebastián, killing 100 crew.
Santa María de la Rosa (Vice-flagship)	Don Martin de Villafranca	1587. San Sebastián.	945	26	84	238	322	Basque merchantman. New mainmast fitted after storm in Corunna. Sank in Blasket Sound 21 September with only one survivor.
San Salvador	Don Pedro Priego	?1586.	958	25	75	321	396	Damaged by explosion 31 July, killing 200 crew. Captured by English and salvaged 1 August.
San Esteban	Don Felipe de Córdoba	?1586.	736	26	68	204	272	Ran ashore at Doonbeg, Co. Clare, Ireland; sixty captured and hanged 20 September.
Santa Cruz	N/K	?1586. Cantabria.	680	18	40	128	168	Returned.
Santa Marta	N/K	?1586.	548	20	73	182	255	Returned.
Santa Bárbara	N/K	?1586. San Sebastián.	525	12	45	154	199	Returned.
Doncella (urca)	N/K	N/K	500	16	40	135	175	Lost Santander.

Name		Built	Tons displacement	Guns	Crew	Troops	Total complement	Fate
San Buenventura	N/K	?1586. Cantabria.	379	21	55	154	209	Returned.
María San Juan	N/K	?1586. Cantabria.	291	12	54	110	164	Returned.
Asunción (*patache*)	N/K	N/K	60	9	16	18	34	N/K
San Bernabe (*patache*)	N/K	?1586. Cantabria.	69	9	17	17	34	Returned.
Nuestra Señora de Guadalupe (pinnance)	N/K	?1586. Cantabria.	?50	1	12	0	12	N/K
Magdalena (*patache*)	N/K	?1586. Cantabria.	?50	1	14	0	14	N/K
Totals								
Fourteen ships			6,991 tons displacement	243 guns	675 crew	1,964 troops	2,639 total complement	At least six (42.9%) ships survived.

5 – Andalusia Squadron (Admiral Don Pedro de Valdés)

Name		Built	Tons displacement	Guns	Crew	Troops	Total complement	Fate
Nuestra Señora del Rosario (Squadron flagship)	N/K	1587. Ribaedo.	1,150	46	119	345	464	Damaged by collisions with one of the Biscayan squadron and later with the Andalusian *Santa Catalina* 31 July. Surrendered to Drake 1 August and taken to Dartmouth.
San Francisco (Vice-flagship)	N/K	1586. Cantabria.	915	21	85	227	312	Returned.
San Bartolomé	N/K	?1585. Cantabria.	976	27	55	210	265	Returned.

Ship	Captain	Built	Tons displacement	Guns	Crew	Troops	Total complement	Fate
Duquesa Santa Ana	Pedro Maré	N/K	900	23	65	250	315	Lost in Loughros Mor Bay, Rossberg, Co. Donegal, Ireland 25/26 September.
La Concepción	N/K	?1584. Cantabria.	862	20	71	185	256	Returned.
San Juan Bautista	N/K	?1584. Cantabria.	810	31	89	245	334	Returned.
Santa Catalina	N/K	?1585. Cantabria.	730	23	69	238	307	Returned.
Santa María de Juncal	N/K	?1586. Cantabria.	730	20	66	219	285	Returned.
La Trinidad	N/K	?1585. Cantabria.	650	13	54	200	254	Returned.
San Juan de Gargarin	Tomé Cano	?1585. Cantabria.	569	16	40	175	215	Returned.
El Espírito Santo (*patache*)	N/K	1585. Cantabria.	70	10	15	18	33	N/K
Totals								
Eleven ships			8,362 tons displacement	250 guns	728 crew	2,312 troops	3,040 total complement	At least eight (72.7%) of ships survived.

6 – Levant Squadron (Admiral Martin de Bertendona)

Ship	Captain	Built	Tons displacement	Guns	Crew	Troops	Total complement	Fate
Ragazona (Squadron flagship)	N/K	Date N/K. Venice.	1,294	30	80	330	410	Returned.
Lavia (Vice-flagship)	Don Diego Enriquez	Date N/K. Venice.	728	25	71	205	276	Merchantman. Ran ashore in storms at Streedagh, Co. Sligo, Ireland 25 September.

	Commander	Date/Place built	Tons displacement	Guns	Crew	Troops	Total complement	Notes
La Trinidad Valencera	Don Alonso de Luzón	Date N/K. Venice.	1,100	42	75	335	410	Grain ship commandeered to carry siege guns. Lost on reef in Kinnagoe Bay, Northern Ireland 16 September.
Trinidad de Scala	N/K	Date N/K. Genoa.	900	22	65	340	405	Returned.
Juliana	Don de Aranada	Date N/K. Genoa.	860	32	65	290	355	Merchantman. Ran ashore in storms at Streedagh, near Sligo, Ireland 25 September.
San Nicholas Prodaneli	Capt. María Prodaneli	Date N/K. Ragusa.	834	26	68	225	293	Lost off Co. Mayo, Ireland 16–21 September.
Rata Santa María Encoronada	Don Alonso de Leyva	Date N/K. Genoa.	820	35	90	355	445	Ran aground off Fahy, Blacksod Bay, Co. Mayo. Set ablaze. after 21 September.
San Juan de Sicilia	Don Diego Tellez Enríquez	Date N/K. Ragusa.	800	26	60	275	335	Blown up in Tobermory Bay, Isle of Mull, Scotland, by agent of Walsingham 5 November.
Anunciada	Capt. Iveglia	Date N/K. Ragusa.	703	24	79	196	275	Scuttled and set ablaze off Scattery Island, off Kilrush, Co. Clare, Ireland 20 September.
Santa María de Visón	Capt. de Bartolo	Date N/K. Ragusa.	666	18	70	236	306	Merchantman. Ran ashore in storms at Streedagh, Co. Sligo, Ireland 25 September.
San Bautista de la Esperanza	N/K	Date N/K. Catro Urdiales.	300	?12	N/K	N/K	N/K	N/K
Totals								
Eleven ships			9,005 tons displacement	292 guns	723 crew	2,787 troops	3,510 total complement	At least two (18.2%) ships survived.

7 – Squadron of Hulks (Admiral Don Juan Gómez de Medina)

Ship	Captain	Built						Fate
El Gran Grifón (Squadron flagship)		Date N/K. Rostock.	650	38	43	235	278	Driven ashore at Stroms Hellier, Fair Isle, Scotland 28 September.
San Salvador (Vice-flagship)		1565. Danzig.	650	24	53	218	271	?Lost off Ireland.
Castillo Negro	Capt. Pedro Ferrat	Date N/K. Low Countries.	750	27	46	158	204	?Lost off Ireland.
Casa de Paz Grande	N/K	Date N/K. Low Countries.	650	26	70	250	320	Declared unseaworthy after storm at Corunna. Returned.
Barca de Amberg	Capt. Juan de San Martin	1577. Hamburg.	600	23	25	259	284	Sank off Ireland 1 September.
Santiago	Capt. J. de Luna	1551. Baltic.	600	19	32	32	64	Wrecked off Co. Mayo, Ireland 16–21 September.
San Pedro el Mayor (Hospital ship)	N/K	1586. Baltic.	550	18	28	176	204	Stranded on Bolt Tail, Devon 6 November.
Falcon Blanco Mayor	N/K	1586. Low Countries.	500	16	35	182	217	Returned.
El Sansón	N/K	Date N/K. Low Countries.	500	18	31	184	215	Returned.
San Pedro Menor	N/K	1586. Baltic.	500	18	22	175	197	?Lost off Ireland.
Barca de Danzig	Capt. Pedro de Arechaga	1572. Danzig.	450	26	28	150	178	N/K
El Gato	N/K	Date N/K. Low Countries.	400	9	22	40	62	Returned.

Ship	Commander	Date/Origin	tons displacement	guns	crew	troops	total complement	Fate
Santo Andrés de Malaga	N/K	Date N/K. Low Countries.	400	14	25	40	65	Returned.
Cièrvo Volante	Capt. Juan de Permato	Date N/K. Baltic.	400	18	39	130	169	Lost off Co. Mayo, Ireland 16–24 September.
Santa Bárbara	Don Cristobal de Avila	1559. Low Countries.	370	19	25	70	95	N/K. Captain hanged by Medina Sidonia for cowardice.
Casa de Paz Chica	N/K	1560. Riga.	350	15	21	155	176	Returned.
Falcon Blanco Mediano	Don Luis de Córdoba	1564. Low Countries.	300	16	24	57	81	Ran aground at Barna, west of Galway city, Ireland 25 September.
San Gabriel	N/K	1561. Low Countries.	280	4	16	31	47	N/K
Esayas	N/K	1542. Baltic.	280	4	20	35	55	Returned.
Paloma Blanca	N/K	Date N/K. Low Countries.	250	12	30	67	97	Returned.
Perro Marina	N/K	Date N/K. Low Countries.	200	7	18	80	98	Returned.
La Ventura	N/K	Date N/K. Low Countries.	160	4	16	49	65	Returned.
Totals			9,790 tons displacement	375 guns	669 crew	2,773 troops	3,442 total complement	
Twenty-two ships								At least ten (46%) ships survived. Nine known to have been lost.

8 – Portuguese Galleys (Admiral Don Diego Medrano)

Capitana (Squadron flagship)	N/K	N/K	5	53	56	109	Returned.
Princesa	N/K	N/K	5	44	37	81	Returned.
Diana	N/K	N/K	5	47	32	79	Convict Oarsmen mutinied 27 July. Beached at Bayonne; guns salved and hull later broken up.
Bazana	N/K	N/K	5	46	26	72	Wrecked off Bayonne 27 July.
Totals							
Four galleys	N/K		20 guns	190 crew – plus convict oarsmen	151 troops	341 total complement – plus convict oarsmen	Two galleys (50%) survived.

9 – Neapolitan Galleasses (Admiral Hugo de Moncada)

San Lorenzo (Squadron flagship)	N/K	1578. Naples.	600	50	124	245	369	Ran aground off Calais harbour 8 August. Destroyed.
Napolitana (Vice-flagship)	N/K	1581. Naples.	600	50	100	220	320	Returned.
Zúñiga aka Patrona	Capt. Peruchio	1578. Naples.	600	50	120	175	295	Driven by storms to Le Havre, France 4 October; repairs took a year. Last ship to return.
Girona	Capt. Fabrico Spinola	1580. Naples.	600	50	140	229	369	Repaired at Killybegs; wrecked off Lacada Point, Co. Antrim, en route to Scotland 28 October.

Totals Four ships			2,400 tons displacement	200 guns	484 crew	869 troops	1,353 total complement	Two ships (50%) survived.

10 – Auxiliary Squadron – Pataches, Zabras, Caravels, Feluccas (Admiral Agustín de Ojeda)

Ship			displacement	guns	crew	troops	total complement	notes
Nuestra Señora de Pilar de Zaragoza (Squadron flagship)	N/K	1584. Cantabria.	300	11	51	110	161	N/K
Caridad Inglesa	N/K	Date N/K. England.	180	11	36	43	79	Hulk. N/K
San Andrés Escocés	N/K	Date N/K. Dundee.	150	12	29	40	69	Hulk. N/K
El Crucifijo	N/K	N/K	150	8	33	30	63	*Patache.* N/K
La Concepción de Francisco de Latero	N/K	N/K	75	6	40	29	69	*Patache.* N/K
Esperitu Santo	N/K	N/K	75	-	40	20	60	Returned.
La Concepción de Carasa	N/K	N/K	70	5	40	30	70	N/K
Nuestra Señora de Guadalupe	N/K	N/K	70	-	40	20	60	*Patache.* Returned.
San Francisco	N/K	N/K	70	-	37	20	57	N/K
Nuestra Señora de Begoña	N/K	N/K	64	20	40	30	70	*Patatche.* N/K
La Concepción de Capetillo	N/K	N/K	60	10	25	20	45	*Patache.* N/K
Nuestra Señora de Gracia	N/K	N/K	57	5	34	20	54	*Patache.* Returned.

Nuestra Señora del Puerto	N/K	N/K	55	8	33	30	63	Patache. N/K
San Jeronimo	N/K	N/K	50	4	35	20	55	Patache. N/K
Trinidad	N/K	N/K	N/K	2	23	N/K	N/K	Zabra. ?Lost off Ireland.
Nuestra Señora de Castro	N/K	N/K	75	2	26	-	26	Zabra. Captured in Tralee Bay; crew hanged by Sir Edward Denny after 15 September.
Santo Andrés	N/K	N/K	N/K	2	15	N/K	N/K	Zabra. N/K
La Concepción de Valmesda	N/K	N/K	N/K	N/K	27	N/K	N/K	N/K
La Concepción	N/K	N/K	N/K	N/K	31	N/K	N/K	N/K
Santa Catalina	N/K	N/K	N/K	N/K	23	N/K	N/K	Zabra. N/K
San Juan de Carasa	N/K	N/K	N/K	N/K	23	N/K	N/K	Zabra. N/K
Total								
Twenty-one ships				c.106 guns	681 crew	c.462 troops		
129 ships				2,485 guns	7,707 crew plus convict oarsmen in galleys	18,703	26,410 plus convict oarsmen in galleys	

CHRONOLOGY

1527: 21 May Philip II of Spain born in Valladolid, son of Charles V of the Holy Roman Empire, and his consort, Isabella of Portugal.

1533: 25 January Henry VIII marries Anne Boleyn secretly at Westminster. Obviously pregnant, she is crowned queen on **1 June**, nine days after Thomas Cranmer, Archbishop of Canterbury, had divorced Henry from his first wife, the Spanish princess Katherine of Aragon.

1533: 7 September Elizabeth born at Greenwich Palace, only child of Henry VIII and Anne Boleyn.

1534: November Act of Supremacy passed (26 Henry VIII *cap.* 1), making Henry VIII supreme head, on earth, of the Church in England.

1542: 8 December Mary Queen of Scots born at Linlithgow, daughter of James V of Scotland and his second wife, Mary of Guise. She succeeds her father to the throne of Scotland on his sudden death on **14 December**. Her mother is regent until she dies on **11 June 1560** in Edinburgh.

1550: 15 September William Cecil appointed a principal Secretary of State to Edward VI and sworn one of the king's Privy Council. He becomes surveyor of Princess Elizabeth's estates and is knighted on **11 October 1551**.

1554: 25 July Philip of Spain marries Elizabeth's half-sister, the Catholic Mary I, at Winchester Cathedral, two days after their first meeting. He shares her title and honours during their marriage.

1555: 7 June Mary obtains a papal bull from Paul IV confirming that she and Philip are monarchs of Ireland.

1556: 16 January Philip becomes King of Spain after his father, Charles V, abdicates. His wife Mary is his consort in Spain and *Queen of the Spanish East and West Indies and of the Islands and Mainland of the Ocean Sea.* Their joint style and title now is: *Philip and Mary, by the*

Grace of God, King and Queen of England, Spain, France, Jerusalem, both the Scillies and Ireland, Defenders of the Faith, Archdukes of Austria, Dukes of Burgundy, Milan and Brabant, Counts of Habsburg, Flanders and Tyrol.

1558: 24 April Mary Queen of Scots marries François, Dauphin of France, son of Henri II, in Notre Dame Cathedral, Paris.

1558: 17 November Elizabeth I succeeds Mary as queen on her death. Cecil is appointed Privy Councillor and Secretary of State. Philip offers to marry her – but Elizabeth delays her reply and instead, he marries Elizabeth of Valois, eldest daughter of Henri II of France in 1559. (She dies after a miscarriage in 1568 and he takes as his fourth wife, his niece, Anne of Austria.)

1559: 16 January Mary Queen of Scots and her husband assume the style and title: *François and Mary, by the Grace of God, of Scotland, England and Ireland, King and Queen* and include the arms of England in her heraldry.

1559: 10 July Mary Queen of Scots' husband ascends the French throne as François II.

1560: 5 December Mary Queen of Scots widowed. She returns to Scotland on **19 August 1561**, landing at Leith, near Edinburgh.

1565: 29 July Mary Queen of Scots marries her second husband, Henry Stuart, Lord Darnley, son and heir of the Earl of Lennox. He is proclaimed 'King of Scots'.

1566: 19 June Mary's only child James (later James VI of Scotland and from **1603**, James I of England) born in Edinburgh Castle.

1567: 10 February Henry, Lord Darnley, syphilitic husband of Mary Queen of Scots, murdered at Kirk o' Field, Edinburgh.

1567: 13 March Battle of Oosterweal – traditionally seen as the beginning of the Dutch revolt in the Spanish Netherlands. Between 700 and 800 Protestant rebels killed by a 1,000-strong Spanish force.

1567: 15 May Mary Queen of Scots marries James, Earl of Bothwell, according to Protestant rites at Holyrood House, Edinburgh.

1567: 15 June Mary Queen of Scots surrenders to the Scottish Protestant lords; Bothwell flees to Denmark where he dies, insane, eleven years later.

1567: 24 July Mary Queen of Scots forced to abdicate in favour of her baby son, who is crowned James VI at Stirling five days later. Her half-brother, the Earl of Moray, becomes regent of Scotland on **22 August**.

1568: 13 May After Mary Queen of Scots escapes from imprisonment, her forces are defeated at the Battle of Langside, near Glasgow, by Moray's army. Three days later she escapes across the Solway Firth and enters England, becoming the guest (and prisoner) of Elizabeth for the next eighteen years.

1569: 14 November Catholic Earls of Northumberland and Westmorland, with 300 armed horsemen, break into Durham Cathedral and destroy English prayer books there, later marching south in an uprising against Elizabeth. The rebellion is put down ruthlessly by Elizabeth's forces.

1570: 25 February Pope Pius V excommunicates Elizabeth by the papal bull *Regnans in Excelsis,* thereby depriving 'the pretended queen' of her throne and absolving her Catholic subjects of any allegiance to her.

1570: April Second Treasons Act (13 Elizabeth *cap.* 1) of Elizabeth's reign, makes it treason to 'imagine, invent, devise, or intend the death or destruction, or any bodily harm' to the queen 'or to deprive or depose her' from the 'style, honour or kingly name of the imperial crown of this realm'. It also becomes treason to claim that Elizabeth is 'a heretic, schismatic, tyrant, infidel or a usurper of the crown'.

Another Act, passed in this Parliamentary session, criminalises the importation of papal bulls or 'writings, instruments and other superstitious things from the See of Rome' (13 Elizabeth *cap.* 2).

1570: autumn Francis Walsingham appointed English ambassador to France.

1571: 25 February Cecil raised to peerage as Lord Burghley and is appointed Lord Treasurer of England in **1572**.

1572: 2 June Thomas Howard, Fourth Duke of Norfolk, executed for treason on Tower Hill.

1572: 24 August St Bartholomew's Day massacre of Protestant Huguenots in Paris and elsewhere in France.

1573: 20 December Francis Walsingham made a Privy Councillor and appointed a joint Principal Secretary of State, becoming Elizabeth's spymaster. He is knighted on **1 December 1577**.

1578: 1 **January** John Hawkins appointed Treasurer of the Navy on the death of his father-in-law Benjamin Gonson.

1578: Philip reinforces his army in Flanders and appoints his nephew, Alexander Farnese (later Duke of Parma), as its commander.

1579: 18 **July** Desmond Rebellion begins in Ireland with invasion of a small force of Irish, Spanish and Italian troops landing at Smerwick Harbour on the west coast (now Ard na Caithne). James Fitzmaurice Fitzgerald proclaims a holy war sanctioned by Pope Gregory XIII. The rebellion is finally snuffed out in 1583.

1580: 25 **August** Spanish forces capture Lisbon. Portugal is annexed. Philip thus acquires an important Atlantic naval base and the small but well-equipped Portuguese fleet.

1580: 10 **September** Six hundred papal troops land at Smerwick as reinforcements for Desmond Rebellion. They are besieged by English forces and surrender on 10 **October**. With the exception of their commander, all are killed and their bodies thrown into the sea.

1581: 22 **July** Dutch States General issues a declaration of independence from Spanish rule.

1582: 26 **July** Álvaro de Bazán, First Marquis of Santa Cruz, defeats a largely French mercenary fleet supporting Dom Antonio, Prior of Crato and pretender to the Portuguese crown, at the battle of São Miguel, in the Portuguese Azores.

1583: 9 **August** Santa Cruz proposes the invasion of England to Philip after his defeat of Portuguese, French and English adventurers at the naval battle of Terceira in the Azores.

1584: 19 **January** Spanish ambassador Bernardino de Mendoza expelled from England following Throckmorton plot against Elizabeth.

1584: 23 **June** Santa Cruz appointed 'Captain general of the Ocean Sea' by Philip.

1584: 10 **July** Dutch Protestant leader William of Orange ('William the Silent') assassinated in Delft in the Netherlands by Balthazar Gérard, a French Catholic.

1584: 30 **September** Philip Howard, eldest son of Thomas Howard, Fourth Duke of Norfolk (beheaded 1572 for treason) is received into the Catholic Church by the fugitive priest William Weston at Arundel Castle, Sussex.

1584: 19 October Walsingham's and Burghley's 'Bond of Association' obliges all its signatories to kill anyone who attempts to usurp the crown or tries to assassinate Elizabeth.

1584: 31 December Treaty of Joinville signed secretly between Spain, Henri, Third Duke of Guise (cousin of Mary Queen of Scots) and the French 'Catholic League' promising support for the Catholic cause in France.

1585: March Act for the Surety of the Queen's Person (27 Elizabeth *cap.* 1) outlaws any attempt to assassinate Elizabeth I in the interests of any pretended successor and permits legally 'the pursuing and taking revenge' on such a pretender.

1585: 24 April Cardinal Felice Peretti di Montalto succeeds Gregory XIII as Pope Sixtus V.

1585: May Charles Howard, Second Baron Effingham, appointed Lord High Admiral of England.

1585: 10 August Elizabeth signs the Anglo-Dutch Treaty of Nonsuch, pledging to assist the rebel Dutch provinces in the Spanish Netherlands. As well as providing an annual subsidy of 600,000 florins, a 7,000-strong English army is sent to the Low Countries under Robert Dudley, Earl of Leicester.

1585: 7–17 October Sir Francis Drake occupies ports in Galicia in north-west Spain, sacking churches. He later raids the Canary Islands, pillages Spanish towns in the Caribbean, and returns to Portsmouth with loot valued at almost £9,000,000 at today's prices.

1585: 24 October Philip decides to invade England and overthrow Elizabeth and in **December** requests Parma to draw up invasion plans.

1586: January Philip agrees that Santa Cruz should also draw up an invasion strategy. The admiral submits his requirements on **12 March**, asking for 156 ships with 55,000 troops to land in England, supported by 400 auxiliary vessels. His plans are rejected as too expensive.

1586: 24 March Walsingham writes to Leicester claiming that the Spanish threat to England 'will prove nothing this year and I hope less the next'.

1586: 15 May Philip Howard, Earl of Arundel, is arraigned in the Star Chamber at Westminster on charges that he tried to flee England without royal permission; that he had been converted to the Church of Rome and was conspiring to be restored as Duke of Norfolk. He is fined £10,000 and is imprisoned in the Tower of London 'during the Queen's pleasure'.

1586: 20 June Parma's proposals for an invasion arrive in Madrid, suggesting that 30,000 infantry and 500 cavalry should be ferried in flat-bottomed barges from Flanders to England, landing between Dover and Margate, Kent.

1586: 20–21 September Anthony Babington and fourteen others executed for high treason.

1586: 11 October Elizabeth's commissioners arrive at Fotheringay Castle, Northamptonshire, to try Mary Queen of Scots for high treason. The trial continues in the Star Chamber Court, Westminster and Mary is condemned on **25 October**.

1586: 17 November Philip orders his kingdoms of Naples and Sicily to dispatch ships and munitions to Spain.

1587: 1 February Elizabeth signs Mary's death warrant.
   Hawkins proposes, unsuccessfully, that six English warships should be stationed off the Spanish coast to warn of Armada preparations.

1587: 8 February Mary Queen of Scots beheaded at Fotheringay.

1587: 29 April–1 May Drake raids Cadiz in a pre-emptive strike against Armada ships, and destroys about 10,000 tons of Spanish shipping.

1587: 18 June Drake captures the Portuguese carrack *São Felipe* off the Azores with her cargo of spices, ivory and silks from the East Indies, valued at £18,000,000 at today's prices.

1587: 16 July Santa Cruz's Armada sails to Azores to rendezvous with the Spanish treasure fleet and escort it safely home in **September**.

1587: 29 July Pope Sixtus V signs a treaty with Philip for governing a Catholic England, allowing him to bestow the English crown on anyone he chooses. Sixtus deposits 1,000,000 ducats in a Rome bank to help fund the 'Enterprise of England' – but stipulates that 50 per cent is payable only after the Spanish land and the remainder in equal instalments every two months thereafter.

1587: 4 August English garrison of the port of Sluis in the Low Countries surrender to Parma's forces after a siege of fifty-three days.

1587: 21 December Charles Howard appointed to command English naval forces against the expected Spanish invasion of England. Dutch station their ships to blockade Dunkirk.

1588: 9 February Santa Cruz dies at Lisbon, aged sixty-one.

1588: 11 February Alonso Pérez de Guzmán, Seventh Duke of Medina Sidonia, succeeds Santa Cruz as commander of the Armada, despite his lack of naval experience and his reluctance: 'But sir, I have not health for the sea, for I know by the small experience that I have had afloat that I soon become sea-sick and have many humours [fevers].'

1588: 8 March English and Spanish commissioners begin peace negotiations in Ostend, moving to Bourbourg, near Dunkirk, on **23 May**.

1588: 6 April Elizabeth orders the lord lieutenants to arm their counties.

1588: 12 May Henri III of France flees Paris after Catholic citizens riot; Guise in control of the French capital.

1588: 30 May Armada sails from Lisbon.

1588: 3 June Howard and Drake concentrate their naval forces at Plymouth, leaving Sir Henry Seymour's squadron to guard the Dover Straits.

1588: 19 June Armada puts into Corunna in north Spain after its supplies are found to be rotting and storms scatter the fleet off Cape Finisterre. Some stragglers are driven north and are sighted off the Scilly Isles, southwest of Cornwall.

1588: 27 June Armada council of war at Corunna advises Philip to delay sailing because of provisions shortage.

1588: 1 July Philip orders the invasion to be launched as soon as possible, brushing aside Sidonia's doubts and objections: 'I have dedicated this enterprise to God ... Pull yourself together then and do your part.'

1588: 4 July English fleet departs Plymouth for a pre-emptive strike on the Armada in Corunna but adverse winds and fears that the Spanish ships might escape them, force Howard to return to Plymouth for resupply after two weeks at sea.

1588: 21 July Armada sails from Corunna. Storms force four galleys to flee to the French coast; *Bazana* is wrecked near Bayonne. The carrack *Santa Ana* seeks shelter in Le Havre, where she remains.

1588: 23 July Elizabeth orders militia in England's southern counties to mobilise.

1588: 26 July Forty ships of the Armada separated from main force by gales; the last straggler rejoins on 30 July.

1588: 29 July Armada sights Cornwall's Lizard peninsula.

1588: 30 July Sidonia sends his flagship's tender to reconnoitre the Cornish coast as the Armada enters the English Channel: a Falmouth fishing boat is captured. Howard's fleet is warped out of Plymouth.

1588: 31 July English fleet sighted by the Armada: Sidonia hoists his holy banner as a signal for his fleet to prepare for battle. First shots are fired as Howard attacks the centre and rear of the Armada. Fighting continues for four hours before the English fleet breaks off. *Nuestra Senõra del Rosario*, flagship of the Andalusian squadron, later collides with the *San Salvador* which suffers an explosion, killing two hundred of her crew and badly damaging her after-decks and steering. She is taken in tow, but the *Rosario* is involved in a second collision, with the *Santa Catalina*. *Rosario*, unable to steer, is abandoned.

Sidonia sends a message to Parma that arrives in Dunkirk on **6 August**.

1588: 1 August Drake captures the *Rosario*. Sidonia sends another message to Parma.

1588: 2 August Fighting off Portland Bill.

1588: 3 August Howard divides his fleet into four squadrons of around twenty-five ships each, commanded by himself, Frobisher, Hawkins and Drake.

1588: 4 August Fighting off the southern tip of the Isle of Wight. Sidonia writes again to Parma seeking supplies of small-calibre shot.

1588: 5 August Both Spanish and English fleets becalmed.

1588: 6 August Armada anchors in Calais Roads, four miles (6.44 km) off the French town and twenty-four (38.62 km) from Dunkirk, where Parma, still in Bruges, had not begun embarkation of his invasion army.

Anglo-Spanish peace talks at Bourbourg broken off.

1588: 7–8 August English send in eight fireships at midnight – scattering the Armada. The galleass *San Lorenzo* runs aground outside Calais harbour after colliding with the *Rata Encoronada*.

Parma begins to embark his invasion army; 16,000 men join their vessels at Nieuport.

1588: 8 August Battle of Gravelines. During the nine-hour action, *María Juan* sinks. The badly damaged galleons *San Felipe* and *San Mateo* are run aground off Ostend and are captured by Dutch ships but *San Felipe* later sinks.
  The Armada is in danger of wrecking on shoals off the coast of Flanders.
  Parma completes embarkation of troops at Dunkirk.

1588: 9 August Council of war aboard Armada flagship *San Martin* decides to re-enter English Channel to escort Parma's invasion force. If winds are contrary, however, it would head around the north coast of Scotland to return to Spain.

1588: 10 August Sidonia tells Armada crews they are returning to Spain. Seymour's squadron remains in English Channel; remainder of English fleet pursue Armada northwards.

1588: 12 August Short of ammunition and food, the English fleet abandons the chase as the Armada passes the Firth of Forth in Scotland.

1588: 19 August Elizabeth makes her speech of defiance at Tilbury Fort overlooking the Thames estuary.

1588: 20 August Elizabeth orders the disbanding of her army.

1588: 21 August Armada rounds the northern coast of Scotland and enters North Atlantic.

1588: 31 August Parma stands down his invasion fleet.

1588: 1 September–5 November At least twenty-seven Armada ships founder on the north and west coasts of Ireland and Scotland. *San Juan de Sicilia* blown up in Tobermory Bay, by John Smollett, one of Walsingham's agents.

1588: 21 September Sidonia returns to Santander in northern Spain. He reports to Philip: 'The misfortunes and miseries that have befallen us ... are the worst that have been known on any voyage.' Of the 129-strong Armada that had departed for England, at least fifty had been wrecked or sunk, with 12,500 casualties.

1588: 22 September Sir William Fitzwilliam, lord deputy of Ireland, orders the arrest and execution of all Spanish survivors from the shipwrecks on the west coast of Ireland.

1588: 6 November Hospital ship *San Pedro Mayor* wrecked on Bolt Tail, Devon.

1588: 12 November Spanish Council of State urges the continuation of the war with England. Philip told them: 'I, for my part, shall never fail to strive for the cause of God and the good of these kingdoms, as much as I can.'

1588: 24 November Service of thanksgiving for victory over Armada in St Paul's Cathedral, London.

1589: 14 April Philip Howard, Earl of Arundel, tried in Westminster Hall for arranging a secret Mass inside the Tower for the success of the Armada. He is attainted and condemned to death for treason. Elizabeth I does not sign his death warrant.

1589: 28 April Privately funded English expedition of 126 vessels and 23,000 men under Drake and Sir John Norris departs for attack on Armada survivors in Santander and to instigate a Portuguese rebellion to put the pretender Dom Antonio on the Portuguese throne.

1589: 4 May English fleet arrives off Corunna and attacks the town.

1589: 26 May English forces land at Peniche, forty-five miles north of Lisbon, arriving in the suburbs of the Portuguese capital on **2 June**. After an ineffective attempt at a siege, they retreat to Cascaes.

1589: 29 June English troops sack Vigo and set it ablaze. Drake fails to find the Spanish treasure fleet.

1589: 8 July–September English expedition returns to Plymouth almost empty-handed. Eleven thousand soldiers and sailors had died of disease or had been killed in action.

1589: Late October Court of Inquiry into Drake's and Norris's expedition.

1590: 6 April Death of Walsingham at his London home in Seething Lane, near the Tower of London, probably from testicular cancer, leaving debts of £27,000. He is buried the following night in Old St Paul's Cathedral.

1594: 15 November Death of Sir Martin Frobisher in Plymouth after he received a gunshot wound at the siege of the Spanish-held Fort Crozon during the battle for Brest, in western France. His heart is interred in St Andrew's Church, Plymouth the same day and his body later buried in St Giles-without-Cripplegate, London.

1595: 19 October Philip Howard, Earl of Arundel, dies from malnutrition – some claim poison – in the Tower. His body is buried in the church of St Peter ad Vincula, within the fortress, but it is exhumed and reburied in 1624 in the Fitzalan Chapel at Arundel Castle and again in the Catholic cathedral in Arundel in 1971. He was beatified by Pope Pius XI in 1929 and canonised by Paul VI on 25 October 1970.

1596: 12 January Death of Sir John Hawkins from dysentery off Puerto Rico.

1596: 28 January Death of Sir Francis Drake from dysentery: buried at sea near Puerto Bello, Colón, Panama.

1596: 20 June Howard and Robert Devereux, Second Earl of Essex, attack Spanish naval forces at Cadiz. Sidonia's slow response was blamed for creating the opportunity for the English to sack the city.

1597: 22 October Lord High Admiral Charles Howard created First Earl of Nottingham.

1598: 4 August Death of Burghley at his London house, Burghley House in The Strand. Buried in St Martin's Church, Stamford, Lincolnshire, on **29 August**.

1598: 13 September Death of Philip in El Escorial, near Madrid, following severe attacks of gout, dropsy and fever, aged seventy-one after reigning as king of Spain for forty-two years and two hundred and forty days.

1603: 24 March Death of Elizabeth I at Richmond Palace, from bronchopneumonia and septicaemia caused by her rotten teeth, aged sixty-nine after reigning for forty-five years and one hundred and twenty-seven days.

1604: 28 August James I of England ratifies the Treaty of London ending the nineteen-year-old Anglo-Spanish war. The Treaty halts English support for the rebellion in the Spanish Netherlands and stops further English attacks on Spanish trading vessels.

1624: 14 December Death of Charles Howard, Second Baron Effingham and first Earl of Nottingham, at Haling House, Croydon, Surrey.

DRAMATIS PERSONÆ

ENGLAND

Edward VI (1537–53). Long-awaited legitimate heir of Henry VIII by his third wife, Jane Seymour. Proclaimed king, 31 January 1547. His governments imposed Protestant policies upon state and church, including the use of prayer books in English. Died of tuberculosis after an attack of measles; Greenwich Palace, 6 July 1553.

Mary I (1516–58). Fourth and only surviving child (from at least six pregnancies) of Henry VIII and his first wife, the Spanish princess Katherine of Aragon, widow of Henry's elder brother Arthur, who died in 1502. Proclaimed queen, 18 July 1553. Returned England to Catholicism and married *Philip*, son of Charles V of Spain, at Winchester on 25 July 1554. Died childless from ovarian or stomach cancer, St James' Palace, London, 17 November 1558.

Elizabeth I (1533–1603). Daughter of Henry VIII and his second wife, Anne Boleyn. Succeeded her half-sister *Mary I* as Queen, 17 November 1558. Catholic Europe saw her as an illegitimate usurper and heretic. Re-established Protestantism as state religion; privately encouraged English privateers to attack Spanish assets and provided military and financial assistance to the Dutch rebels in the Spanish Netherlands. She was mercurial, sometimes unable to decide key issues, and notoriously penny-pinching. Died unmarried, probably from broncho-pneumonia and dental sepsis, Richmond Palace, 24 March 1603.

ELIZABETH'S GOVERNMENT AND COURT

Cecil, William, Baron Burghley (1520–98). Statesman and chief minister to Queen Elizabeth. Secretary to Lord Protector Somerset and imprisoned in the Tower on Somerset's fall, 1549. One of two Secretaries of State to Edward VI, 1550–3 and administrator of Princess Elizabeth's lands. Knighted 11 October 1551. On accession of Elizabeth, again Secretary of State. Created Baron Burghley, 25 February 1571 and appointed Lord High Treasurer, July 1572. Deaf from 1590 and a martyr to gout. Died 4 August 1598, after collapsing, probably from a stroke or a heart attack, at his London house, Burghley House in The Strand. Robert Cecil, his only surviving son by his second wife, became the queen's principal adviser.

Devereux, Robert, Second Earl of Essex (1566–1601). Created a knight banneret for his bravery at the battle of Zutphen in 1586 and became a favourite of *Elizabeth I*. He joined Drake's and Norris's expedition to Spain and Portugal in 1589 without the queen's consent and was forced to obey her letter ordering him 'at his uttermost peril' to return home immediately. The following year he married *Walsingham*'s daughter Frances, widow of Sir Philip Sidney, enraging Elizabeth. In 1596, he commanded the successful English raid on Cadiz with *Lord Howard of Effingham* and Sir Walter Raleigh. Three years later, Essex was appointed lieutenant and governor-general of Ireland but his attempts to suppress the rebellion led by Hugh O'Neill, Earl of Tyrone, in Ulster were disastrous, and he was deprived of his offices. In 1601 he tried to raise a rebellion in London and was executed on 25 February on Tower Green.

Dudley, Robert, Earl of Leicester (1533–88), fifth son of the executed John Dudley, Duke of Northumberland. Proclaimed Lady Jane Grey (his sister-in-law) queen at King's Lynn, Norfolk, in 1553 but later pardoned by *Mary I*. Became favourite of *Elizabeth I* and was suspected of murdering his first wife, Amy Robsart, at Cumnor, Berkshire, in 1560. Leicester launched the association for the protection of Elizabeth in 1584 and the next year was appointed commander of the English forces sent to the Low Countries to assist the rebels against the Spanish. In January 1586, he became governor of the Dutch United Provinces. After being recalled, he was appointed lieutenant general of the land forces mustered at Tilbury, Essex, to repel the Spanish invasion. He died of a 'continual burning fever' at his house at Cornbury, Oxfordshire, on 4 September 1588.

Fitzwilliam, Sir William (1526–99). Administrator; lord deputy of Ireland, 1571–5 and 17 February 1588–11 August 1594. Vice-treasurer and treasurer-at-war, Ireland. Ordered the arrest and execution of all Spanish survivors of the Armada ships wrecked on the west coast of Ireland on 22 September 1588. Punitive expedition in counties Westmeath, Donegal, Sligo, Leitrim and Tyrone against Spanish fugitives and those Irish hiding them, 4 November–23 December 1588. Died at Milton, Northamptonshire, 22 June 1599 and buried at Marham, Norfolk.

Radcliffe, Henry, Fourth Earl of Sussex (?1530–93). Constable of Portchester Castle, Hampshire, 1560, and warden and captain of Portsmouth, 1571. Succeeded his brother as earl 1583 and was heavily involved in the defences of Hampshire and the Isle of Wight, for which he was rewarded by being made a Knight of the Garter in April 1589.

Radcliffe, Thomas, Third Earl of Sussex (c.1525–83). Lord Lieutenant of Ireland, 1559–64. Appointed Lord President of the North in 1569 and put down the rebellion of the *Earls of Northumberland* and *Westmorland*, pursuing the rebels into Scotland.

Walsingham, Sir Francis (c.1532–90). *Elizabeth's* Minister and spymaster. Ambassador in Paris, 1570–3; witnessed the massacre of the Huguenots in Paris on St Bartholomew's Day, 24 August 1572. Privy Councillor and joint Secretary of State 20 December 1573 and knighted on 1 December 1577. Elizabeth starved him of funds for his network of spies in England and across Europe. Died at his home in Seething Lane, London, with debts of £27,000, on 6 April 1590. Buried the following night in Old St Paul's Cathedral.

NAVAL AND MILITARY COMMANDERS

Bingham, Sir Richard (1528–99). Soldier; from 1584, governor of the Irish province of Connacht with his brothers George and John serving as assistant commissioners. He fought for the Dutch rebels as a volunteer in the Low Countries in 1578. Sent to Ireland in 1579 to assist in the suppression of the second Desmond Rebellion. Presided over Galway Assizes early in 1584 when he declared more than seventy death sentences on rebels. Later the same year he successfully besieged Castle Cloonoan, in Clare, afterwards slaughtering the garrison. Died, Dublin, 19 January 1599 and buried in Westminster Abbey.

Borough, William (1536–99). Naval commander. Appointed Comptroller of the Queen's ships in 1580. Hanged ten masters of captured pirate vessels at Wapping on the River Thames in June 1583. Vice-admiral during *Sir Francis Drake's* raid on Cadiz in April 1587 and afterwards acquitted of charges of mutiny and cowardice. Commanded the galley *Bonavolia* in the Thames estuary during the Armada campaign.

Drake, Sir Francis (1540–96). Vice-admiral and second-in-command of English fleet during the Armada campaign; swashbuckling privateer and navigator. Called '*El Draque*' by the Spanish. Born in Tavistock, Devon, the eldest of twelve sons of the Protestant farmer Edmund Drake. Second cousin of *Sir John Hawkins* and accompanied him in selling African slaves to the Spanish in the Caribbean. Knighted by *Elizabeth* on board his ship *Golden Hind* at Deptford, 4 April 1581 after his circumnavigation of the world in 1577–80. In 1585 Drake sacked the Spanish ports of Santo Domingo in Hispaniola and Cartagena in today's Columbia and captured the Spanish fort of San Augustine in Florida. Sacked Cadiz and destroyed some of the Armada shipping, 1587. Together with Sir John Norris, led a privately funded English expedition 1589 to attack surviving Armada warships in Spain and to instigate a Portuguese uprising in support of the pretender Dom Antonio. This proved unsuccessful and Drake fell out of favour for some years. Died of dysentery during expedition to West Indies and was buried at sea near Puerto Bello, Colón, Panama, 28 January 1596.

Frobisher, Sir Martin (1539–94). Navigator and naval commander. Undertook three voyages to New World, landing in north-east Canada, 1576–8. Commanded the *Triumph* in campaign against Armada and led one of *Howards'* squadrons. Knighted and appointed commander of squadron in Narrow Seas 1588–9. In November 1594, he was involved in the siege and relief of Brest, France and received a gunshot wound during the siege of the Spanish-held Fort Crozon. He died at Plymouth on 15 November.

Hawkins, Sir John (1532–96). Naval commander, privateer and slaver. Undertook three slaving voyages to Sierra Leone 1562–8; during last, most of his ships were destroyed by a Spanish fleet and Hawkins had to land some of his crews in Mexico because of lack of food. Appointed Treasurer of the Navy 1 January 1578 and introduced new designs for faster, more manoeuvrable warships. Commanded *Victory* in Armada campaign and the rear squadron during fighting in the English Channel. Knighted by *Howard* after the action off the Isle of Wight. Died at sea off Puerto Rico in 1596 while serving with *Drake* on an expedition to the West Indies.

Howard, Charles, Second Baron Effingham and later **Earl of Nottingham** (1536–1624). Eldest son of William Howard, first son of Thomas Howard, Second Duke of Norfolk and his second wife, Agnes Tilney. Married Katherine Carey, eldest daughter of *Elizabeth*'s second cousin, Lord Hunsdon, in 1563. Commanded cavalry during the 1569 northern rebellion. Lord Chamberlain 1574–85. Appointed Lord High Admiral of England in May 1585. Commissioner at trial of *Mary Queen of Scots*. Commanded the English fleet during skirmishes against the Armada up the English Channel in 1588; fought Battle of Gravelines and chased the survivors into Scottish waters. Created Earl of Nottingham in 1596 after his successful raid that year on shipping in Cadiz and appointed lieutenant general of all England in 1599. Commissioner at *Essex*'s trial, 1601. Commissioner for union with Scotland, 1604 and at trial of gunpowder plot conspirators, 1606.

Norris, Sir John (?1547–97). Soldier. Whilst a captain under Sir Walter Devereux, First Earl of Essex in Ulster in 1573, Norris massacred two hundred Scots at Rathlin Island, afterwards killing several hundred of their women and children. In 1577, he commanded English volunteers in the Low Countries fighting the Spanish in support of the Dutch rebels. He had three horses shot from under him at the battle of Rijmenam on 2 August 1578 and relieved Steenwijk two years later. Returned home in 1584 and appointed president of Munster in Ireland that July. Commanded a small English army in Low Countries in 1585 and was knighted by *Leicester* the following year after his relief of the town of Grave. Under Leicester, marshal of the camp at west Tilbury during the Armada campaign and with *Drake*, led the unsuccessful expedition to northern Spain and Lisbon in 1589. In 1591–3, fought for Henri IV of France, in support of the Protestant cause in Brittany, seizing the Spanish fortress of Crozon, outside Brest. After further inconclusive military service in Ireland, he died at Mallow, probably from gangrene from old wounds.

Wynter, Sir William (d.1589). Naval commander. Surveyor of Navy, 1549–89; master of ordnance, 1557–89. Knighted 1573. Commanded *Vanguard* during Armada campaign.

CATHOLICS EXECUTED OR IMPRISONED IN ENGLAND

Babington, Anthony (1561–86). Conspirator whose correspondence with Mary Queen of Scots, containing plans for a foreign invasion, a Catholic uprising and the assassination of Elizabeth, was the major factor in her subsequent indictment and execution. Executed at Tyburn, 20 September 1586.

Campion, St Edmund (1540–81). Jesuit martyr. Joined Jesuits 1573 and ordained priest 1578. Chosen for mission to England with Robert Parsons 1580. Arrested at Lyford, Berkshire, on 17 July 1581 and taken to Tower of London, where he was racked three times. Executed at Tyburn, 1 December 1581. Beatified in December 1886 and canonised by Paul VI in 1970.

Howard, St Philip, Earl of Arundel (1557–95). Eldest son of *Thomas*

Howard, Fourth Duke of Norfolk. Became a Catholic in 1584 and imprisoned after attempting to escape from England in 1585. Condemned to death for allegedly arranging Mass for the success of the Spanish Armada in the Tower of London, but not executed. Died in the Tower of London from malnutrition and ill treatment, although some claimed he was poisoned. Canonised by Pope Paul VI on 25 October 1970.

Howard, Thomas, Fourth Duke of Norfolk (1536–72). Inherited the title from his grandfather, the third duke on his death in 1554. Too trusting and politically naïve, he became embroiled in the Catholic conspiracies in London and planned to marry *Mary Queen of Scots* and was executed in 1572.

Parry, William (died 1585). Conspirator. Secretly became a Catholic around 1579. Accused in 1585 of conspiring to kill *Elizabeth I* and executed 2 March 1585, Palace Yard, Westminster.

Percy, Blessed Sir Thomas, Seventh Earl of Northumberland (1528–72). Elder son of Sir Thomas Percy, attainted and executed in June 1537 for his prominent role in the Pilgrimage of Grace rebellion against Henry VIII. Mary I favoured him as a staunch Catholic and granted him the Earldom of Northumberland in 1557. After promises of Spanish military assistance in 1569, Northumberland, together with *Charles Neville, Sixth Earl of Westmorland,* rebelled in 1569 with the aim of freeing *Mary Queen of Scots* and restoring England to Catholicism. After the revolt failed, Northumberland fled to Scotland but was handed over to the English authorities in exchange for £2,000 and he was beheaded in the market place at York on 22 August 1572. Beatified by Pope Leo XIII in May 1895.

Throckmorton, Francis (1554–84). Member of a large West Midlands Catholic family who acted as an intermediary between *Mary Queen of Scots* and her agent in Paris, Thomas Morgan. Executed at Tyburn on 10 July 1584 for his role in plotting a French invasion of England; the Spanish ambassador *Bernardino de Mendoza* was expelled from England in January 1584 for his role in the conspiracy.

EXILED CATHOLICS

Allen, Dr William, later **Cardinal of England** (1532–94). Leader of the exiled English Catholics in Europe during *Elizabeth I*'s reign. Principal of St Mary's Hall, Oxford, in 1556 but fled to the Spanish Netherlands in 1561. Founded a seminary college at Douai, in the Low Countries (now in northern France), funded by Pope *Gregory XIII* but it was expelled in 1578 and re-established in Rheims, in the Champagne-Ardennes region of France, under the protection of the Guise family. Allen supported plans to enthrone *Philip II* of Spain in England – with him appointed Papal Legate, Archbishop of Canterbury and Lord Chancellor in a Catholic government. *Sixtus V* made him a cardinal on 7 August 1587 at the request of Philip II. Buried in the Church of the Holy Trinity, adjoining the Venerable English College in Rome.

Arundel, Charles (?1540–87). Second cousin to *Thomas Howard, Fourth Duke of Norfolk*. Devotee of Mary Queen of Scots. Fled England in the aftermath of the Throckmorton plot of 1583.

Englefield, Sir Francis (*c.*1520–96). Imprisoned for celebrating Mass before Princess Mary, 1551. Lost his seat on the Privy Council on *Elizabeth I*'s accession and fled to Valladolid, Spain, before May 1559. *Mary Queen of Scots*' agent in Spain and later *Philip II*'s English secretary. Outlawed for high treason in 1564 and estates confiscated in 1585. Blind for the last twenty years of his life. Buried at Valladolid.

Neville, Charles, Sixth Earl of Westmorland (1543–1601). With *Sir Thomas Percy, Seventh Earl of Northumberland*, rebelled in 1569 with the aim of freeing *Mary Queen of Scots* and restoring England as a Catholic realm. After the rebellion failed, he fled to the Spanish Netherlands, living at Louvain on a pension from *Philip II* of Spain. In 1580, appointed colonel of a regiment of English refugees fighting for Spain and the following year went on pilgrimage to Rome. Died, heavily in debt, at Nieuport, 16 November 1601.

Sanders, Nicholas (*c.*1530–81). Fled to Rome after *Elizabeth*'s accession and ordained priest. His hopes of a cardinalate were dashed by the death of Pius V in 1572 and he went to Madrid but *Philip*'s caution frustrated his attempts to gain Spanish military assistance for the English Catholics. Published *De visibili Monarchia Ecclesiae* in 1572, giving the first account of the sufferings of Catholics in England. Papal commissary during 1579 invasion of Ireland and after its defeat, spent two years as a fugitive in south-west Ireland, dying of dysentery and starvation.

Stukeley, Sir Thomas (?1520–78). Privateer for *Elizabeth I* in 1563 but escaped to Spain seven years later where he received a pension from *Philip II*. He later joined a Portuguese expedition against Morocco and died after a cannon ball took off both his legs at the battle of Alcácer Quibir.

SCOTLAND

James VI of Scotland, later succeeding *Elizabeth* as James I of England (1566–1625), Son of *Mary Queen of Scots* and her second husband Henry Stuart, Lord Darnley.

Mary Queen of Scots (1542–87). Only surviving legitimate child of James V of Scotland who died when she was six days old. Widow of *François II* of France, then of Henry Stuart, Lord Darnley and latterly wife to James Hepburn, Fourth Earl of Boswell. She had quartered the arms of England with those of Scotland and France in her personal heraldry and claimed she was the strongest heir presumptive to the English crown through her direct descent from Henry VIII's elder sister Margaret. Fled Scotland in May 1568 to become the guest and prisoner of *Elizabeth I* for nineteen years before her execution at Fotheringay on 8 February 1587.

James Stewart, Earl of Moray (*c.*1531–70). Illegitimate half-brother of *Mary Queen of Scots*, being the bastard son of her father James V and Lady Margaret Erskine, wife of Sir Robert Douglas of Lochleven. Leader of the Scottish Reformation, adviser to Mary Queen of Scots after her return to Scotland in 1561 and the following year defeated the rebellion by George Gordon, Fourth Earl of Huntley, at the Battle of Corrichie, near Aberdeen. Appointed Regent of Scotland in July 1567 after Mary's forced abdication and defeated her forces at the Battle of Langside on 13 May 1568. Assassinated by a supporter of Mary's at Linlithgow, 23 January 1570 when he was fatally wounded by a gunshot fired out of a window as he passed below in procession.

FRANCE

François II (1544–60). King of France 1559–60. First husband of *Mary Queen of Scots,* marrying her on 24 April 1558 at Notre Dame Cathedral Paris at the age of fourteen. Crowned at Rheims but governance of France was in the hands of his wife's uncles, François and Charles de Guise. François II died, aged sixteen, at Orléans from a brain abscess caused by an ear infection.

Henri III (1551–89). King of France 1574–89 and elected monarch of Poland 1573–5. His Edict of Beaulieu in 1576 granted concessions to French Huguenots and triggered the formation of the Catholic League. Fled Paris in May 1588 after *Henry Guise, Third Duke of Guise* entered the city. After Guise's assassination, imprisoned his son but Parliament preferred criminal charges against him. Stabbed by a Dominican friar Jacques Clément at Saint Cloud, Hauts-de-Seine, on 1 August 1589, his assassin immediately killed by the royal guards. He died the following morning, naming the Protestant Henry of Navarre as the new King of France.

Guise, Henri, Third Duke of Guise (1550–88) and cousin of *Mary Queen of Scots.* Helped plan the St Bartholomew's Day massacre of Huguenots in Paris in 1572 and formed the Catholic League. Nicknamed *Le Balafré* ('the Scarred') after being wounded in the cheek by a harquebus shot during the Battle of Dormans on 10 October 1575 against German mercenaries fighting for the Protestant cause in France. On 9 May 1588, Guise entered Paris after Catholic rioting in the city, forcing the French king *Henri III* to flee. After appointing Guise 'Lieutenant General of France', he summoned him on to the Château de Blois 23 December 1588 where Guise was assassinated.

NETHERLANDS

Justin of Nassau (1559–1631). Illegitimate son of *William, Prince of Orange* and his mistress Eva Elincx. Appointed lieutenant admiral of Zeeland, 28 February 1585. Governor of Breda, 1601–25, when he surrendered the city to the Spanish after an eleven-month siege.

William I, Prince of Orange (1533–84). 'William the Silent' was the main leader of the Dutch revolt until his assassination. Joined Calvinist church 1574. Survived an assassination attempt on 18 March 1582 in Antwerp, when he was wounded in the face by a pistol fired by the Spaniard Juan de Jáuregni. Killed by a pistol shot in the chest, fired at close range by a French Catholic, Balthazar Gérard, in the Prinsenhof in Delft, in the Netherlands after *Philip II* offered 25,000 crowns as a reward to any assassin who killed this 'pest on the whole of Christianity and the enemy of the human race'. William's last words were reportedly: 'May God have pity on my soul: may God have pity on this poor people.'

SPAIN

Philip II of Spain (1527–98). 'Philip the Prudent' acceded to the throne on the abdication of his father Charles V in January 1556. King of Spain, Portugal, Naples and Sicily. During his second marriage (of four) to *Mary I* in 1554–8, was also King of England and Ireland. In 1560, led a Holy

League of Spain, Venice, Genoa, the Papal States and the Knights of Malta against the Ottoman Turks, destroying the Turkish fleet at the battle of Lepanto in 1571. Dutch subjects rebelled against Spanish rule in the Netherlands from 1568 and their States General declared they no longer recognised Philip as king in 1579. *Elizabeth I*'s alliance with the Dutch and *Drake*'s attacks on Spanish assets led to Philip's plans to invade England. He was also at war with Protestant Henri IV of France in 1590–8. Died in his palace of El Escorial, near Madrid, on 13 September 1598.

AMBASSADORS

de Figueroa, Gómez Suárez, Fifth Count de Feria (?1520–71), later Duke of Feria. Captain of Spanish Guard 1558 and prominent counsellor to *Philip II*. Anglophile. Appointed Philip's personal representative in England at end of 1557. Remained in England until May 1559.

de Mendoza, Bernardino (*c*.1540–1604). Spanish ambassador in London 1578–84 and supporter of the cause of *Mary Queen of Scots*. Son of the Count of Corunna, served as a cavalry captain with Spanish forces in the Low Countries 1567–75. Implicated in the *Throckmorton* plot and expelled from London in January 1584, becoming Spanish ambassador in Paris from November that year. Acted as paymaster to the French Catholic League but after a cataract operation, he became blind in 1590 and resigned because of poor health. Died in the convent of San Bernardo of Madrid.

NAVAL AND MILITARY COMMANDERS

de Bazán, Álvaro, First Marqués of Santa Cruz (1526–88). Captain general of the navy and of the ocean. Commanded galleys of Naples in 1568 and commanded the reserves during the battle of Lepanto, 1571. Captured the Azores from supporters of Dom Antonio, Prior of Crato, following the naval battle of Terceira in 1583. On 9 August 1583, suggested invading England in a letter to *Philip II*. Died at Lisbon, 9 February 1588.

de Bertendona, Martin (died 1604). Commander of the Armada's Levant squadron in *La Regazona*. Brought his flagship safely home and in 1589 was involved in the defence of Corunna against *Drake*'s and *Norris*'s expedition.

Farnese, Alexander, Duke of Parma (1545–92). Mother was half-sister to *Philip II*. Fought against the Turks in the naval battle of Lepanto, 1571; Governor of Netherlands and commander of Spanish forces against the

Dutch rebels, 1578. Successfully besieged Antwerp, July 1584–August 1585; captured the port of Sluis, August 1587. Failed to rendezvous with Medina Sidonia's Armada.

de Guzmán, Alonso Pérez, Seventh Duke of Medina Sidonia (1550–1615). Commander-in-chief of Spanish Armada, unwillingly succeeding *Santa Cruz* on his death in February 1588, because of his lack of military experience and fear of seasickness. After a cautious campaign up the English Channel, Medina Sidonia was sent into convalescence but retained his posts of captain general of the ocean and of Andalusia. His slow response to the English attack on Cadiz in 1596 brought criticism in Spain, as did his loss of a squadron in fighting against the Dutch off Gibraltar in 1606.

de Oquendo, Miguel y Sequra (died 1588). Fought in the battle of Terceira under *Santa Cruz* in 1583. Commander of the Guipúzcoa squadron of Spanish Armada but his ship caught fire and he died soon afterwards.

de Recalde, Juan Martinez (1532–88). Commanded Spanish naval forces in Netherlands, 1572–80 and in the latter year, was naval commander in the expedition to the west coast of Ireland. Commanded the Biscayan squadron in the Armada campaign.

de Toledo, Fernando Alvárez, Third Duke of Alba (1507–82). Governor and captain-general of Spanish Netherlands 1567–73.

de Valdés, Diego Flores (*c.*1530–95). Spanish admiral and chief of staff and adviser to Medina Sidonia. Cousin and bitter enemy of *Pedro de Valdés*, commander of the Armada's Squadron of Andalusia. Joined Spanish navy in 1550, serving in Peru and Chile in 1555 and in the Caribbean from 1565. Commander of the Chilean fleet, 1581–4, protecting Spain's South American trade against English pirates. After return of Armada, imprisoned in Burgos.

de Valdés, Pedro (1544–1615) Spanish admiral, commander of the Armada's Squadron of Andalusia from 1587. Fought against the Ottoman Turks in the eastern Mediterranean; against French privateers off the coast of Florida and in the Gulf of Mexico in 1566–73 and in the campaign of 1582–3 in the Portuguese Azores. Cousin and bitter enemy of *Diego Flores de Valdés*, Medina Sidonia's chief of staff. His flagship *Nuestra Señora de Rosario* was captured by *Sir Francis Drake* after she was badly damaged in several collisions. Ransomed in February 1593. (He may have been the inspiration for the 'great pirate Valdés' in Shakespeare's *Pericles*,

Prince of Tyre, written in 1607 or early 1608.) Served as captain general of Cuba 1602–8 and created Marqués of Canalejas. Died at Gijón.

THE VATICAN

Gregory XIII (1502–85). Pope 1572–85. Reforming Pope who laboured to stem the tide of Protestantism by founding or supporting a number of seminary colleges for priests. After the St Bartholomew's Day massacre in Paris in 1572, he held a celebratory *Te Deum* mass in Rome and struck a commemorative medal inscribed 'VGOTIORUM STRAGES' ('Massacre of the Huguenots'). Sent papal troops to support the second Desmond Rebellion in Ireland in 1579–80. The English Jesuits persuaded him in 1580 to water down *Pius V*'s bull excommunicating *Elizabeth I*; English Catholics were now advised to obey her while awaiting her overthrow.

Pius V (1504–72). Pope 1566–72. On 25 February 1570, he published the bull *Regnans in Excelsis* that excommunicated *Elizabeth I* and deprived this 'pretended queen' of her throne and absolved her Catholic subjects of any loyalty or allegiance to her. Their disobedience would also attract excommunication.

Sixtus V (1520–90). Pope 1585–90. Imposed new taxes and sold appointments to repair Vatican finances after the papacy of *Gregory XIII*. Although he admired her greatly, agreed to renew the excommunication of *Elizabeth I* and to grant a subsidy to *Philip II*, payable only after the Spanish Armada landed in England. He also excommunicated Henri IV of France.

GLOSSARY

almain rivets Light body armour, replaced by the CORSLET.

argosy Large merchant ship, its name derived from *Ragusino*, modern-day Dubrovnik in Croatia.

armour Worn from the thigh upwards by officers, pikemen and heavy cavalry.

arquebus *See* HARQUEBUS.

arroba Spanish measurement of liquid volume equivalent to 3.5 gallons (15.91 litres).

barque Three-masted sailing vessel, square-rigged on the fore and main masts with a fore-and-aft spanker sail rigged on the mizzen.

boom Floating barrier of large tree-trunks, chained together, to bar entry by attacking ships to harbours or rivers.

bowsprit Long wooden spar projecting forward from a ship's bows to which extra sails are secured.

brigantine Small two-masted oared GALLEY.

butt A large cask. Capacity varied but may be estimated at 108 gallons (477 litres).

cable length Measurement of distance stretching 100 FATHOMS (188 m), equal to 10 per cent of NAUTICAL MILE (0.188 km).

caliver Short-barrelled shoulder-fired firearm, superseding the HARQUEBUS.

cannon Muzzle-loaded ordnance with 7.25 in (18.42 cm) calibre bore, firing roundshot of between 30–50 lbs (13.61–22.68 kg) at ranges of between 300 and 2,000 yards (274.32–1,828.8 m). *See* also: CULVERIN, DEMI-CANNON, DEMI-CULVERIN, DRAKE, FALCON, FOWLER, MINION, MUSKET, SAKER, SERPENTINE and SLING.

caravel Lightly-armed three-masted ship rigged with LATEEN sails, of between 80 and 130 tons (81.28–132.09 tonnes) displacement.

carrack Three- or four-masted ship type developed in late fifteenth century for service in the Atlantic with tall superstructures at the bow and stern. GALLEONS were developed from this design of merchant ship.

corslet Breast and tasset plates protecting the upper half of the body and the thighs, replacing the flexible ALMAIN RIVETS.

cromster Dutch shallow-draught ship displacing 200 tons (203.21 tonnes) armed with CULVERINS and DEMI-CULVERINS.

culverin Muzzle-loading ordnance with 5.25 in (13.34 cm) calibre, firing shot of about 18 lbs (8.16 kg) at ranges of between 400 and 2,400 yards (365.76–2,194.56 m). *See* also CANNON, DEMI-CANNON, DEMI-CULVERIN, DRAKE, FALCON, FOWLER, MINION, MUSKET, SAKER, SERPENTINE and SLING.

currier Larger calibre shoulder-fired firearm that fired short arrows or quarrels.

dagg An early form of single-shot pistol.

demi-cannon Ordnance with a calibre of 6.25 ins (15.88 cm), firing a 32 lb (14.52 kg) shot between 320 and 1,700 yards (292.61–1,554.48 m). *See* also CANNON, CULVERIN, DEMI-CULVERIN, DRAKE, FALCON, FOWLER, MINION, MUSKET, SAKER, SERPENTINE and SLING.

demi-culverin Ordnance with 4.25 in (10.8 cm) calibre, firing shot weighing about 9 lbs (4.08 kg) over ranges of between 400 and 2,500 yards (365.76–2,286 m). *See* also CANNON, DEMI-CANNON, CULVERIN, DRAKE, FALCON, FOWLER, MINION, MUSKET, SAKER, SERPENTINE and SLING.

dice-shot Sharp pieces of iron scrap fired by ships' guns as an anti-personnel munition, particularly to defeat enemy boarders.

drake Short gun similar to CULVERIN. *See* also CANNON, DEMI-CANNON, CULVERIN, DEMI-CULVERIN, FALCON, FOWLER, MINION, MUSKET, SAKER, SERPENTINE and SLING.

falcon Small cannon of 2.5 ins (6.35 cm) calibre, firing shot of 3lbs (1.36 kg) weight.

fanega Spanish measurement of dry volume equal to two bushels (70.48 litres).

fathom Measurement of depth, equal to six feet (1.88 m), originally derived from the distance between the fingertips of a man standing with his arms outstretched.

felucca Small Spanish LATEEN-rigged sailing vessels, used for reconnaissance and carrying dispatches.

flyboat Fast two-masted gunboat, displacing 140 tons (142.25 tonnes) or less, capable of operations in shallow waters.

fore-and-aft-rig Sails set along the line of ship's keel.

fowler Light breech-loading gun used close-range against enemy crews.

galleass Three-masted ship developed from a large merchant galley, propelled by sails and up to thirty-two oars, each worked by five rowers, sitting side by side on wooden benches.

galleon Ocean-going ship with three or four masts evolved from CAR-RACK in second half of sixteenth century, displacing between 450 and 1,500 tons (457.22–1,524.07 tonnes). Lower superstructures and lengthened hulls provided additional stability in heavy seas. Sometimes termed GREAT SHIPS in English documents.

galley Shallow-draft ship with LATEEN sails running on one or two masts, with banks of oars on each side. Highly manoeuvrable and, with ordnance mounted in bows and stern, effective gun platforms, but poor performers in northern waters. Galleys made their final appearance in naval warfare in the Russo-Turkish war at the Battle of Chesma on 5 July 1770, between Anatolia and the island of Chios in the eastern Mediterranean, although galleys were used by the Knights of Malta during Napoleon's siege of Valetta in 1798.

great ships *See* GALLEON.

horse Contemporary collective noun for cavalry, whether LANCES or LIGHT HORSE.

hoy Coastal vessel of around sixty tons (60.96 tonnes). The name is derived from the Middle Dutch *hoey*.

hulk Large three-masted, wide-beamed cargo ship.

jack Protective leather jacket for infantry, often with metal plates sewn on.

knot Measurement of a vessel's speed equal to one NAUTICAL MILE (1.852 km) an hour.

lances Heavy cavalry, wearing three-quarter armour and armed with lance, sword, pistol and dagger.

last Measure of gunpowder equivalent to 24 barrels, each holding 100 lbs (45.36 kg).

lateen sail Large triangular sail on a long yard, mounted FORE-AND-AFT. Still used on Arab dhows.

league Measurement of distance, equal to three NAUTICAL MILES (5.556 km).

lee The side of a ship or an area of water sheltered, or away from the wind.

leeward The direction away from the wind, or down-wind.

levanter Large sailing ship built for service in the Mediterranean.

light horse Cavalry with only light personal protection, armed only with a spear and pistol.

luff Windward side of a vessel. To 'luff' is to steer its bows round to the wind.

lunula Spanish Armada's crescent-shaped battle formation, adopted to protect its supply ships during passage up English Channel.

militia Citizen force of partially trained soldiers, funded by English counties.

minion Small gun of 3.25 in (8.26 cm) calibre, firing a 4 lb (1.81 kg) shot between 300 and 1,600 yards (274.32–1,463.04 m). *See* also CANNON, DEMI-CANNON, CULVERIN, DEMI-CULVERIN, DRAKE, FALCON, FOWLER, MUSKET, SAKER, SERPENTINE and SLING.

morion Visorless helmet with curved brim.

musket Light breech-loaded gun in swivel mounting, sometimes firing large arrows as anti-personnel weapon. Alternatively, a heavy matchlock firearm, 4.5 feet (1.37 m) long, fired from the shoulder but employing a forked rest because of its weight. Superseded the CALIVER.

nautical mile Measurement of distance 6,076 ft in length (1,852 m) equal to one minute of arc along the long meridian.

patache Larger Spanish version of PINNACE, displacing up to 180 tons (182.89 tonnes). Sometimes also called ZABRAS.

petronel Cavalry pistol.

pike Long-spear like weapon, 16–18 ft (4.88–5.49 m) long used by infantry to defend against cavalry attack. Those carried on ships were much shorter.

pipe A large wooden cask holding 105 gallons (477 litres) of water or wine.

pinnace Two-masted vessel, displacing up to 70 tons, sometimes with oars, used for reconnaissance and carrying dispatches. The Spanish version is PATACHE or ZABRA.

prize An enemy ship captured at sea. Proceeds from the sale of the vessel and its contents were shared amongst the officers and crew of the ship that captured it, proportionally to their rank.

quintal A measurement of weight, equal to 102 lb (46.28 kg).

Queen's ships English Royal Navy ships, funded by the exchequer.

run before the wind To sail in the same direction as the wind.

saker Small gun of 3.25 in (8.26 cm) calibre, firing a 5 lb (2.27 kg) shot, between 330 and 1,700 yards (301.75–1,554.48 m). *See* also CANNON, DEMI-CANNON, CULVERIN, DEMI-CULVERIN, DRAKE, FALCON, FOWLER, MINION, MUSKET, SERPENTINE and SLING.

serpentine Light breech-loaded gun. *See* also CANNON, DEMI-CANNON, CULVERIN, DEMI-CULVERIN, DRAKE, FALCON, FOWLER, MINION, MUSKET, SAKER and SLING.

sling Type of small gun, used against enemy crews at close quarters.

See also CANNON, DEMI-CANNON, DRAKE, CULVERIN, DEMI-CULVERIN, FALCON, FOWLER, MINION, MUSKET, SAKER and SERPENTINE.

socorro A designated battle group of Spanish ships, deployed to reinforce areas of danger to the Armada formation.

tack To sail obliquely against the wind.

tercios Spanish army unit, or large regiment, with 3,000 men.

urca Round-hulled tub-like freight ship.

warp To move a becalmed ship by hauling on the anchor cable. The anchor is then moved forward by the ship's boat, dropped ahead and the process repeated.

weather gauge A position to WINDWARD to other ships, advantageous in battle. When a vessel has to beat to windward, it heels under the pressure of the wind, restricting its gunnery. However, if a ship has the weather gauge, when it turns downwind to attack, it may alter course at will and is able to bring its port and starboard batteries to bear on its enemy.

windward Or 'weather': upwind from a point of reference.

zabra *See* PINNACE.

NOTES

Prologue

1 TNA, SP 12/1/7. Printed in Loades, *Elizabeth I*, pp.36–7 and Starkey, *Elizabeth*, pp.241–2, where it is cogently argued that her speech was made on 17 November rather than the traditionally accepted date of three days later. Elizabeth had arranged for her agent, Sir Nicholas Throckmorton, to inform her of Mary's death but his journey to Hatfield was delayed. When he arrived, his news was 'stale'. See: Strickland, *Lives of the Queens of England*, vol. 3, p.102.

2 *Feria Dispatch*, p.336.

3 Naunton, *Fragmenta Regalia*, p.7; Strickland, op. cit., vol. 3, p.102.

4 For more information about this disease, called the *sudor Anglicus,* see: Mark Taviner, Guy Thwaites and Vanya Grant, 'The English Sweating Sickness 1485–51: A Viral Pulmonary Disease', *Medical History,* vol. 42 (1998), pp.96–8 and by the same authors, 'The English Sweating Sickness', *New England Jnl of Medicine,* vol. 336 (1997), pp.580–2.

5 *CSP Spain,* vol. 4, pt 2, pp.881–2. Mary's voice was said to be 'rough and loud like a man's' and could be heard some distance away.

6 *CSP Domestic Henry VIII,* vol. 10, p.51.

7 Succession to the Crown: Marriage Act 1536; 28 Henry VIII *cap.* 7.

8 Succession to the Crown Act: 35 Henry VIII *cap.* 1.

9 Somerset, *Elizabeth I,* p.13.

10 Mumby, *Girlhood of Queen Elizabeth,* p.29.

11 *CSP Spain,* vol. 10, p.206.

12 In early August 1553, one of her officials wrote a memorandum for Mary, inquiring how she 'is answered of lead and bell metal of abbeys, colleges and suchlike: what remains and where ... How the jewels, plate, ornaments, goods and chattels of dissolved monasteries, colleges and chantries and of all persons attainted since 4 February 1536 are answered' (TNA, SP 11/1/22). In April 1554, she had £10,000 in

proceeds from the sale of church bells available to pay royal debts (TNA, SP 11/4/6).

13 The religious houses re-founded by Mary were: the Observant Franciscan friars adjacent to Greenwich palace (April 1555); Westminster Abbey (November 1556); the Charterhouse at Sheen, Surrey (January, 1557); the Bridgettines at Syon, Middlesex (April 1557); the Dominican Nuns at King's Langley, Hertfordshire (June 1557); the Savoy Hospital (November 1556), between the City of London and Westminster and the Fraternity of Jesus within St Paul's Cathedral, London. The houses at Greenwich and the Savoy had been founded by Mary's grandfather, Henry VII in 1499 and 1505. See: Rex, *The Tudors*, p.160.

14 *CSP Venice*, vol. 6, p.1074.

15 *CSP Spain*, vol. 11, p.220–1.

16 *CSP Venice*, vol. 6, p.1058.

17 Ibid., p.1058.

18 The execution took place on 6 July 1554. See: Machyn, *Diary*, p.66. See also Neale, *Queen Elizabeth*, p.48.

19 TNA, SP 11/4/2. Damaged but in Elizabeth's hand. Missing portions have been supplied from an eighteenth-century copy in BL Harleian MS, 7,190, article 2, ff.125r–126r.

20 *CSP Spain*, vol. 13, pp.166–7 and *CSP Domestic Mary*, fn. p.53. High tide on 17 March 1554 came at one o'clock in the afternoon, so she must have written the letter at around noon at Westminster.

21 Somerset, op. cit., p.53.

22 Marcus *et al., Elizabeth I: Collected Works*, p.48.

23 Machyn, *Diary*, p.60.

24 News of Elizabeth's release was included in an account of events at court sent by Robert Swift the younger to the Earl of Shrewsbury on 20 May: LPL, MS 3,206, f.263.

25 Marcus *et al.*, op. cit., p.46.

26 The title 'King of Ireland' was created by Henry VIII in 1542 after he was excommunicated and was therefore not recognised by the Catholic states. Pope Paul IV issued a papal bull recognising Philip and Mary as King and Queen of Ireland on 7 June 1555.

27 Rex, op. cit., p.155.

28 Neale, op. cit., p.56; Somerset, op. cit., pp. 64–5. A thousand copies of the seditious pamphlet had been seized by Sir William Gerard, Lord Mayor of London.

29 Worsley & Souden, *Hampton Court Palace*, p.44.

30 *CSP Venice*, vol. 6, p.1548.

31 *CSP Spain*, vol. 13, pp.372–3.

32 Loades, *Mary Tudor*, pp.380–3.

33 Porter, *Mary Tudor: The First Queen*, pp.404–5.

34 *Feria's Dispatch*, pp.331, 335.

35 Philip II to the Princess Dowager of Portugal; Brussels, 4 December 1558. *CSP Spain*, vol. 13, p.440.

36 *CSP Spain*, vol. 13, p.441. The first list included the 'French robe of cloth of gold, adorned with crimson velvet and thistles of curled gold' which Philip wore on his wedding day on 25 July 1554 at Winchester Cathedral. There was also the velvet cap, decorated with precious stones and pearls, which he noted was 'sent to me by the queen in the house where I spent the night before entering London [on 18 August 1554] and I wore it on my head on that occasion'. Another item was 'a dagger which the Queen gave his majesty in England, complete with its stones and chain and the sheath with its stones and pearls, nothing being missing, enclosed in a case'. Philip added this comment: 'This was sent to me by the Queen with Lord Pembroke one Garter day [23 April].'

37 TNA, SP 12/1/7; printed in Marcus *et al.*, op. cit., pp.51–2.

38 *CSP Spain (Simancas)*, vol. 1, p.7.

39 Rex, op. cit., p.185.

40 Mary I was also short-sighted, so much so that she could not 'read or do anything else without placing her eyes quite close to the object', Hayward, *Annals of the first four years of the Reign of Queen Elizabeth*, fn. p.7.

41 Hayward, op. cit., p.7.

42 Philip II to Count de Feria: Brussels, 10 January 1559. *CSP Spain (Simancas)*, vol. 1, pp.22–3; Somerset, op. cit., p.136.

43 Memorandum from Count de Feria to Philip II; London, late February 1559; *CSP Spain (Simancas)*, vol. 1, p.35.

44 de Feria to Philip II; London, 19 March 1559. *CSP Spain (Simancas)*, vol. 1, p.37.

45 Neale, op. cit., p.79.

46 Elizabeth of Valois was the third of Philip's four wives. His first was Maria Manuela, daughter of John III of Portugal, who died in 1545. Their only offspring was Carlos, Prince of Asturias, who died unmarried in 1568. His second was Mary I of England. After Elizabeth died following a miscarriage in 1568, he married his niece Anne of Austria in 1570. This marriage produced four sons and a daughter. Three

sons died young and the fourth, Philip, succeeded his father in 1598.

47 Somerset, op. cit., p.135. For Elizabeth's address on 10 February 1559 to Parliament on her determination to remain single, see: TNA, SP 12/2/22.

48 Rex, op. cit., p.185.

49 1 Elizabeth *cap.* 1.

50 1 Elizabeth *cap.* 2.

CHAPTER 1: **The Enemy Within**

1 Archer and Douglas, *English Historical Documents 1558–1603,* p.806.

2 Mary was the widow firstly of François II of France, then of the syphilitic Henry Stuart, Lord Darnley, and finally of dashing James Hepburn, Fourth Earl of Bothwell whom she last saw after the defeat of her army at the Battle of Carberry Hill, near Musselburgh, East Lothian, on 15 June 1567. Bothwell fled to Scandinavia but was imprisoned at Dragsholm Castle, Denmark, for ten years. He died there insane, on 14 April 1578, aged forty-four. His alleged mummified body reportedly could be seen in nearby Fårevejle church until around twenty years ago.

3 Mary's army lost more than four hundred killed. Its main body never entered the fray because her general, Archibald Campbell, Earl of Argyle, with unfortunate timing, fell sick just as the battle began. She watched the fighting from Court Knowe, near Cathcart Castle, one mile (1.6 km) to the south. The site of the battlefield is marked by a monument erected in 1887 at National Grid reference: NS 57869 61716.

4 James Stewart, Earl of Moray, was the bastard son of Mary's father James V by Lady Mary Erskine, wife of Sir Robert Douglas of Lochleven. A leader of the Scottish Reformation, in June 1559 Moray had cleansed churches in Perth of 'idolatrous' imagery and in September 1561 he disrupted Masses conducted by Mary's priests at Holyrood.

He was assassinated on 23 January 1570 in Linlithgow, West Lothian, by James Hamilton of Bothwellhaugh, a supporter of Mary's. In one of the earliest cases of assassination using a firearm, Hamilton fired from an upper window, fatally wounding the regent as he passed in procession. The location for the attack was significant; Mary was born in Linlithgow Palace, now a roofless ruin alongside a small inland loch. Moray was buried in St Giles' Kirk, Edinburgh, and is commemorated by a monumental brass, showing the seated figures of Religion and Justice, engraved by the royal goldsmith, James Gray.

5 Margaret, who died on 18 October 1541, was grandmother to Mary Queen of Scots, having married James IV of Scotland in 1503.

6 Haigh, *Reformation and Resistance in Tudor Lancashire*, p.49.

7 The rood screen separated nave and chancel in Pre-Reformation churches. On top of the screen stood the crucified Christ, flanked by figures of the Blessed Virgin Mary and St John. These were favourite targets for Protestant reformers during the reign of Edward VI, were reinstated under Mary I but were ordered to be dismantled by Elizabeth in 1561. One must feel some sympathy at the plight of local churchwardens, faced with frequent weathercock changes in government policies on religion which they had to implement at the expense of the parish.

8 McCann, 'The Clergy and the Elizabethan Settlement at Chichester', pp.100–1; Birt, *Elizabethan Religious Settlement*, pp.427–30; Duffy, *Stripping of the Altars*, pp.494 and 577.

9 Cox, 'Ecclesiastical History', pp.74–5.

10 See my *House of Treason* for an account of the vicissitudes of the ambitious Howard family under the Tudors.

11 Dickens, 'The first stages of Romish Recusancy in Yorkshire', pp.163 and 166.

12 Prudently, Mary had been moved further south to Tutbury from Bolton Castle, North Yorkshire, in late January 1569 to forestall any attempt to free her by Catholic supporters in northern England.

13 Elizabeth was surprised that Sussex doubted the fidelity of her people as she believed she had 'many faithful and loyal subjects in that country'. However, if any person incited mutiny within the royalist ranks she recommended 'the speedy executions of two or three' as a salutary example. Sharp, *Memorials of the Rebellion of 1569*, p.50.

14 Sharp, ibid., p.189; Fletcher & MacCulloch, *Tudor Rebellions*, p.151.

15 BL Harleian MS 6,990, f.44. Printed in Sharp, op. cit., pp.42–3. The proclamation was also published at Staindrop, Co. Durham, and Richmond, north Yorkshire.

16 Fletcher & MacCulloch, op. cit., p.98.

17 De Spes to the Duke of Alba; London, 1 December 1569. *CSP Spain (Simancas)*, vol. 2, p.213.

18 The removal of Northumberland's accoutrements was intended 'that all others, by his example, for evermore hereafter beware how they

commit or do like crime or fall in shame or rebuke'. BL Cotton MS Vespasian C, xiv, f.583.

19 De Spes to Philip II; London, 3 December 1569. *CSP Spain (Simancas)*, vol. 2, p.213. More than two weeks later, he reported the unruly return home of the London levies – 'miserable fellows' – who had 'slashed and cudgelled Captain Leighton, one of [their] leaders who has come [back] to court badly wounded to complain of his own soldiers'. Ibid., p.218.

20 Philip II to the Duke of Alba; Madrid, 16 December 1569. *CSP Spain (Simancas)*, vol. 2, p.217.

21 Aside from the deserters, Bowes lost only five killed and sixty-seven wounded during the siege.

22 Sharp, op. cit., p.119.

23 Contarini to the Doge and Signory; Angers, 17 January 1570. *CSP Venice*, vol. 7, p.439.

24 De Spes to Philip II; London, 9 January 1570. *CSP Spain (Simancas)*, vol. 2, p.225.

25 Northumberland was beatified by Pope Leo XIII in May 1895. William Tessimond appeared before a court in York in 1572 for possessing the relic of hair from Northumberland's beard which he cut off while the head was displayed in the tollbooth. See: Walsham, 'Miracles and the Counter-Reformation ...', p.794.

26 Westmorland died at Nieuport in the Netherlands on 16 November 1601.

27 Contarini to the Doge and Signory; Angers, 17 January 1570. *CSP Venice*, vol. 7, p.439.

28 These included a Durham alderman, a priest called Plumtree, forty constables and fifty serving men in Durham. BL Harleian MS 6,991, ff.31–3. Three hundred and twenty were executed in that county.

29 McCall, 'Executions after the Northern Rebellion', pp.85 and 87.

30 Sharp, op. cit., p.170. Henry Carey, First Baron Hunsdon (1526–96), was the son of Elizabeth's aunt, Mary Boleyn, and William Carey, an esquire of the body to Henry VIII. Mary, of course, was Henry's mistress before Anne Boleyn and there has been persistent speculation that Carey and his sister Catherine were the king's illegitimate children.

31 *CSP Venice*, vol. 7, pp.448–51.

32 Felton was beatified by Pope Leo XIII in 1886.

33 13 Elizabeth *cap.* 1. This was repealed on 28 July 1863 but until as late as 1967, it remained treason under the Succession to the Crown Act

1707 to maintain that Parliament could not control the succession. The first Treason Act of Elizabeth's reign was in 1558 (1 Elizabeth *cap. 5*).

34 13 Elizabeth *cap*. 2.

35 Parmiter, 'The Imprisonment of Papists in Private Castles', p.16.

36 BL Harleian MS 290, f.88.

37 Williams, *A Tudor Tragedy*, pp.199–200. Bailly (1542–1625) was released from the Marshalsea prison, probably in 1573, and died in Belgium.

38 Robinson, *The Dukes of Norfolk,* p.63; Williams, op. cit., pp.200–2.

39 Hutchinson, *House of Treason,* p.192.

40 *CSP Domestic Elizabeth 1581–90,* p.48. On 3 May 1581 the Privy Council had ordered Norton to examine 'a Jesuit naming himself Briant and if he refuses to confess the truth, then to put him to torture and by the pain and terror of the same, to wring from him the knowledge of such things as shall appertain'.

41 See: Merriman, *American Historical Review,* vol. 13, fn. p.484.

42 HMC Salisbury, vol. 1, p.526.

43 BL Add. MS 48,027, ff.80–125*v*; Hutchinson, *House of Treason,* p.201.

44 Merriman, op. cit., p.481.

45 Parmiter, op. cit., p.16.

46 *APC,* vol. 8, p.73. Wisbech Castle, originally constructed by William the Conqueror, was largely rebuilt in brick in 1478–83 and was surrounded by a moat. It was later demolished and a house built on the site in 1816. Other castles identified by Sir Francis Walsingham probably in the spring of 1579 as locations to imprison recusants were: Banbury, Oxfordshire; Framlingham, Suffolk; Kimbolton, Huntingdonshire (where Katherine of Aragon died); Portchester in Portsmouth harbour; Devizes, Wiltshire; Melbourne, Derbyshire; Halton, Cheshire; Wigmore, Herefordshire and Barnard Castle, Co. Durham. See: BL Harleian MS 360, art. 38 (ff.65*r* and *v*).

47 Fénelon, *Correspondance Diplomatique,* vol. 3, p.27.

48 Ibid., p.27.

49 Brennan, 'Papists and Patriotism ...', p.6.

50 Meyer, *England and the Catholic Church ...,* p.242.

51 Carini, *Mons. Niccolò Ormaneto, nunzio alla corte di Filippo II,* pp.84 *et seq.*

52 Queen Mary I, Elizabeth's predecessor.

53 Elizabeth was implicated in the conspiracy that led to Wyatt's

Rebellion in 1554 because of her relationship with two of the ring-leaders, Sir William Pickering and Sir James Crofts. The treason case against her was dropped through the intervention and influence of her great-uncle, William Howard. See Somerset, *Elizabeth I*, pp.47–55.

54 *CSP Vatican*, vol. 2, p.551.

55 Duffy, *Fires of Faith*, p.93.

56 Loomie, *Spanish Elizabethans*, p.8.

57 Marble Arch, on the edge of Hyde Park, is the site of Tyburn. Story was beatified by Pope Leo XIII in 1886.

58 13 Elizabeth *cap.* 3.

59 Meyer, op. cit., pp.239–40.

60 Elizabeth kept a crucifix and candles on the altar of the Chapel Royal to the fury of her chaplains and bishops who regarded these objects as 'dregs of popery'. See: Rex, *The Tudors*, p.186.

61 Stählin, *Sir Francis Walsingham und seine Zeit ...*, fn. p.527.

62 *CSP Vatican*, vol. 2, p.45.

63 Fénelon, op. cit., vol. 4, p.330.

64 Gregory had become Pope on 13 May 1572 on the death of Pius V, who was canonised by Pope Clement XI in May 1712. Gregory prob-ably believed that the Huguenots were involved in a *coup d'état* and was seemingly unaware of the extent of the massacre, so subsequent criticism of him may be a little harsh. He is best remembered for introducing the Gregorian calendar into Catholic countries in 1578.

65 See E. Howe, 'Architecture and Vasari's Paintings of the Massacre of the Huguenots', *Jnl Warburg & Courtauld Institute*, vol. 39 (1976), pp.258–61.

66 Merriman, op. cit., p.484.

67 Walton, *Intelligence Analysis ...*, p.50. These responsibilities span the activities of today's Secret Intelligence Service (MI6), Security Service (MI5) the police Special Branch and the electronic eavesdropping agency, the Government Communications Headquarters (GCHQ).

68 More than 1,310 seminary priests landed in England between 1574 and 1588 but no more than 150 were active in any one year, even in the peak year of 1585. See: McGrath & Rowe, 'Anstruther Revisited', pp.2 and 6–7.

69 See: Law, 'Cuthbert Mayne and the Bull of Pius V', pp.141–4. Mayne was executed at Launceston, Cornwall on 29 November 1577. He was canonised by Pope Paul VI on 25 October 1970.

70 TNA, SP 12/114/22. See also: Parmiter, op. cit., p.18.

71 TNA, SP 12/141/29.

72 23 Elizabeth *cap.* 1.

73 De Mendoza to Philip; London, 6 April 1581. *CSP Spain (Simancas)*, vol. 3, p.97.

74 Twelve seminary priests, headed by the Jesuit William Weston, staged exorcisms at Peckham's home in Denham in 1585–6, when several of his servants and adolescents were said to be possessed by demons. They used the girdle worn by the Jesuit martyr Edmund Campion (executed in 1581) to cause the 'devils excruciating pain'. One witness believed that five hundred people were reconciled to the Catholic faith because of this incident; others estimated the number at three to four thousand. See: Walsham, op. cit., pp.800 and 802–3.

75 Merriman, op. cit., p.497.

76 The Spanish explorer Hernán Cortés (1485–1547) conquered the Aztec empire in present-day Mexico in 1519–21.

77 *CSP Spain (Simancas)*, vol. 3, pp.384–5; Merriman, *op.cit.*, pp.492–9.

78 Soldiers armed with a harquebus, an early form of musket.

79 *CSP Vatican*, vol. 2, p.19.

80 Ibid., p.54.

81 *CSP Vatican*, vol. 3, p.208.

82 *CSP Domestic Elizabeth, 1581–90*, p.130.

83 A Jesuit witness reported Throckmorton 'made a very holy and edifying end. He would not ask pardon of the Queen ... at the hour of his death [he] said she ought to ask pardon of God for her heresy and misgovernment in allowing innocent men to be killed every day' (Edwards, *Plots and Plotters* ..., p.99). Lord Hunsdon corroborated this account: 'He died very stubbornly, never asking Her Majesty's forgiveness nor would willingly have anybody to pray of them' (TNA, SP Scot. 52/35/18).

84 See: *A new Ballade declarynge the dangerous shootyng of the Gunne at the Courte ...* by 'W.E.' – William Elderton.

85 *CSP Domestic Elizabeth, 1581–90*, p.126.

86 *CSP Domestic Elizabeth, 1581–90*, p.127. The Spanish ambassador claimed that Edward Arden, his wife Mary and the priest Hugh Hall were to be executed; however, the woman's body would not be quartered as this was illegal under English law. Her sentence was deferred because she was pregnant. *CSP Foreign Elizabeth*, vol. 18, pp.651–2. See also: Read, *Mr Secretary Walsingham*, vol. 2, fn. p.381.

87 BL Cotton MS Caligula B v, f.159. A brief on the issues contained in the Bond for Parliamentary debate, drawn up by Walsingham's clerk, is in ff.222–3v.

88 Hatfield House CP 13/177 and BL Add. MS 48,027, f. 251*v*.

89 27 Elizabeth *cap*. 1.

90 TNA, SP 12/176/22. See: Graves, *Profiles in Power*, p.94. Burghley had drawn up similar plans in October 1562 when Elizabeth was suffering from a dangerous smallpox infection which deprived her of speech for some time.

91 BL Add. MS 48, 027, ff.242–47*v*.

92 BL Lansdowne MS 43, article no. 3; 3ff.

93 Hutchinson, *Elizabeth's Spymaster*, p.146.

94 A broadsheet written by Thomas Deloney and printed in London by Richard Jones in 1586, celebrated the event. Entitled *A joyful song made on behalf of all her majesties faithful subjects of the great joy which was made in London at the taking of the late traitorous conspirators,* it included crude woodcuts of the conspirators and carried this snappy verse:

> O Englishmen with Roman harts what Devil bewitch you
> To seek the spoil of Prince and Realm like Traitors most untrue
> Why is your duty forgot unto your Royal Queene?
> That you your faith and promise breake O viperous band
> uncleane ...
> Blessed be God who knew your thoughts had brought your
> treasons out.

> (Society of Antiquaries of London, *Broadsides*, Henry VIII–Elizabeth, 1519–1603, f.83.) STC 6557.

95 For more on Elizabeth's cynical plan to avoid responsibility for Mary's death, see: Read, 'The Proposal to Assassinate Mary Queen of Scots'.

96 For a full account of Mary Queen of Scots' trial and execution, see my book *Elizabeth's Spymaster*, pp.169–202. An eye-witness account of the section by Richard Fletcher, dean of Peterborough, is in BL, Add. MS 48,027 ff.653–8*v* with a sketch of the scene at f.650. Other accounts are in Cotton MS Caligula B, v, ff.175*v*–6 and Hatfield House CP 16/17 and 164/170.

CHAPTER 2: **Rumours of War**

1 Murdin, *Collection State Papers*, vol. 1, p.592.

2 Veracruz, in the Gulf of Mexico, was founded by Hernán Cortés after landing there on Good Friday 1519, naming it Villa Rica de la Vera Cruz. *Villa Rica* ('rich village') came from the abundance of gold found by the Spanish – and *Vera Cruz* ('True Cross') a reference to the religious festival held on the day he came ashore.

3 This was Hawkins' third slaving voyage. The first Englishman known to have traded in slaves was the London merchant John Lock who brought five slaves from Guinea back to England in 1555.

4 Mattingly, *Defeat of the Spanish Armada*, p.85. There were insufficient supplies in *Minion* to feed the survivors of the attack, so one hundred crewmen volunteered to be put ashore elsewhere on the Mexican coast – where they were later taken prisoner.

5 Somerset, *Elizabeth 1*, p.416.

6 Ibid., p.537.

7 On uninhabited Grand Cayman, in the Caribbean, the English killed twenty alligators: 'There were crocodiles, which did encounter and fight with us. They live both in the sea and land. We took divers and made very good meat of them. Some of the same were ten feet (3.05 m) in length.' Corbett, *Spanish War*, pp.22–3. For an account of Drake's planned campaign, see BL Lansdowne MS 100, f.98.

8 Martin & Parker, *The Spanish Armada*, p.91.

9 Mattingly, op. cit., p.82.

10 Ibid., p.82.

11 Martin & Parker, op. cit. pp.95–6. Escalante published one of the first geographies of China in Seville in 1577, entitled: *Discourse of the Navigation made by the Portuguese to the Kingdom and Provinces of the Orient and the existing Knowledge of the Greatness of the Kingdom of China*. In contrast to the ponderous title, the book was only two hundred pages long, a reflection of how little was known about China at the time. Six years later, Escalante published his *Discourses on the Military Art*.

12 Martin & Parker, op. cit., p.96.

13 *CSP Domestic Elizabeth, 1581–90*, p.11.

14 Corbett, *Spanish War*, pp.61–3.

15 *CSP Domestic Elizabeth, 1581–90*, pp.305, 323, 324. In 1583, English merchants had reported that Santa Cruz had been ordered by Philip to command two hundred and fifty galleys for an invasion, to be launched from Cherbourg in France 'and there receiving aid from the French king to cut over to Portsmouth'. Hatfield House CP 162/148.

16 There were also riots on the Isle of Sheppey in Kent that February. In Sussex, markets were reported well supplied with grain but 'the prices are high, wheat being at 3s 4d (17p, or £441 in 2013 spending power) a bushel (a dry measure of volume, equivalent to 9.9 litres). *CSP Domestic Elizabeth, 1581–90*, pp.305 and 323. The famine continued: on 2 January 1587 a proclamation was published, 'foreseeing

the general dearth of corn and other victuals, partly through the unseasonableness of the year past', ordering markets to be supplied with foodstuffs 'at reasonable prices'. It also criticised the 'uncharitable greediness of such as be great corn-masters'. BL Lansdowne MS 48, f.120 and STC 8161.

17 Read, *Mr Secretary Walsingham*, vol. 3, p.219.

18 BL Harleian MS 6,993, f.125; Hutchinson, *Elizabeth's Spymaster*, p.205.

19 Read, op. cit., vol. 3, p.220.

20 Poyntz was the brother-in-law of Sir Thomas Heneage, treasurer of Elizabeth's Privy Chamber, and a student of the Inner Temple in London. He was an acknowledged double agent and was used by Walsingham to feed disinformation to the Spanish government. He worked for Mendoza, now Spanish ambassador in Paris.

21 *CSP Domestic Elizabeth, 1581–90*, p.340.

22 Martin & Parker, op. cit., pp.96–8.

23 Philip II to Count de Olivares; Madrid, 11 February 1587. *CSP Spain (Simancas)*, vol. 4, p.16. The Infanta was the ten-year-old Isabella Clara Eugenia, Philip's daughter by his third wife, Elizabeth of Valois. She eventually married Albert VII, Archduke of Austria, but died in 1633 without issue. Mary's will, written by her secretary Claude Nau, with corrections in her own hand, was drawn up in February 1577 and is in BL Cotton MS Vespasian C xvi, f.145. An extract, with notes by Robert Beale, clerk to Elizabeth's Privy Council, is in BL Add. MS 48,027, f.530.

24 Mattingly, op. cit., p.83.

25 Martin & Parker, op. cit., p.104.

26 See, for example, estimates of Spain's annual revenues drawn up in c.1584–9 in BL Add. MS 63,742, ff.99–105.

27 Welwood, *Most Material Transactions* ..., pp.8–9; Read, op. cit., vol. 3, fn. pp.285–6 and the 'Life of Sutton' in *Biographia Britannica, or the Lives of the Most Eminent Persons who have Flourished in Great Britain*, six vols (London, 1747–66), vol. 6, pp.3, 852. There is no mention of Sutton's involvement in this conspiracy in the twenty-seven folios of his *Life*, written in the seventeenth century and now in BL Lansdowne MS 1,198.

28 *CSP Spain (Simancas)*, vol. 4, p.127. Sixtus was the first pope to declare that abortion was homicide.

29 Meyer, *England and the Catholic Church* ..., p.329.

30 *CSP Spain (Simancas)*, vol. 4, p.51.

31 Ibid., p.114.

32 Ibid., pp.116–18. The king noted on the memorandum: 'The papers that came did not say that [Mary's] letter was written in her hand, although considering the quality of the matter and the way that it is dealt with, it may be inferred that it was so. If Don Bernardino [Mendoza] has the original, it would not be bad to see how it can safely be brought hither, as I do not believe it is here now. But we have a copy ...'

33 Sir Francis Englefield to Philip II; Madrid, 17 June, 18 June, 22 June, 1587. *CSP Spain (Simancas)*, vol. 4, p.112.

34 The English spy codenamed 'B.C.' reported that initially Philip awarded Dudley a pension of six crowns a day. 'If I had my alphabet [his cipher for use in a letter-substitution code] I would say more touching his lewd speech.' (BL Harleian MS 295. f.190.) Did the youth grow into the 'Mr Dudley' whom the exiled priest Robert Persons mentions in 1590 as being one of the seminary priests being sent to England that year? (HMC Salisbury, vol. 4, p.69.) Conversely, in BL Lansdowne MS 53, article 79, is an account of Anne Burnell who claimed in London that she was the daughter of Mary I and Philip. Bizarrely, she had the arms of England tattooed on her back. However, she was shown to be insane, caused 'by her great misery and penury' and having been ejected by her husband.

35 Sixtus V to Philip II; Rome, 7 August 1587. *CSP Spain (Simancas)*, vol. 4, pp.132–3.

36 Olivares to Philip II; Rome, 16 March 1587. Ibid., pp.38–9.

37 Martin & Parker, op. cit., p.105.

38 Olivares to Philip II; Rome, 2 March 1587. *CSP Spain (Simancas)*, vol. 4, p.28.

39 The full text of the treaty is in Meyer, op. cit., p.454. See also: McGrath, 'Papists and Puritans...', p.199.

40 Welwood, op. cit., pp.8–9; Read, op. cit., vol. 3, p.285.

41 The information came from Oda Colonna, nephew of one of the cardinals, who had been captured and questioned by the Dutch. Initially, no one put any credence to his claims. Martin & Parker op. cit., p.106.

42 Strype, *Annals*, vol. 3, book 2, pp.551–2.

43 *CSP Domestic Elizabeth, 1581–90*, p.386; Corbett, op. cit., pp.192–3.

44 A quintal was a measurement of weight, equal to 102 lb (46.28 kg). The capacity of a butt, a large cask, varied, but generally was around 108 gallons (477 litres).

45 *CSP Domestic Elizabeth, 1581–90*, pp.383 and 388.

46 Rowse, *Tudor Cornwall*, p.395.

47 *CSP Domestic Elizabeth, 1581–90*, pp.387, 391, 394 and 399.

48 Laughton, *Defeat of the Spanish Armada*, vol. 1, pp.58–62.

49 *CSP Spain (Simancas)*, vol. 4, p.24. Mendoza, the Spanish ambassador in Paris, described Raleigh as being 'very cold about these naval preparations and is secretly trying to dissuade the queen from them'. In January 1587, he reported 'several conversations' with Raleigh 'and signified to him how wise it would be to offer his services' to Philip as 'the queen's favour to him could not last long'. Raleigh allegedly agreed to prevent the expeditions to Spain or Portugal sailing from England (ibid, p.1).

50 *Rainbow* had been launched a few months earlier and was built on the lines of a galleass. She was commanded by Henry Bellingham.

51 Among the London ships were: *Merchant Royal* (400 tons), *Susan* (350 tons), *Edward Bonaventure* (300 tons), *Margaret and John* (210 tons), *Solomon* (200 tons), *George Bonaventure* (150 tons), *Thomas Bonaventure* (150 tons), *Minion* (200 tons). See: Corbett, *Drake and the Tudor Navy*, vol. 2, fn. p.68. A subsequent Spanish description of Drake's fleet was: 'Two *capitanas* of at least five hundred tons; two *almirante* of the same burden; another ship of the same build; two galleasses of extreme beauty each two hundred tons; seven ships of one hundred and fifty tons and thirteen large frigates of from fifty to sixty tons.' (*CSP Venice*, vol. 8, p.275.)

52 BL Lansdowne MS 56, f.175. The agreement was signed by Drake and examined and verified by Richard May, public notary.

53 *CSP Spain (Simancas)*, vol. 4, p.97.

54 Ibid., p.63.

55 Thomas Fenner to Walsingham; Plymouth, 11 April 1587. *CSP Domestic Elizabeth, 1581–90*, p.401.

56 Hopper, *Sir Francis Drake's Memorable Service*, p.5.

57 Corbett, *Spanish War*, pp.103–4.

58 The messenger was said to be 'a base son' (a bastard), of John Hawkins.

59 Hopper, op. cit., pp.28–9.

60 Neale, *Essays*, p.174 and Martin & Parker, op. cit., p.106. Mendoza was said to have three informants within the English embassy – but these may all have been the same person.

61 Hopper, op. cit., p.29.

62 Cadiz was still recovering from a huge fire that devastated its older districts in 1569.

63 Mattingly, op. cit., p.96.

64 Ibid., p.97.

65 According to a French account of Drake's attack. Corbett, *Spanish War*, p.117.

66 One had to be beached to prevent it sinking.

67 BL. Lansdowne MS 53, f.23.

68 Drake to Mr John Foxe 'preacher'; from *Elizabeth Bonaventure*, 7 May 1587; BL Harleian MS 167, f.104. Drake added a postscript in his own hand: 'Our enemies are many but our Protector commands the whole world. Let us all pray continually and our Lord Jesus will help us, in good time mercifully.' Foxe, the Protestant polemicist, never received the letter as he had died before Drake had written it.

69 Oria *et al.*, *La armada Invencible*, document 14 bis.

70 Mattingly, op. cit., p.107.

71 BL Harley MS 167, f.104r. Probably written by Robert Leng.

72 De Acuña's reputation was damaged badly by his part in the fighting at Cadiz. He later served in the Armada merely as an officer without an individual command.

73 Oria *et al.*, *La armada Invencible*, p.230.

74 Martin & Parker, op. cit., p.109.

75 Hopper, op. cit., p.7.

76 Baldwin, 'William Borough', *ODNB*, vol. 6, p.671.

77 BL Lansdowne MS 52, article 39.

78 Hopper, op. cit., p.42.

79 Ibid., p.19.

80 Corbett, *Spanish War*, pp.107–8.

81 *CSP Venice*, vol. 8, p.283.

82 Laughton, op. cit., vol. 2, p.101. Borough's defence against Drake's charges is in BL Lansdowne MS 52, article 31. An account of the general court martial on board the *Elizabeth Bonaventure* on 30 May 1587 is in BL Add. MS 12,505.

83 'Pompeo Pellegrini' (alias Anthony Standen) to Jacomo Manucci, 3 July 1587. BL Harleian MS 296, f.44. Manucci was a Florentine who worked for Walsingham in France in 1573–4 before being imprisoned. Returning to London, he lived in the parish of St Andrew Undershaft, as a controller of a section of the English spy network in Europe.

84 BL Harleian MS 6,994, f.76. Walsingham's plan was supported by Lord Admiral Howard and the Lords Cobham and Hunsdon of the Privy Council.

85 Murdin, op. cit., vol. 2, p.592.

CHAPTER 3: **Ramparts of Earth and Manure**

1 *CSP Domestic Elizabeth, 1581–90,* p.483.

2 His real name was Johannes Müller (1436–76). His *Ephemeris* was employed by the explorer Christopher Columbus to successfully predict the lunar eclipse of 29 February 1504, thereby impressing the inhabitants of Jamaica (where he was stranded) and persuading them to give him food. The name Regiomontanus was given to Müller by the Protestant reformer Phillip Melanchthon in 1534. Königsburg, then the capital of east Prussia, is present-day Kaliningrad, capital of Russia's *Oblast* of the same name.

3 Mattingly, *Defeat of the Spanish Armada,* p.167.

4 BL Cotton MS Caligula C ix, f.2.

5 Elizabeth wanted, at all costs, to avoid fighting a war on two fronts as her father, Henry VIII, had done in 1513 and again in the 1540s.

6 Martin & Parker, *The Spanish Armada,* p.103. Maxwell (1553–93) adopted the double-headed Imperial eagle flag of the Holy Roman Empire as his personal banner. He was imprisoned but released after the Armada had limped back to Spain. Later, at the head of the clan Maxwell, he invaded Annandale, the ancient lands of the clan Johnstone, but his force was ambushed at Dryfe Sands, near Lockerbie, on 3 December 1593 and seven hundred of his men were killed. Legend has it that as he tried to surrender, his outstretched arm was completely severed by a sword before he was hacked to pieces.

7 *CSP Domestic Elizabeth, 1581–90,* p.314.

8 Ibid., p.322.

9 BL Harleian MS 296, f.48. In reality, Sixtus V refused to listen to the proposals of those who offered to assassinate her. This was in stark contrast to the policy of his predecessor, Gregory XIII, whose secretary of state declared: 'There can be no doubt that while that guilty woman of England holds the two noble Christian kingdoms [England and Ireland] she has usurped, and while she is the cause of such great harm to the Catholic faith and the loss of so many millions of souls, whoever moves her from this life with the due end of God's service, not only would not sin but would be doing a meritorious deed, especially as the sentence still stands which Pius V of holy memory pronounced upon her.' See: McGrath, *Papists and Puritans...,* p.195.

10 *CSP Domestic Elizabeth, 1581–90,* p.484.

11 *CSP Domestic, Elizabeth Addenda 1580–1625,* p.232. The Bristol merchants were named as Thomas and Humphrey Hollman, William Swanley, Robert Pentecost, Robert Alder, William Dawson, Ralph

and Richard Sadler and Richard James. The domiciles of John Roberts, Robert Barratt and Francis Poyllis were not stated.

12 Mendoza to Philip II; Paris, 5 April 1587. *CSP Spain (Simancas)*, vol. 4, p.62.

13 BL Cotton MS Vespasian C viii, f.207.

14 Mendoza to Philip II; Paris, 12 July 1587. *CSP Spain (Simancas)*, vol. 4, p.123.

15 Ousley later served as a gentleman volunteer in Drake's ship *Revenge* against the Armada and Lord Admiral Howard revealed his reward: 'It has pleased her majesty, in respect of his good service ... in Spain, in sending very good intelligence thence, and now since in our late fight against the Spanish fleet, to grant him the lease of [the rectory of] St Helen's in [Bishopsgate] London.' *CSP Spain (Simancas)*, vol. 4, fn. p.123.

16 Read, *Secretary Walsingham ...*, vol. 3, p.290.

17 BL Harleian MS 6,994, f.76.

18 For comparison, the budget for today's British intelligence and security agencies, MI5, MI6 and GCHQ (the equivalent of the USA's FBI, CIA and NSA) totalled £2.2 billion in 2013.

19 *CSP Spain (Simancas)*, vol. 4, p.123.

20 Deacon, *History of the British Secret Services*, p.20.

21 The North Foreland.

22 Philip to Parma; El Escorial, 4 September 1587. *CSP Spain (Simancas)*, vol. 4, pp.136–7.

23 Martin & Parker, op. cit., p.119.

24 TNA, SP 9/210/33.

25 *CSP Domestic Elizabeth, 1581–90*, p.472.

26 Ibid., p.486.

27 In May 1544.

28 Laughton, *Defeat of the Spanish Armada*, vol. 1, p.213.

29 *Hardwick Papers*, vol. 1, p.360.

30 *CSP Domestic Elizabeth, 1581–90*, p.470.

31 *APC*, vol. 16, p.168; *CSP Domestic Elizabeth*, p.507; Fernandez-Armesto, *Spanish Armada: The Experience of War*, p.111. Burghley admitted he suffered sleepless nights worrying about the Thames defences, which cost £1,470. Richard Gibbes, one of Walsingham's agents in Lisbon, who posed as a Scotsman, was questioned about the suitability of various English rivers and harbours for use by the Armada ships. Misleadingly, he told them that the River Thames was 'very ill, full of sands within and without sight of land, and [it was]

impossible to bring in a navy'. See: Deacon, op. cit., p.20.

32 BL Add. MS 44,839.

33 *CSP Domestic Elizabeth, 1581–90*, p.304.

34 Boynton, *Elizabethan Militia*, p.129.

35 TNA, MPF 1/134.

36 McDermott, *England and Spain: A Necessary Quarrel*, p.187.

37 The southern maritime counties had only two sakers, two minions and two falcons each in March 1587. Ibid., p.184.

38 Sir George was the son of Lord Hunsdon. History supported his argument: more than 2,000 French troops had landed on the Isle of Wight in 1545.

39 TNA, SP 12/168/4. Repairs to the keep and walls of Carisbrooke Castle were undertaken in March 1587, together with the excavation of an outer ditch.

40 *APC*, vol. 14, p.229.

41 The protruding bastions provided flanking fire against attackers attempting to scale the walls.

42 Boynton, op. cit., p.130.

43 *CSP Domestic Elizabeth, 1581–90*, p.440.

44 O'Neill & Stephens, *Norfolk Archaeology*, vol. 28, pp. 5–6.

45 *APC*, vol. 15, p.351.

46 *The effect of certain branches of the Statute made in Anno. XXXIII Henry. VIII touching the maintenance of Artyllery and the punishment of such as vse vnlawfull games, very necessary to be put into execution* (Society of Antiquaries Proclamations, vol. 4, Elizabeth, 1558–90, f.26).

47 *APC*, vol. 14, pp.110 and 212.

48 Hogg, 'England's War Effort', p.25.

49 Boynton, op. cit., p.141.

50 Hughes & Larkin, *Tudor Royal Proclamations*, vol. 2, pp.541–2.

51 HMC Foljambe, p.40. Walsingham's contribution was larger than any other member of the English nobility or Privy Council, save for Sir Christopher Hatton and the Earl of Essex.

52 *APC*, vol. 15, pp.88–9; BL Add. MS 21,565, f.21.

53 BL Add. MS 21,565, f.21.

54 Boynton, op. cit., p.143.

55 Ibid., p.143.

56 'Billmen' carried 'pole arms' such as halberds or spears, some developed from agricultural implements.

57 *CSP Domestic Elizabeth, 1581–90*, p.75.

58 Ibid., p.485.

59 In Huntingdonshire, one of the captains was named as 'Oliver Cromwell', commanding two hundred men (Murdin, *Collection State Papers,* vol. 2, p.601). After losing most of his money supporting the royalist cause in the civil war, he died in 1655, aged ninety-two, after reputedly falling into a fire whilst drying himself after a bath. Cromwell was the uncle and godfather of the 'Lord Protector' of the same name (born in 1599), who ruled England as a republic in the mid-seventeenth century.

60 *CSP Domestic Elizabeth, 1581–90,* p.521.

61 McGurk, 'Armada Preparations in Kent', p.80.

62 Martin & Parker, op. cit., p.255.

63 A type of helmet with a peak and protective cheek pieces.

64 *CSP Domestic Elizabeth, 1581–90,* p.520.

65 HMC Foljambe, p.35.

66 McGurk, op. cit., p.71.

67 TNA, SP 12/199/93.

68 HMC Foljambe, pp.33 and 39.

69 Loomie, *Spanish Elizabethans,* p.7.

70 BL Lansdowne MS 50, items 19–21.

71 *CSP Domestic Elizabeth, 1581–90,* p.445.

72 Ibid., p.449. Some had also fallen on hard times. Samuel Lewknor joined Parma's army in the early 1580s and was wounded in the arm whilst serving as a captain. He had married the daughter of a Brabant merchant but was crippled financially by a costly lawsuit over her dowry. Penniless, Lewknor begged a passport back to England in 1590. Five years later, he published *The Estate of English Fugitives* in which he warned that Spain's motives in helping English exiles was to 'sow sedition' or ensure their deaths in Philip's military service. Loomie, op. cit., p.10.

73 *CSP Domestic Elizabeth, 1581–90,* p.472.

74 Ibid., p.463.

75 See: Watson, *Historical Account of the Town of Wisbech* (Wisbech, 1827), p.127 and Hutchinson, *Elizabeth's Spymaster,* pp.305–6.

76 Covington, *Trail of Martyrdom …,* p.70.

77 *CSP Domestic Elizabeth, 1581–90,* p.425.

78 Ibid., p.458.

79 Boynton, op. cit., p.149.

80 Sir Richard Knightly, who was organising construction of new beacons in Hampshire in December 1586, wrote to Sir Edward Montague,

seeking an estimate 'for the number of trees needed for a beacon ... I think you must set down more than three to a beacon unless your trees [are] a great deal bigger than ours.' HMC Montague, p.12. The earliest mention of a beacon system is in 1324, dealing with thirty-one in the Isle of Wight and the system was still operational in 1745 when Prince Charles Stewart – 'Bonnie Prince Charlie' – was expected to land on the south coast and again in 1804 when Napoleon Bonaparte threatened invasion. (White, 'The Beacon System in Kent', pp.78–9 and 91.)

81 Kitchen, 'The Ghastly War Flame: The Beacon System in Essex', p.42. An almost contemporary map of the beacon sites in Kent is in BL Add. MS 62,935.

82 Invasions were considered unlikely to be launched in the winter months. In December 1580, the Hampshire justices were told to stand down their beacon watch 'in consideration of the extremity and sharpness of the weather'.

83 Boynton, op. cit., p.134; Kitchen, op. cit., p.42.

84 *CSP Domestic Elizabeth, 1581–90,* pp.339–40.

85 Surrey Local History Centre LM/1945.

86 White, 'Beacon System in Hants', p.279.

87 *APC,* vol. 15, pp.xi and 17.

88 The Privy Council were told that Poole was suffering 'decay and dis-ability' and so they thought it 'convenient [that] they shall be spared for the present and eased of that burden'. *APC,* vol. 16, p.23.

89 *CSP Domestic Elizabeth, 1581–90,* p.473, *APC,* vol. 15, p.59.

90 Revd. J. Silvester-Davies, *History of Southampton* (Southampton, 1883), p.253.

91 *CSP Domestic Elizabeth, 1581–90,* p.477; *APC,* vol. 15, p.60.

92 *APC,* vol. 15, p.92.

93 By comparison, the navy strength at the time of Henry VIII's death in January 1547 was fifty-three ships, displacing a total of 10,000 tons.

94 Laughton, op. cit., vol. 1, p.23.

95 Martin & Parker, op. cit., p.33.

96 Ibid., pp.34–5.

97 McDermott, op. cit., p.77.

98 TNA, SP 12/208/79, f.181.

99 The ship had been bought for the navy from Sir Walter Raleigh for £5,000, the sum being deducted from his debts to the queen. She was launched on 12 June 1587.

100 TNA, SP 12/208/87 f.201*v*.
101 TNA, SP 12/209/40 f.77.

CHAPTER 4: **The Great and Most Fortunate Navy**

1 Laughton, *Spanish Armada*, vol. 1, p.175.
2 In Rome, Pope Sixtus believed Santa Cruz's death was caused by the admiral's 'disgust at two orders issued by the king; first that Don Pedro de Fuentes of the house of Toledo was to sail with the marqués [and] the other that [he] was to obey the Duke of Parma'. *CSP Venice*, vol. 8, p.343.
3 Santa Cruz's body was exhumed in 1643 and reburied in the convent of San Francisco.
4 *CSP Venice*, vol. 8, p.339.
5 Mattingly, *Defeat of the Spanish Armada*, p.192.
6 In early January, the Venetian envoy listed three thousand as dead from disease and a thousand were sick. A further one thousand had deserted.
7 *CSP Venice*, vol. 8, p.329.
8 This Venetian ship was commandeered in 1587 while she was along-side in a Sicilian port. She had been hired to transport troops to Lisbon.
9 *CSP Venice*, vol. 8, p.336. The Spanish planned to build temporary wooden fortifications to protect their bridgehead in Kent.
10 Ibid., pp. 337–8.
11 *CSP Spain (Simancas)*, vol. 4, pp.187–8.
12 Ibid., p.200.
13 Thompson, 'Medina Sidonia…', p.198.
14 *CSP Venice*, vol. 8, p.340.
15 A *real* was a small Spanish silver coin, 0.8 inch diameter (20.3 mm), eight of which were worth a silver dollar.
16 Medina Sidonia to Juan de Idiáquez; San Lúcar de Barrameda, 16 February 1588. *CSP Spain (Simancas)*, vol. 4, pp.207–8; and printed in full in Duro, *La armada Invencible*, vol. 1, pp.414–17. Most of Medina Sidonia's income came from foreign trade (particularly from England) and this had slumped during the hostilities, although he was accused of conniving at illegal trade for his own profit. See: Thompson, op. cit., p.213 and Braudel, *La Méditerranée* …, pp.575–6. In fact, despite his protests of poverty, Medina Sidonia contributed 7,827,358 *maravedis*, or £2,245, towards the Armada costs.
17 *CSP Venice*, vol. 8, p.319.

18 Oria *et al.*, *La armada Invencible*, vol. 1, p.148; Thompson, op. cit., p.213; Martin & Parker, *Spanish Armada*, p.125.

19 *CSP Spain (Simancas)*, vol. 4, p.209.

20 Mattingly, op. cit., p.196.

21 He took over command of the English forces after Leicester's return to England.

22 Lincolnshire Archives – 8ANC/58. ?March 1588.

23 Fernandez-Armesto, *Spanish Armada, the Experience of War*, p.15.

24 *CSP Venice*, vol. 8, p.341.

25 See: de Courcy Ireland, 'Ragusa and the Spanish Armada'. Some historians believe that as many as twenty-three Ragusan ships served with the Armada of which twelve were galleons; ibid., pp.254–5.

26 *CSP Venice*, vol. 8, p. 332.

27 Ibid., p. 340.

28 Ibid., p.351.

29 Oria *et al.*, op. cit., pp.112, 124, 125, 136; Duro, op. cit., vol. 1, p.385; Thompson, op. cit., p.207.

30 *CSP Spain (Simancas)*, vol. 4, pp.225–6.

31 *CSP Spain (Simancas)*, vol. 4, pp.232–3 and 239.

32 *CSP Venice*, vol. 8, pp.331 and 336.

33 *CSP Spain (Simancas)*, vol. 4, p.201.

34 *CSP Venice*, vol. 8, pp.329 and 331. The threat of an English invasion to put the pretender Dom Antonio on the Portuguese throne may have been one of the chief motivations behind the Armada. See: Armstrong, 'Venetian Dispatches', pp.673–4 and Thompson, op. cit., p.203.

35 *CSP Venice*, vol. 8, pp.332 and 335.

36 *CSP Spain (Simancas)*, vol. 4, p.202.

37 Walsingham had been suffering from a recurrent fever which left him so weak: 'as that neither my hand or arm can endure the use of my pen'.

38 *Hardwick Papers*, vol. 1, pp.360–1.

39 *CSP Spain (Simancas)*, vol. 4, p.191.

40 Ibid., p.201. Elizabeth's instructions to her chief negotiator, Dr Valentine Dale, are in Hatfield House CP 17/2.

41 Mattingly, op. cit., p.180.

42 Mattingly, op. cit., p.223; Mousset, *Dépêches diplomatiques*, p.380.

43 *CSP Venice*, vol. 8, p.344. Later Gritti reported the bribe amounted to 500,000 crowns.

44 The Holy Roman Empire, ruled by Rudolf II from 1576, encompassed Germany, Austria, the present-day Czech Republic, northern Italy, western Poland and Switzerland.

45 *CSP Venice*, vol. 8, p.345.

46 Ibid., p.363.

47 *Fugger Newsletters*, (1924), p.122.

48 Anabaptists only recognised the baptism of adult believers.

49 William Allen, *Admonition*, p.xi. It was signed: 'From my lodging in the palace of St Peter, Rome, the 28th of April 1588'. An Italian translation was made solely for the information of the Pope and the Duke of Parma. A Spanish agent in London had warned at the end of March of an English plot to poison Allen, 'I can assure you the matter is being arranged.' *CSP Spain (Simancas)*, vol. 4, p.239.

50 Ibid., p.289; Meyer, *England and the Catholic Church ...*, fn. p.326.

51 Parma to Philip II; Bruges, 21 July 1588. *CSP Spain (Simancas)*, vol. 4, p.351.

52 Mendoza to Philip II; Paris, 5 April 1588. *CSP Spain (Simancas)*, vol. 4, p.258.

53 Ibid., pp.240–1.

54 Ibid., p.252.

55 Ibid., p.265.

56 The 'Earl of Surrey' was Philip Howard, Earl of Arundel. William Vaux, Third Baron Vaux of Harrowden (1535–95) was convicted for recusancy and committed to the Fleet by the Privy Council. He was tried in the Star Chamber in February 1581 on charges of harbouring the priest Edmund Campion, together with his brother-in-law Sir Thomas Tresham. Vaux was gaoled and fined £1,000. The Fleet prison was located in Farringdon Street, on the eastern banks of the Fleet River, outside the western walls of the City of London. It was built in 1197 but was destroyed three times: during the Peasants' Revolt of 1381, the Great Fire of London in 1666 and during the Gordon Riots of 1780. It was finally demolished in 1846.

57 Bedingfield held Elizabeth under house arrest during her time at Woodstock.

58 Although the earl's brother, Sir William Stanley, listed under Lancashire, 'is a good Catholic'.

59 *CSP Spain (Simancas)*, vol. 4, pp.184–6. The document ends: 'I wish to God my old own bones were of any service to his majesty in the cause for I would willingly die in service of the Catholic faith under the protection of his majesty, whom God bless.'

60 *CSP Spain (Simancas)*, vol. 3, pp.80–6.

61 A quintal is a measurement of dry weight, equal to 102 lb or 46.28 kg.

62 A fanega of beans is equivalent to two bushels (70.48 litres).

63 An arroba is a measurement of liquid volume equal to 3.5 gallons (15.91 litres).

64 A pipe was a large wooden cask holding 105 gallons (477 litres).

65 Hatfield House CP 17/23.

66 In contrast, in the English fleet, preachers were recorded in the ship's companies of the *Ark Royal, Elizabeth Jonas, Revenge, Lion, Bear* and *Rainbow*.

67 *CSP Spain (Simancas)*, vol. 4, pp.284–5.

68 Fernandez-Armesto, op. cit., p.52.

69 Fernandez-Armesto, op. cit., pp.8–10; *CSP Spain (Simancas)*, vol. 4, pp.269–70 and 284–6; *CSP Domestic, Elizabeth, 1581–90*, p.16. In March 1588, Burghley, alarmed at the cost of the fleet's provisions, reduced the beef ration at two pennies the pound and introduced alternate fish days. *CSP Domestic, Elizabeth, 1581–90*, p.468.

70 In April 1588, Parma had just over nine hundred Irish soldiers under Sir William Stanley, who had defected and handed over the town of Deventer to the Spanish, and eight hundred and four Scots, commanded by Archibald Peyton. An intelligence report from Flanders claimed the brutality and ill-conduct of Irish soldiers in Parma's army was so bad that the Spanish had nicknamed them *los savages perdidos* – the 'evil savages'. *CSP Domestic, Elizabeth, 1581–90*, p.446.

71 H. O'Donnell, 'The Requirements of the Duke of Parma for the Conquest of England' in Gallagher & Cruickshank (eds), *God's Obvious Design*, pp.96–7.

72 BL Cotton MS Vespasian cviii, f.105*v*.

73 *CSP Spain (Simancas)*, vol. 4, pp.261–2.

74 Whitehead, *Brags and Boasts*, pp.58–78.

75 *CSP Venice*, vol. 8, pp.351–2.

76 Mattingly, op. cit., pp.202–3; Martin & Parker, op. cit., p.128.

77 A naval custom, observed in the sixteenth century in Spain and other Catholic countries. Boys would say the *Pater Noster* before a bell was tolled three times, a process repeated twice more.

78 *Harleian Miscellany*, vol. 1, pp.111–14.

79 TNA, SP 94/3, f.227*r*.

80 *CSP Spain (Simancas)*, vol. 4, pp.245–52.

81 Naish, 'Documents Illustrating the History of the Spanish Amada', pp.21–2.

82 *CSP Spain (Simancas)*, vol. 4, p.273.

83 BL Harleian MS 288, f.187; Read, *Secretary Walsingham*, vol. 2, p.423.

84 Gómez-Centurión, *La Invencible ...*, p.70.

85 *CSP Domestic Elizabeth, 1581–90*, pp.483 and 486.

CHAPTER 5: **First Sighting**

1 *CSP Spain (Simancas)*, vol. 4, p.357.

2 AGS CS 2a/278, f.167 and AGS CMC 2a/772.

3 It was later found to be 'unserviceable'.

4 Medina Sidonia to Philip II; *San Martin*, 10 June 1588. *CSP Spain (Simancas)*, vol. 4, p.309.

5 *CSP Venice*, vol. 8, p.362.

6 Medina Sidonia to Philip II; *San Martin*, Corunna, 24 June 1588. *CSP Spain (Simancas)*, vol. 4, p.316.

7 Ibid., pp.328–9.

8 Ibid., pp.330–2. The hulks returned safely to Corunna on 6 July. The two prizes that sank had both sailed from Dublin; one with a cargo of wheat and tanned hides, bound for Biscay, and the other was carrying charcoal to France, together with two friars, one a Bernardin and the other a Franciscan.

9 Maura, *El designio de Felipe II ...*, pp.258–61.

10 AGS Estado 455/320–1.

11 Memorandum from Juan de Idiáquez to Philip II; 2 July 1588. *CSP Spain (Simancas)*, vol. 4, p.332.

12 Bodleian Library – Douce Prints a.48; McGrath, *Papists and Puritans*, p.200.

13 This is a reference to Philip's landing at Southampton to marry Mary on 20 July 1554. Olivares was a member of his entourage.

14 Olivares to Philip II; Rome, 8 July 1588. *CSP Spain (Simancas)*, vol. 4, pp.333–4.

15 Ibid., pp.321–4. Don Pedro de Valdés complained to Philip a few days later that after expressing his opinions at the council of war, Medina Sidonia was 'looking upon him with an unfriendly eye and had used expressions towards him which had greatly grieved him'.

16 Oria *et al.*, *La armada Invencible*, pp.210–14; Naish, 'Documents illustrating the History of the Spanish Armada', p.23; Martin & Parker, *Spanish Armada*, pp.143 and 163.

17 *CSP Spain (Simancas)*, vol. 4, pp.327–8.

18 Ibid., pp.329–30.

19 Duro, *La armada Invencible,* vol. 2, pp.169–70.

20 Ibid., p.199.

21 *CSP Spain (Simancas),* vol. 4, pp.334–5.

22 Martin & Parker, op. cit., p.145.

23 *CSP Spain (Simancas),* vol. 4, fn. p.338.

24 Building operations began in 1587. The fortress is now joined to the mainland by a breakwater and houses the Museo Arqueológico e Histórico.

25 AGS GA 225/55–6.

26 Laughton, op. cit., vol. 1, p.176.

27 England had a total of 1,392 merchant ships in 1588, of which 183 displaced more than one hundred tons. (Revd J. Silvester Davies, *History of Southampton* (Southampton, 1883), p.481.) On 31 March 1588, an embargo was placed on shipping of every county, not so much to obtain ships but to prevent their crews departing on voyages. The Royal Navy still has contingency plans to hire civilian ships for various logistic roles in time of hostilities, known by the acronym STUFT, or Ships Taken Up From Trade.

28 A list of Seymour's ships on 23 July includes 'a ship of Romney [the *John Young*] sent to seize by order touching Brasbridge, pirate, his prize'. TNA, SP 12/213/14.

29 Laughton, op. cit., vol. 1, pp.189–90. On 13 June, the lord admiral told Walsingham that his crews 'behaved admirably; none have mutinied though all know they are short of rations. Kindly handled they will bear want and run through fire and water but their want of victuals is distressing.' (*CSP Domestic Elizabeth, 1581–90,* p.488.) Howard commandeered a cargo of rice, almonds and other goods from the *Mary of Hamburg* at Plymouth to help meet the shortfall in provisions.

30 Lincolnshire archives, 8ANC10/114; The Hague, 5 April 1588.

31 It was then called 'the Hermitage Bulwark' as it was built on the site of a monastic house dissolved three years before.

32 A.D. Saunders, 'Tilbury Fort and the Development of Artillery Fortifications in the Thames Estuary', *Antiquaries' Jnl,* vol. 28 (1960), pp.155–6. Costs at Tilbury amounted to £247 8s 4d for timber for the drawbridges, gates and palisades and three hundred labourers at eight pence a day. *CSP Domestic, Elizabeth, 1581–90,* p.550. Additional expenditure was requested on 8 October.

33 William Page (ed.), *Victoria County History of Kent,* vol. 2 (London, 1926), p.296.

34 Laughton, op. cit., vol. 1, pp.206–7.

35 The Nore is located midway between Havengore Creek in Essex and Warden Point in Kent.

36 Borough based his successful defence on a chart of Cadiz that amply demonstrated the perils of the *Golden Lion*'s station assigned by Drake. See: Baldwin, 'William Borough', *ODNB*, vol. 6, p.671. Borough died in November 1598, having become one of the Brethren of Trinity House. In his will, he left £10 towards a dinner for them to be held in remembrance of him. (TNA, PROB 11/92, ff.229–30.)

37 HMC Foljambe, p.43.

38 *CSP Domestic Elizabeth, 1581–90,* pp.489–90.

39 *CSP Domestic Elizabeth, 1581–90,* p.488.

40 TNA, SP 12/211/56.

41 Strype, *Annals,* vol. 3, pt 2, p.544 and HMC Bath p.28.

42 *CSP Domestic Elizabeth, 1581–90,* p.487; Laughton, op. cit., vol. 1, pp.192–3.

43 *CSP Domestic Elizabeth, 1581–90,* p.489; Laughton, op. cit., vol. 1, pp.195–7. Howard was frustrated by the weather: 'We can do [no] good as this wind is, for its holds here at west and south-west and blows up so hard that no ship here but her majesty's great ships dare ride in this sound but are fain to go into the haven … We are not able by any means to get the weather [get to windward] of this harbour …'

44 TNA, SP 12/211/47.

45 Laughton, op. cit., vol. 1, pp.221–2.

46 TNA, SP 9/210/34. Seymour dictated this letter, to Walsingham, as he had 'strained his hand with hauling a rope whereby I cannot write so much as I would'.

47 Laughton, op. cit., vol. 1, pp.278–4.

48 Palavicino was a Genoese banker who settled in England where he accumulated a large fortune and was employed in the financial business of Elizabeth's government. He was knighted in 1587.

49 Stade was a prominent port of the Hanseatic League until eclipsed by Hamburg.

50 TNA, SP 12/212/66, f.139.

51 The crew and guns from *Diana* were saved but her hull was broken up. One of her slaves, the Welshman David Gwynn, later boasted how he freed his fellow slaves, killed the Spanish crew and captured the other three galleys. History has unfortunately refuted his tall tale. See: Mattingly, *Defeat of the Spanish Armada*, p.247.

52 Martin & Parker, op. cit., p.146.

CHAPTER 6: **Action This Day**

1 Laughton, *Defeat of the Spanish Armada*, vol. 1, p.289.
2 It was the thirty-fourth anniversary of Philip's landing at Southampton to marry Mary I of England.
3 Graham, *The Spanish Armadas*, p.98.
4 *Fugger Newsletters,* 1926, pp.165, 169.
5 Mendoza to Philip II; Paris, 24 July 1588. *CSP Spain (Simancas)*, vol. 4, p.353.
6 Medina Sidonia to Philip; *San Martin,* 'in sight of the Lizard', 30 July 1588. *CSP Spain (Simancas)*, vol. 4, pp.357–8.
7 Parker, '*El Testamento politico*', pp.22–4 and 29.
8 Gentlemen and members of the aristocracy were apparently exempt from the ban on playing bowls.
9 Barratt, *Armada 1588*, p.47. In the second part of a 1624 tract entitled *Vox Populi* (which deals with Prince Charles Stuart's escapades in Spain), there is a report of a sitting of the *Cortes* (the Spanish parliament), which was discussing policy towards England. The Duke of Braganza said: 'Did we not in 1588 carry our business to England so secretly ... as in bringing our navy to their shores, while their commanders were at bowls upon the Hoe at Plymouth?' The story of the bowls game was therefore then current and was within living memory.
10 Warping is an agonisingly slow method of moving a becalmed ship by hauling on the anchor cable, usually assisted by a capstan. The anchor is then taken forward by the ship's boat, dropped ahead and the process repeated *ad nauseam*. Some ships may also have been simply towed out by their boats.
11 A position to windward to other ships, advantageous in battle.
12 Martin & Parker, *The Spanish Armada*, pp.146 and 149.
13 Graham, op. cit., p.100.
14 In contrast, King Philip had been advised by a bloodthirsty Italian, Cavaliere Fra Tiburtio Spanocchi, to take 'the honourable decision to declare war' but perhaps it only 'sufficed to set foot on the enemy's territory'. See: *Fugger Newsletters*, 1926, p.152.
15 *CSP Spain (Simancas)*, vol. 4, p.440.
16 To 'luff' is to steer a ship's bows round to the wind.
17 Parker, op. cit., p.29.
18 Laughton, op. cit., vol. 1, p.302.
19 Duro, *La armada Invencible,* vol. 2, p.230.
20 Martin & Parker, op. cit., p.149.

21 *CSP Spain (Simancas)*, vol. 4, p.441.

22 Mattingly, *Defeat of the Spanish Armada*, p.259.

23 *Harleian Miscellany*, vol. 1, p.120.

24 Barratt, op. cit., p.57.

25 Calderón listed those remaining on the *San Salvador*: sixty-four seamen; Captain Pedro de Priego, 'who was badly burnt and had ninety-four soldiers; Captain Don Francisco de Chaves, who was unhurt and had one hundred and thirty-three soldiers; Captain Geronimo de Valderrama, with ninety-two soldiers ... also unhurt'. See: *CSP Spain (Simancas)*, vol. 4, p.441. English accounts put the dead at about one hundred and twenty in the explosion (Laughton, op. cit., vol. 2, p.56).

26 Martin & Parker, op. cit., p.151.

27 Oria *et al.*, *La armada Invencible*, pp.352–3; Martin & Parker, op. cit., p.152; fn. p.164.

28 Laughton, op. cit., vol. 2, p.135.

29 Lord Admiral Howard to Walsingham; *Ark Royal*, Plymouth, 31 July 1588. TNA, SP 12/212, f.167.

30 Laughton, op. cit., vol. 1, p.290.

31 Medina Sidonia to Parma; on board *San Martin*, two leagues off Plymouth, 31 July 1588. *CSP Spain (Simancas)*, vol. 4, p.358.

32 Mattingly, op. cit., pp.263–4.

33 A private ship belonging to Sir Walter Raleigh.

34 Laughton, op. cit., vol. 2, p.136.

35 James A. Froude, *English Seamen of the Sixteenth-century* (London, 1896), p.264.

36 Amazingly Winslade survived the queen's justice and is recorded as fighting for Spain in 1600 in a regiment of foreign pensioners in the Netherlands under the command of the renegade English soldier Sir William Stanley (Loomie, *Spanish Elizabethans*, p.203). His interrogation is described in Surrey Local History Centre, Loseley MS LM/1339/370. The Spanish saw Winslade as a loyal 'well-born gentleman [who] has endured much suffering' (McDermott, *England and Spain: The Necessary Quarrel*, p.369).

37 Two barques landed the Spanish prisoners ashore at Dartmouth. The prize survey of the *Rosario* listed twenty-six brass cannon and two of iron mounted on carriages. Costs associated with the prize at Torbay included £2 'to a man of my lord admiral's that came for the powder of the Spaniard and so came by post to Portsmouth'; £5 for dried fish to feed the prisoners and £1 10 for 'guarding and watching of the

Spaniards two days and a night at their landing'. See: Laughton, op. cit., vol. 2, pp.190–4. The *Rosario* was later taken to Plymouth and committed to the charge of George Cary and Sir John Gilbert, the latter unfortunately responsible for filching some of the eighty-five casks of wine on board. The more honest Cary wrote to Walsingham in despair over the thefts of the prize's goods: 'Watch and look never so narrowly they will steal and pilfer'. See: *APC,* vol. 16, pp.xxiv–v.

38 Barratt, op. cit., p.62; Martin & Parker, op. cit., pp.152–3; Mattingly, op. cit., p.266.

39 Barratt, op. cit., pp.62–3.

CHAPTER 7: Firestorm

1 Laughton, *Defeat of the Spanish Armada*, vol. 2, p.63.

2 HMC Foljambe, p.48. Lord Chandos, lord lieutenant of Gloucestershire, for example, was instructed to appoint a provost marshal for 'the arrest and punishment of idle vagabonds to prevent the spread of false rumours' (Gloucestershire Archives, GBR/H/2/1 f.1).

3 HMC Foljambe, p.50.

4 Gerson, 'English Recusants and the Spanish Armada', p.590.

5 McDermott, *England and Spain: the Necessary Quarrel*, p.244.

6 TNA, SP 12/211/95.

7 *CSP Spain (Simancas)*, vol. 4, pp.372–3.

8 Ibid., p.480.

9 In 1584, the Member of Parliament Job Throckmorton claimed in a debate that 'God had vowed himself to be English' and went on to describe the Pope as Antichrist, Catherine de Medici (mother of Henri III of France) as 'an adder whose brood is left to pester the earth' and Philip of Spain as 'idolatrous and incestuous'. It was not just foreign royalty that drew his ire: 'A Frenchman was as vile a man that lives and no villainy can make him blush.' As a boy, he had 'heard it said that falsehood was the very nature of a Scot'. Sir Christopher Hatton, later Lord Chancellor, reprimanded him for 'speaking sharply of princes' and Throckmorton was thrown into the Tower. See: Brennan, 'Papists and Patriotism ...', p.8 and Neale, *Elizabeth and her Parliaments*, pp.28, 168 and 169–73.

10 Mattingly, *Defeat of the Spanish Armada*, p.311.

11 McDermott, op. cit., p.241.

12 *CSP Spain (Simancas)*, vol. 4, p.378.

13 A Spanish spy in London reported on 7 September that the Dutch

musketeers had mutinied because they had not 'been paid a penny' and had killed their colonel and lieutenant colonel. 'They are said to have fortified themselves in a castle near Sandwich but I hear from another quarter they have now been pacified and embarked' to return home to the Netherlands. *CSP Spain (Simancas)*, vol. 4, p.421.

14 Martin & Parker, *The Spanish Armada*, pp.255 and 257; P. Clark, *English Provincial Society from the Reformation to the Revolution; Religion, Politics and Society in Kent 1500–1640* (Hassocks, 1977), p.249.

15 On 2 August, Leicester told the Privy Council: 'I have put these forts [Tilbury and Gravesend] in as good strength as time will permit but there must be planks sent in with all haste and workmen to make [gun] platforms.' R.P. Cruden, *History of Gravesend and the Port of London* (London, 1843), p.237.

16 *APC*, vol. 16, pp.174–6.

17 Ibid., p.183.

18 Laughton, op. cit., vol. 1, pp.319.

19 Ibid., p.321.

20 Hogg, op. cit., pp.34–5.

21 Laughton, op. cit., vol. 1, p.331.

22 BL Cotton MS Caligula D i, f.420. The spelling of the letter, written in English, has quaint lapses into the Scottish vernacular.

23 Martin & Parker, op. cit., p.63.

24 *CSP Spain (Simancas)*, vol. 4, p.397.

25 BL Cotton MS Otho E ix, f.185*v*.

26 *CSP Spain (Simancas)*, vol. 4, p.460.

27 Martin & Parker, op. cit., p.155.

28 TNA, SP 94/3/11; *CSP Spain (Simancas)*, vol. 4, p.359.

29 Parker, 'El testamento politico ...', p.31.

30 *CSP Spain (Simancas)*, vol. 4, p.442.

31 BL Cotton MS Julius F x, f.114; Corbett, *Drake and the Tudor Navy*, vol. 2, p.227. The *Delight* was owned by Sir William Wynter, Surveyor of the navy.

32 A 'crock'(or crook) was the forked wooden or metal rest on which the heavy harquebus was rested when it was aimed and fired.

33 BL Cotton MS Julius F x, f.114. This account suggests that the cannon were fired rapidly like muskets in a land battle.

34 *CSP Foreign Elizabeth*, vol. 22, p.5. The sailor also repeated what he had heard from 'the Spanish captains that they meant to carry off the English women to Spain and that the king's [Philip's] commission

instructed them to massacre everyone they met in England, even the children'. As this comes from an English source, the report's veracity may be tainted.

35 Corbett, op. cit., vol. 2, p.228.

36 BL Cotton MS Julius F x, f.114.

37 Graham, *The Spanish Armadas,* p.117; Parker, 'The Dreadnought Revolution', p.269.

38 TNA, SP 12/213/71, f.164.

39 Medina Sidonia to Don Hugo de Moncada; on board the royal galleon *San Martin,* 2 August 1588. *CSP Spain (Simancas),* vol. 4, p.359.

40 Named after 'The Spit' a sandbank that stretches south from the shore of Hampshire for 3.1 miles (5 km). Spithead, later the traditional anchorage for the Royal Navy, is fourteen miles (22.5 km) long with an average breadth of four miles (6.5 km). On 2 August, Seymour had written to the Privy Council warning them of a possible Spanish landing on the Isle of Wight. See Laughton, op. cit., vol. 1, p.300.

41 Martin & Parker, op. cit., p.157.

42 Fernandez-Armesto, *The Spanish Armada: The Experience of War,* p.159.

43 Both fleets would have seen four stacks in 1588 instead of the three 'Needles' of today. A 120-foot (36.58 metres) rock, nicknamed 'Lot's Wife', stood just to the north of the central stack. It collapsed in 1764.

44 BL Cotton MS Julius F x, f.115.

45 One of the Spanish pilots reported 'there is a risk in passing here because there is a castle on the mainland called Hurst which is the strongest in England. Its artillery reaches into the channel.' Repairs to the central tower, built by Henry VIII in the 1530s as one of his coastal artillery forts, had been completed in 1585. Around eight hundred roundshot and two lasts of gunpowder had been ordered for the castle early in 1588. See: Jude James, *Hurst Castle: An Illustrated History* (Lymington, 2003), p.21.

46 St Helen's Roads had its own dangers: submerged shoals off the island's Horsestone Point, and a prominent rock, later nicknamed 'Ben Ben', off a plateau of rocks extending six hundred yards (548.64 m) south of Nettlestone Point, between present-day Ryde and Bembridge on the Isle of Wight. There are thirteen wrecks recorded in the area.

47 Barratt, *Armada 1588,* p.81.

48 Medina Sidonia asked for smaller calibre roundshot – 4, 5 and 10 lbs (1.81, 2.27 and 4.54 kg) in weight 'in as large a quantity as possible'.

49 Medina Sidonia to Parma; 'Royal galleon, off the Isle of Wight', 4 August 1588. *CSP Spain (Simancas)*, vol. 4, p.360.

50 A large galleon.

51 Laughton, op. cit., vol. 1, p.13.

52 *CSP Spain (Simancas)*, vol. 4, pp.398–9.

53 Ibid., p.443.

54 Parker, op. cit., p.32; Martin & Parker, op. cit., p.160.

55 Fernandez-Armesto, op. cit., p.160; Laughton, op.cit., vol. 2, p.40. The wounded received a collective bonus of £80.

56 Eighteen miles (28.97 km) but Carey's landsman's estimate of the distance is too great: the fighting was much closer to land.

57 TNA, SP 12/213/40, f.97. In France, the Venetian ambassador Giovanni Mocenigo later reported that Spanish reports of the battle off the Isle of Wight claimed they had 'got the best of it, sinking fifteen ships, among them the flagship. The rest fled towards Dover ... where the body of the English fleet is lying. They said that three ships which had lost their masts were captured and one large ship took fire. A Breton, who was taken by Drake ... has come home. He declares that a galleass attacked the flagship and with the first broadside cut down her masts and at the second sank her and that Drake escaped in a boat under cover of the thick smoke.' *CSP Venice*, vol. 8, p.373.

58 BL Cotton MS Otho, E, ix, f.214r.

59 BL Add. MS 33,740, ff.2–3. Four hundred had already been supplied to the fleet from Hampshire. The Earl of Sussex wrote to Walsingham the same day reporting receipt of a letter from Howard requesting powder and shot 'saying he has a very great want [of it] indeed' but pointing out that if he sent the five lasts of gunpowder he had received from the Tower of London, 'there would be none left'. See Laughton, op. cit., vol. 1, p.323.

60 Laughton, op. cit., vol. 1, p.331.

61 *CSP Foreign Elizabeth*, vol. 22, p.85.

62 A Lancashire gentleman who was also imprisoned for his adherence to the Catholic faith.

63 Hammond was 'an old aged woman... a laundress in the Tower'.

64 BL Add. MS 48,029, f.102.

65 Ibid., f.81.

66 Norfolk, *Lives of Philip Howard... and Anne Dacres his wife*, pp.87–9.

67 Archer, *Progress, Pageants and Entertainments of Queen Elizabeth*,

pp.196–7. Montague had spoken against the Act of Supremacy of 1559, arguing that a Catholic settlement was imperative because of the dangers from abroad that would result from Protestantism becoming England's national religion. He warned: 'I fear my prince's sure estate and the ruin of my native country. May I then, being her true subject, see such peril grow to her highness and agree to it?' See Brennan, op. cit., p.5.

68 AGS Estado 693/30.

69 Medina Sidonia to Parma; 'from the Armada before Calais'. 6 August 1588. *CSP Spain (Simancas)*, vol. 4, pp.362–3.

70 BL Sloane MS. 262/62.

71 AGS 594/113. Letters written from the Armada on 25 July about the departure from Corunna did not arrive in Flanders until 2 August. Martin & Parker, op. cit., p.182.

72 Oria *et al.*, *La armada Invencible*, p.42. See also Martin & Parker, op. cit. p.168.

73 Martin & Parker, op. cit., pp.171–2.

74 Parma to Philip II; Bruges, 8 August 1588. *CSP Spain (Simancas)*, vol. 4, p.366.

75 Medina Sidonia to Parma; 'Galleon *San Martin*', 7 August 1588. *CSP Spain (Simancas)*, vol. 4, pp.364–5.

76 AGS 594/113.

77 Laughton, op. cit. vol. 2, p.9. Wynter may have been suffering from wishful thinking; none of the Spanish ships was burnt.

78 *CSP Spain (Simancas)*, vol. 4, pp.443–4. The fireship attack became one of the cheapest tactical achievements of the Tudor period. Replacement value of the eight burnt vessels was later estimated at £5,111 10s.

79 Many believed that Asculi was an illegitimate son of Philip II.

80 Martin & Parker, op. cit., p.175–6.

81 Ibid., p.176.

82 Laughton, op. cit., vol. 1, pp.347–9.

83 *CSP Spain (Simancas)*, vol. 4, pp.377 and 383. The English initially wanted to wait for high tide to float out the *San Lorenzo* but then tried three times to burn her.

CHAPTER 8: **Fleeing for Home**

1 TNA, SP 12/213/64.

2 AGS Estado 594/182. Asculi eventually landed in Dunkirk on 9 August, begging leave to return to the Armada, which Parma refused.

'I am very unhappy to be out of whatever events may happen to the
Armada but as God has ordained otherwise, it cannot be helped and
my only wish is to serve your majesty and do my duty in a manner
worthy of my birth,' he told Philip later.

3 Corbett, *Drake and the Tudor Navy'*, vol. 2, pp.258–9. A roundshot
destroyed the bed 'of a certain gentleman lying weary thereupon' in
the stern of *Revenge.*

4 Laughton, *Defeat of the Spanish Navy*, vol. 2, pp.102–3.

5 Coarse hemp called oakum.

6 *CSP Spain (Simancas)*, vol. 4, p.444.

7 Probably Seymour's *Rainbow.*

8 A small shield.

9 Barratt, *Armada 1588*, p.114.

10 *CSP Spain (Simancas)*, vol. 4, pp.444–5.

11 Ibid., p.401.

12 Barratt, op. cit., p.120.

13 An old measurement of length, approximating to eighteen inches.
Thus eight cubits would be around twelve feet (3.66 m) of water in
the lower decks of the Spanish ships.

14 Barratt, op. cit., pp.112–13. There were reports that Medina Sidonia
had been wounded with a gash on one leg during the Battle of
Gravelines. The captain general had given his boat-cloak to Gongora.
Another of his cloaks covered a wounded ship's boy in his cabin
below. See Mattingly, *Defeat of the Spanish Armada*, p.308.

15 Duro, *La armada Invencible,* vol. 2, p.405.

16 Laughton, op. cit., vol. 2, p.10.

17 Ibid., p.58; Martin & Parker, *The Spanish Armada*, p.179; Duro, op.
cit., vol. 2, pp.271 and 400.

18 Laughton, op. cit., vol.2, pp.10–11.

19 Duro, op. cit., vol. 2, p.407.

20 TNA, SP 12/213/64, f.148.

21 TNA, SP 12/213/65, f.150.

22 Laughton, op. cit., vol. 2, p.40.

23 TNA, SP 12/213/71, f.165.

24 Don Pedro de Mendoza's Biscayan vice-flagship *El Gran Grin* was
also badly damaged by the recoil of her guns.

25 Sir William Borlas, governor of Flushing, to Walsingham, 13 August
1588. *CSP Foreign Elizabeth*, vol. 22, p.104. Another report from a
Spanish spy in London suggested that Browne and his companion
in arms were hanged. Philip noted on the margin of this despatch:

'You will know very well who this is.' *CSP Spain (Simancas)*,vol. 4, p.372. A third report, by Richard Esherton, provost of the Merchant Adventurers' Company in Flushing, said prisoners had told him the two Englishmen had been killed in the fleet action off Gravelines. *CSP Foreign Elizabeth*, vol. 22, p.113.

26 *CSP Foreign Elizabeth*, vol. 22, p.111. There is no 'Tostal' or any name resembling it, among the mayors or sheriffs of London in the sixteenth century up to 1588. The fate of these two Englishmen is unknown.

27 *CSP Spain (Simancas)*, vol. 4, p.445.

28 Duro, op. cit., vol. 2, p.407; Oria *et al.*, *La armada Invencible*, p.325. See also: Martin & Parker, op. cit., p.180.

29 Barratt, op. cit., p.129.

30 Fernandez-Armesto, *The Spanish Armada: The Experience of War*, p.202.

31 *CSP Spain (Simancas)*, vol. 4, p.403.

32 Laughton, op. cit., vol. 2, p.65.

33 BL Add. MS 33,740, f.6. The resolution carried the 'protestation that if our wants of victuals and munitions were supplied, we would pursue them to the furthest they dared [to] have gone'.

34 *CSP Spain (Simancas)*, vol. 4, p.403.

35 BL Add. MS 32,092, f.102.

36 *CSP Spain (Simancas)*, vol. 4, p.384. Valdés was held at the home of Sir Francis Drake's kinsman, Richard Drake, at Esher, Surrey, south-west of London, together with the infantry captains Don Alonso de Çayas and Don Vasco de Mendoça y de Silva. Here, they received 'the best usage and entertainment that may be'. About forty of 'the better sort' of prisoner were lodged in merchants' houses in London. Presumably they gave their parole – promising not to attempt escape. See: Laughton, op. cit., vol. 2, p.136.

37 Laughton, op. cit., vol. 2, pp.24–9.

38 Gerson, 'English Recusants and the Spanish Armada', p.594.

39 *CSP Domestic Elizabeth, 1581–90*, p.527. Sixty-year-old Shrewsbury had impeccable credentials as a supporter of Elizabeth; he had served as keeper of Mary Queen of Scots 1569–83 and, as lord high steward, had presided over the trial of Thomas Howard, Fourth Duke of Norfolk in 1571.

40 *CSP Domestic Elizabeth, 1581–90*, p.526.

41 Laughton, op. cit., vol. 2, p.93. The information came from 'Mr Nevinson', Scott's scoutmaster, who may have misunderstood Drake.

42 Laughton, op. cit., vol. 2, p.54.

43 *CSP Domestic Elizabeth, 1581–90*, p.527.

44 Duro, op. cit., vol. 2, pp.407–8.

45 Medina Sidonia was catching up on his sleep and left orders not to be disturbed. He took no part in the court martials and Cuéllar reported he 'kept [to] his cabin and was very unhappy and did not want anyone to speak to him'.

46 Duro, op. cit., vol. 2, p.337.

47 *CSP Spain (Simancas)*, vol. 4, p.447.

48 Laughton, op. cit., vol. 2, p.54.

49 *CSP Spain (Simancas)*, vol. 4, p.404.

50 Ibid., p.447.

51 Olivares to Philip II; Rome, 8 and 19 August 1588. Ibid., pp.368 and 385.

52 Gritti to the Doge and Senate of Venice; Rome, 20 August 1588. *CSP Venice*, vol. 8, p.379. Sixtus had a pet plan to rebuild the Church of the Holy Sepulchre in Jerusalem in Rome. 'It would be possible to buy it from the Turks but he did not want to prove to the world that he had abandoned all hope of recovering it by [force of] arms,' Gritti reported. The Pope was piqued that the Spanish army 'would be sufficient for this purpose' but was now engaged in a war with England, rather than helping achieve his ambitions in the Holy Land.

53 Philip to Bernardino de Mendoza and Medina Sidonia; El Escorial Palace, San Lorenzo, *CSP Spain (Simancas)*, vol. 4, pp.384–5.

54 Lippomano to the Doge and Senate of Venice; Madrid, 20 August 1588. *CSP Venice*, vol. 8, p.378.

55 Mendoza to Philip II; Paris, 20 August 1588. *CSP Spain (Simancas)*, vol. 4, p.586. Stafford to Walsingham; Paris, 19 August 1588. *CSP Foreign Elizabeth*, vol. 22, p.115.

56 *CSP Spain (Simancas)*, vol. 4, pp.410–11.

57 Mattingly, op. cit., pp.320–1.

58 The Queen's usher was charged with preparing for her reception at any house where she was to stay.

59 *CSP Domestic Elizabeth, 1581–90*, p.525.

60 Ibid., p.529.

61 *The Queenes most excellent Maiestie, being minded in this daungerous time to intertain a certain number of captaines and souldiers for the garding of her royall person ... by this proclamation straightly to charge and command that all and every person and persons ... do observe and keep such rates and prices for all kinds of victuals,*

horsemeate, lodging and other necessaries ... Proclamation signed at St James', 17 August 1588.

62 Leicester means his own quarters at West Tilbury.

63 Christy, 'Queen Elizabeth's visit to Tilbury', p.47.

64 Ibid., p.52.

65 John Stow, *A Summarie of the Chronicles of England ... unto 1590* (London, 1590), p.751. This was the home of Mr Edward Rich, a justice of the peace for Essex.

66 Thomas Deloney, *The Queenes Visiting of the Campe at Tilburie* ... f.3.

67 Karen Hearne, 'Elizabeth I and the Spanish Armada', p.131.

68 BL Harleian MS 6,798, f.87. A late sixteenth-century copy, reprinted in Marcus *et al.*, *Elizabeth I: Collected Works*, pp.325–6.

69 Leicester to the Earl of Shrewsbury; Tilbury Camp, 15 August 1588. LPL MS 3,198, f.284.

70 BL. Cotton MS Otho, E ix, f.180r reprinted in Ellis, *Original Letters ...*, vol. 3, p.142. Was this a rumour deliberately spread on Elizabeth's behalf to add more drama and poignancy to her speech?

71 BL Cotton MS Caligula D, i, f.420.

72 *CSP Domestic Elizabeth, 1581–90*, p.519.

73 Enclosed in a dispatch from Madrid, 29 September 1588. *CSP Venice*, vol. 8, p.395.

CHAPTER 9: **Shipwrecked upon an Alien Shore**

1 *CSP Ireland, Elizabeth, August 1588–September 1592*, p.68. Fenton (1539–1608), a zealous Protestant, had been arrested as a debtor the previous year on the orders of the then governor Sir John Perrot and ignominiously paraded in chains through the Dublin streets. Quickly released, he was knighted in 1589.

2 TNA, SP 63/137 no.1, ii, f.4. The orders fell into the hands of Sir Richard Bingham, governor of the Irish province of Connacht, at the end of September.

3 The wrecks of two possible Armada casualties between Bergen and Sognefjorden in Norway, are marked on a map of the area dated 1590.

4 *CSP Spain (Simancas)*, vol. 4, p.448. The charts supplied to the Armada covered no further north than Scotland's Moray Firth and the Beara Peninsula, north of Bantry Bay in the far south-west of Ireland. See: Martin & Parker, *The Spanish Armada*, p.212.

5 Lime had been mixed with the flour used to make the ship's biscuit which was a staple of the Armada's rations.

6 *CSP Spain (Simancas)*, vol. 4, pp.393–4.

7 Until 1708, it was the capital of the Shetlands.

8 Martin & Parker, op. cit., p.212.

9 BL Cotton MS Caligula D. i, f.292. There had been four pilots on board the *San Martin* – one of them an Englishman – but three had died at sea. See: Mattingly, *Defeat of the Spanish Armada*, p.331.

10 Sir George Carey, governor of the Isle of Wight, reported in early September that a Southampton fishing barque which had arrived from the Shetland Islands had seen 'a very great fleet of monstrous ships … [on] a course to run betwixt Orkney and Fair Isle' on 18 August. Laughton, op. cit., vol. 2, pp.137–8.

11 *CSP Spain (Simancas)*, vol. 4, p.448.

12 Divers from RAF Lossiemouth found a wreck in 1997, five fathoms (30 metres) down off Kinlochbervie, north-west Sutherland, with iron guns and four anchors. It was initially believed to be the remains of an Armada ship, but fragments of Italian majolica pottery, manufactured between 1570 and 1610, suggest that it was a merchantman which sank in the 1590s or even after 1600. See: D.H. Brown and C. Curnow, 'A Ceramic Assemblage from the seabed near Kinlochbervie, Scotland', *International Jnl of Nautical Archaeology*, vol. 33 (2004), p.29 and P. Robertson, 'A Shipwreck near Kinlochbervie, Sutherland, Scotland', ibid., p.14.

13 Martin & Parker, op. cit., p.213.

14 The wreck was discovered by divers in February 1971 and recovered artefacts are on display in the Tower Museum, Union Hall Place, Londonderry.

15 The bishop was executed by the English in 1612.

16 Probably Kelly's captains, Richard and Henry Ovenden, foster-brothers of Hugh O'Neill, Third Earl of Tyrone.

17 AGS GM 262/147 appendix, document 34.

18 AGS Estado K-1567. appendix, document 23.

19 They were well treated by James VI who arranged for them to be clothed and given money. Eventually thirty-two Spanish were taken by two Scottish vessels to Bordeaux and repatriated.

20 *CSP Spain (Simancas)*, vol. 4, p.508.

21 Rodríguez & Aladrén, 'Irish Wrecks of the Great Armada …' in Gallagher & Cruickshank, *God's Obvious Design*, pp.146–7.

22 Mendoza, then Spanish ambassador in London, had arranged his

escape. See: *CSP Spain (Simancas)*, vol. 4, pp.454–5.

23 This was most likely William Stacey. His brother-in-law, Captain Alonso de la Serna, a prisoner in London's Bridewell gaol, died at the end of September, probably from typhus.

24 *CSP Ireland Elizabeth, August 1588–September 1592*, pp.26 and 28; Martin & Parker, op. cit., p.216.

25 Ibid., p.29.

26 Ibid., p.6.

27 Ibid., p.35; Martin & Parker, op. cit., p.216.

28 *CSP Ireland Elizabeth, August 1588–September 1592*, p.43.

29 Gallagher & Cruickshank, *God's Obvious Design*, pp.238–9.

30 Evelyn Hardy, *Survivors of the Armada*, p.41 and Robert Gibbings, *Lovely is the Lee* (London, 1945), pp.22 *et seq*.

31 Falls, *Elizabeth's Irish Wars*, p.166. A gallowglass was a Scottish professional soldier in the service of Irish clan chieftains. Douglas (*Downfall of the Spanish Armada ...*) considers this story dubious as M'Cabb's employer, William Burke, held seventy-two Spanish prisoners including a bishop, a friar and three noblemen.

32 Rodríguez & Aladrén, op. cit., p.145.

33 Clancy to Sir Richard Bingham; fields of Liscannor, 16 September 1588. *CSP Ireland Elizabeth, August 1588–September 1592*, pp.29–30.

34 Mutton Island (*Oileán Caorach*) is so named because its shape resembles that of a leg of mutton. Spanish Point is directly north-west of the island.

35 Martin & Parker, op. cit., pp.216–17.

36 Ibid., p.217.

37 Ibid., p.218; Rodríguez & Aladrén, op. cit., p.154. The wreck of the *Santa María de la Rosa* was discovered in 1968 and its remains showed that she had hit the rock amidships which tore out her keel when she dragged on her anchor.

38 Four hundred Spanish prisoners were executed at Galway prison.

39 Douglas, *Downfall of the Spanish Armada in Ireland*, p.118.

40 Bagwell, *Ireland under the Tudors*, vol. 3, p.179.

41 TNA, SP 63/139/25, f.83.

42 Martin & Parker, op. cit., p.222; Rodríguez & Aladrén, op. cit., pp.150–1.

43 *CSP Ireland Elizabeth, August 1588 – September 1592*, p.97.

44 The shipwreck is depicted on the reverse of banknotes issued by the First Trust Bank in Northern Ireland. The wreck was discovered by

divers in June 1967 and six gold chains recovered – including one 8 feet (2.78 m) long – belonging to Spanish officers. There were also forty-five pieces of gold and jewellery, including a ring, inscribed in Spanish: 'I have nothing more to give you.' The *Girona* artefacts are now in the Ulster Museum.

45 *CSP Ireland Elizabeth, August 1588–September 1592*, p.68.

46 AGS GM 244.42 Appendix, document 26; AGS Estado 2219/64, Appendix document 29.

47 TNA, SP 63/139/25, f.83.

48 Martin & Parker, op. cit., p.219.

49 Bagwell, op. cit., vol. 3, p.176.

50 Gallagher & Cruickshank, *God's Obvious Design*, pp. 238–9. The monastery was the Abbey of Staad, allegedly founded by St Molaise, two miles (3.22 km) west of Grange and one and a half miles (2.5 km) from Streedagh Strand. The west wall of the nave is still standing with a doorway, but coastal erosion has eaten away the edge of the low sea cliff to just 6.5 yards (6 m) from the ruined wall. Archaeological investigation in 2000 suggested an ecclesiastical presence at Staad to at least the latter part of the first millennium AD and perhaps earlier.

51 *CSP Ireland Elizabeth, August 1588–September 1592*, p.93.

52 Ibid., p.61.

53 Bagwell, op. cit., vol. 3, pp.183–4 and 188. In revenge, the Spanish beheaded four hundred Dutch prisoners.

54 *CSP Ireland Elizabeth, August 1588–September 1592*, p.47.

55 Rodríguez & Aladrén, op. cit., p.152.

56 The site of the wreck is at National Grid reference HZ 2117 7007.

57 A writer describing Fair Isle 150 years later claimed the baldness came from Scales – the genetic skin disease *Ichtyosis vulgaris* although it seems more likely to have been scalp *psoriasis* or *alopecia areto*. Monteith, *Description of the Isles of Orkney ...*, p.53.

58 Monteith, op. cit., p.54.

59 Rodríguez & Aladrén, op. cit., p.155; Martin & Parker, op. cit., p.215.

60 AGS Estado K-1568, document 140.

61 *CSP Ireland Elizabeth, August 1588–September 1592*, p.108. One gold wedge eventually was sent to Queen Elizabeth.

62 Martin & Parker, op. cit., p.224.

63 The site of the wreck is at National Grid reference NM 51 55.

64 *Certain Advertisements out of Ireland, concerning the Losses and Distress happened to the Spanish Navy, upon the West Coasts of Ireland in their Voyage intended from the Northern Isles beyond*

Scotland toward Spain, printed at London by J. Vautrollier for Richard Field, 1588.

65 *Hardwick Papers*, vol. 1, pp.363–4.

66 *CSP Ireland Elizabeth, August 1588–September 1592*, p.38.

67 Quinn, 'Spanish Armada Prisoners Escape from Ireland', pp.117–18; Hatfield House CP 186/2; TNA, SP 63/137/17 and SP 63/149/30.

68 AGS GA 247 and 249.

69 Rodríguez & Aladrén, op. cit., pp.156–7.

70 *CSP Ireland Elizabeth, August 1588–September 1592*, p.38.

71 Rodríguez & Aladrén, op. cit., p.158.

72 *CSP Ireland Elizabeth, August 1588–September 1592*, p.38.

73 *CSP Spain (Simancas)*, vol. 4, p.465.

74 The seventh crusade in 1250.

75 Martin & Parker, op. cit., pp.238–9.

76 *CSP Spain (Simancas)*, vol. 4, pp.432–3.

77 *CSP Venice*, vol. 8, p.390.

CHAPTER 10: 'God Be Praised for all His Works'

1 *Harleian Miscellany*, vol. 1, p.157. Marten was the sewer in Elizabeth's privy chamber.

2 Waters, 'The Elizabethan Navy and the Armada Campaign', p.125.

3 Sigüenza, *La fundación de Monasterio ...*, p.120.

4 *CSP Spain (Simancas)*, vol. 4, p.467.

5 Martin & Parker, *The Spanish Armada*, p.242.

6 *CSP Ireland Elizabeth August 1588–September 1592*, p.127.

7 Martin & Parker, op. cit., pp.241–2.

8 Meyer, *England and the Catholic Church ...*, p.340. Visible signs of mourning were forbidden in Spain that November. See *Fugger Newsletters* (1924), p.130.

9 *CSP Venice*, vol. 8, p.404.

10 *CSP Domestic Elizabeth, Addenda*, p.255.

11 *CSP Venice*, vol. 8, p.396.

12 Ibid., p.411.

13 Martin & Parker, op. cit., pp.240–1.

14 *CSP Venice*, vol. 8, p.405.

15 Ibid., p.399. However, some reports suggested that Philip refused requests by Medina Sidonia to come to court: 'He was forbidden and ordered to go home as his majesty had no desire to speak to him.' See: *Fugger Newsletters* (1926), p.182.

16 *CSP Ireland Elizabeth, August 1588–September 1592*, pp.126–7. The

information came from Edward Walsh who had arrived in Waterford from Bilbao. 'The ships' companies were so weak that they were taken to their lodgings in wagons.'

17 Pierson, *Commander of the Armada*, pp.74–6.
18 *Fugger Newsletters* (1926), p.181.
19 *CSP Spain (Simancas)*, vol. 4, p.466.
20 Ibid., p.474.
21 *CSP Venice*, vol. 8, p.406.
22 Ibid., p.412.
23 Ibid., p.407.
24 *CSP Foreign Elizabeth*, vol. 22, p.104.
25 Ibid., p.113.
26 Laughton, *Defeat of the Spanish Armada*, vol. 2, p.150. Wynter told Walsingham that Parma had 'retired in some haste with certain troops of horse from Bruges up into Brabant … fearing some sudden revolt'. The sailors who had been recruited to serve in the invasion fleet 'run away daily, many of whom he has caught … and imprisoned sharply'. Ibid., p.150.
27 *CSP Venice*, vol. 8, p.399.
28 Ibid., p.402.
29 Ibid., p.407.
30 *CSP Spain (Simancas)*, vol. 4, p.474.
31 AGS Estado 1261/115; 6 September 1588.
32 Martin & Parker, op. cit., p.254.
33 *CSP Spain (Simancas)*, vol. 4, p.502.
34 Parker, 'The Dreadnought Revolution', pp.278–9.
35 Martin & Parker, op. cit., pp.189–90 and 194.
36 Thompson, 'Spanish Armada Guns', p.358.
37 For an excellent detailed discussion on Spanish artillery shortcomings in both equipment and technique in the Armada ships, see Martin & Parker, op. cit., pp.184–205.
38 Laughton, *Defeat of the Spanish Armada*, vol. 2, pp.250–3.
39 TNA, E 351/225 and AO1/1686/23.
40 For full discussion on the artillery, see Thompson, 'Spanish Armada Guns', pp.355–71.
41 *Fugger Newsletters,* 10 November 1588 (1924), p.182.
42 *CSP Domestic Elizabeth, 1581–90*, p.557.
43 Martin & Parker, op. cit., p.251.
44 Meyer, op. cit., p.341.
45 *CSP Venice*, vol. 8, p.401. Mendoza had been operated on some years

earlier for a cataract. He said he was so blind that he could 'only just see objects dimly, as if through a dark glass'.

46 *CSP Spain (Simancas)*, vol. 4, p.470.

47 Mocenigo to the Doge and Senate of Venice; Paris, 19 August 1588. *CSP Venice*, vol. 8, p.378.

48 Meyer, op. cit., p.342. According to Plutarch, Caesar wrote these words in a letter in 47 BC announcing his victory at the battle of Zela in northern Turkey at the end of the Pontic campaign.

49 Duro, *La armada Invencible*, vol. 1, p.217.

50 *CSP Foreign Elizabeth*, vol. 22, p.111. They claimed that Philip had sent him 'the crown and sceptre of England, blessed by the Pope'.

51 On 27 September a worried Ralph Lane wrote to Burghley expressing his 'no small grief [that] he understands her majesty is displeased with him for sending so great a list of the captains and officers remaining in her majesty's pay'. He explained that when the army was disbanded, the officers were ordered to remain in readiness. *CSP Domestic Elizabeth, 1581–90*, p.545.

52 *The Queenes Maiestie being given to vnderstand that diuers souldiers vpon the dissoluing of the campe at Tilberie in the countie of Essex have in the way homeward sold diuerse their armors and weapons* ..., St James' Palace, 25 August 1588. The parsimony was widespread. Elizabeth also faced a mutiny by her troops forming the garrison at Ostend whose only lodging was 'lying upon straw, the better part scant, much less fire, not so much as a candle to answer the alarms'. They assured the queen of their 'readiness to yield up their lives in her service' but prayed 'they may be allowed six months' pay to cherish themselves and supply their wants'. *CSP Foreign Elizabeth*, vol. 22, p.166.

53 Laughton, op. cit., vol. 2, pp.138–41.

54 Ibid., p.96.

55 Ibid., p.97.

56 In November, Francis Cotton told Burghley that he had been 'solicited, even with tears, to represent the lamentable distress of the men engaged on the [defensive] works at Portsmouth who had not received one penny since April last'. *CSP Domestic Elizabeth, 1581–90*, p.561.

57 Laughton, op. cit., vol. 2, p.159.

58 Fernandez-Armesto, *The Spanish Armada: The Experience of War*, p.226.

59 BL Lansdowne MS 144, f.53.

60 Or was it a pejorative slang reference to those depicted? The coarse term 'prick' for the male member is known to have been used in

standard English in 1592 and the possible *double entendre* may be an example of bawdy Tudor humour.

61 A silver medal with the queen's head on the obverse may have been awarded to her commanders in the Armada campaign. On the reverse is the image of a bay tree, believed to be immune from lightning strikes. This symbolises Elizabeth herself who protects the island on which the tree stands while lightning destroys a ship in the background.

62 Meaning they feared no danger.

63 *CSP Spain (Simancas)*, vol. 4, p.419. Messia was sent to England to spy by Santa Cruz.

64 Somerset, *Elizabeth I*, p.595.

65 *CSP Spain (Simancas)*, vol. 4, p.420. The previous week Messia had seen Leicester riding through the London streets 'splendidly accompanied and [showing] every appearance of perfect health, as if he would have lived for five years'. A man called Smith claimed to have killed Leicester by bewitching him, but the Privy Council released him from custody after deciding that the earl died more prosaically from malaria.

66 Longleat House MS DU/Vol. 3, ff.91–102.

67 *CSP Spain (Simancas)*, vol. 4, p.431.

68 *CSP Venice*, vol. 8, p.404.

69 Nichols, *Progresses ...*, vol. 3, p.537.

70 *APC*, vol. 16, p.292.

71 Nichols, *Progresses ...*, vol. 3, p.540.

72 *SAC*, vol. 23 (1871), p.114.

73 L.F. Salzman, *The Town Book of Lewes 1542–1701* (Sussex Record Society, 1946), p.36.

74 R. Wilson (ed.), *Three Lords and Three Ladies of London* (London, 1912).

75 Raymond, *Pamphlets and Pamphleteering ...*, p.119.

76 *A Skeltonical Salutation*, published by T. Cooke (London, 1589), without pagination, but ff. 3–4.

77 The prick of a horseman's spur.

78 Deloney, *A joyful new Ballad ...*, 1588.

79 Richard Leigh had been imprisoned in the Tower in 1588. Aged twenty-seven, he was executed at Tyburn on 30 August that year, together with five other Catholics: Edward Shelley, Richard Martin, Richard Lloyd, John Roche and Margaret Ward. Leigh was beatified in 1929.

80 Anon., *Copy of a Letter sent out of England ...*, 1588.

81 For discussion on the Armada portraits, see: Sir Roy Strong, *Portraits*

of Queen Elizabeth I (Oxford, 1963).

82 Nicholas, *Progresses* ..., vol. 3, p.539.

83 Leahy, *Elizabethan Triumphal Processions*, pp.75–6.

CHAPTER 11: **The English Armada**

1 LPL, MS 647, ff.235–8.

2 Wernham, *Expedition of Sir John Norris and Sir Francis Drake* ..., p.xiii; 'Queen Elizabeth and the Portugal Expedition', p.3; F.C. Dietz, *The Exchequer in Elizabeth's Reign* (Northampton, Massachusetts, 1923), pp.84–6 and 100–1.

3 F.C. Dietz, *English Public Finance 1558–1640* (London, 1932), p.59. The Parliament summoned in February 1589 voted two new subsidies and taxes which would bring in £280,000 over the next four years.

4 Wernham, 'Queen Elizabeth', p.5.

5 Cambridge University Library Hh. 6.10, ff.1–59.

6 *CSP Domestic Elizabeth, 1581–90*, p.545.

7 Ibid., p.551.

8 Mendoza to Philip II; Paris, 29 September 1588. *CSP Spain (Simancas)*, vol. 4, p.454.

9 Ibid., p.470.

10 The Spanish abandoned the siege of Bergen-op-Zoom on 3 November and Parma sent his troops into winter quarters.

11 *CSP Domestic Elizabeth, Addenda,* p.254; *CSP Venice*, vol. 8, pp.426 and 435.

12 *Hardwick State Papers*, vol. 1, pp.365 and 367–8.

13 *CSP Foreign, Elizabeth*, vol. 22, p.227.

14 Wernham, *Expedition* ..., p.xxix.

15 BL Lansdowne MS 103, f.93.

16 *CSP Spain (Simancas)*, vol. 4, p.525.

17 *APC*, vol. 18, p.297.

18 HMC Southampton, p.126.

19 *CSP Domestic Elizabeth, 1581–90*, p.568.

20 Rowse, *Tudor Cornwall*, p.398.

21 Wernham, *Expedition*, p.xxi. The owners of the Dutch flyboats submitted a petition to Drake and Norris 'not to be compelled to join in the expedition as their ships were unprovided with victuals and other things necessary for such a voyage'. Furthermore, the ships' detention was, they said, 'a violation of the treaty between her majesty and the States' of Holland. *CSP Domestic Elizabeth, 1581–90*, p.591.

22 Rowse, op. cit., p.399.

23 Another name for armour.

24 Wernham, *Expedition*, pp.126–7.

25 Wernham, 'Queen Elizabeth ...', p.24.

26 BL Add. MS 12,497, f.183.

27 Hatfield House CP 18/82. 'From my study, some few days before my departure' and endorsed: 'The Earl of Essex before his departure to the voyage of Portugal.'

28 *CSP Domestic Elizabeth, 1581–90*, p.592.

29 Contarini to the Doge and Senate; Madrid, 24 May 1589. *CSP Venice*, vol. 8, p.439.

30 Wernham, *Expedition*, p.222.

31 Ibid., p.146. Thirty were killed by the fall of masonry.

32 Ibid., p.153.

33 *CSP Venice*, vol. 8, pp.438–9.

34 Wernham, *Expedition*, p.xlv.

35 Somewhat lamely, Norris and Drake told the Privy Council that they had met up with Essex off Cape Finisterre but were 'unable to send him home earlier as they could not spare the services of the *Swiftsure*'. *CSP Domestic Elizabeth, 1581–90*, p.604.

36 BL Stowe MS 159, f.370.

37 *CSP Spain (Simancas)*, vol. 4, p.554.

38 *CSP Domestic Elizabeth, 1581–90*, p.603.

39 Corbett, *Drake and the Tudor Navy*, vol. 2, p.326.

40 Wernham, *Expedition*, p.137.

41 Ibid., p.182.

42 MacCaffrey, *Elizabeth I: War and Politics 1588–1603*, p.87.

43 *CSP Spain (Simancas)*, vol. 4, p.549.

44 *APC*, vol. 18, p.49.

45 Leahy, *Elizabethan Triumphal Processions*, p.80.

46 Hatfield House, CP 18/54.

47 BL Lansdowne MS 59, f.105.

48 A fother was the equivalent of a cartload in the sixteenth century, or nineteen and a half hundredweight (990.65 kg).

49 Hatfield House, CP 18/26.

50 Rodger, *The Safeguard of the Sea*, p.274.

51 *CSP Venice*, vol.8, p.437.

Epilogue

1 Giovanni Mocenigo to Doge and Senate of Venice; San Dié, 21 November 1588. *CSP Venice*, vol. 8, p.413.

2 Charlotte Sneyd (transl.), *A Relation ... of the Island of England about the year 1500* CS (London, 1847), pp.24–5.

3 S. Daultrey, 'The Weather of NE Europe during the Summer and Autumn of 1588' in Gallagher & Cruickshank, *God's Obvious Design*, pp.114–16 and 138.

4 Daultrey, op. cit., pp.117–36.

5 See: Douglas, Lamb and Loader, 'A Meteorological Study ...', 1978.

6 *CSP Spain (Simancas)*, vol. 4, p.450.

7 They had been captured with Pedro de Valdés when the *Rosario* surrendered.

8 *CSP Spain (Simancas)*, vol. 4, pp.438 and 455.

9 Ibid., p.551.

10 Martin & Parker, *Spanish Armada*, p.226.

11 Ibid., p.227.

12 The money was held in a large chest. An iron-strapped replacement for the original, made in 1623, is on display in the museum of Chatham's Royal Naval Dockyard. It has five locks, each key held by a different person. The 'Chatham Chest' was amalgamated with the Greenwich naval hospital in 1802. Its minutes and accounts for 1594–1987 are held in the Medway Archives and Local History Centre in Chatham under the reference CH 108.

13 Keevil, *Medicine and the Navy*, vol. 1, p.54.

14 *CSP Venice*, vol. 8, p.414.

15 Both ships ran aground before being set ablaze by their captains. Sir Walter Raleigh described graphically how they grounded, 'tumbling into the sea heaps of soldiers so thick as if coals had been poured out of a sack in many portholes at once. Some were drowned and some stuck in the mud.' Then they blew up, 'many Spanish drowned themselves; many, half burnt, leapt into the water, very many hanging by the ropes' ends by the ships' sides, under the water, even to the lips; many swimming with grievous wounds, stricken under water and put out of their pain ... [There was] a huge fire and such tearing of the ordnance in the *Great Philip* ... if any man had a desire to see Hell itself, it was there most lively coloured.' See: Graham, *The Spanish Armadas*, p.214.

16 Two English sailors were hanged for molesting a woman in Cadiz and Essex chivalrously allowed 1,500 nuns to leave the city. 'Such a gentleman has not been seen before among heretics,' Philip observed.

17 Pierson, *Commander of the Armada*, p.212.

18 *CSP Spain (Simancas)*, vol. 4, p.635.

19 The burial registers for St Paul's church has this record by the vicar John Tremaine: 'the twenty-third day July, the year of our Lord God 1595, on the which day the church, tower, bells and all other things pertaining to the same, together with the houses and goods was burned and spoiled by the Spaniards in the said parish, being Wednesday ...' He recorded the burials of Jenkin Keigwyn of Mousehole 'being killed by the Spaniards' and 'James of Newlyn was slain by enemies ... likewise Teek Cornall'.

20 McGrath & Rowe, 'Anstruther Analysed ...', pp.8–9.

21 Parmiter, 'Imprisonment of Papists ...', pp.29–30.

22 Brennan, 'Papists and Patriotism ...', p.10.

23 See LPL MS 250, ff.170–5.

24 Hutchinson, *House of Treason*, pp.217–18; 220–1.

25 Quinn, *Sir Francis Drake as seen by his Contemporaries*, pp.13–14.

26 His soft organs were buried in St Andrew's church Plymouth and his body was taken to London and buried in St Giles-without-Cripplegate.

27 Mattingly, *The Defeat of the Spanish Armada*, p.343.

28 Barratt, op. cit., pp.244–9.

29 Hutchinson, *Elizabeth's Spymaster*, pp.253–4.

30 Michael Graves, *Profiles in Power: Burghley* (London, 1998), p.100.

31 Parotitis is inflammation of the parotid glands, the largest of the salivary glands at the back of the mouth. Elizabeth must have suffered intense pain when salivating or eating – hence her refusal to consume any food. See: Clifford Brewer, *The Death of Kings* (London, 2000), p.151 and Graham, op. cit., p.273.

32 Rex, *The Tudors*, p.235.

33 Philip III's ratification of the Treaty of London, dated 15 June 1605, is in TNA, E30/1705.

BIBLIOGRAPHY

LIST OF ABBREVIATIONS

Add. MS Additional Manuscript

AGS CMC Archivo General de Simancas, Mayor de Cuentas

AGS CS Archivo General de Simancas, Contaduria del Sueldo

AGS Estado Archivo General de Simancas, Secció de Estado

AGS GA Archivo General de Simancas, Guerra Antigua

AGS GM Archivo General de Simancas, Guerra y Marina

APC Acts of Privy Council

Arch. Cant. Archaeologia Cantiana, journal of the Kent Archaeological Society

BL British Library

Bull. Bulletin

CP Cecil Papers, Salisbury MSS, Hatfield House, Hertfordshire

CRS Catholic Record Society

CS Camden Society

CSP Domestic Calendar of States Papers, Domestic, in reign of Elizabeth

CSP Foreign Calendar of State Papers, Foreign, in reign of Elizabeth

CSP Ireland Calendar of State Papers, Ireland, in reign of Elizabeth

CSP Milan Calendar of State Papers, Milan

CSP Spain Calendar of State Papers, Spain preserved in ... the Archives of Simancas

CSP Venice Calendar State Papers, Venice

CSP Vatican Calendar of State Papers preserved in Rome, in the Vatican archives

ed. edited, editor(s)

EHR English Historical Review

fn footnote

HMC Historical MSS Commission

HJ Historical Journal

Jnl journal

LPL Lambeth Palace Library

MM Mariner's Mirror, journal of the Society for Nautical Research

MS/MSS manuscript/manuscripts

NRS Naval Records Society

n.s. new series

ODNB Oxford Dictionary of National Biography

r recto

rev. revised

SAC Sussex Archaeological Collections, journal of Sussex Archaeological Society

STC Short Title Catalogue

Trans Transactions

TNA The National Archives, Kew, Surrey

TRHS Transactions Royal Historical Society

v verso

vol.(s) volume(s)

PRIMARY SOURCES
Manuscript

MINISTERIO DE CULTURA, SPAIN
ARCHIVO GENERAL DE SIMANCAS, VALLADOLID

Contaduria Mayor de Cuentas (AGS CMC)

2a/772 – Papers of *San Francisco,* vice-flagship of Armada's Andalusian squadron, with Medina Sidonia's new ration orders; 9 July 1588.

Contaduria del Sueldo (AGS CS)

2a/278 f.617 – Account of putrid provisions thrown overboard in the Armada; 30 June 1588.

Secció de Estado (AGS Estado)

455/320–1 Copy of Medina's dispatch to Parma of 10 June 1588, annotated by Philip II.

594/113 – Parma to Philip II; Bruges, 7 August 1588.

594/182 – Prince of Asculi to Philip II; Dunkirk, 12 August 1588.

693/30 – Complaint by the town of Emden about the removal of navigation marks from the 'banks of Flanders', 13 September 1588.

2,219/164, Appendix, document 29: Irish merchants Philip Roche and Edward Walsh; Waterford, 5 January 1589.

K-1568/185, Appendix, document 23 – Testimony of the boatswain of *Trinidad Valencera*; London, 3 December 1588.

 – 140 – Letter from Captain Marolín de Juan; Le Havre, 27 December 1588.

Guerra Antigua (AGS GA)

225/55–6 – Don Pedro de Valdés to Philip II; Corunna, 15 and 19 July 1588.

247 and 249 – Documents on Armada losses sent to Philip II by Beltrán del Salton; 10 April 1589.

Guerra y Marina (AGS GM)

244/42, Appendix, document 26 – Pedro Combarro to Domingo de Berganza; Santander, 1 January 1589.

262/147, Appendix, document 34 – Testimony of Juan Lázaro, helmsman of the *Trinidad Valencera*.

BODLEIAN LIBRARY, OXFORD

Douce Prints

a.48 – *A Declaration of the Sentence and deposition of Elizabeth the vsurper and pretensed Quene of Englande;* Antwerp, 1588 (Mutilated).

BRITISH LIBRARY, LONDON

Additional MSS

12,497, f.183 – Earl of Essex to the Privy Council; April 1589.

12,505 – Proceedings of a General Court held on board the *Elizabeth Bonaventure*, 30 May 1587 before Sir Francis Drake on mutineers of the ship *Golden Lion*, commanded by Captain Marchant.

21,565, f.21 – List of bishops within the Province of Canterbury 'that have sent certificates of their provision for horse and armour'.

32,092, f.102 – Privy Council letter to John Whitgift, Archbishop of Canterbury, seeking public prayers against the success of the Armada; Richmond Palace, 2 August 1588.

33,740, ff.2–3 – Privy Council letter to Lord High Admiral Howard that a 'good number of the best and choicest shot of the trained bands' of Kent should be sent immediately to the coast 'to double man the ships'; Richmond Palace, 4 August 1588.

> f.6 – Resolution of a council of war of English naval commanders 'to follow and pursue the Spanish fleet until we have cleared our own coast ...'; 11 August 1588.

44,839 – Map of Thames Estuary from Lambeth to Tilbury Hope made by Robert Adam, Surveyor of the Works, showing the route taken by Elizabeth I from Westminster to Tilbury Fort, August 1588.

48,027 (Yelverton MS 31), ff.83–125*v* – Papers relating to the imprisonment, trial and execution of Thomas Howard, Fourth Duke of Norfolk, 1570–2.

> – ff.242–247*v* – Documents relating to Dr William Parry, including two accounts of his execution and speech on the scaffold.
>
> – ff.249–251*v* – Bond of Association for the safety of Elizabeth (19 October 1584) and oath of allegiance to Bond of Association allegedly signed by Mary Queen of Scots at Wingfield, 5 January 1584.
>
> – ff.636–650*v* – Papers relating to the execution of Mary Queen of Scots, 1587, including a pencil-and-ink drawing of the execution at Fotheringay Castle on 8 February at f.650.
>
> ff.654–658*v* – 'A Report of the manner of the execution of the Scottish Queen performed 8 February Anno 1586 in the great hall within the castle of Fotheringay, with relation of speeches uttered and actions happening in the said execution, with the delivery of the said Scottish Queen to Mr Thomas Andrews esquire, sheriff of the county of Northampton, unto the end of the said execution' by Richard Fletcher, Dean of Peterborough.

48,029 (Yelverton MS 33) – f.81 – Confession of Sir Thomas Gerard; 25

October 1588.

> – f.102 – Confession of William Bennet, priest, a prisoner in the Counter gaol, Wood Street. 16 October 1588.

62,935 – Map of warning beacons in Kent by W[illiam] L[ambarde]; August 1585.

63,742, ff.99–105 – Estimates of the annual revenues of Spain, c.1584–9.

Cotton MSS

Caligula B v, f.159 – Instrument of an Association for the Preservation of the Person of Queen Elizabeth I, signed at Hampton Court, 19 October 1584.

> – f.175v–176 – Account of the execution of Mary Queen of Scots at Fotheringay Castle, 8 February 1586.

Caligula C ix, f.2 – Letter from Elizabeth to James VI of Scotland denying any responsibility for the death of his mother, Mary Queen of Scots; 14 February 1587.

Caligula D i, f.292 – Letter from William Ashby to Sir Francis Walsingham describing the seizure of Scottish and Dutch fishing boats in the Shetland islands; Edinburgh, 18 September 1588.

f.420 – Letter from James VI of Scotland to Elizabeth; Edinburgh, 4 August 1588.

> – f.420 – Letter from Elizabeth to James VI of Scotland; London, August 1588.

Julius F x, ff.111–17. 'A Relation of Proceedings' – possible official English account of the action against the Armada.

Otho E ix, f.180v – Edward Radcliffe to Earl of Sussex, reporting Elizabeth's visit to the camp at Tilbury, Essex; Burntwood, Essex, 20 August 1588.

f.185r – Letter from Lord High Admiral Howard to Sir Francis Walsingham, requesting reinforcements from Portsmouth; 'from aboard her majesty's good ship, *Ark Royal*, 1 August 1588.

f.187 – Letter from William Hawkins, mayor of Plymouth, to the Privy Council providing news of the Spanish Armada.

f.214v – Letter from Walsingham to Burghley, arranging for more gunpowder and shot to be sent to Lord High Admiral Howard; 4 August 1588.

Vespasian C viii, f.207 – Letters to Sir Francis Walsingham from 'Mr Hunter of Lisbon' describing his imprisonment in that city and the armaments there; 10 February 1589.

C xiv, f.583 – Order to remove the Earl of Northumberland's banner and stall plate as a Knight of the Garter; St George's Chapel, Windsor, 27

November 1569.

C xvi, f.145 – Will of Mary Queen of Scots, drawn up at Sheffield in February 1577 by her secretary Claude Nau, with corrections in her own hand.

Egerton MSS

2,541, f.1 – 'Queene Elizabeth's whole army at sea against the Spanish forces in anno 1588; list of ships, crews and names of captains'.

Harleian MSS

167, f.104 – Sir Francis Drake's account of his raid on Cadiz in a letter to John Foxe, 'preacher'; written in *Elizabeth Bonaventure*, 7 May 1587.
   – f.104r. Account of Drake's raid on Cadiz by one of his crew, probably Robert Leng.

288, f.187 – Sir William Stafford to Sir Francis Walsingham; Paris, 25 April 1588.

290, f.88 – Letter from Mary Queen of Scots to the Duke of Norfolk urging him to escape from house arrest; 31 January 1571.

295, f.190 – Letter from the English spy 'B.C.' on the preparations of the Spanish Armada; Madrid, 28 May 1588.

296, f.44 – 'Pompeo Pellegrini' (alias Anthony Standen) to Jacomo Manucci, on the results of Drake's raid on Cadiz, 3 July 1587.
   – f.46 – Letter, partly in cipher, in the same hand as 'Pompeo Pellegrini', signed 'B.C.' and endorsed 'from Mr Standen' on the verso; Florence, 28 August 1587.
   – f.48 – Letter from Stephen Paule to Sir Francis Walsingham warning of an attempt to poison Elizabeth; Venice, 7 November 1587.

360, article 38, ff.65r and v – Plan to intern English Catholics in ten castles, in Sir Francis Walsingham's handwriting, undated but probably before spring 1579.

6,798, f.87 – Speech by Elizabeth I to her troops at West Tilbury, Essex, 19 August 1588.

6,990, f.44 – Proclamation by the Earls of Northumberland and Westmorland; Darlington, 16 November 1569.

6,991, ff.31–33. Memorandum on the 1569 Rebellion written by Lord Huntingdon to Cecil; York, 10 October 1573.

6,993, f.125 – Letter from Sir Francis Walsingham in which he dismisses reports of Spanish preparations to invade England as 'Spanish brag', March 1586.

6,994, f.76 – Letter from Sir Francis Walsingham to Burghley, calling for Drake to attack the Spanish bullion fleets and cautioning

Burghley to protect the true identity of his agent Pompeo Pellegrini; 26 July 1587.

7,190, article 2, ff.125r–126r – Eighteenth-century copy of Elizabeth I's letter to Mary I from the Tower, 17 March 1554.

Lansdowne MSS

43, no.3, 3ff – Letter from William Parry to Lord Burghley; Fetter Lane, London, 2 August 1584.

48, f.120 – Proclamation ordering markets to be supplied with foodstuffs 'at reasonable prices'; Greenwich, 2 January 1587.

50, articles 19–21 – Letters from Henry Radcliffe, Fourth Earl of Sussex about a planned rebellion by Catholics 'in the country near Portsmouth, Hampshire; June 1586.

52, article 31 – Captain William Borough's defence against the charges laid against him by Sir Francis Drake, May 1587.

– article 39 – Captain William Borough's account of his 'misunderstanding' with Sir Francis Drake, 30 April 1587.

– article 40 – *Discourse of what courses were best taken for the resistance of the Spanish navy*, by William Borough: 26 February 1589.

53, article 3, 3ff – Speech of Mr William Parry at his execution; Great Palace Yard, Westminster, 2 March 1585.

– f.23 – Account of the fighting off Cadiz by Francisco de Benito de Maiora; St Mary's Port, 'nine of the clock at night', 29 April 1587.

– article 79 – Account of Anne Burnell who claimed to be the daughter of Mary I and Philip of Spain.

56, f.175 – Agreement between Sir Francis Drake and the London Merchant Adventurers covering the supply of ships and the division of spoil for the attack on Cadiz; signed 28 March 1587.

59, f.105 – Proclamation forbidding any who served with the expedition to Spain and Portugal from approaching the royal court; 1589.

100, f.98 – Drake's plan for his campaign in Galicia and the Caribbean in 1585.

103, f.93 – Authority to Anthony Ashley to keep a 'true journal' of proceedings during the expedition to Spain and Portugal; 1589.

Sloane MSS

262/62 – Diary of the English peace commissioners in Flanders.

Stowe MSS

159, f.370 – Letter from Ralph Lane describing the English landing at Peniche, Portugal, 26 May 1589.

UNIVERSITY OF CAMBRIDGE LIBRARY, CAMBRIDGE

MSS
Hh.6.10. ff.1–59 – Disputation of Puritan Ministers in London; November 1588.

GLOUCESTERSHIRE ARCHIVES, GLOUCESTER

Gloucester Borough Records
GBR/H/2/1, f.1 – Privy Council letter to Lord Chandos, seeking the appointment of a provost marshal for the arrest and imprisonment of 'idle vagabonds', 1588.

HATFIELD HOUSE, HERTFORDSHIRE
MSS OF THE MARQUIS OF SALISBURY

Cecil Papers
13/77 – Mary Queen of Scots signed bond 'to be an enemy to all those that attempt anything against Queen Elizabeth's life'; Wingfield, 5 January 1585.

16/17 – Circumstances of the execution of Mary Queen of Scots, bearing Burghley's holograph.

17/2 – Instructions to Dr Dale, negotiating a peace treaty with Spain.

17/23 – Depositions by two Dutch sailors who served with the Spanish Armada.

18/26 – Letter from the Privy Council to Lord Burghley seeking licences to export corn, 1589.

18/54 – Appeal by twenty-five captains who had served on the expedition to Portugal for further service.

18/82 – Letter from Robert, Earl of Essex, to Vice-Chamberlain Heneage.

162/148 – Advertisements of merchants 'touching practises against England', [1583].

164/17 – Account of execution of Mary Queen of Scots.

166/83 – Numbers and names of ships that served against the Spanish Armada.

186/2 – Claim for compensation, following the escape of thirty Spanish prisoners from Dublin Bay in the stolen pinnance, *Swallow*, 1588. (Misdated in HMC Salisbury, vol. XIC (London 1923), p.813, as 1601).

Maps
CPM Supp.11 – *Map of Ulster and his nearest nigthbores.*

INNER TEMPLE LIBRARY, CITY OF LONDON

Petyt MSS

Series 538, vol. 43, ff.304–14 – *An Antidote against Jesuitism'* written in Burghley's hand; draft dated 158– but probably 1583. Final version is in vol. 37, ff.177 *et seq.*

LAMBETH PALACE LIBRARY, LONDON

MSS

250, ff.170–15 – Proceedings at the arraignment of Philip Howard, Earl of Arundel, in Westminster Hall, 14 April 1589.

647, ff.235–8 – Letter from William Fenner to Anthony Bacon; Plymouth, 1589.

3,198, f.284 – Leicester to the Earl of Shrewsbury; Tilbury Camp, 15 August 1588.

3,206, f.263 – Robert Swift the younger to the Earl of Shrewsbury, providing news from court, including the release of Princess Elizabeth from the Tower; London, 20 May 1554.

LINCOLNSHIRE ARCHIVES
LINCOLN RECORD OFFICE, LINCOLN

8ANC/58 – 'Note of such information as I had of some shipmasters that came from the [Gibraltar] straits who were eye-witness to all that is underwritten'; Peregrine Bertie, Thirteenth Baron Willoughby de Eresby; ?March 1588.

8ANC10/114 – Lord Willoughby to the Dutch States General, reminding them of their agreement to supply ships against any enterprise by Spain against England; The Hague, 5 April 1588.

LONGLEAT HOUSE, WARMINSTER, WILTSHIRE

DU/Vol. 3, ff.91–102 – 'State of the debt charged upon the deceased Earl of Leicester for exceeding his allowance in the time of his lieutenant generalship in the Low Countries', 1588.

NATIONAL ARCHIVES, KEW, SURREY

Admiralty records

AO1/1686/23 – 1588 Accounts of Treasurer of Navy.

Exchequer records

E 30/1705 – Ratification of the Treaty of London, ending the Anglo-Spanish war, by Philip III of Spain; Valladolid, 15 June 1605.

Maps

MPF 1/134 – Richard Popinjay's map of Hampshire, Portsmouth and the Isle of Wight, 1587, showing fortifications and potential landing beaches. Scale: 1 inch to the mile.

MPF 1/318 – Drake's chart, used in his attack on Cadiz in 1587, dated that year and signed by his vice-admiral William Borough.

State Papers – Domestic

SP 11/1/22 – Memoranda for Queen Mary on financial issues; early August 1553.

SP 11/4/6 – Estimate for payment of royal debts; ?April 1554.

SP 11/4/2 – Letter from Princess Elizabeth to Mary I: Westminster, 'about noon' 17 March 1554.

SP 12/1/7 – Elizabeth's charge to Sir William Cecil and her Council; Hatfield, 17 (or ?20) November 1558.

SP 12/2/22 – Elizabeth I's address to Parliament declaring her determination to remain unmarried; 10 February 1559.

SP 12/114/22 – John Aylmer, Bishop of London, to Walsingham; London, 21 June 1577.

SP 12/141/29 – Account of attempts to convert Catholics in York Cathedral, August 1580.

SP 12/168/4 – Sir George Carey, governor of the Isle of Wight, complains to Sir Francis Walsingham about his poor resources to defend the island; February 1584.

SP 12/168/9; SP 12/181/26; SP 12/187/3 – Reports on the fortifications of Portsmouth and the Isle of Wight.

SP 12/176/22 – Lord Burghley's proposals for a 'Grand Council' to govern England in the event of the queen's assassination, 1584–5.

SP 12/197/13 – Hampshire people requested to lend labourers to dig trenches.

SP 12/198/64 – Instructions to Justices of the Peace on the maintenance and operation of warning beacons, 1587.

SP 12/199/93 – Lord Burghley to the deputy lieutenants of the maritime counties with directions for a new review of horse and foot within the realm; March 1587.

SP 12/208/79, f.181 – Letter from Lord High Admiral Howard to Lord Burghley, reporting on the condition of the queen's ships; 12 February 1588.

SP 12/208/87, f.201*v* – Letter from Lord High Admiral Howard to Lord Burghley reporting on the *Ark Royal*; 28 February 1588.

SP 12/209/40 f.77 – Letter from Sir Francis Drake to the Privy Council, urging a pre-emptive strike on the Armada before it sailed; Plymouth, 30 March 1588.

SP 12/210/33 – *Such means as are considered to put the forces of the Realm in order to Withstand any Invasion.*

SP 12/211/47 – Sir Francis Godolphin's report of a Mousehole barque sighting Armada ships on 23 June 1588.

SP 12/211/56 – Proclamation ordering martial law against possessors of papal bulls, books, pamphlets; Greenwich, 1 July 1588.

SP 12/212/66 f.139 – Lord Burghley to Sir Francis Walsingham on financial problems, 19 July 1588.

SP 12/212/80 f.167 – Lord Howard, Lord High Admiral to Sir Francis Walsingham, *Ark Royal,* Plymouth, 31 July 1588.

SP 12/212/95 – Proclamation against 'wicked and traitorous lies'.

SP 12/213/14 – Names of the ships presently in [Sir Henry Seymour's] fleet; 23 July 1588.

SP 12/213/34 – Report by Lord Henry Seymour listing his ships and their supplies, June 1588.

SP 12/213/40, f.97 – Sir George Carey to Earl of Sussex, reporting fighting off the southern coast of the Isle of Wight; Carisbrooke Castle, 4 August 1588.

SP 12/213/64, f.148 – Lord Howard, Lord High Admiral, to Sir Francis Walsingham, reporting on the battle of Gravelines, in *Ark Royal,* 8 August 1588.

SP 12/213/65 f.150 – Sir Francis Drake to Sir Francis Walsingham reporting on the battle of Gravelines, in *Revenge,* 8 August 1588.

SP 12/213/71, ff.164–5 – Sir John Hawkins to Sir Francis Walsingham, reporting on the battle of Gravelines, in *Victory*, 8 August 1588.

State Papers – Foreign

SP 94/2 f.212 – Estimate of men and ships under the command of Santa Cruz, ?1587.

SP 94/3 f.227r – Spanish Armada reported ready to sail, 7 May 1588.
  f.229 – Estimates of the numbers of men and ships gathered at Lisbon.

State Papers – Ireland

SP 63/137 no. 1, ii, f.4 – Medina Sidonia's sailing instructions for Spain. –17, Partial list of Spanish prisoners remaining at Drogheda, 13 October 1588.

SP 63/139/25 no.1 f.83 – Testimony of James Machary of 'the Cross within the County of Tipperary', 29 December 1588.

SP 63/149, f.30 – Report of Luke Plunkett on the *Swallow*; Dublin, 1589.

State Papers – Scotland
SP 52/35/18 – Letter from Lord Hunsdon to William Davison describing the execution of Francis Throckmorton; Berwick, 23 July 1584.

Will
PROB 11/92 ff.229–30 – Will of William Borough, dated 26 July 1598.

SURREY LOCAL HISTORY CENTRE, WOKING, SURREY

LM/13/29/370 – Examination of 'Tristram Winslade, a Catholic, accused of involvement in a Spanish invasion'; 1588.

LM/1945 – Paper entitled 'A certain and direct way to perceive in the night season or in a misty weather in the daytime whether the beacon the which we have regard unto be on fire or not'.

Printed

SOCIETY OF ANTIQUARIES OF LONDON
BURLINGTON HOUSE, LONDON

Broadsides
T[homas] D[eloney] – *A most ioyfull songe made in the behalfe of all her Maiesties faithfull and louing subjects of the great ioy which was made in London at the taking of the late trayterous conspirators* (London, printed by Richard Jones [1586]). (*Broadsides*, Henry VIII–Elizabeth, 1519–1603, f.83). STC 6557.
W[illiam] E[lderton] – *A new Ballade, declaring the daungerous shootyng of the Gunne at the Court*e (London, Edward White, 1579). (*Broadsides*, Henry VIII–Elizabeth, 1519–1603, f.72).

Proclamations
Reuocation of sundrie her Maiesties subiects remaining beyond the Seas under colour of studie, and yet liuing contrarie to the Lawes of God and of the Realm. And also against the reteyning of Jesuits and Massing Priestes, sources of sedition and other treasonable attempts, Greenwich, 10 January 1581 (London, Christopher Barker, 1581). (*Proclamations*, vol. 4, Elizabeth, 1558–90, f.26B.)
   The effect of certain branches of the Statute made in Anno. XXXIII Henry. VIII touching the maintenance of Artyllery and the punishment of such as vse vunlawfull games, very necessary to be put into execution

(London, Christopher Barker, ?1580). (*Proclamations*, vol. 4, Elizabeth, 1558–90, f.26.)

Against the bringing in, dispersing, uttering and Keeping of bulles from the Sea of Rome, and other Traiterous and Sedicious Libels, Bookes and Pamphlets, Greenwich, 1 July 1588 (London, deputies of Christopher Barker, 1588). (*Proclamations*, vol. 4, Elizabeth, 1558–90, f.45.)

The Queenes most excellent Maiestie, being minded in this daunger-ous time to intertain a certain number of captaines and souldiers for the garding of her royall person under the government and lieutenancy of the Right Hon. Lord Chamberlain … by this proclamation straightly to charge and command that all and every person and persons… do observe and keep such rates and prices for all kinds of victuals, horsemeate, lodg-ing and other necessaries … St James', 17 August 1588 (London, deputies of Christopher Barker, 1588). (*Proclamations*, vol. 4, Elizabeth, 1558–90, f.46.)

The Queenes Maiestie being given to vnderstand that diuers souldiers vpon the dissoluing of the campe at Tilberie in the countie of Essex have in the way homeward sold diuerse their armors and weapons which have been delivered vnto them by the officers of those Counties where they have been levied … and besides the sale of the said armor and weapons have most falsely and slanderously given out that they were compelled to make sale of them for that they received no pay which is most vntruely reported, St James', 25 August 1588 (London, deputies of Christopher Barker, 1588). (*Proclamations*, vol. 4, Elizabeth, 1558–90, f.47.)

Concerning [sic] *the souldiers appointed to serve in her Maiesties seruice beyond the seas vnder the charge of Sir Iohn Norris and Sir Francis Drake,* Richmond, 23 January 1589 (London, deputies of Christopher Barker, 1589). (*Proclamations*, vol. 4, Elizabeth, 1558–90, f.51.)

By the Queenes commaundment forasmuch as it is found by good proofe that many persons which haue serued of late on the seas in the iourney towards Spayne and Portingall, in coming from Plymouth and other portes … have fallen sick by the way and diuers died as infected with the plague …, Nonsuch, 22 July 1589 (London, deputies of Christopher Barker, 1589). (*Proclamations*, vol. 4, Elizabeth, 1558–90, f.55.)

Other printed works

Allen, Cardinal William – *An admonition to the nobility and people of England and Ireland concerninge the present warres made for the esecu-tion of his Holines sengtence by the highe and mightie Kinge Catholike of Spaine* (Antwerp, 1588).

APC – Acts of the Privy Council, n.s., ed. John Roche Dasent;
- vol. 8, 1571–5 (London, 1894).
- vol. 14, 1586–7 (London, 1897).
- vol. 15, 1587–8 (London, 1897).
- vol. 16, 1588 (London, 1897).
- vol. 17, 1588–9 (London, 1898).
- vol. 18, 1589–90 (London, 1899).

Archer, Ian W. and Price, F. Douglas – *English Historical Documents 1558–1603* (London & New York, 2011).

Corbett, Sir Julian S. – *Papers Relating to the Navy during the Spanish War, 1585–7*, NRS (London, 1898).

CSP Domestic Henry VIII – Letters and Papers, Foreign and Domestic, Henry VIII, vol. 10, 1536, ed. James Gairdner (London, 1887).

CSP Domestic Mary – Calendar of State Papers Domestic Series Mary I 1553–58, ed. C.S. Knighton, rev. ed. (London, 1998).

CSP Domestic Elizabeth – Calendar of State Papers, Domestic Series, of the Reign of Elizabeth, 1581–90, ed. Robert Lemon (London, 1865).

- *Addenda, Calendar of State Papers, Domestic Series, of the Reigns of Elizabeth and James I, Addenda, 1580–1625*, ed. Mary Anne Everett Green (London, 1872).

CSP Foreign Elizabeth – Calendar of State Papers, Foreign, of the Reign of Elizabeth, vol. 9, 1569–71, ed. Allan Crosby (London, 1874).

- vol. 18, July 1583–July 1584, ed. Sophie Crawford Lomas (London, 1914).
- vol. 21, pt 1, 1586–8, ed. Sophie Crawford Lomas (London, 1927).
- vol. 22, July–December 1588, ed. Richard Bruce Wernham (London, 1936).

CSP Ireland Elizabeth – Calendar of State Papers Relating to Ireland, of the Reign of Elizabeth I, August 1588-September 1592, ed. Hans Claude Hamilton (London, 1885).

CSP Milan – Calendar of State Papers Existing in the Archives of Milan, ed. Allen B. Hinds, vol. 1 (London, 1912).

CSP Spain – Calendar of Letters and State Papers Spain, vol. 4, pt 2, 1531–3, ed. Pascual de Gayangos (London, 1882).

- vol. 10, 1550–2, ed. Royall Tyler (London, 1914).
- vol. 11, 1553, ed. Royall Tyler (London, 1916).
- vol. 13, 1554–8, ed. Royall Tyler (London, 1954).

CSP Spain (Simancas) – Calendar of Letters and State Papers Relating to English Affairs, Preserved in, or Originally Belonging to, the Archives of Simancas, vol. 1 (1558–67), ed. Martin A.S. Hume (London, 1892).

– vol. 2, 1568–79, ed. Martin A. S. Hume (London, 1894).

– vol. 3, 1580–6, ed. Martin A. S. Hume (London, 1896).

– vol. 4, 1587–1603, ed. Martin A. S. Hume (London, 1899).

CSP Vatican – Calendar of State Papers Relating to English Affairs Preserved Principally at Rome in the Vatican Archives and Library, vol. 2, 1572–8, ed. J.M. Rigg (London, 1926).

CSP Venice – Calendar of State Papers Relating to English Affairs Existing in the Archives of Venice, vol. 6, 1556–8, ed. Rawdon Brown (London, 1877).

– vol. 7, 1558–80, ed. Rawdon Brown and G. Cavendish Bentinck (London, 1890).

– vol. 8, 1581–91, ed. Horatio F. Brown (London, 1894).

Deloney, Thomas – The Queenes Visiting of the Campe at Tilburie with Her Entertainment There to the Tune of Wilson's Wilde (London, 1588). STC 6565.

Ellis, Henry – Original Letters Illustrative of English History, 2nd s., (4 vols, London, 1827).

Fénelon, Bertrand de Salignac de la Mothe – Correspondance Diplomatique de Bertrand de Salignac de la Mothe Fénelon, Ambassadeur de France en Angleterre, de 1568–75, ed. A. Teulot, seven vols (Paris & London), 1838–40.

Feria's dispatch – 'The Count of Feria's Dispatch of 14 November 1558' ed. and translated, J. Rodriquez Salgado and S. Adams in Camden Miscellany, vol. 28, C.S. fourth s., vol. 29 (London, 1984) pp.302–44.

Fugger Newsletters – The Fugger Newsletters, being a selection of unpublished letters from the correspondents of the House of Fugger, 1568–1605; ed. Victor von Klarwill; translated by Pauline de Chary. First s. (London, 1924); second s. translated by L.S.R. Byrne (London, 1926).

Hardwick Papers – Miscellaneous State Papers from 1501 to 1726, two vols (London, 1778).

Harleian Miscellany – ed. William Oldys and Thomas Park, nine vols (London, 1808–12).

Hayward, Sir John – Annals of the first four years of the Reign of Queen Elizabeth, ed. John Bruce, C.S. (London, 1840).

HMC – Historical Manuscripts Commission Reports.

– 'Bath' – MSS of the marquis of Bath, preserved at Longleat, Wiltshire, vol. 2 (London, 1907); vol. 5 (Talbot, Dudley and Devereux Papers, 1533–1659), (London, 1980).

– 'Foljambe' – *MSS of Rt Hon. Francis J. Salville Foljambe of Osberton, Nottinghamshire* (London, 1897).

– 'Montague' – *MSS of Lord Montague of Beaulieu* (London, 1900).

– 'Salisbury' – *MSS of the Most Hon. the marquis of Salisbury at Hatfield House*, vol. 1, pt I (London, 1883); vol. 4 (London, 1892) and vol. 5 (London, 1904).

– 'Southampton' – *MSS of the Corporations of Southampton and King's Lynn* (London, 1887).

Hopper, Clarence (ed.) – *Sir Francis Drake's Memorable Service done Against the Spaniards in 1587, written by Robert Leng, Gentleman, one of his co-Adventurers and Soldiers*, C.S. (London, 1863).

Hughes, Paul and Larkin, James – *Tudor Royal Proclamations*, three vols (New Haven & London, 1969).

Laughton, John Knox – *The Defeat of the Spanish Armada Anno 1588*, two vols, NRS (London, 1894).

'Machyn – Diary' – *The Diary of Henry Machyn, Citizen and Merchant-Taylor of London, 1550–1563*, ed. John Gough Nichols, C.S., vol. 42 (London, 1847).

Marcus, Leah S., Mueller Janel and Rose, Mary Beth – *Elizabeth I: Collected Works* (Chicago & London, 2000).

Mousset, A. – *Dépêches diplomatiques de M. de Longlée, résident de France en Espagne 1582–90* (Paris, 1912).

Mumby, Frank – *The Girlhood of Queen Elizabeth, a Narrative in Contemporary Letters* (London, 1909).

Murdin, William – *Collection of State Papers Relating to Affairs in the Reign of Queen Elizabeth 1571–96*, two vols (London, 1759).

Naish, George P.B. – *Documents Illustrating the History of the Spanish Armada, Naval Miscellany*, vol. 4, NRS, vol. 92 (1952), pp.2–84.

Naunton, Robert – *Fragmenta Regalia* (reprinted London, 1824).

Oria *et al.* – *La armada Invencible: Documentos procedentes de Archivo General de Simancas*, ed. E. Herrera Oria, M. Bordouan and A. de la Plaze (Valladolid, 1929).

Raleigh, Sir Walter – *Judicious and Select Essayes and observations* (London, 1650).

Sharp, Sir Cuthbert – *Memorials of the Rebellion of 1569* (London, 1840).

Strype, John – *Annals of the Reformation*, six vols (Oxford, 1824).

Wernham, R.B. – *The Expedition of Sir John Norris and Sir Francis Drake to Spain and Portugal, 1589*, NRS (London, 1988).

SECONDARY SOURCES

Equivalent monetary values were calculated using: Lawrence H. Officer and Samuel H. Williamson, 'Purchasing Power of British Pounds from 1245 to Present'. URL: www.measuringworth.com/ppoweruk.

Archer, Elizabeth *et al.*, *Progress, Pageants and Entertainments of Queen Elizabeth* (Oxford, 2007).

Armstrong, E., 'Venetian despatches on the Armada and its results', *EHR*, vol. 12 (1897), pp.659–706.

Bagwell, Richard, *Ireland Under the Tudors*, three vols (London, 1890).

Baldwin, R.C.D., 'William Borough' in *ODNB*, vol. 6, pp.670–2.

Barratt, John, *Armada 1588: The Spanish Assault on England* (Barnsley, 2005).

Birt, H., *The Elizabethan Religious Settlement* (London, 1907).

Boynton, L., *The Elizabethan Militia* (London, 1967).

Braudel, F., *La Méditerranée et le monde méditerranéen a l'époque de Philippe II*, 2 vols (2nd ed., Paris, 1966).

Brennan, Gillian E., 'Papists and Patriotism in Elizabethan England', *Jnl Recusant History*, vol. 19 (1998–9), pp.1–15.

Carini, F.M., *Mons. Niccolò Ormaneto, nunzio alla corte Filippo II* (Rome, 1894).

Corbett, Julian S., *Drake and the Tudor Navy*, two vols (London, 2nd ed., 1899).

Covington, Sarah, *The Trail of Martyrdom: Persecution and Resistance in Sixteenth Century England* (Notre Dame, Indiana, 2003).

Cox, J., 'Ecclesiastical History' in *Victoria County History, Hampshire*, ed. A. Doubleday, five vols (Westminster, 1903), vol. 2, pp.1–231.

Christy, Miller, 'Queen Elizabeth's visit to Tilbury in 1588', *EHR*, vol. 34 (1919), pp.43–61.

Colthorpe, Marion, 'Queen Elizabeth I at Tilbury and in Kent', *Arch. Cant.*, vol. 104 (1987), pp.83–6.

Deacon, Richard, *History of the British Secret Services* (London, 1969).

Dickens, A.G., 'The First Stages of Romanist Recusancy in Yorkshire', *Yorkshire Archæological Jnl*, vol. 35 (1941), pp.157–82.

Dietz, Brian, 'The Royal Bounty and English Merchant Shipping in the sixteenth and seventeenth-centuries', *MM*, vol. 77 (1991), pp.5–20.

Douglas, Ken, *The Downfall of the Spanish Armada in Ireland* (Dublin, 2009).

Duffy, Eamon, *The Stripping of the Altars* (Cambridge, 1992).

– *Fires of Faith: Catholic England under Mary Tudor* (New Haven & London, 2009).

Duro, C.F., *La armada Invencible*, two vols (Madrid, 1884–5).

Edwards, Francis, *Plots and Plotters in the Reign of Elizabeth I* (Dublin, 2002).

Falls, Cyril, *Elizabeth's Irish Wars* (London, 1950).

Fernandez-Armesto, Felipe, *The Spanish Armada: The Experience of War* (London, 1988).

Fletcher, Anthony and MacCulloch, Diarmaid, *Tudor Rebellions*, fourth ed. (London, 1997).

Frye, Susan, 'The Myth of Elizabeth at Tilbury', *Sixteenth Century Journal*, vol. 23 (1992), pp.95–114.

Gallagher, P. & Cruickshank, D. W. (eds), *God's Obvious Design: Papers for the Spanish Armada Symposium, Sligo, 1988* (London, 1990).

Gerson, Armand J., 'The English Recusants and the Spanish Armada', *American Historical Review*, vol. 22 (1917), pp.589–94.

Gómez-Centurión, C., *La Invencible y la empresa de Inglaterra* (Madrid, 1988).

Graham, Winston, *The Spanish Armadas* (London, 1972).

Graves, Michael, *Profiles in Power: Burghley* (London, 1998).

Haigh, Christopher, *Reformation and Resistance in Tudor Lancashire* (Cambridge, 1975).

Hardy, Evelyn, *Survivors of the Armada* (London, 1966).

Hearn, Karen, 'Elizabeth I and the Spanish Armada: A Painting and its Afterlife', *TRHS*, vol. 14 (2004), pp.123–40.

Hogg, O.F.G., 'England's War Effort against the Spanish Armada' *Jnl Society for Army Historical Research*, vol. 44 (1966), pp.25–43.

– 'Elizabethan Artillery', *Jnl Royal Artillery*, vol. 65 (1938), pp.130–43.

Hutchinson, Robert, *Last Days of Henry VIII* (London, 2005).

– *Elizabeth's Spymaster* (London, 2006).

– *House of Treason* (London, 2009).

Ireland, J. de Courcy, 'Ragusa and the Spanish Armada of 1588', *MM*, vol. 64 (1978), pp.256–61.

Joad, Raymond, *Pamphlets and Pamphleteering in Early Modern England* (Cambridge, 2003).

Keevil, J.J., *Medicine and the Navy*, four vols (Edinburgh, 1957–63).

Kitchen, Frank, 'The Ghastly War Flame: Fire Beacons in Sussex until the mid-17th Century', *SAC*, vol. 124 (1986), pp.179–93.

– 'The Ghastly War Flame: the Beacon System in Essex', *Essex Jnl*, vol. 23 (1988), pp.41–4.

Law, T.G., 'Cuthbert Mayne and the Bull of Pius V', *EHR*, vol. 1 (1886), pp.141–4.

Leahy, William, *Elizabethan Triumphal Procession* (Aldershot, 2005).

Levin, Carole, *'The Heart and Stomach of a King': Elizabeth I and the Politics of Sex and Power* (Philadelphia, 1994).

Loades, David, *Mary Tudor* (Oxford, 1989).

– *Elizabeth I: The Golden Age of Gloriana* (London, 2003).

– 'Thomas Fenner', *ODNB*, vol. 19, pp.301–2.

Loomie, Albert J., *The Spanish Elizabethans: English Exiles at the Court of Philip II* (New York, 1963).

MacCaffrey, Wallace T., *Elizabeth I: War and Politics 1588–1603* (Princeton, 1992).

Martin, Basil, *Sir John Hawkins*, ODNB, vol. 25, pp.919–27.

Martin, Colin, 'A 16th-century Siege Train: the Battery Ordnance of the 1588 Spanish Armada', *International Jnl of Nautical Archaeology and Underwater Exploration*, vol. 17 (1988), pp.57–73.

– and Parker, Geoffrey, *The Spanish Armada*, rev. ed. (London, 1999).

Maura Gamazo, G., Duke of Maura, *El designio de Felipe II y el episodio de la armada invencible* (Madrid, 1957).

Mattingly, Garrett, 'Aspects de la propaganda religieuse', *Travaux d'Humanisme et Renaissance*, vol. 28 (Geneva, 1957), pp.325–39.

– *The Defeat of the Spanish Armada* (London, 2nd ed., 1983).

McCall, H.B., 'Executions after the Northern Rebellion', *Yorkshire Archæological Jnl*, vol. 18 (1887), pp.74–86.

McCann, Timothy, 'The Clergy and the Elizabethan Settlement in the Diocese of Chichester' in *Studies in Sussex Church History*, ed. M.J. Kitch (Falmer, Sussex, 1981), pp.99-123.

McDermott, James, *England and Spain: A Necessary Quarrel* (New Haven & London, 2005).

McGrath, Patrick, *Papists and Puritans under Elizabeth I* (London, 1967).

– and Rowe, Joy, 'Anstruther Analysed: the Elizabethan Seminary Priests', *Jnl Recusant History*, vol. 18 (1986), pp.1–13.

McGurk, J.N., 'Armada Preparations in Kent and Arrangements made after the Defeat', *Arch. Cant.*, vol. 85 (1970), pp.71–93.

Merriman, Roger Bigelow, 'Some Notes on the Treatment of English Catholics in the Reign of Elizabeth', *American Historical Review*, vol. 13 (1908), pp.480–500.

Meyer, Arnold, *England and the Catholic Church under Queen Elizabeth* (London, 1916).

Monteith, Sir Robert, *Description of the Isles of Orkney and Zetland* (Edinburgh, 1711).

Neale, J.E., *Queen Elizabeth* (London, 1934).

– *Elizabeth and her Parliaments 1584–1601* (London, 1957).

– *Essays in Elizabethan History* (Oxford, 1958).

Nichols, John, *Progresses and Public Processing of Queen Elizabeth* three vols (London, 1823).

Norfolk, Fourteenth Duke of, *Lives of Philip Howard, earl of Surrey and of Anne Dacres, his wife,* first ed. (London, 1857).

ODNB, *Dictionary of National Biography,* new ed., ed. H.G.G. Matthews and Brian Harrison, sixty vols (Oxford, 2004).

O'Neill, B.H. and Stephens, W.E., 'A Plan of the Fortifications of Yarmouth in 1588', *Norfolk Archaeology,* vol. 28 (1945), pp.1–6.

Parker, Geoffrey, 'El testamento politico de Juan Martinez de Recalde', *Revista de historia naval,* vol. 60 (1988), pp.7–44.

– 'The *Dreadnought* Revolution of Tudor England', *MM,* vol. 82 (1996), pp.269–300.

Parmiter, Geoffrey de C., 'The Imprisonment of Papists in Private Castles', *Jnl Recusant History,* vol. 19 (1988–9), pp.16–38.

Pierson, Peter, *Commander of the Armada: the seventh duke of Medina Sidonia* (New Haven & London, 1989).

Porter, Linda, *Mary Tudor: The First Queen* (London, 2007).

Quinn, David, 'Spanish Armada Prisoners Escape from Ireland', *MM,* vol. 70 (1984), pp.117–18.

– *Sir Francis Drake as seen by his Contemporaries* (Providence, 1996).

Read, Conyers, *Mr Secretary Walsingham and the Policy of Queen Elizabeth,* three vols (Oxford, 1925).

– 'The Proposal to Assassinate Mary Queen of Scots at Fotheringay', *EHR,* vol. 11 (1925), pp.234–5.

Rex, Richard, *The Tudors* (Stroud, 2003).

Robinson, John Martin, *Dukes of Norfolk* (Chichester, 1995).

Rodger, N.A.M., *The Safeguard of the Sea: A Naval History of Great Britain,* vol. 1, 660–1649 (London, 1997).

Rodríguez, D. Higueras and Aladrén, M.P. San Pío, 'Irish Wrecks of the Great Armada: the Testimony of the Survivors, in Gallagher & Cruickshank (eds), *God's Obvious Design* (London, 1990).

Rowse, A.L., *Tudor Cornwall: Portrait of a Society* (London, 1941).

Russell, Percy, 'Fire Beacons in Devon', *Trans. Devon Association*, vol. 87 (1955), pp.250–302.

– 'White's Schedule of the Dorset Beacons', *Proceedings Dorset Natural History and Antiquarian Field Club*, vol. 81 (1959), pp.103–6.

Saunders, A.D., 'Tilbury Fort and the Development of Artillery Fortifications in the Thames Estuary', *Antiquaries' Jnl*, vol. 40 (1960), pp.152–74.

Scott, James R., 'Pay List of the Forces, Raised in Kent to Resist the Spanish Armada', *Arch. Cant.*, vol. 11 (1877), pp.388–91.

Sharpe, Kevin, *Selling the Tudor Monarchy: Authority and Image in 16th Century England* (New Haven & London, 2009).

Somerset, Anne, *Elizabeth I* (London, 2002).

Stählin, Carl, *Sir Francis Walsingham und seine Zeit ... Mit einem Porträt*, one vol. (all published), (Heidelberg, 1908).

Starkey, David, *Elizabeth: Apprenticeship* (London, 2001).

Strickland, Agnes, *Lives of the Queens of England from the Norman Conquest*, six vols (London, 1866).

Thompson, I.A.A., 'The Appointment of the Duke of Medina Sidonia to the Command of the Spanish Armada', *HJ*, vol. 12 (1969) pp.197–216.

– 'Spanish Armada Guns', *MM*, vol. 61 (1975), pp.355–71.

Walsh, M.K., *Destruction by Peace: Hugh O'Neill after Kinsale* (Monaghan, 1986).

Walsham, Alexandra, 'Miracles and the Counter-Reformation Mission to England', *HJ*, vol. 46 (2003), pp.779–815.

Walton, Timothy, *Challenges in Intelligence Analysis* (Cambridge, 2010).

Waters, D.M., 'The Elizabethan Navy and the Armada Campaign', *MM*, vol. 35 (1949), pp.92–127.

Wark, K.K., *Elizabethan Recusancy in Cheshire* (Manchester, 1971).

Welwood, James, *Memoirs of the most Material Transactions in England in the last One Hundred Years Preceding the Revolution in 1688* (London, 1820).

Wernham, R.B., 'Queen Elizabeth and the Portugal Expedition of 1589', *EHR*, vol. 66 (1951), pp.1–26; 194–218.

White, H.T., 'The Beacon System in Hampshire', *Proceedings Hampshire Field Club*, vol. 10 (1930), pp.252–78.

– 'The Beacon System in Kent', *Arch. Cant.*, vol. 46 (1934), pp.77–96.

– 'Fire Beacons in Devon', *Trans. Devon Association*, vol. 87 (1955), pp.250–302.

Whitehead, B.T., *Of Brags and Boasts: Propaganda in the Year of the Armada* (Stroud, 1994).

Williams, Neville, *A Tudor Tragedy: Thomas Howard, Fourth Duke of Norfolk* (London, 1964).

Worsley, Lucy and Souden, David, *Hampton Court Palace* (London & New York, 2005).

INDEX